EXPLORING DIGITAL LIBRARIES

·········

Foundations, practice, prospects

Karen Calhoun

facet publishing

© Karen Calhoun 2014

Published by Facet Publishing
7 Ridgmount Street, London WC1E 7AE
www.facetpublishing.co.uk

Facet Publishing is wholly owned by CILIP: the Chartered Institute
of Library and Information Professionals.

British Library Cataloguing in Publication Data
A catalogue record for this book is available from the British
Library.

ISBN 978-1-85604-820-0

First published 2014

Text printed on FSC accredited material.

Typeset from author's files in 10/14 pt Palatino Linotype and
Myriad Pro by Facet Publishing Production.
Printed and made in Great Britain by CPI Group (UK) Ltd,
Croydon, CR0 4YY.

For Maxwell and Emilie,
in the hope they will treasure their generation's
libraries as I have mine.

· · · · · · · · ·

Contents

·········

List of figures and tables

Figures

Tables

·········

Preface

The emergence of digital libraries in the early 1990s was a turning point and a critical component of the worldwide, world-changing shift to networked information. The turning point crystallized from myriad disparate elements that had influenced and combined with one another, in the process creating something entirely new. The high energy and important outcomes of that first, formative digital library decade created further winds of change that in turn produced more vigorous activity. More than 20 years on, we can observe a young, multidisciplinary field of digital library research and practice that has now reached a new intersection of dynamic forces – one dominated by the social web. This is the context in which I wrote this book.

The intention of the book is to help advance learning, professional discourse, research and practice at this particular moment in the evolution of digital libraries. I have done my best to take a broad, international perspective. At one level, I have approached the subject generally: the foundations, current practice and prospects of digital libraries. A second structural theme runs through the book as well: digital libraries in the context of the web-based communities they serve. In particular I explore the possibilities of a shift toward a community-centered perspective based on what digital libraries contribute or might contribute in a time of large-scale, web- and network-driven societal change.

The book attempts to place insights gleaned from the record of digital libraries' first decade, the second decade's literature of research and practice, conversations with several digital library experts, and my own research and experiences into an overarching framework that can make sense of an enormous amount of activity. Over the course of twenty-some years, thousands of people from multiple disciplines and domains have contributed to this young field of endeavor. The book's structure, topics and analyses reflect my own perspective, interpretations and knowledge of all this work; it may be an understatement to say there are other perspectives. I have cited many sources in this book, not only to place the chapters and sections in the context of related work, but also to guide those who wish to explore specific topics in more depth or from other points of view.

The challenges facing libraries, including digital libraries, are momentous. In this book, I have tried to lay out the issues and opportunities in a way that invites progress toward addressing the issues and seizing the opportunities. While it explores the past and present, the book looks forward. Thus, I have written mainly for the individuals and groups who will define and carry out the next stages of the digital shift in libraries, cultural memory institutions and information infrastructures: practicing professionals, graduate students and their professors. In addition, library and information science leaders and researchers may find some of the book's analytical frameworks of interest. Finally, the second half of the book may contain some relevant material for those interested in the broad question of the social roles of libraries in the digital age.

Chapter 1 of the book traces the emergence of the field and offers a definition of 'digital libraries' in an environment of multiple perspectives and continuous change. Chapter 2 describes the outcomes of the first decade of digital libraries (1991–2001) that continue to shape digital library research and practice today: among them the transformation of scholarly communication processes, the open access movement, large-scale digitization, and working digital libraries. Chapter 3 introduces a concept map that identifies the key themes and challenges of digital libraries' second decade (2002–12). Chapters 4 and 5 discuss digital libraries and the web through the lens of collections and collection building, with Chapter 4 devoted to repositories and Chapter 5 examining hybrid libraries (collections containing both digital and non-digital resources).

The second half of the book turns to the social roles of digital libraries and their value in their communities. Chapters 6 to 8 explore digital libraries in the context of a framework of actual and potential social roles, with Chapter 6 laying out the framework, Chapter 7 examining the nature of online communities, and Chapter 8 looking into the prospects of open access repositories. Chapters 9 and 10 offer a visual framework for considering the possibilities of digital libraries as social platforms on the web, with Chapter 9 exploring the influence of the social web on scholarship, and Chapter 10 examining a number of opportunities afforded by the social web to go beyond what digital libraries have achieved in their first two decades.

A great deal has been written and said about specific aspects of digital libraries, but not that much that examines their progress or prospects in terms of their overarching societal or community impact. In addition to this book's aim to summarize a large body of research and practice into a manageable resource for teaching and learning, it has the goal of encouraging new discourse and reflection about digital libraries' contributions to democratic societies. Recognizing that we find ourselves in a chaotic social and technical environment, facing significant uncertainty about the future, it is more important than ever to collectively take up this conversation.

Acknowledgements

The process of creating this book has involved examining the work of hundreds of researchers and practitioners who took the time to collect their thoughts and write. I want to start by thanking them, as this book builds on what they studied, learned and shared. The digital library field has produced a large body of literature, impossible for any one person to absorb, so I apologize in advance for any key contributions I have missed, and I welcome hearing about them.

Many individuals have personally supported me through the lengthy process of forming and articulating the ideas in this book. First and foremost, I would like to thank my husband for his unflagging patience and support during the 16 months or so when I was devoting any free time that I had to writing. Second, without the encouragement, generosity and flexibility of Rush Miller, university librarian at the University of Pittsburgh, I would not have been able to write this book.

Many have helped to guide the writing. Among them, I want to thank Howard D. White, professor emeritus of Drexel University's College of Information Science and Technology, whose teaching and advice resulted in my first steps, over 30 years ago, toward professional research, writing and publication. More recently, my friend and former colleague Lorcan Dempsey, OCLC's chief strategist and vice president of research, has helped to shape my thinking over the past decade; he was the first to make me believe that I could write this book, and he has been generous with looking at drafts, helping me sort out ideas and referring me to useful sources. Sheila Corrall, professor and chair of the University of Pittsburgh's library and information science program, took time from an incredibly busy year to read drafts and provide very specific help and guidance; I cannot thank her enough. In addition, the encouragement, enthusiasm and comments of Helen Carley and Sarah Busby, my editor and former editor at Facet Publishing, have been most welcome.

Early conversations with Ron Larsen, dean and professor of Pitt's School of Information Sciences (SIS), and Stephen Griffin, visiting professor at SIS and a former program director at the National Science Foundation (NSF), helped me to understand the impact and outcomes of NSF's Digital Library Initiatives. Aaron Brenner, head of Pitt's digital library program, helped from the writing's beginning to the final drafts with contributions of time, critiques and suggestions. Jordan Hatcher, an expert in intellectual property and internet law, kindly found time to talk with me about legal language. Elvia Arroyo-Ramirez, at the time a new graduate of the University of Pittsburgh, brought the perspective of a new professional to reviewing early chapters and helped me to find this book's voice.

The later chapters of this book incorporate the results of interviews with nine well known digital library experts. I am grateful for their willingness to share their experience and insights, which have underpinned and enriched these chapters. They are:

- William Arms, professor emeritus, Computing & Information Science, Cornell University
- Jill Cousins, executive director, Europeana
- Ricky Erway, senior program officer, OCLC Research and former associate co-ordinator of the American Memory program at the Library of Congress
- Rose Holley, digital library specialist, National Archives of Australia and former manager of the Australian Newspaper Digitization Program at the National Library of Australia
- Carl Lagoze, associate professor, School of Information, University of Michigan
- Clifford Lynch, executive director, Coalition for Networked Information
- Deanna Marcum, managing director, ITHAKA S+R
- Oya Rieger, associate university librarian for digital scholarship and preservation services, Cornell University Library
- Roy Tennant, senior program officer, OCLC Research.

I also want to express my gratitude to Dawn and Jim Metz, owners of an inn in the small town of Ligonier, where I spent three highly productive writing retreats. Their warm hospitality and wonderful house gave me space and peace to fill these pages. I also benefited greatly from the space and kind support of two public libraries; my thanks are due to Diana Falk and her staff of the Norwin Public Library and to Janet Hudson and her staff of the Ligonier Valley Public Library.

I did not realize what the journey of writing this book was going to entail when I first began. Perhaps if I had fully realized the scope of what I was setting out to do, I would not have started. I want to express my heartfelt appreciation to those I have acknowledged here; they made the journey possible. Finally, I am grateful to the many other colleagues, friends and family who contributed to completing this book, perhaps without knowing they were doing so.

Karen Calhoun

·········

Glossary

This glossary provides brief, informal definitions of terms in the context of digital libraries; some of the terms have other meanings in different contexts.

ACM Association for Computing Machinery

altmetrics A subfield of bibliometrics that includes quantitative measures based on engagement and impact in the context of the social web

API Application Programming Interface; a machine interface that allows and responds to requests for services from other computer programs and/or allows data to be exchanged

ARL Association of Research Libraries (US)

artifacts Physical items in library, museum or archival collections

arXiv A subject-based repository of pre-prints in the fields of mathematics, physics, astronomy, computer science, quantitative biology, statistics, and quantitative finance

ASEO Academic search engine optimization; the creation, publication, and modification of scholarly content in a way that makes it easier for academic search engines to both crawl and index it

associative indexing A form of information organization and retrieval based on the relationships (links) between things; a concept often credited to Vannevar Bush and his idea for the 'memex'

authentication The automated process of validating the identity of a person or computer

authorization The automated process of providing the appropriate rights to access information or carry out particular actions

BASE Bielefeld Academic Search Engine; BASE collects and indexes digital academic content from repositories and other sources worldwide

BIBFRAME An undertaking by the Library of Congress and the library community to determine a transition path for MARC21 to linked data standards

bibliometrics A research method in library and information science that uses quantitative assessment and statistics to describe publication patterns. One bibliometric method is citation analysis

BnF Bibliothèque nationale de France

branding In the context of this book, the process of successfully communicating the identity, intent and nature of a digital library to the target audiences it aims to serve

business model How a product, service or organization will generate income and/or cover costs

business processes Activities that produce services or projects. Some library business processes are selecting, acquiring, describing and managing, supporting discovery and access, circulating or linking and preserving collections

CERN European Organization for Nuclear Research

citation management tools Tools that support scholarly research and writing; they capture, organize and maintain citations (references) and enable using the captured data in multiple ways, most commonly to create lists of references or bibliographies

citizen science A form of research collaboration involving members of the public in scientific research projects that address real-world problems

cloud services Web-based applications that are accessed via common web browsers and whose infrastructure is hosted on the network (i.e., 'in the cloud')

CNI Coalition for Networked Information

Creative Commons licenses A set of template copyright licenses available to the public that allow for certain types of free, worldwide distribution of copyrighted works. Creative Commons (creativecommons.org) is the best known of several new models for licensing rights to content

CrossRef A reference linking service operated by a consortium of publishers; the official DOI registration agency for scholarly and professional publications

crowdsourcing A massive collaboration technique that enables individuals, working as a virtual group, to collectively accomplish a shared, large and significant goal

cyberinfrastructure An infrastructure of high-speed networks, computing and data systems, repositories, and instruments that supports data-intensive research environments and enables advanced capabilities

DARPA Defense Advanced Research Projects Agency (US)

data curation Activities including selection, organization and access, preservation, maintenance and archiving of scientific data

deep web The part of the web that is not indexed by common search engines; also called the invisible or hidden web

deposit mandates Policies requiring authors to make their work available via open access in a particular repository or repositories

destination site On the web, a site that people visit by going directly to its URL through typing or bookmarks

digital curation A series of activities that support creating, acquiring, appraising, repurposing, accessing, and preserving digital collections

digital divide The gap between those with and without access to quality information resources and to information and communications (ICT) technologies

digital libraries 1. A field of endeavor with participants chiefly from the computer, library and information sciences, publishing, the cultural heritage sector, and education; 2. Systems and services, often openly available, that support the advancement of knowledge and culture, contain managed collections of digital resources, and often use an architecture centered on a repository

digital preservation The active management and appraisal of digital information over its entire life cycle, from creation and active use to selection, transfer and preservation, access and re-use

digitization The process of converting a physical item into a digital format, sometimes known as digital reformatting

disclosure In the library context, the results of activities to make library content discoverable and visible in or from external systems and services, especially search engines and on high-traffic sites

discovery service In the library context, a type of web-based user interface that provides for unified, integrated search and retrieval based on a pre-harvested, centralized index to heterogeneous resources

DLF Digital Library Federation

DLI Digital Libraries Initiative, a US-based digital library research program that began in the early 1990s

DOAJ Directory of Open Access Journals

DOI Digital Object Identifier, a type of identifier used to identify scholarly publications

DRIVER Digital Repository Infrastructure Vision European Research;

DRIVER harvests and provides access to content from repositories in 38 countries

DSpace A well known open source software package for building and managing repositories

Dublin Core A small set of metadata elements used to describe digital resources; maintained by the Dublin Core Metadata Initiative

EAD Encoded Archival Description, used to create electronic finding aids for archival materials

EDM Europeana Data Model

eLib The Electronic Libraries Programme, a UK-based digital library development program that ran from 1994 to 2001

EPrints A well known open source software package for building and managing repositories

e-research Data- and computationally-intensive, distributed, collaborative research activities that use advanced information and communication technologies; see also **cyberinfrastructure**

ERM E-resource management system

Europeana A portal to a multi-lingual online collection of millions of digitized items from European museums, libraries, archives and multi-media collections

fair dealing, fair use A legal provision that provides exceptions to copyright law when the use of copyrighted material is for the purposes of non-commercial research or study, criticism, review or reporting. It is related to the US concept of 'fair use'

Fedora Flexible Extensible Digital Object Repository Architecture; an open source software system for providing a core repository service

FRBR *Functional Requirements for Bibliographic Records*, a conceptual model for metadata developed by IFLA that provides a framework for expressing a work in terms of its attributes and relationships to other objects/resources

Gold open access The provision of open access by publishing in an open access journal

Google 5 The five libraries that entered into a 2004 agreement with Google to mass-digitize their collections; this developed into the **Google Library Project**, with more research library participants

Green open access The provision of open access by publishing in journals and self-archiving a copy on the web or in an open access repository

HathiTrust A membership organization for creating a shared repository of digital collections; most of the content is from libraries that participated in the Google Library Project

HTML Hypertext Markup Language, a simple language used on the web for marking up and formatting text and linking to other objects

HTTP Hypertext Transfer Protocol, the basic protocol of the web for communication between browsers and websites

hybrid library Combinations of traditional collections, licensed e-resources and openly available digital collections produced in-house or elsewhere

i2010 Digital Libraries A European Commission plan, announced in 2005, to build a European digital library by 2010; Europeana developed from this initiative

identifiers In the digital library domain, references to digital objects that are intended to be long-lasting or persistent; an essential characteristic of a digital library resource. Some examples of identifiers discussed in this book are DOIs, PURLs, URIs, and ORCIDs

IEEE A professional association for advancing technology. Originally the acroynym stood for Institute of Electrical and Electronics Engineers, but the scope of the association is now much broader; therefore the organization is now known simply as IEEE

IFLA International Federation of Library Associations

IMLS Institute of Museum and Library Services (US)

institutional repository A repository for collecting, preserving and disseminating, in digital form, the intellectual output of an institution

interoperability The provision of uniform, coherent access for users to diverse information from different, independently managed systems

IR Information retrieval

ISO International Organization for Standardization

JISC Joint Information Systems Committee (UK)

JSTOR A digital library subscription service for scholarly journals, primary sources and books

Kahn-Wilensky architecture Principles for the design of a digital library that is open in its architecture, with four main components: a repository, mechanisms to support search, identifier systems, and user interfaces. The architecture could contain additional components for supporting other services

knowledgebases Digital registries (machine- or human-readable, usually both) that collect and organize metadata and content needed for specific functions, like managing access rights information

landing page The web page that appears when a user clicks on a link from a search engine result list or other referring site

learning management systems Integrated software applications for supporting network-based learning environments

Library 2.0 A conceptualization of the 'next generation' library, characterized by user interaction, participation and user-centered design

library management systems Integrated software applications, generally based on relational databases, that support the business processes of libraries

linked data The framework for publishing and consuming semantic web content, which consists of interlinked, structured data. Linked data can also refer to the collection of interrelated, linked datasets in the web of data

LIS Library and information science

LOCKSS Lots of Copies Keep Stuff Safe, a community effort and open source system allowing libraries to collect, preserve and provide access to digital content

long tail A concept made popular by Chris Anderson of *Wired* magazine that refers to obscure, low-use content as the 'long tail' of a demand curve. His hypothesis is that network-level aggregation and disclosure of these obscure items will also generate demand and open new markets for their use

MARC Machine-Readable Cataloging

mashups Interactive web applications that gather content from diverse sources to create new services. An example is the combination of Google Maps content with other information displayed to a user

mass digitization The digitization of very large, whole collections of content, with no or minimal selection

mediated deposit Self-archiving that is accomplished through a mediator, e.g., a manager of an institutional repository

metadata Structured information that describes, explains, locates and otherwise makes it easier to retrieve and use an information resource (NISO definition)

MIT Massachusetts Institute of Technology

MOOC Massive open online course

NCBI National Center for Biotechnology Information (US)

NDIIPP National Digital Information Infrastructure and Preservation Program (US)

NDLTD Networked Digital Library of Theses and Dissertations

needs assessment A process that studies user needs, wants and tasks in order to use this information in designing or selecting systems or services

NIH National Institutes of Health (US)

NISO National Information Standards Organization (US)

NLA National Library of Australia

NSF National Science Foundation (US)

OAI Open Archives Initiative

OAI-ORE Open Archives Initiative Object Reuse and Exchange; a set of standards for the description and exchange of aggregations of web resources

OAI-PMH Open Archives Initiative Protocol for Metadata Harvesting

OAIS Open Archival Information System

OASIS Organization for the Advancement of Structured Information Standards

OCLC Online Computer Library Center

OCR Optical character recognition, an automated process for creating a digital representation of text

OECD Organization for Economic Cooperation and Development

online communities Network-based spaces in which participants communicate and interact, share and distribute content, and build or maintain relationships. Examples of types of online communities are support, interest-based, gaming and knowledge communities

open access The provision of online, free-of-charge access to content that is also free of most copyright and licensing restrictions

open source software Software for which the source code is freely available. To be open source software, it should be licensed under an Open Source Initiative (OSI)-compliant open source software license (http://opensource.org has details)

OpenDOAR Directory of Open Access Repositories

OpenURL A standard for enabling linking from one information resource to another; OpenURLs work by capturing and transferring metadata about an information resource to another service, then retrieving and displaying the information resource to the user

ORCID Open Researcher and Contributor ID

orphan works Copyrighted works whose owner is unknown or cannot be located. Orphan works are a problem because potential users of the orphan works have no one to seek permission from when doing clearances

PageRank The link analysis algorithm used by the Google search engine, based on the principle of associative indexing and named after Larry Page, a co-founder of Google

PDA Patron Driven Acquisitions, a model for licensing and purchasing e-books 'just in time,' based on library user selections

peer review The professional evaluation of a work by a colleague in the same field

personas In user-centered design, a representation of the goals and behavior of a hypothesized type of user. Personas, typically developed from user interviews, are used to guide service design, development or enhancement

portal A term used in the library community to refer to a service for simplifying searching across and linking from and to diverse collections and making it easier to authenticate and authorize access to licensed resources. Portal implementations in the first half of the 2000s were generally associated with metasearch or federated searching

post-prints Digital representations of scholarly articles after they have been peer-reviewed

pre-prints Digital pre-publications (drafts) of scholarly articles

PubMed Central A subject-based repository of biomedical and life sciences journal literature operated by the National Center for Biotechnology Information (US). PubMed Central also has centers in Europe and Canada

PURL Persistent Uniform Resource Locator

RDA *Resource Description and Access*, an international standard for cataloging and the successor to AACR2 (the *Anglo-American Cataloging Rules* second edition revised)

RDF Resource Description Framework, a method supporting interoperability that allows structured and semi-structured data to be mixed, exposed and shared across different applications

referee See **peer review**

reference linking Linking from one information resource to another

reference management tools See **citation management tools**

registries Databases that store specific types of information needed for enabling the exchange of data between systems

RePEC Research Papers in Economics; a subject-based repository

repositories Open access digital libraries of research-quality resources. They can be subject- or institutionally based, or they can be aggregations of repositories

ROAR Registry of Open Access Repositories

RSS Really Simple Syndication; supports subscription and automatic, immediate distribution of content so that users receive updates

scholarly communication The communication activity of scholars, for example how they communicate as writers, cite each others' work, choose channels for disseminating their work and collaborate with other scholars

Scopus A database of citations and abstracts for scholarly journal articles

self-archiving Depositing a digital copy of a work on the web (e.g., on a personal or group web page or in a repository) to provide open access to it

semantic web A common framework that enables large-scale integration of, and reasoning on, data on the web and allows data to be shared and re-used across boundaries. Also known as 'a web of data' that can be processed by machines

SEO Search engine optimization

serials crisis Continual, above-inflation increases in the costs of subscriptions to scholarly content, while the budgets of subscribing libraries remain static or decline

SGML Standard Generalized Markup Language, a system for creating markup languages and a precursor to XML

SHERPA RoMEO A searchable database of publisher's policies regarding self-archiving of journal articles

SIP Simple Publishing Interface, a publishing protocol facilitating the exchange and re-use of data in multiple applications and systems

social web A phrase used to refer collectively to the websites, tools and services that facilitate interactions, collaboration, content creation and sharing, contribution and participation on the web. Examples include e-mail and discussion forums, bookmarking, wikis and blogs, microblogs, media sharing services and social networks

socio-technical systems In digital libraries, systems that support not only information seeking and discovery but also community interaction and collaboration. Socio-technical system design is based on the interplay between technologies, information, and people

SRU/SRW Protocols for internet search queries maintained by the Library of Congress. SRU (an OASIS standard) is the Search/Retrieve URL Service and SRW is the Search/Retrieve Web Service. SRU/SRW draw on the model for Z39.50 but are not as complex

SSRN Social Science Research Network; a subject-based repository

standards Established technical norms, requirements, specifications, processes or practices that are ratified, proposed or in draft form, accepted, or recommended by international, regional or national organizations

subject-based repository A repository for collecting a providing access to digital objects related to a subject or group of subjects; also called a discipline-based repository

success factor A requirement or necessary condition for achieving an organization's or project's mission

SWORD Simple Web-Service Offering Repository Deposit, an interoperability standard facilitating deposit in repositories

syndication The automatic distribution of web content to multiple other sites

target audience A specific group (or groups) of people for whom a product or service is intended

TEI Text Encoding Initiative

TEL The European Library

TRAC Trustworthy Repositories Audit and Certification

UKOLN UK Office for Library and Information Networking

URI Uniform Resource Identifier

usability A quality attribute that assesses how easy user interfaces are to use (Jakob Nielsen)

user-centered design A philosophy and process for designing interactive systems in which the needs and practices of end-users receive extensive attention; sometimes called human-centered design

value proposition A brief, clear statement of the benefits of using a particular service or product, e.g., what problems it solves for the user

VIAF Virtual International Authority File

VLEs Virtual learning environments

VREs Virtual research environments

W3C World Wide Web Consortium, an international standards body that works on the creation and maintenance of web standards. W3C develops specifications (called recommendations) that describe the building blocks of the web. Tim Berners-Lee is the director of W3C

Web 2.0 A conceptualization of the web as a platform for participation, emphasizing user interaction, sharing of content and social networking

web referrer An online site or service that drives visits and visitors to another site

web services, web APIs Enabling technologies that support the machine-to-machine exchange and re-use of content between sites

WoS Web of Science; a citation index to scholarly literature

XML eXtensible Markup Language, a subset of SGML that provides a simple, flexible text format. XML has played an important role in the publication and exchange of data on the web

Z39.50 A standard protocol for searching collections on remote systems, gathering and displaying a unified set of results; used in early digital library efforts to achieve interoperability

CHAPTER 1

·········

Emergence and definitions of digital libraries

Overview

This chapter traces the first decade of progress in digital libraries (1991–2001), with emphasis on the foundational innovations, vision, motivations, new technology, funding and early programs that prompted their emergence and rapid development. It next turns to the question of how to define the concept of 'digital libraries' in an environment of multiple perspectives and continuous technological and societal change. The chapter's intent is to orient the reader to the field as well as to ground the rest of the book in the context of the aspirations and efforts of many diverse communities and individuals.

The emergence of digital libraries (1991–2001)

This book places the beginning of digital libraries in 1991, the year in which the National Science Foundation (NSF) in the US sponsored a series of workshops on how to make digital libraries a reality, not just a dream. At the same time, digital libraries are an outcome of the revolution in computing, telecommunications and information systems that began almost 40 years ago, around 1965. This section frames the emergence of digital libraries as a recognized field of endeavor in terms of four requirements for viability and growth: a compelling vision, strong motivating factors, technology and funding.

A compelling vision

Many authors (Arms, 2000; Fox, 1993a; Lesk, 2004; Tedd and Large, 2005) trace the vision of digital libraries to a post-World War 2 paper by Vannevar Bush called *As We May Think* (1945) and a book called *Libraries of the Future* by J. C. R. Licklider (1965). Licklider's research for the book was sponsored by the US Council on Library Resources (Clapp, 1965, ix). Bush, at that time director of the US Office of Scientific Research and Development, called for a new approach to information organization and discovery based on the visionary concept of a 'memex' – a fast, flexible and efficient desktop device enabling associative indexing and instant access to both a vast library and a scientist's personal files.

The ideas and writings of Licklider, a professor of computer science at MIT, vice president of a high-technology company and imminent researcher for the Defense Advanced Research Projects Agency (DARPA), eventually led to ARPANET, a system of networked computers that preceded the internet. At the outset Licklider's *Libraries of the Future* focuses less on technology and more on solving the basic limitations of printed materials and the bricks-and-mortar libraries of the time:

> If books are intrinsically less than satisfactory for the storage, organization, retrieval, and display of information, then libraries of books are bound to be less than satisfactory also. We may seek out inefficiencies in the organization of libraries, but the fundamental problem is not to be solved solely by improving library organization at the system level. Indeed, if human interaction with the body of knowledge is conceived of as a dynamic process involving repeated examinations and intercomparisons of very many small and scattered parts, then any concept of a library that begins with books on shelves is sure to encounter trouble
>
> Licklider, 1965, 5

Noting that 'the "libraries" of the phrase, "libraries of the future", may not be very much like present-day libraries,' and 'in the present century, we may be technically capable of processing the entire body of knowledge in almost any way we can describe,' Licklider went on to create a prescient list of criteria for the future library that reflects both the progress and aspirations of 21st-century libraries (Licklider, 1965, 1, 20, 36–9).

Key developments from 1965 to the early 1990s

Licklider laid out his challenging 'libraries of the future' vision in 1965. Over the next 25 years, the technologies needed to build digital libraries became not only available but affordable – for example, digital storage, processors, connectivity, natural language processing, text formatting and scanning, optical character recognition (OCR), indexing and more (as discussed by Lesk, 2004, 16–89). Perhaps most importantly, the promise of the internet (dedicated in its earliest years to research-oriented use) for public and commercial use had captured the public imagination as well as the interest of the private sector and research professionals (Weingarten, 1993; Stoker, 1994; Ginsparg, 2011).

The computer and information sciences

Computer and information scientists made enormous progress in information retrieval theory and systems between 1965 and 1990. Computer scientists advanced the knowledge and understanding of architecture and systems, and information scientists complemented their work (Arms, 2012, 581). Howard D. White and Kate McCain's renowned analysis of the structure of the information science discipline between 1972 and 1995 indicates that the discipline was principally focused on information retrieval and user-system relationships; bibliometrics; automated library systems and online catalogs; science communication; and user theory (White and McCain, 1998). All of these created a solid foundation for the emergence of new research on digital libraries.

Online information industry

The online information industry predates the internet and the web. It had its start in the 1970s and by the early 1990s, it was a US$12 billion industry (1992 dollars), serving mainly the business sector (Calhoun, 1994, 2). There was, however, a segment of the industry called 'scientific, technical and diversified online services' that served primarily research and education; the market leaders in the early 1990s were Mead Data Central (NEXIS/MEDIS), Dialog and InfoPro Technologies (BRS/ORBIT) (Calhoun, 1994, 4–5). Dialog dates to 1972 (O'Leary, 1993).

In the early 1990s the online information industry took the form of online host services that mounted databases and software from which subscribers could retrieve information using first, dedicated terminals and later, personal computers. The firms that offered these services relied on content providers (database producers, publishers, abstracting and indexing services) and reliable, commercially available telecommunications networks (providing dial-up services). The supply of online content was already relatively large by the early 1990s; online databases grew from around 300 in 1979 to nearly 5200 in 1993 (Calhoun, 1994). CD-ROM database vendors had also entered the market for digital information by that time.

The growing adoption of personal computers not just by businesses and other organizations but also in homes, together with the advent of internet access (which was faster and cheaper than the existing commercial networks) led to both amazing opportunities and large challenges for the most successful online services and content providers of the time. The internet has long roots, and many had been aware of its potential for years. For example, in a 20-year retrospective piece he wrote in 2011, the well known physicist Paul Ginsparg notes that he first used e-mail on the original ARPANET, which preceded the internet, while a freshman at Harvard in 1973.

Online information industry services and content providers (e.g., publishers and professional societies) were faced with managing the disruptive risks and opportunities of the 'information superhighway' and full-text digital content in order to maintain (or improve) their positions – or else risk extinction. This same set of new conditions encouraged the entry of many new players providing online information and services.

Libraries, standards and automation

Libraries were early adopters of online information systems, and highly trained reference librarians served as intermediaries conducting searches of the very expensive online services, which had expert, non-intuitive interfaces *not* designed for end-user searching. In addition, for library information technology and technical services operations, the first distribution of MARC (Machine-Readable Cataloging) records from the Library of Congress in 1968 (Avram, 1969) was a great leap forward. Over the ensuing years MARC had a transformative influence on libraries, as did the founding in 1967 of the first shared computerized cataloging system based on MARC, the Ohio College Library Center (now OCLC Online Computer Library Center; Kilgour, 1969).

The MARC record and these new systems quickly created a new plane for library technological advances. MARC made it possible to aggregate large structured datasets to underpin the conversion from printed to online catalogs of library holdings; the first generation of robust automated systems for libraries; and many new services in libraries (for example, interlibrary lending became much easier, faster and less costly). All of these developments together put libraries in a position to be early adopters of many new information technologies, the internet and the web. Thanks to this long foreground, libraries were also ready for digital library collections, systems and services (Calhoun, 2003, 282).

The Follett report

In the UK, a great deal of experience and knowledge of the latest information technologies and networks, predating the internet and the web, led up to the Follett report (1993). The UKOLN (UK Office for Library and Information Networking) had been established in 1990 (Stoker, 1994, 119). Just two examples that reflect the current topics of the 1980s are from Brindley, who was writing about strategy for the 'electronic campus' and the shift from print and CD-ROM to online dissemination of scholarly content (Brindley, 1988; 1989); and from Law, an expert on library automation since the 1970s, who among other topics was writing about projects to get the nation's academic library catalogs online (Law, 1988). The logical extension of all this work was the Follett report, which placed academic libraries high on the UK national agenda for higher education and quickly generated large-scale national funding for the development of 'electronic' or 'virtual' libraries (the eLib Programme, discussed later in this chapter).

Archives and other professional communities

A foundational development that came out of the archives, humanities computing, linguistics and other professional communities was the Text Encoding Initiative (TEI), which produced a standard for encoding scholarly texts in machine-readable form. TEI, intended to support data interchange in humanities research, can be traced to a conference of the Association for Computers and the Humanities in 1987. The then newly available Standard Generalized Markup Language (SGML) was the spark needed to kick off the development of TEI and a new way of supporting textual research on the network (Ide and Sperberg-McQueen, 1995).

Daniel Pitti (1997) describes how the advent of the internet inspired the archival community to renew its efforts to bring geographically distributed primary resources together in a way that would enable universal intellectual access. Foundational (pre-internet) work was accomplished from 1981 to 1984 when a US National Information Systems Task Force of the Society for American Archivists paved the way to a MARC standard for the encoding of records describing archives and manuscripts. MARC records provide for the online discovery of archives and manuscript collections at the collection level, and in a library context; but machine-encoded finding aids were needed to actually lead to the materials in the collection. Archivists' next step was to develop a standard, computer-based encoding structure for finding aids. This work began in 1993 and produced the Encoded Archival Description or EAD standard. SGML is the technology underlying EADs. The development of EAD and experience with SGML were momentous developments that aligned the archival community's work with the web and the networked digital environment that was emerging.

Other developments

Given the limits of this space and my time to conduct the necessary research, this section's mini-analysis of the conditions leading to digital libraries from 1965 to the early 1990s is far from complete. I have merely touched on the work of some disciplines, organizations and communities of practice and not discussed others' contributions at all. In addition to the roles played by early research on the internet (which goes back to the 1970s) and by computer and information scientists, the online information industry, archives and libraries, the efforts of countless researchers and implementers intersected with, ran parallel with, or contributed directly to the origins of digital libraries. These include the individuals and groups who developed the internet and web standards, open systems and other core aspects of networking; those who pioneered new ways of marking up and encoding text; the geospatial or informatics communities; teaching and learning communities; and more. While recognizing these many contributions, I have focused this and the next chapter chiefly on the roles of computer and information scientists; libraries and the cultural heritage sector; and scholarly communities, content providers and online services.

An ambitious agenda

Christine Borgman (2007, 21), writing of the political aspects of new, large-scale research programs, noted 'visions must be grand to attract attention and the promised outcomes must be ambitious to attract money.' By the start of the last decade of the 20th century, computer and information scientists, scholarly content providers and libraries were ready to embrace an ambitious agenda. They were ready for the next steps toward the systems that Bush and Licklider had envisioned in 1965. Building the first digital libraries was not just feasible: it was the logical next step for researchers and professionals in many fields. Elements of the vision of digital libraries that fueled scholarly and public interest in the first decade of digital library research and development, starting around 1991 included:

- easy, fast, and convenient access to the world's information (regardless of where that information is stored) at any time, from anywhere in the world
- effective storage and organization of massive amounts of text, multimedia and data beyond the bounds of what even the largest single library could provide
- organization and access to materials in many languages
- greatly improved searching and browsing capabilities
- interoperability enabling the cross-searching of many diverse collections at once
- direct, instant delivery of information and data to multiple users at the same time
- transformative improvements in support for research and education globally; better support for interdisciplinary work and scholarly collaboration across institutions and around the world
- significant cost savings over traditional (duplicative) methods for cataloging, storing and preserving analog materials.

Strong motivating factors

As if the grand opportunities were not enough, two more powerful motivating factors converged in the early 1990s to make the time right for digital libraries. One was a sense of urgency to solve the pressing issue of an explosion of scholarly information; the other, already mentioned, was a sense of opportunity that arose in firms and communities of practice supporting scholarship. First, publishers, professional societies and indexing services seized on technological advances to improve the information storage and retrieval systems they used. Second, libraries and cultural organizations saw an opportunity to preserve and extend access to valuable collections through digitization.

A sense of urgency
Runaway growth

Both scholars and librarians have considered digital libraries to solve large-scale, long-standing challenges. Chief among them is the need to make an increasingly overwhelming volume of material accessible and available. Writing at the conclusion of World War 2, Bush (1945) noted the 'growing mountain of research' and that the difficulty posed by an explosion of scientific publications 'extended far beyond our present ability to make real use of the record.' In the UK the sense of urgency was similar, in that it was centered on the perception of runaway growth, but of a different nature. UK national attention was focused on specific problems facing UK higher education and academic libraries – increasing costs for materials coupled with a huge expansion in student populations – and the opportunity to solve them by effectively harnessing the technologies of the global information revolution (Carr, 2002).

The notions of runaway growth were fueled by other early predictions as well. Although his methodology was later called into question (Molyneux, 1994), librarian Fremont Rider's conclusion in *The Scholar and the Future of the Research Library* (1944) – that research libraries would double in size every 16 years – firmly established a sense of urgency around solving the problem of runaway library growth.

How much information?

Rider's methods may have been flawed, but he was not wrong about runaway growth in the world's information, including scholarly information. Figure 1.1 pulls estimates from a report of how much information was

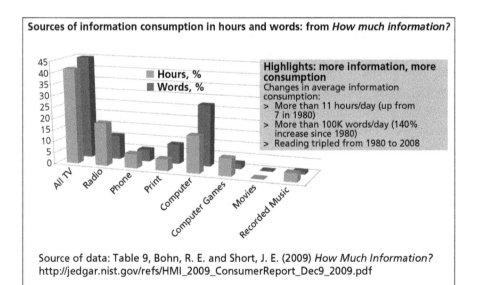

Source of data: Table 9, Bohn, R. E. and Short, J. E. (2009) *How Much Information?* http://jedgar.nist.gov/refs/HMI_2009_ConsumerReport_Dec9_2009.pdf

Figure 1.1 Validation of the predictions of runaway growth: more information and more consumption

consumed by Americans, from what sources, in 2008 compared to 1980 (Bohn and Short, 2009). The bars in Figure 1.1 compare estimated 2008 information consumption in hours and words.

As it turns out, there was and continues to be an information explosion, although not perhaps in the ways that Rider and digital library pioneers anticipated. Much more information does exist, and people spend more of their time consuming more of it. Bohn and Short estimate that the number of hours of information consumption per person grew 2.6% a year from 1980 to 2008 (2009, 7). The size of research library collections has not doubled every 16 years, but the amount of information available and of interest to an academic community has exceeded that growth rate; there is more to read than ever, and reading has increased since 1980: this is because there are now so many more ways to consume words (text). The report estimates that a third of the words that people consume come through interactions with computers, and the overwhelmingly preferred way to receive words is via the internet.

A new world
Scholarly communication
'Scholarly communication' alludes to the communicative activity of scholars (people engaged in creating original scholarly works), in particular how they communicate as writers, linkers (e.g., citing others' work), submitters/ disseminators (the choice of formal and informal communication channels, e.g., journals, conferences, wikis, blogs), and collaborators (Borgman and Furner, 2002, 6). Quite a few groups, classes of individuals and tools contribute to the *process* of scholarly communication, but stand outside scholarly communication itself: a few of these are peer reviewers, tenure review boards, evaluation tools or systems (e.g., citation counts), editors, publishers, professional societies, online information services, libraries, and of course readers/information seekers and those who annotate or comment on scholarly work informally.

Innovation in the process of scholarly communication was already well under way by the early 1990s, and the early achievements of online information services, publishers, professional societies and indexing services are impressive. At the time when digital library work got under way, major scholarly societies and publishers saw new opportunities and were keenly interested in developing better systems for publishing full-text journals and articles.

Mercury and CORE

Two early projects, Mercury and CORE, influenced the rapid development of new kinds of networked, online retrieval systems that made papers from many independent sources appear as one integrated service. Mercury began in 1991; it was a pre-web solution for bringing together computer science articles from three different scholarly publishers. It validated new concepts for converting, storing and delivering page images from distributed sources over the Carnegie Mellon University's campus network (Arms, 2012, 581). CORE was an early project and key influencer of methods for scanning document collections. It ran from 1991 to 1995, digitizing about 400,000 pages from 20 chemistry journals and demonstrating successful ways to build a full-text index for retrieval and display of digitized documents (Arms, 2012, 588). Chapter 2 discusses other early projects (TULIP, Red Sage and others).

The scholarly content providers and services that supported these projects brought a sense of opportunity and substantial resources to early digital library research and development, and these projects had a powerful impact. Indeed, together with many subsequent investments by scholarly societies, publishers and indexing and online service providers, the early projects eventually transformed scholarly publishing and the expectations of faculty and researchers that scholarly content will be not only online, but also interlinked.

Digitization

Librarians and other professional communities also drove the development of early digital libraries and the technologies underpinning them. Early efforts to preserve the treasures held in library collections, archives and museums through digital reformatting (digitization) took off in the early 1990s; these are also discussed in Chapter 2. By 1995, there were baseline standards, working principles, and a small but growing community of digitization specialists available for digital imaging projects for texts, pictorial images and more. This field of specialization eventually grew beyond the library and cultural heritage community and spawned mass digitization projects and the public's growing demand for books in digital form (e-books).

Technology
The last barriers removed

As mentioned already, personal computers, the internet and the web were also catalysts enabling research and development of digital libraries; these technologies were firmly in place before the web's first iteration in 1989 (attributed to Tim Berners-Lee, then at CERN) and the enthusiastic take-up of the Mosaic browser starting in 1993 (the US National Center for Supercomputer Applications at the University of Illinois had developed Mosaic) (Ginsparg, 2011, 5). These new innovations scaled up the size of prior opportunities to build services for collections stored in digital forms, retrievable over networks.

Arms (2000, 10) reported a series of technical developments in the early 1990s that 'removed the last fundamental barriers to building digital libraries':

- Storing information on computers became significantly less costly.
- Major advances had been made in the quality of personal computer displays.
- Receiving information over the internet became fast, affordable and reliable.
- Portable personal computers had become affordable and powerful.

The Kahn Wilensky architecture

The general principles for the design of a digital library that is 'open in its architecture and which supports a large and extensible class of distributed digital information services' were laid out by Kahn and Wilensky (Kahn and Wilensky, 1995; Arms, 1995). Kahn and Wilensky strongly influenced how early digital libraries were built by technologists. Micah Altman (2008) characterizes the 'Kahn-Wilensky architecture' as having four main types of components:

- *repositories*, ranging from file systems to distributed storage systems for content
- mechanisms to support *search* (indexing or metadata)
- *identifier systems* for identifying and locating digital objects
- *user interfaces* to perform user services (for example searching, browsing, visualization, delivery).

This is not an exhaustive list. Other components of digital library architecture include, for example, security systems for authenticating users, services to aggregate search results from multiple sources, and tools for supporting collaboration and other types of interaction.

Interoperable, web-based digital libraries

By 1991, computer scientists already had extensive experience with the development of information retrieval (IR) systems. Fox and Sornil (2003) wrote: 'DLs can be regarded as extended IR systems with multiple media and federation.' As web search and retrieval tools improved and gained acceptance over the course of the decade, digital library researchers and professionals sought new approaches to integrate their methods with web technology and the network. Lorcan Dempsey (1994), then at UKOLN, offered a prescient analysis of how the internet and web would generate entirely new kinds of systems and move information creation, publication and discovery to the network. This is indeed what has happened. He also foresaw the immense challenges that libraries would face aligning and integrating their traditional knowledge organization practices, metadata silos and fragmented information systems with the new networked environment – things he has continued to write and speak about today.

Computer scientists and librarians began to respond to the challenges. For example, early in the new millennium, Cornell and the University of Virginia began work on Fedora (Flexible Extensible Digital Object and Repository Architecture), a new system for digital library architecture. The intent was to provide a new framework for interoperable, web-based digital libraries (Payette and Staples, 2002). As will be discussed in Chapter 3, interoperability (the provision of uniform access to diverse information stored on different computer systems in different locations) has proved to be an ongoing challenge facing digital library developers.

Hybrid libraries

Interoperability became increasingly important as digital library projects, publishers, professional societies, indexing and online services brought content online and demand grew for unified access to content locked up in separate systems with separate interfaces. Furthermore, libraries began looking for ways to integrate the digital content with their predominantly non-digital collections (printed books and journals, prints, slides, maps, analog sound recordings and films, government documents, etc.) Rusbridge (1998) usefully described library collections in four categories: *legacy* (non-digital), *transitional* (legacy resources that have been or will be digitized), *new* digital resources (those expressly created as digital) and *future* digital resources. This book refers to the third and fourth categories as *born digital* resources. Rusbridge called for the development of technologies, systems and services for the 'hybrid library,' which would integrate all four categories of resources. As discussed in Chapter 5, from early days to the present, the necessity of accommodating the requirements of hybrid libraries has been a key driver in the field of digital libraries and the profession of librarianship.

Funding

This section provides a high-level summary of key national and international funding sources and programs in the first decade of digital libraries. A subsequent section, which contains a review of early large-scale digital library programs, also contains information about funding. The next chapter also incorporates information about funding from foundations, membership organizations, individuals, commercial or non-profit entities, universities and national libraries.

Funding streams

Federal and international agencies, national libraries, higher education institutions, public and private sector organizations, even individuals – all provided streams of funding for the early development of digital libraries. First-decade digital library funding tended to gravitate to national or local institutional levels, or it was invested as a result of the strategic capital budgeting decisions of commercial firms. The variety of streams has resulted in many technical advances, diverse digital libraries, and a complex landscape.

Large-scale efforts

Large-scale efforts tended to be funded by international bodies, government agencies, foundations and non-profit organizations. Some libraries invested heavily in digital library programs in keeping with their missions to support historical and cultural studies, provide a national research information infrastructure and preserve their nations' creative output (examples from Australia, France, the Netherlands, New Zealand, the UK, the US and elsewhere are represented in the next chapter). As noted previously, the investments of scholarly societies, publishers and indexing and online services also considerably advanced the early efforts to put scholarly content online; the amounts invested are unknown but collectively it must have been substantial.

Universities and institutions

It should also be mentioned that the funding from many universities and institutions supporting individual library projects, when taken as a whole, probably surpasses the financing provided by the centrally organized programs. Daniel Greenstein and Suzanne Thorin's report (2002) of a survey conducted by the Digital Library Foundation indicated that in 2000 responding libraries spent an average of over US$1 million each on digital conversion and digital library personnel (see their Table 3.1). University library projects at that time focused predominantly on digitization of cultural heritage materials.

Other sources

In a few cases the vision, commitment and financial resources of single individuals produced lasting and influential digital libraries. Brewster Kahle, for example, founded the Internet Archive in 1995, providing the capital himself. In 2003 one journalist reported that 'the ten million-dollar annual budget [of the Internet Archive] continues to come primarily out of Kahle's pocket' (Womack, 2003). Chapter 2 continues the discussion of how a variety of types of organizations supported the emergence of digital libraries as a new field of endeavor.

The one universal digital library

National agendas have contributed to the sense of urgency that spurred the eventual development of digital libraries in many countries. The dream of one universal, global digital library has been relevant everywhere to some degree, and it still is (see Arms, 2005, for a discussion of the user's viewpoint). However, while digital libraries are relevant globally, with some notable exceptions they have been funded at the national or local level. Writing for the 2007 issue of the *Annual Review of Information Science and Technology*, David Bearman (2007, 223–4) stated that 'although the vision of a singular "Digital Library" was what captured the popular and political imagination, and was promoted especially by Vice President Al Gore in the 1992 election campaign, through the 1990s the United States government supported "digital libraries" in the plural.' Bearman's perspective is supported by a review of the *Source Book on Digital Libraries* (Fox, 1993b), which reports on a series of NSF invitational workshops that preceded the NSF's call for the Digital Library Initiative (DLI-1) proposals. That work in the foreground of funded projects had two long-lasting outcomes: a preference for the term 'digital library' over 'electronic library' and a shift from the goal to 'develop a prototype national digital library' (singular) toward funding opportunities for the development of digital libraries (plural). The last chapter of this book returns to a consideration of the dilemma created for digital library implementers as a result of the disunion between who funds digital libraries and who benefits from them.

Early digital library projects

UK, US and multinational programs had considerable influence on digital library development and they produced significant outcomes that defined the way forward as digital libraries continued to evolve. The key projects included:

UK eLib Programme (eLib)

The driving force for the commissioning of eLib was the Follett report (1993), which reviewed the system of UK academic libraries in light of the problems of huge expansion of undergraduate populations, rising costs for library materials and the opportunities of new forms of information storage, access and retrieval over networks. Recommending that the problems be addressed through the use of information technology, the Follett report was highly influential and released the funding for eLib (Dempsey, 2006b). Managed by the Joint Information Systems Committee (JISC), eLib ran for seven years (1995–2001) and involved 70 projects. For more information see the first feature article in the first issue of *Ariadne*, which itself grew out of eLib (Kirriemuir, 1996). Pinfield (2004) offers a detailed review of eLib's influential outcomes.

DLI-1

The first large-scale funding for digital libraries in the US began in 1994 with an initial four-year Digital Library Initiative (DLI-1) sponsored by NSF, the National Aeronautical and Space Agency (NASA) and DARPA (Defense Advanced Research Projects Agency) (Arms, 2000, 62–3; National Science Foundation, 1993). The projects emphasized mainly technical aspects of digital libraries (Mischo, 2004, 6) and were led for the most part by computer scientists. Behavioral, social and economic issues got little attention during the first round of NSF funding.

DLI-2

In 1998 NSF issued a second call for proposals (National Science Foundation, 1998a; Griffin, 1999; Mischo, 2004). DLI-2 began with more concern for the social, behavioral and economic aspects of digital libraries and attracted funding from multiple agencies, including national libraries and the Institute of Museum and Library Services (IMLS).

Other US national programs

Arms (2012) reports on American Memory, a digital library that started in 1995 as a result of the Librarian of Congress' establishment of a project to digitize five million items and make them available on the web within five years (see Table 2.1 in this book). Arms, Blanchi and Overly (1997) discussed the technical building blocks, which came from the National Digital Library Project (NDLP) at the Library of Congress. The US National Institutes of Health (NIH) engaged early with digital library efforts. In February 2000 they launched the digital library PubMed Central, which as of this writing contains 2.7 million articles. The US PubMed Central was developed and is managed by the US National Center for Biotechnology Information (NCBI) (Humphreys, 2000).

Joint NSF/JISC international projects

In 1998 NSF called for proposals for multi-country, multi-team projects. In the UK, JISC issued a matching call. Six projects were funded jointly by NSF and JISC to explore cross-domain resource discovery, digital archiving, search and retrieval for musical information, reference linking, subject gateways, and metadata for multimedia digital objects (Chowdhury and Chowdhury, 2003, 56–7).

European Commission (EC)

Even before the first decade of digital library research and practice, the European Commission devoted substantial attention and funding to library-related programs. As Dempsey (2006b) notes, 'the first EU call for proposals in the libraries area was as far back as July 1991. The motivating framework for this and later calls was established in the Libraries Action Plan, a document first circulated in 1988.' Digital library programs were funded under the European Union's Framework Programmes, beginning with the Third. Funding for digital library research has continued at generous levels (http://cordis.europa.eu; see also Collier, Ramsden and Zhao, 1995; Dempsey, 1995; Dempsey, 2006b).

Projects in China and India

A considerable body of digital library research and development has occurred in China and India. Zhou (2005) and Shen et al. (2008) describe a number of large-scale digital library projects in China, starting with the introduction of CALIS (Chinese Academic Library Information System) in 1998, followed by CADLIS (Chinese Academic Digital Library), completed in 2005. Kumar (2010) and Das, Sen and Dutta (2010) describe digital library research and development in India, which began early in the new millennium and now includes open repositories, a number of cultural heritage digital libraries and the Digital Library of India.

Other projects

A number of large-scale, ambitious projects were inspired by democratic ideals and attracted multiple sources of funding and voluntary support:

Project Gutenberg

Project Gutenberg (www.gutenberg.org) is the first and oldest digital library. It began in 1971 as an idea from Michael Hart, who, given free computer time at the University of Illinois, decided to type in the US *Declaration of Independence* and then tried (unsuccessfully) to send it to everyone on the campus network (Hart, 1992). Gutenberg's goal has been to provide public domain e-texts a short time after they enter the public domain, for free, using only volunteers and donations to get the work done.

Internet Archive

Brewster Kahle started the Internet Archive in 1995. The Internet Archive (IA) has numerous components, but the Wayback Machine, which provides access to archived versions of an estimated 220+ million websites, may be the best known. The IA is an advocate for universal and free access to knowledge and it founded a co-operative project called the Open Content Alliance to build and preserve a massive digital library of multilingual digitized text and multimedia content (Dougan, 2010).

The Million Books project

The Million Books project (www.ulib.org; the first project of the Universal Digital Library) began with some preliminary test projects that led to an initial grant from NSF in 2000 (Linke, 2003; St Clair, 2008). Raj Reddy, an award-winning computer science professor at Carnegie Mellon University, continues to inspire and direct it. The Universal Digital Library's mission is to foster creativity and free access to all human knowledge; its purpose is to make digital texts freely available to anyone who can read and has access to the network (www.ulib.org/ULIBAboutUs.htm). Partners came from China, Egypt, India and the US. It reached and exceeded its goal of a million scanned books in 2007. Collections are represented on mirror sites in China and India.

Definitions of digital libraries
The definition used in this book

The definition of 'digital libraries' that underpins this book has two parts. Digital libraries are:

1 A field of research and practice with participants from many disciplines and professions, chiefly the computer, information and library sciences; publishing; the cultural heritage sector; and education.
2 Systems and services, often openly available, that (a) support the advancement of knowledge and culture; (b) contain managed collections of digital content (objects or links to objects, annotations and metadata) intended to serve the needs of defined communities; (c) often use an architecture that first emerged in the computer and information science/library domain and that typically features a repository, mechanisms supporting search and other services, resource identifiers, and user interfaces (human and machine).

My intention is to provide a practical definition that reflects the current situation, but can evolve as digital libraries evolve in the context of the web. Lagoze (2010, 25–31) has persuasively discussed the trend of digital libraries toward the resource-centered architecture of the web (mentioned again in subsequent chapters of this book). The definition used in this book refers for the most part to the traditional repository-centered architecture, because this model remains characteristic of most digital libraries today. Through the chapters of this book, I attempt to make the case that the important characteristics of digital libraries are (in this order) the social roles they play;

the communities they serve; the collections they gather for those communities; and the enabling technologies that support them. Social roles and communities are more likely to abide over time; collections and enabling technologies are more likely to shift.

Other definitions of digital libraries
Different perspectives

At the start of digital libraries' first decade, what came to be called a digital library had a number of names – electronic library, virtual library, library without walls. The first decade's explosion of activity and funding for digital library research and practice engendered many diffuse definitions of the phrases *digital library* or *digital libraries*. Some of the principal authors during this first decade paid little heed to definitions; others' discussions of definitions are lengthy. Considered as a whole, the digital library literature contains an enormous amount about how to define digital libraries. Fox et al. (1995, 24) suggest an explanation: 'the phrase "digital library" evokes a different impression in each reader.'

The public on the one hand, and those involved in building digital libraries, on the other, naturally had a variety of perspectives on the nature of digital libraries, when they were first conceived. The following list represents a few of these initial perspectives:

- a computerization of traditional libraries (people in general)
- a framework for carrying out the functions of libraries in a new way with new types of information resources (librarians)
- a new set of methods to innovate and improve fee- or membership-based indexing, full-text repositories and hyperlinking systems (publishers, online information services, professional societies, indexing services)
- a distributed text-based information system (computer and information scientists)
- a collection of distributed information services (computer and information scientists)
- a distributed space of interlinked information (computer and information scientists)
- a networked multimedia information system (computer and information scientists)
- a space in which people can collaborate to share and produce new knowledge (those working on collaboration technologies)
- support for formal and informal teaching and learning (educators).

Arguably the most comprehensive and thoughtful discussion of first-decade digital library definitions is by Borgman (1999 and 2000, 35–52), who notes that the many definitions arise because 'research and practice in digital libraries are being conducted concurrently' and by individuals and teams from different fields. Borgman made sense of the definitions that had emerged by 2000 by grouping and discussing them in a variety of ways, including:

- orientation (research-oriented versus practice-oriented definitions)
- concept of a library (narrow – library as a collection of content supporting information retrieval – versus broad – library as a continuous and trusted social entity)
- emphasis (definitions emphasizing collections, a particular type of content or communities versus those with an emphasis on institutions or services).

A sample of definitions

Table 1.1 builds out from the core of definitions considered by Borgman in 1999 and 2000. It offers a sample of definitions, considers their principal facets and cites their sources. The sample is far from comprehensive but attempts to show the progression of definitions from those emphasizing the enabling technologies of digital libraries (text analysis, distributed retrieval systems, metadata, indexing and knowledge representation, data communication networks, intelligent agents, interface design, multimedia storage, etc.) toward a new generation of definitions that place more emphasis on the communities and social roles of digital libraries. A number of authors have made the point that early research engendered definitions that focused more on technical issues and less on the broader social context of digital libraries (for example, Lagoze, 2010, 6).

Discussion

The DELOS definition offers a framework for understanding, planning and evaluating digital libraries. Another model is the '5S' framework (Streams, Structures, Spaces, Scenarios, and Societies) introduced in the dissertation of Marcos André Gonçalves (2004), which has been used to inform the development of a curriculum for digital library education and for other purposes. Another influential definitional model – one that pushes beyond read-only digital library repositories – is the one proposed by Lagoze and others (2005). This paper introduced a more flexible, richer information model for digital libraries based on an 'information network overlay' for modeling resources, their descriptions and relationships. It represented breakthrough thinking that led to new possibilities for digital libraries that facilitate 'the creation of collaborative and contextual knowledge environments.'

Table 1.1 A progression of digital library definitions

Definition	Facets	Source and comments
'The library of the future will be based on electronic data ... contain both text and graphics and be widely available via electronic networks. It is likely to be decentralized ...'	• Digital data (collections) • Multimedia • Services (widely accessible) • Networked • Distributed • Enabling technologies	Lesk, Fox and McGill, 1993, 12, 19–24 This was a white paper for NSF created in 1991. It led to the series of NSF workshops and the first NSF call for proposals. The focus of the definition and white paper was on enabling technologies and maintaining US national competitiveness.
'A service; an architecture ... a set of information resources, databases of text, numbers, graphics, sound, video, etc.; a set of tools and capabilities ... [with] users ... [and] contributors ...' Another key assumption: For use on the network	• Services (networked; with tools/capabilities) • Architecture (enabling technologies) • Digital data (collections) • Multimedia • Community-based (users/contributors)	Borgman, 1993, 122
'Systems providing a community of users with coherent access to a large, organized repository of information and knowledge ... enriched by the capabilities of digital technology ... span[ning] both print and digital materials ... provid[ing] a coherent view of a very large collection of information ... integrat[ing] materials in digital formats ... such as multimedia, geospatial data, or numerical datasets ... [characterized by] continuity [with] traditional library roles and missions ... [and with] many digital repositories ... appear[ing] to be a single digital library system ...'	• Systems • Community-based • Services (coherence; collected and organized) • Enabling technologies • Distributed, interoperable • Digital and non-digital data (hybrid) • Multimedia • Extension of existing libraries	Lynch and Garcia-Molina, 1995
'A large collection of the full contents of high use materials including books, journals, course materials, and multimedia learning packages, which can be directly accessed by students and staff' [with personal computers]	• Multimedia • Terms and conditions (licensed content) • Collection • Digital data (digitized)	Zhao and Ramsden, 1995 ELINOR project; concerned with digital library development for teaching and learning. Led to insights and progress on copyright and publisher content licensing issues (see Collier, Ramsden and Zhao, 1995). *(Continued on next page.)*

Table 1.1 *(continued)*

Definition	Facets	Source and comments
'Organized collections of digital information. They combine the structuring and gathering of information, which libraries have always done, with the digital representation of information that computers have made possible.'	• Services (organized, structured and gathered) • Digital data (collections) • Extension of existing libraries • Computers (enabling technologies)	Lesk, 1997, xx, xxii Lesk also stressed the importance of the economics of digital libraries: 'We know how to build a digital library … we do not know how to make it economically supportable.'
'The definition of the digital library will require an understanding of the role and nature of public institutions in a postindustrial society.' 'A realm of free speech and association as well as an information market place.'	• Extensions of existing libraries (but not as collections; rather in their societal roles) • Social (emphasis on social aspects)	Lyman, 1996 Emphasizes the social role of libraries offering free and equal access to knowledge and ponders the question of how digital libraries might support the traditional role of the library as a 'marketplace of ideas' and the public interest in education and democratic participation.
'Organizations [i.e., institutions] that provide the resources, including the specialized staff, to select, structure, offer intellectual access to, interpret, distribute, preserve the integrity of, and ensure the persistence over time of collections of digital works so that they are readily and economically available for use by a defined community or set of communities.'	• Organizations (institutions) • Digital data (collections) • Community-based • Services (selecting, collecting, organizing, providing access, delivering, preserving)	Waters, 1998 The definition developed by the Digital Library Federation. Services encompass a curatorial role. See also Deegan and Tanner (2002, 22)
1 Digital libraries are a set of electronic resources and associated technical capabilities for creating, searching, and using information. 2 Digital libraries are constructed – collected and organized – by [and for] a community of users, and their functional capabilities support the information needs and uses of that community.	• Digital data (collections) • Enabling technologies • Services (collecting, organizing, searching, using information) • Community-based • Use- and user-centered • Emphasis on social aspects (life cycle of information)	Shortened version of Borgman, 2000, 42. This definition has been very influential in the digital library field. From the beginning, Borgman has stressed the importance of the social aspects of digital libraries.
'Sociotechnical systems – networks of technology, information, documents, people, and practices.'	• Systems • Networked • Community-based • Use- and user-centered (work practices and people) • Emphasis on social aspects • Systems • Enabling technologies • Collections	Bishop, Van House and Buttenfield, 2003 Emphasis on balancing the needs of people with the requirements for collections and enabling technologies.

Table 1.1 (continued)

Definition	Facets	Source and comments
'A tool at the center of intellectual activity having no logical, conceptual, physical, temporal, or personal borders or barriers to information. Generally accepted conceptions have shifted from a content-centric system that merely supports the organization and provision of access to particular collections of data and information, to a person-centric system that delivers innovative, evolving, and personalized services to users. Conceptions of the role of Digital Libraries have shifted from static storage and retrieval of information to facilitation of communication, collaboration, and other forms of dynamic interaction … [and] the capabilities of Digital Libraries have evolved from handling mostly centrally located text to synthesizing distributed multimedia document collections, sensor data, mobile information, and pervasive computing services.'	• Service (Tool) • Systems • Use- and user-centered • Community-based • Social (communication, collaboration, dynamic interaction) • Multimedia • Mobile • Terms and conditions (policies)	Candela et al., 2007 A conceptual definition from the DELOS Digital Library Manifesto (Candela et al., 2006). Defines six core components of digital libraries: content, users (both humans and machines), functionality, quality, policy (e.g., rights) and architecture. The Manifesto contains a useful discussion of digital library definitions.

Other authors have also contributed insightful commentary on how to define digital libraries, rather than specific or formal definitions or frameworks (two examples are Chowdhury and Chowdhury, 2003, 4–9; Chowdhury and Foo, 2012, 2–4). Bill Arms offers an informal definition ('a managed collection of information, with associated services, where the information is stored in digital formats and accessible over a network,' but at the same time Arms has consistently emphasized that digital libraries must be understood as an 'interplay of people, organizations and technology' (2000, ix, 2). The already cited article by Peter Lyman offers another, quite different perspective; I recommend it to anyone with an interest in libraries' (and digital libraries') roles supporting the public good. The IFLA/UNESCO manifesto on digital libraries (www.ifla.org/digital-libraries/manifesto), which contains a definition of a digital library, also emphasizes the role of digital libraries in bridging the 'digital divide' (discussed in Chapter 6).

Levy and Marshall's article (1995, 78, 80, 82–3) is particularly important because it applies a work-oriented (ethnographic) perspective, noting that the emergence of digital libraries challenges the assumptions but not the basic character of libraries as an interplay of collections, enabling technologies, and services supporting the work that communities of users want to do. Noting 'an infrastructure by itself does not constitute a library' and 'the highest priority of a library, digital or otherwise, is to service the research needs of its constituents,' their article presaged the ensuing shift away from enabling technologies and digital collections as ends in themselves and toward user-centered design and networked services supporting collaborative work.

A few definitional issues

There are many challenges associated with attempting to define digital libraries. Some of the issues discussed by various authors include the following:

Distributed digital libraries

Some digital libraries are central archives that provide digital content storage and deliver services from a single system; others' content and services are distributed in multiple locations on the network. Still others aggregate the content of many digital libraries (repositories of repositories). Suleman (2012; 17–21) discusses centralized and distributed digital libraries. It should be noted here that digital libraries that are crawled and indexed by common or academically oriented search engines are discoverable in search engine results as if they were aggregated. The definition of digital libraries in this book covers some of these but excludes the virtual aggregations offered by common search engines like Google or Bing. The academic search engine Google Scholar, however, has characteristics of a digital library (it has a social role and it is intended for scholars' use). Beel, Gipp and Wilde (2010, under section 2.1) further discuss academic search engines, including Google Scholar, PubMed and IEEE Explore.

Hybrid libraries

As already noted, Rusbridge coined the term 'hybrid library' to refer to combinations of traditional collections, licensed e-resources and openly available digital collections produced in-house or elsewhere. Some digital content is directly accessible; other content can be linked to; still other content is represented only by citations (metadata). Schwartz (2000) writes 'the hybrid library is the context within which most academic digital libraries are found – the ecosystem of the digital library, as it were.' Chowdhury and Chowdhury (2003, 6–7) confirm this view; in their book they use the phrase 'digital libraries' to denote both digital-only and digital-plus-analog (hybrid) libraries. As Bearman (2007, 223) remarks, an assumption that a digital library contains only digital works is overly limiting; it is necessary to include within the scope of digital libraries those that 'service some physical items in addition to digital content.' The definition of digital libraries in this book includes hybrid libraries provided that the amount of digital content directly available or accessible through links exceeds the content represented by metadata only. Databases of metadata only fall outside the definition.

'Library' or 'digital library'?

As library collections are increasingly dominated by online content, the concepts of 'digital libraries' and 'libraries' are less distinguishable than they were in the 1990s, when digital libraries began to emerge. Chapter 5 discusses the possible convergence of strategic agendas for digital libraries and traditional libraries. However, the definition provided in this book does not conflate digital libraries and libraries.

Preservation

Deegan and Tanner's definition (2002, 22) is a set of principles emphasizing the curatorial role of digital libraries as managed collections, requiring that digital objects be selected, made accessible, and preserved as *long-term, stable resources*. The definition of digital libraries used in this book does not explicitly require a preservation mission.

Open or restricted content?

As discussed in Chapter 4 of this book, digital library innovations have led to rapid growth in the availability of open, freely available digital content and a culture of open data interchange. The definition used in this book notes that digital libraries are often open. However, the definition does not exclude fee-based or restricted-access digital libraries such as those produced by publishers and other e-resource providers, provided they are intended to serve defined communities. Borgman (2000, 46–7) and Chowdhury and Chowdhury (2003, 8–9) also discuss this issue. The definition in this book includes, for example, open or fee-based digital libraries from scholarly publishers, professional societies, aggregators like JSTOR or the Directory of Open Access Journals. It also includes library or consortially provided, cloud-based library discovery layers that provide access to a substantial amount of open, licensed and/or fee-based digital content.

Global digital library

Borgman proposed a working definition of a 'global digital library' as 'a useful construct that encompasses all the digital libraries that are connected to and accessible through a global information infrastructure' (2000, 48). Such a construct does not exist as of this writing. The world wide web, in and of itself, or its representation in a search engine like Google, falls outside the definition of a digital library that is used in this book.

Conclusion

This chapter has traced the antecedents of digital libraries to 1965 and J. C. R. Licklider's challenging vision for 'libraries of the future,' which, he noted, 'may not be very much like present-day libraries.' Key developments from 1965 to 1990 in computer and information science, telecommunications and networks, online publishing, personal computer ownership, libraries, archives and other professional communities – not to mention the internet and web – prepared the ground for an ambitious digital library research and development agenda. The vision for digital libraries was grand, and it attracted top research and professional talent and generous funding.

Early projects in the US and UK, programs funded by the European Commission, scholarly publishing projects, a number of projects inspired by democratic ideals, and many other initiatives led to groundbreaking innovations and the emergence of a new field of endeavor. Multifaceted and surrounded by dynamic technological and societal conditions, digital libraries are challenging to define, because they evoke diffuse impressions and continually evolve. The chapter concludes with a practical definition that underpins the use of the phrase 'digital libraries' in this book.

The next chapter examines the outcomes of digital libraries' exhilarating first decade: a new field of endeavor; transformative change in the processes of scholarly communication and in how (and where) people look for information; new ways of organizing, interlinking, and aggregating digital content; large-scale digitization; digital preservation; the open access movement; and working digital libraries.

CHAPTER 2

·········

Outcomes of digital libraries'
first decade

Overview

This chapter identifies and discusses a set of significant outcomes from the first decade of digital library research and practice (1991 to 2001). It describes accomplishments that set the dominant themes and continue to shape the field of digital libraries today. The chapter's overall purpose is to offer a framework for understanding the productive work of thousands of people during that period, one that reveals the interplay of people (producers and providers of digital libraries), enabling technologies and the collections, services and communities they support. Figure 2.1 visualizes the framework and seven elements within it. The chapter discusses the elements in the following order:

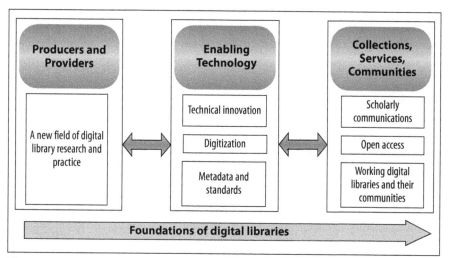

Figure 2.1 Key outcomes of the first decade of digital libraries

1 A new field of research and practice
2 The transformation of scholarly communication processes
3 Open access
4 Technological innovations
5 Digitization and digital preservation
6 Metadata and standards
7 Working digital libraries and the communities they serve.

These are the elements that formed the foundations as digital libraries moved into their second decade.

A new field of research and practice
The disciplines of digital libraries

As noted by Lynch, the first decade of research, development and practice in digital libraries was characterized by 'an enormous, exhilarating flowering of innovation, creativity and experimentation' (2000). From 1991 and into the new millennium, large numbers of projects were generously funded internationally and nationally by government agencies and foundations, institutions, public- and private-sector organizations and individuals around the world. At local levels, universities invested considerable funding in digital library research, prototyping and operations. The flowering was plentiful but diffuse: Lynch begins a later article with the remark that 'the field of digital libraries has always been poorly-defined, a 'discipline' of amorphous borders and crossroads' (2005). In a pre-print of a conference paper, Nguyen (2011) offers a long view based on a systematic study of 20 years' development of the peer-reviewed literature. Nguyen's results from an analysis of Scopus suggest that peer-reviewed papers have come from computer science (63%), library and information science (26%) and many other fields (11%).

Community building and organizational support

Early digital library community building, which took place through conferences, foundations, associations, co-operatives, partnerships and projects, brought far-flung digital library developers and practitioners together and contributed substantially to their efforts. These early community building efforts produced an active field of digital library research and practice as well as working digital libraries.

With respect to conferences, the computer science section of IEEE and the Association for Computing Machinery (ACM) began hosting conferences in 1995 and 1996 respectively. National and international library associations as well as many other associations and organizations now host digital library conferences; interested individuals could attend one or more conferences each month, if they so desired (*D-Lib Magazine* (www.dlib.org/groups.html) maintains a list of digital library conferences).

The foundations, associations, membership organizations and others that have been major supporters of digital library development are too numerous to describe in this short section, but without their contributions, digital libraries would not have emerged.

Education for digital librarianship

A variety of training programs as well as formal courses in digital libraries had begun to appear by the end of the first decade, and more developed over the ensuing years. Ma, Clegg and O'Brien (2009) provide an overview of trends and the results of their study of education for digital libraries from 1999 to 2006, as digital libraries were emerging. Ma's results echo the earlier findings of Spink and Cool (1999) and Liu (2004). One well known co-operative project to develop a digital library curriculum combined experts from both library and information science and computer science (Yang et al., 2009). Tammaro (2007) reported on work being done in Europe to develop digital library education; earlier, Liu (2004) had reported on programs being offered in the UK, the Netherlands and elsewhere. Sheila Corrall (2011, 57–60) offers a more recent evaluation of progress and the continuing debate around educating library professionals for the specific requirements of digital library environments.

The literature of digital libraries

The founding of D-Lib Magazine and Ariadne

Bill Arms and some colleagues founded *D-Lib Magazine* (www.dlib.org) in 1995. It has proved to be a key resource tracking the progress of digital libraries and the interdisciplinary field that grew up around them (see also Chapter 3). Much of what was happening in the NSF-funded projects was reported in *D-Lib*. *Ariadne* (www.ariadne.ac.uk) grew out of the eLib program in the UK (Dempsey, 2006a) and has served a similar function (Tedd, 2002) for UK projects, particularly those funded by JISC, an important agency supporting UK higher education and libraries, computing and research. Published by UKOLN, *Ariadne's* first issue is dated January 1996.

Blogs and e-discussion lists

Since its beginnings the digital library community has embraced the web and its new forms of communication and participation. Roy Tennant has been blogging about digital libraries since 1997 (Tennant, 2004b, vii) and his blog The Digital Shift (www.thedigitalshift.com) has been widely influential. Since 1990 the current awareness newsletter *Current Cites* has been a good source for digital library topics. Charles Bailey Jr (www.digital-scholarship.org/cwb) has created and maintained online bibliographies since 1996; they have been a valuable source for learning about and tracking selected digital library topics. The Dublin Core Metadata Initiative has maintained public online news since 1995 and a public e-mail list since 1996.

Publication patterns over time

An informal quantitative analysis of publications on digital library topics suggests that articles began to appear in the early 1990s and grew to a peak in 2005 and 2006. This publication pattern is illustrated by Figure 2.2, which

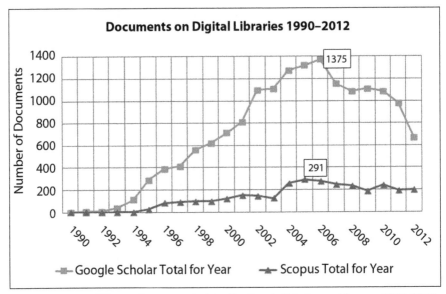

Figure 2.2 Digital library documents indexed in Google Scholar and Scopus, 1990–2012 (articles with the words 'digital library' or 'digital libraries' in the title)

is a snapshot of the count of items indexed by Google Scholar with either 'digital library' or 'digital libraries' in the title for each year from 1990 to 2012. The counts were captured in June 2013. The reader should consider that there may be a time lag before newer papers are indexed in Google Scholar; this time lag contributes to the lower number of articles found for 2011 and 2012.

For comparison the same search was done using Scopus (an Elsevier-owned subscription database of citations and abstracts from primarily peer-reviewed academic journals and conference proceedings). Scopus is a competitor to another commercially available product for tracking scholarly citations, the Web of Science (WoS) from Thomson-Reuters. The pattern of the Scopus curve is the same as the Google Scholar curve, with articles growing to a peak in 2005 and 2006, but remaining fairly steady through 2010. This analysis was inspired by Christine Borgman's (2009) keynote address at a Joint Conference on Digital Libraries, in which she briefly noted the clustering pattern of the usage of 'digital library' in Google Scholar indexes.

The results visualized in Figure 2.2 are not unexpected: they are consistent with studies comparing Google Scholar, Web of Science and Scopus from Meho and Yang (2007), De Sutter and Van Den Oord (2012) and Harzing (2012 and 2013). Google Scholar's coverage of many document types (e.g., dissertations and theses, reports, conference presentations, working papers and posters, pre-prints, and more) is the reason for the higher number of documents indexed in Google Scholar compared to Scopus, which indexes articles from primarily peer-reviewed sources. The results of this quantitative analysis are also consistent with the history of national-level research and development funding for the digital library field, as described in Chapter 1. Ambitious projects produced a growing number of publications during the years following 1994 – when large-scale funding began – until about 2006, when the many research findings produced under the largest grants had appeared in the literature.

The impact of shifts in funding

After 2005, large-scale funding for digital library research from US federal agencies diminished. In a 2005 article Stephan Griffin, then a program director at NSF, noted plans for a third US digital libraries program (beyond DLI-1 and DLI-2), as documented in the 2003 NSF-sponsored Chatham Workshop (Larsen, Wactlar and Friedlander, 2003). This third program did not materialize as expected. Similarly Lynch, reviewing a decade's work in digital libraries, noted:

As of 2005, it seems a virtual certainty that substantial programmatic US government funding of digital libraries research in terms of the construction of prototype systems is at an end, at least for the near future. The novelty of constructing digital libraries as a research end in itself has run its course . . .

Lynch, 2005

After 2003 other NSF funding priorities came to the fore, such as cyberinfrastructure, e-science and the stewardship of digital data (Atkins et al., 2003). Chapter 8 returns to these topics.

The literature of digital library practice

Around the start of the new millennium, the digital library field of endeavor began to include many more publications reporting the results of practitioners. By 2007 a large number of university research libraries had introduced digital library programs. For example, in a survey conducted on behalf of the Association of Research Libraries (ARL) in January 2006, results indicated that over half of ARL libraries had or planned to have working institutional repositories of locally produced digital works (Bailey et al., 2006). In February 2006, a little over half of the members of the ARL libraries responded to a survey about digitization activities; nearly all of those who responded (97%) reported they were engaged in these operations in their libraries (Mugridge, 2006).

The transformation of scholarly communication processes
Early projects

Robert Wilensky, principal investigator of a DLI-2 project that began in 1999 wrote 'our practice of disseminating, accessing and using information, especially scholarly information, is still largely informed by the nature of pre-electronic media' (2002). He, like many others working in the field of digital libraries at that time, advocated the development of new enabling technologies and new publishing models that would transform and substantially improve scholarly information dissemination and use. Hans Geleijinse of Tilburg University, a leader and early adopter of digital library technologies in the Netherlands, provides an excellent description of how Tilburg began innovating its scholarly information services in the early 1990s (Geleijinse, 1999).

The first decade of digital libraries research and practice made significant progress toward transforming scholarly communication processes. Chapter 1 discussed Mercury and CORE, two early influential projects. Others include:

TULIP (The University Licensing Program)

A project organized by Elsevier in 1991, TULIP tested the (pre-web) networked, desktop delivery of e-journals with nine universities. A parallel experiment with Tilburg University ran from 1992 to 1995 (Elsevier, 2012). The work evolved eventually to a web-based service for finding and delivering a large number of scholarly journals. The projects provided Elsevier with technical lessons and the university partners with a better understanding of e-journal distribution and access issues associated with electronic journals. At the University of Michigan, which had been a TULIP partner, the experiences of project participation, combined with early experimentation with SGML, positioned Michigan to continue contributing to digital library development (Bonn et al., 1999). Participation in TULIP was an important stepping stone for other university participants as well.

Red Sage

Red Sage was supported by the University of California-San Francisco, Bell Labs and Springer-Verlag and ran from 1992 to 1996. The three partners assembled a large group of participating commercial publishers, scholarly societies, and university presses to build a digital library for the health sciences and serve as a laboratory to inform the transition from print-based to digital systems (Lucier and Brantley, 1995). The participating publishers in Red Sage benefited not only from technology transfer but also from a better understanding of the economic and social issues associated with the electronic delivery of journals.

UK e-publishing projects

This was a large set of projects beginning in 1995 in the context of eLib (described in Chapter 1). The projects were organized into seven program areas, among them on-demand publishing, digitization, electronic document delivery and e-journals (Rusbridge, 1995). The experiences of these projects provided many UK universities with new skills and abilities to exploit information technology innovations (Kirriemuir, 1996).

DeLIver (Desktop Link to Virtual Engineering Resources)

The DeLIver testbed project was funded by professional societies, commercial publishers and federal agencies and began in 1998. It considerably advanced research and development of web-based access to full-text journals and articles (Mischo, 2004, 7–10). Scholarly societies and publishers subsequently used the project's design insights and specific technologies to establish or improve their own full-text repositories and hyperlinking systems.

e-Depot

The Dutch national library extended its responsibility for the legal deposit of all Dutch publications to the digital era by making the decision to build an 'e-Depot' in 1993 (Oltmans and Lemmen, 2006, 63). This was a project that demonstrated to the digital library field what archiving, preservation and legal deposit programs could look like in the digital age, and how national libraries could strike innovative, large-scale, mutually beneficial agreements with commercial publishers and online information service providers. In 2010 the Dutch national library announced that it would upgrade e-Depot to become a 'National Platform for Digital Publications.' The new platform is intended to aggregate e-content (as e-Depot has done) but also to deliver content from the national library's ambitious mass digitization program to digitize all Dutch printed publications since 1470, some 730 million pages. The initial stage of the project involves partnerships with Google and Proquest (Janssen, 2011).

Open access

The open access movement was another key outcome of the first decade of work in digital libraries. Among the early influencers is Stevan Harnad. In 1990 he published a paper (now frequently cited) that advocated extending the idea of an electronic archive to include digital prepublications of scholarly articles (*pre-prints*). The purpose was to harness the nascent forms of digital scholarship to take scholarly collaboration to a new level and 'substantially restructure the pursuit of knowledge.' The copyright laws were among the obstacles he listed to realizing the goal.

There was reason for optimism: by the next year (1991), the Los Alamos research institute had begun to instantiate such a new model for digital scholarship and collaboration (Harnad, 1999). The new model featured *self-archiving* of pre-prints and final refereed drafts. An early instantiation was the Los Alamos Physics Archive, which eventually became arXiv.org (see Table

2.1 at the end of this chapter). Physicist Paul Ginsparg had developed the physics archive from the idea of a 'centralized automated repository and alerting system . . . a solution [that would] democratize the exchange of information' (Ginsparg, 2011).

The foundation stones for what became a strong global movement for *open access* to scholarship included:

- the opportunity to greatly improve scientific inquiry and the advancement of knowledge
- an innovative re-conceptualization of the scholarly communication process for the digital era
- open online archives (repositories)
- the concept of self-archiving.

Advocacy and advocates for open access sprang up quickly, as further discussed in later sections of this chapter and in Chapters 4, 6 and 8.

A new world of scholarly research, teaching and learning

The impacts of these early projects and later investments in new systems by scholarly societies, publishers, indexing services, research institutes and open access advocates were enormous. If a time machine were to transport a set of graduate students and faculty members from 1990 to today, they might find their contemporary colleagues' scholarly sources and practices almost unrecognizable. As Clifford Lynch, director of CNI, wrote in his review of the ways in which information technology has changed academic libraries:

> In the late 1980s, the world of scholarly communication, teaching, and research began to change as a result of networking and advanced information technology. We entered a decade characterized by an enormous, exhilarating flowering of innovation, creativity, and experimentation. The idea of networked information emerged . . . International information sharing and collaboration were greatly facilitated. The use of the Net became critical in many forms of scholarly communication. Pre-prints and technical reports became widely distributed on the Net, democratizing access to this critical information and speeding up the rate of communication . . . Scholarly communication became much more interactive through the use of technologies as mundane as mailing lists or as sophisticated as collaboratories.
>
> Lynch, 2000

Rapid adoption and changing work practices

Surprisingly rapid integration of the new systems and databases for electronic resources into everyday practices for research, teaching and coursework followed the digital transformation of the scholarly communication process. By fall 2001, a survey (Friedlander, 2002) of over 3000 faculty, graduate students and undergraduates found that while the use of print sources remained important, 35% of faculty and 49% of graduate students reported they were relying exclusively or almost exclusively on electronic sources for their research. Undergraduates were even more willing to shift to online research practices, with 49% reporting they used electronic sources exclusively or almost exclusively. Over time these trends have grown considerably stronger.

Technical innovations

This section covers the outcomes of first-decade research and practice that advanced the enabling technologies of digital libraries. It begins with an outcome of DLI-funded digital library research at Stanford called PageRank. It next turns to outcomes that advanced interoperability. A third subsection considers outcomes that enable interlinking across digital sources. A fourth subsection considers the genesis of open access repositories.

PageRank

The physicist Paul Ginsparg (2011) concludes his retrospective on the 20th anniversary of the physics open archive with the insight 'the Internet, World Wide Web, search engines, and other developments described here all initially stemmed from the academic community's need to transmit, retrieve, and organize information'. Indeed, the academic community's information needs drove many technological innovations and influenced what digital libraries produced in their first decade. A new world of scholarship was one of those outcomes. Another outcome that arose from the early work of the digital library field was an innovation that has changed the world for everyone – PageRank.

In April 1998 at the Seventh International World Wide Web Conference, Stanford graduate students Sergey Brin and Larry Page presented the results of research they had conducted as part of a team working on one of the six NSF DLI-1 projects (see Chapter 1). That project, under the leadership of Hector Garcia-Molina and others, was called the Stanford Integrated Digital Library Project. Brin and Page's conference paper (1998) presented a prototype of Google and its underlying system for efficiently crawling and indexing the web, called PageRank. PageRank uses the link structure of the web to produce what might be called 'associative indexing' – an approach much like that envisioned by Vannevar Bush in 1945 when he proposed the 'memex.'

PageRank (further described by Page et al., 1999) had its beginnings in the Stanford project's attempts to discover powerful new ways to find information (Stanford University. Digital Library 2005a, 2005b; Google, 2012). Brin and Page presented their conference paper in April 1998. In September 1998 they founded Google, whose well known mission is 'to organize the world's information and make it universally accessible and useful.'

Comparing the Google mission to the stated purpose of the Stanford Integrated Digital Library Project, funded under DLI-1 and continuing in DLI-2, suggests that these projects influenced Brin and Page's bold vision for Google. The following quote from the Stanford award abstract demonstrates this strong connection (National Science Foundation, 1998b):

> This project – the Stanford Integrated Digital Library Project (SIDLP) – is to develop the enabling technologies for a single, integrated and 'universal' library, proving uniform access to the large number of emerging networked information sources and collections. These include both online versions of pre-existing works and new works and media of all kinds that will be available on the globally interlinked computer networks of the future. The Integrated Digital Library is broadly defined to include everything from personal information collections to the collections that one finds today in conventional libraries and the large data collections shared by scientists. The technology developed in this project will provide the 'glue' that will make this worldwide collection usable as a unified entity, in a scalable and economically viable fashion.
>
> Hector Garcia Molina, National Science Foundation, 1998b

Among the outcomes of the first decade of digital libraries, the contribution of the Stanford Digital Library Project to the creation of PageRank made significant progress toward the dream of a universal library. Google 'emerged from the [DLI] funded work and has changed working styles for virtually all professions and private activities that involve a computer' (Paepcke, Garcia-Molina and Wesley, 2005).

Early support for interoperability

One vision of digital libraries that fueled this first decade's efforts included the notion that digital libraries would reflect a distributed environment; in other words, they would bring together diverse collections of information on different computer systems in different locations around the world. Interoperability and integration of search results in an understandable display for the user are the prerequisites for cross-searching, retrieval and display of diverse, distributed, complex digital objects.

'Interoperability' (in this context, the provision of uniform, coherent access to diverse information from different, independently managed systems) has proved to be a great and ongoing digital library challenge. Chapter 3 discusses the grand challenge of interoperability and the progress that has been made, starting with efforts using Z39.50, a protocol for information retrieval that pre-dates the web. The following section picks up the interoperability thread with an outcome of early digital library work, the Open Archives Initiative.

The Open Archives Initiative

The Open Archives Initiative (OAI, www.openarchives.org) was instrumental in defining a new framework for interoperable digital libraries. OAI has had a significant impact on how scholars distribute, share and discover research. Its origin is a meeting held in Santa Fe in October 1999 in response to a call to explore co-operation among scholarly e-print archives (Van de Sompel and Lagoze, 2000; Lagoze and Van de Sompel, 2001). The technical and organizational framework for OAI that emerged from the meeting came to be called the Santa Fe Convention, which was seen as the key to increasing the impact of open repositories and establishing real alternatives to scholars' dependence on traditional journal publishing. The group's work led quickly to the development of the OAI Protocol for Metadata Harvesting (OAI-PMH).

OAI-PMH

Participants at the OAI Santa Fe meeting representing arXiv.org, the California Digital Library, CogPrints, RePEc (a repository of papers in economics) and NCSTRL (a repository of technical reports in computer science) left the meeting with the intention to be early adopters of the Santa Fe Convention. The technical specifications for OAI-PMH (the metadata harvesting protocol) were released in May 2001 (Lagoze and Van De Sompel, 2001; Lagoze et al., 2002). The intent was for OAI-PMH to be the 'appropriate catalyst for the federation of a broad cross-section of content providers.' OAI-PMH represented a fresh, easier-to-implement approach to achieving inter-operability for distributed digital libraries.

By adopting OAI-PMH, individual repositories make their metadata accessible in a standards-based way for harvesting by providers of search and discovery services. The framers of OAI-PMH intentionally chose a low-barrier, easy-to-implement approach. Many adopted OAI-PMH to enable interoperability with other metadata providers and allow harvesting of their data stores, thereby making their digital libraries more widely known. This strategy has paid off extremely well for making the content of open access repositories visible in search engine results. Perhaps more than any other first-decade digital library technical innovation, OAI-PMH has been a major factor in the rapid growth of open access repositories around the world.

Identifiers

Digital library researchers and builders have understood the central importance of persistent identifiers from the earliest days of digital library work. Identifiers are an essential component of the Kahn-Wilensky architecture of digital libraries (see Chapter 1). Bermès (2006) introduces and explains the critical role of identifiers in the context of digital library projects. The keen appreciation of persistent identifiers continues to be a defining characteristic of digital library research and practice (Chapters 3 and 9 further discuss identifiers).

The Handle System and DOIs

The Handle System and DOIs were key outcomes of first-decade digital library research. Kahn and Wilensky first developed the Handle System (www.handle.net) in 1993 (Kahn and Wilensky, 2006, 115). Today, handles are used to identify journal articles, technical reports, books, theses and dissertations, government documents, metadata and more. The International DOI Foundation's implementation of the Handle System is the DOI (Digital Object Identifier) system (International DOI Foundation, 2012). DOIs were rapidly taken up by publishers and implemented as a critical part of the infrastructure for digital publishing. For example, DOIs are now used by CrossRef (www.crossref.org), a consortium of nearly 4000 publishers.

URLs versus persistent identifiers

URLs are Uniform Resource Locators. Although the word 'locator' is embedded in the phrase from which URL is derived, URLs are unreliable for locating and linking to things over time (see, for example, Nelson and Allen, 2002). Everyone is familiar with broken links on the web.

Aware of the difficulties that web developers were having maintaining usable URLs, OCLC Research (1996) developed and made software freely available to help developers manage URLs in a way that would reduce the need for maintenance and provide long-term stability. This is the PURL (Persistent Uniform Resource Locator) software, which provides for flexible naming and resolution of URLs. OCLC completed a collaborative project to re-architect and release the PURL software as open source in 2007 (OCLC Research, 2007).

Over time, best practices for web developers and digital library implementers favor Uniform Resource Identifiers (URIs), the technology for naming and addressing resources on the web (www.w3.org/Addressing; Baker and Dekkers, 2003). Chapter 3 returns to the discussion of URIs and how they relate to digital libraries.

Reference linking

There is another enabling technology related to digital library interoperability. Information seekers expect to be able to link directly and immediately between sources such as an article and its references, from citations in a database or online index, or from references in a catalog or bibliography. This functionality is called 'reference linking.' The Open Journal demonstration project (Hitchcock et al., 1998) confirmed the value of links for providing faster and more direct access to more information, enhancing the effectiveness of information retrieval and adding value to electronic resources. It also influenced the development of what became widely used solutions for reference linking by scholarly publishers and online information services.

OpenURLs

Reference linking is particularly important in a hybrid library, where some of the resources may be represented by online citations but the text to which the citation refers is available only in print. Another application of reference linking is providing user access to the appropriate online version of an article, given the set of sources to which that user has access. Caplan and Arms' article (1999) on reference linking for journal articles provides a useful generic statement of the problem that reference linking solves: 'given the information in a standard citation, how does one get to the thing to which the citation refers?'

Reference linking works best if the links persistently identify what users want to link to. Unfortunately, persistent identifiers do not exist for everything (or even most things). Early digital library research identified other methods for linking that have become familiar and widely adopted: OpenURLs and services based on them, such as SFX from Ex-Libris, a library system vendor active in the development of OpenURLs. Van de Sompel and Hochstenbach noted:

> The omnipresence of the World Wide Web has raised users' expectations [for interlinking] . . . When using a library solution, the expectations of a net-traveler are inspired by his hyperlinked Web-experiences. To such a user, it is not comprehensible that secondary sources, catalogues and primary sources, that are logically related, are not functionally linked.
>
> Van de Sompel and Hochstenbach, 1999a, 1999b, 1999c

An OpenURL provides a standardized way for an information service to capture and transfer metadata about an information object in one location, transport this data to another information service, then display the information object to the user. The digital library community's interest in OpenURL was immediate; it was approved for fast-track standardization by NISO, and it became an approved standard in 2004.

While the utility of OpenURLs in practice suggests some new work to improve linking, as suggested by Blake (2002), Chandler (2009) and Trainor and Price (2010), OpenURLs are now widely deployed by publishers and aggregators, library subscription agents, library system vendors, consortia and libraries.

The emergence of open access repositories

Two first-decade outcomes led to the emergence of open access repositories, a type of digital library that has had a substantial impact on the world's access to scholarly content. The origins of these outcomes can be traced to the OpCit Project and OAI-PMH.

At the end of the 1990s NSF and JISC funded six international digital library projects. One was the Open Citation Project (OpCit), with participants from Southampton University, Cornell University and the Los Alamos National Laboratory (National Science Foundation, 2001). Hitchcock et al. (2002) tell the story of OpCit. The key, lasting technical outcome of the OpCit project enabled many to build open access repositories by producing the open source software called GNU EPrints. By the time OpCit concluded, the EPrints software (www.eprints.org) was being used by nearly 60 archives. As of this writing (June 2013), ePrints software is being used by 505 of the 3430 repositories tracked by the Registry of Open Access Repositories (http://roar. eprints.org). EPrints can be said to have stimulated the subsequent development of other repository software (like DSpace) and the building of many open access repositories (see Chapters 4 and 8).

Digitization and digital preservation

Digital content is often created through digital reformatting. *Reformatting* converts an original object (that is, an object in its original form, like text or images) to a digital one that is easier not only to preserve, but also to compress for storage and manipulate with computer programs. This conversion process is called 'digitization,' the process of converting a physical item into a digital representation or facsimile. Digitization relies on a number of enabling technologies, including scanning and OCR but also digital photography, re-recording and other techniques. Many types of materials held by libraries, museums and archives might be digitized: maps, music (printed and recorded), manuscripts, photographs and images of many kinds, videos, oral histories, thee-dimensional objects and microfilm or microfiche.

The following sections briefly describe the key outcomes of first-decade digital library work involving digitization and preservation:

- large-scale digitization of scholarly journals
- some early defining projects that established the value of digitization
- national library programs for cultural heritage materials
- contributions to preservation
- the emergence of digitization specialists and best practices.

Scholarly journals: JSTOR and other initiatives

JSTOR (see Table 2.1 at the end of this chapter) is an example of an organization with roots in the first decade of digital libraries. JSTOR (www.jstor.org) is not a publisher, but an independent non-profit organization founded to help academic libraries and publishers. Initially funded in 1994 and officially launched in 1997, it is a key first-decade outcome because of its substantial influence on the development and creation of digital libraries of scholarly content, how journals are preserved, library management of shelf space for journal back files, the visibility and usage of older materials, and more (Guthrie, 1997; Guthrie, 2001). As of this writing JSTOR provides access to archival and current issues of more than 1400 scholarly journals.

Other early projects to digitize scholarly journals include DIEPER at Göttingen University (Schwartz, 1999), the Australian Cooperative Digitization Project (ACDP) (Burrows, 1999); and NACSIS-ELS ('the Japanese JSTOR'), which was launched in 1997 (Miyazawa, 2005).

Early defining digitization projects

A number of early projects demonstrated the exciting potential of digitization, especially for broadening access and opening the study of cultural heritage materials to new audiences, freed of the boundaries of time and place. Four of these projects are:

1 Perseus Digital Library
2 Dunhuang Caves
3 Gutenberg Bibles
4 Greenstone.

Perseus Digital Library (www.perseus.tufts.edu)

The Perseus Digital Library (see Table 2.1 at the end of the chapter) focuses on primary materials related to classical Greco-Roman culture. Its development began in 1987 at Harvard and the project moved to Tufts University in 1993 (Crane, 1996). Perseus led the way in testing what happens when libraries move online, how digital technologies would live up to their promise (or not) and how to create an infrastructure for digital libraries that others could learn from. Perseus first appeared on the web in 1995. Perseus' culture of participation allows not only faculty, but also student researchers and citizen scholars, to interact with the art and archaeology, history, language and literature, philosophy and science of the classical world (Crane et al., 2012).

Dunhuang Caves

A large library of ancient Buddhist texts, tablets, prints and artifacts was discovered in 1900 in a cave near Dunhuang, China. Eventually an entire complex of hundreds of caves, containing artifacts and painted walls, was discovered in the area. Dunhuang had been a caravan stop on the Silk Road from central Asia to China. Scholars soon visited the sites and took various treasures back to their own countries. In 1993, the International Dunhuang Project (IDP) began to develop an international database of collaboratively produced and shared digitized representations of the objects. A wealth of additional information about the project (including a timeline and the database) is on the IDP site (http://idp.bl.uk/idp.a4d). IDP demonstrated that digitization provides a way to virtually re-gather treasures that are dispersed around the world.

Gutenberg Bibles

In 1996, Keio University in Japan led an impressive project to create digital facsimiles of its own and several others' surviving Gutenberg Bibles. The project was called HUMI (Humanities Media Interface). The online site (www. humi.keio.ac.jp/treasures/incunabula/B42) makes the study of Gutenberg's early printing accessible to everyone and enables side-by-side comparisons of two copies (Keio's and Cambridge University's) of these incredibly rare books.

Greenstone (www.greenstone.org)

The first New Zealand digital library project was organized by computer science researchers at the University of Waikato in 1995. The Waikato team's efforts had long-term significance because their efforts produced Greenstone – open source, freely available, multilingual digital library software for use by others (Witten et al., 1999; Witten, Bainbridge and Nichols, 2009). Early experiences of the Waikato researchers with United Nations and humanitarian and development organizations eventually led to Greenstone's adoption in many countries around the world, including developing countries. As of this writing, Greenstone supports digital libraries in South America, Asia, Africa, the Middle East, Europe and North America (results from June 2013 search of opendoar.org). In New Zealand, Greenstone is the basis of the highly popular PapersPast, a project of the National Library of New Zealand (see Table 2.1 at the end of the chapter). The global implementation of Greenstone revealed the potential of digital libraries to address not just multilingualism but also the *digital divide* (see Chapter 6).

National library programs

This subsection presents a tiny number of additional examples of early national library digitization projects. Some national library digitization projects have already been mentioned in Chapter 1 (e.g., American Memory). National library projects not only produced sites that have enabled broad, online, public global access to previously hidden cultural heritage materials, but also the lessons learned from the projects strengthened and guided the development of the digital library field.

Sounds.bl.uk

This service of the British Library goes back years; the digital library part of the story begins in 1992, when the British Library began adopting digital audio technology for the purpose of broadening access to its world-class sound recordings archive. The mission of the earliest project, 'Project Digitise,' was dual – access and preservation (Copeland, 1994). That first project focused on the conversion and cataloging of recordings on wax cylinders from the collection of A. L. Lloyd (an authority on folksongs) and from a collection of ethnographic field recordings. Many other projects followed, notably the Archival Sound Recordings project from 2004–9 (JISC, 2007, 5–8), funded under the extensive JISC Digitisation Programme, which continues today (www.jisc.ac.uk/digitisation). As of this writing, the most recent digital library-related initiative out of the BL Sound Archive is http://sounds.bl.uk, which went live in January 2012 (see Table 2.1).

Gallica

Gallica, the digital library of France, grew out of digitization activities at the Bibliothèque nationale de France (BnF) that began in the 1990s. Gallica first launched in 1997 with digitized content of books and journals, manuscripts, many types of images, maps, and more. The BnF has exemplified an assessment-based approach to digital library development (see, for example, Assadi et al., 2003, which inspired a whole series of digital library usage and user studies in France and elsewhere). In addition, Gallica has exemplified a commitment to continuous improvement in its use of digital library technologies, for example implementing OAI-PMH for publishing Gallica metadata and harvesting from other digital repositories (Delorme, 2011) and experimenting with linked data and semantic web approaches (see Chapter 10).

The BnF's next wave of innovative digital library leadership, announced in May 2011, is a large-scale partnership to digitize half a million copyrighted out-of-print 20th-century French books. Digitization efforts will focus on the national library's legal deposit collections. The large, five-year project will enrich Gallica and be financed by the French Centre national du livre. The Jouve Group, a digital service provider, will do the digitization (Coordination of European Picture Agencies Stock, Press and Heritage, 2011). The BnF's approach to the project, based on an agreement between the French government, the French Publishers Association and the French Society of Literary Authors, promises to avoid the traps and delays of other large-scale digitization projects that have lacked such prior agreements between key stakeholders to address the complex rights and economic issues.

Picture Australia

Picture Australia first began with a image digitization project in 1999. It was the foundation project for the large-scale, highly successful Trove digital library of the National Library of Australia (Cathro, 1999; Cathro, 2001; Cathro and Collier, 2010; Holley, 2010b; see also Table 2.1 at the end of this chapter). Picture Australia was fully integrated into Trove in 2012 (http://trove. nla.gov.au/general/australian-pictures-in-trove). The NLA's achievement with Picture Australia was an important outcome of the first decade of digital libraries because it exemplified a project that substantially progressed the public, open availability of historic photographs. Photographs are important primary sources documenting events, people and daily life, and their digitization has been a key to the public's enthusiasm for digital libraries. Chapter 10 further discusses the importance of digital library image collections on the social web.

Papers Past (http://paperspast.natlib.govt.nz)

Digitization and digital library technologies were quickly adopted to make historic newspapers – an unparalleled primary source – widely available to the public. Digital libraries of newspapers were highly significant outcomes of first-decade work; they greatly enhanced the work of researchers who were aware of the unique value of newspapers, but who faced either crumbling pages or miles of microforms and minimal indexing. Begun in 2001, Papers Past is a highly popular digital library of newspapers maintained by the National Library of New Zealand; it runs on Greenstone software described earlier in this section (see Table 2.1).

The British Library Online Newspaper Archive

This archive also dates from 2001. By 2010, the British Library was providing access to around four million pages of digitized content from British national and regional newspapers from 1600 to 1900, all searchable via a single interface (Deegan, Steinvel and King, 2002; King, 2005; Bingham, 2010).

Individual institutions

In parallel with the large-scale initiatives funded at the national level, individual institutions – principally large research libraries – were building digital libraries and investing in digitization: an average of US$286,000 each in 2000 (Greenstein and Thorin, 2002, 66). Tonta's analysis of digitization activities in Europe (Tonta, 2008) documents the considerable digital library activity in individual institutions there.

Contributions to preservation

Library digitization programs are often linked to the long-term preservation of materials. For example, in the US, three reports of the US Council on Library and Information Resources (CLIR; www.clir.org/pubs/reports) published between 1990 to 2000 trace digital preservation practice in the US (Aaron Brenner, personal communication to the author, 24 May 2012). Chapman and Kenney (1996) articulated early baseline standards and working principles for digital imaging projects to preserve texts; Ostrow (1998) described the issues around preservation and access to digitized images of large historical pictorial collections; and Smith (1999) identified a number of false expectations of digitization as a preservation method. Chapter 6 continues the discussion of digital preservation.

Digitization specialists and best practices

Co-operative efforts to share the development of educational materials, document best practices and deliver training are characteristic of the digital library field. For example, in the US, the Northeast Document Conservation Center (NEDEC) presented a 'School for Scanning' starting in 1995 and helped get projects up and running. Best practices were documented in *A Framework of Guidance for Building Good Digital Collections* (www.niso.org/publications/rp/framework3.pdf), a NISO Recommended Practice. In addition, *RLG DigiNews* (www.oclc.org/research/publications/newsletters/diginews.htm)   provided support and an international forum for sharing news. By the end of the first decade of digital libraries, the training programs, curricula, vehicles for information sharing and the experiences of the projects themselves had produced a sizeable community of digitization specialists with a set of agreed best practices.

Metadata and standards

While *metadata* is often defined as 'data about data,' this book uses the definition published by NISO: 'structured information that describes, explains, locates, and otherwise makes it easier to retrieve and use an information resource' (Guenther and Radebaugh, 2004, 1). One of the most important outcomes of the first decade of digital libraries was a new world of metadata and standards. Arguably, the journey to this new world began in 1995 in Dublin, Ohio.

Dublin Core

As noted in Chapter 1, computer and information scientists' understanding of information retrieval had progressed enormously in the years leading up to the early 1990s. Librarians had been working on knowledge organization and cataloging theory and practice for a century, and from 1967 they had been gaining experience in encoding data (MARC) for use in and across automated library systems. A growing number of developers were working on internet and web standards. Humanities computing experts and archivists had been working on text encoding and finding aids. Fifty-two invited experts in these domains and several others convened for three days in March 1995 to collaboratively consider solutions to a problem: the web was full of valuable information resources but there was no good way to find and navigate to them.

The workshop produced a proposal for a simple resource description record (the Dublin Core Metadata Element Set) and next steps for a standard, scalable, low-cost, interoperable way to describe a wide range of networked information resources (Weibel, 1995). OCLC and the US National Center for Supercomputing Applications (NCSA) had convened the invitational workshop in Dublin, Ohio – thus the name, Dublin Core. Another outcome of the 1995 workshop was the decision to convene an ongoing series of workshops, a series that has been going ever since (www.dublincore.org). The Warwick Framework, an architecture to accommodate a variety of metadata models (Dempsey and Weibel, 1996; Weibel and Lagoze, 1997), came out of the second workshop. The Warwick Framework has had considerable impact on the technical development of digital libraries.

The sixth Dublin Core workshop in 1998 kicked off 'a long co-evolution with the W3C's Resource Description Framework (RDF) and the Semantic Web' (Weibel, 1999; Weibel, 2005). Chapter 3 continues the discussion of RDF and the semantic web.

The Dublin Core workshops have been building consensus through a dynamic process involving many stakeholder communities. OCLC provided support for the Dublin Core Metadata Initiative (DCMI) until it became an independent non-profit in 2008; in 2013 DCMI entered into a partnership with the Association for Information Science and Technology (OCLC Research, 2009; ASIS&T, 2013).

Metadata renaissance

Librarians and digital librarianship

By the time work on digital libraries got under way, librarians had over a century of experience producing bibliographies, catalogs, indexes and finding aids (Calhoun, 2007, 174–5). They also had decades of experience with knowledge organization. For example, the first edition of the Dewey Decimal Classification System was published in 1876; by the 21st century it had been translated into many languages and was being used in over 100 countries (Mitchell and Vizine-Goetz, 2009). Even though libraries had begun to automate by the early 1990s, and the MARC format was widely deployed, library cataloging and classification methods in the early 1990s still reflected a world of information that was fairly stable and relatively small in scale, at least compared to today. Librarians generally produced one type of metadata (descriptive) and used a few indexing vocabularies and document organizing methods (e.g., classification schemes) to manage library collections. The requirements for digital librarians were different.

The needs for scale and many new classes of metadata

Many new types of metadata and knowledge organization methods became necessary as digital libraries and networked electronic resources emerged. The new methods needed to cover content on a scale previously unimagined. Prior, mostly manual, approaches could not scale to meet the need; in addition, the scope of the requirements for metadata and knowledge organization expanded by an order of magnitude. These new conditions resulted on the one hand in a great deal of volatility and on the other an exciting renaissance in metadata research and practice in which I have been fortunate to participate. Lagoze, Lynch and Daniel explained the new landscape for metadata (1996, under sections 6.1–6.3). It was clear that descriptive metadata would still be needed, but that new classes and characteristics of metadata would also be required to:

- support both human and machine-to-machine uses on the network
- encode and mark up documents
- define and manage collections of information resources at the collection level
- support the preservation and archiving of digital objects (digitized and 'born digital')
- create frameworks for accommodating metadata from many different communities (e.g., publishing, geospatial, museum, teaching and learning, multimedia . . .)
- represent and encode objects and metadata using many languages and scripts
- persistently and reliably identify digital objects and their metadata (identifiers)
- convey and adhere to the terms and conditions for use of digital objects and their metadata (rights; authentication and authorization)
- manage digital objects and/or their metadata, e.g., date created, date last modified (administrative metadata)
- describe attributes of digital objects, e.g., content ratings, reviews, usage, etc. (evaluative; statistical)
- define the sources or origins of objects (provenance) or their metadata
- convey relationships to other objects or link to them (linking)
- enable the syndication and exchange of digital objects
- indicate the components of objects and how to access or manipulate them (structural, technical)
- define document types (DTDs)
- move beyond text-based metadata to support many new types of digital media (e.g., images, audio, video).

The preceding list is not comprehensive, but it conveys a sense of the scope of the work that needed to be done.

From a library perspective, during that first decade, an entirely new set of conditions created disruptive change, moving the library field from bibliographic control to distributed systems for metadata management

(Calhoun, 2012b, under 'metadata management'). These new conditions also created a new, multifaceted community of metadata and knowledge organization specialists, who produced an array of new standards, protocols, reference and data models, community-specific schemas/element sets and content rules, crosswalks, application profiles and more. For a quick look at the results of these widely distributed efforts, see Riley and Becker's 'visualization of the metadata universe' (2010).

Working digital libraries

So far this chapter has reviewed first-decade digital library outcomes that built a new field of endeavor, transformed the processes of scholarly communications or delivered key enabling technologies. Early digital library work also produced working digital libraries that continue to attract significant attention today. The final section of this chapter provides information about some of these.

A sample from the first decade

Bearman (2007, 227–30) offers a useful framework for categorizing digital libraries. Table 2.1 at the end of this chapter adapts Bearman's categories to lay out some examples of digital libraries from different countries, their histories and funding sources. The choice of examples is deliberately limited to currently existing, working digital libraries whose roots are in the first decade of digital library research and development. Numbered citations in the right-most column of the table refer to the list of statistical data sources at the end of this chapter. Other citations in the table are incorporated in the list of references at the end of the book.

Discussion of sample digital libraries

The 15 sample digital libraries in Table 2.1 produced lasting, real-world collections and services that have proved highly useful to specific communities of users. Many projects in the first decade of digital library work made transformative technical advances or helpful prototypes, but did not produce working digital libraries. The digital libraries in the sample were chosen to provide a set of comparison cases and facilitate the reader's consideration of why these early digital libraries continue to thrive. This topic will be taken up again in the later chapters of this book.

Conclusion

I have provided a framework that attempts to make sense of the outcomes produced by a momentous, intensively active ten-year period. Thousands of people and hundreds of organizations contributed to these outcomes. Inevitably, and with my apologies, I have given cursory treatment or unintentionally omitted some first-decade activities that are important. The framework I have presented in this chapter reflects my own professional experience, an analysis of many hundreds (but certainly not all) sources, and a resulting perspective. Others' experiences and analyses might yield other useful perspectives on key outcomes. Yet all are likely to agree that the first decade's outcomes considerably advanced the grand vision of digital libraries, as well as creating a new field of research and practice to carry that vision forward.

These outcomes 'set the stage, through examples, for a renaissance in research methods and practices, scientific and cultural communication and creative representation and expression of ideas' (Griffin, 2005, under 'Future Directions'). The renaissance indeed began. Over the next decade of progress in digital libraries (2002–12), amid continuing technical progress, the challenges of online community-building, long-term sustainability and digital library integration with the web came to the fore. The remaining chapters of this book explore how digital libraries are finding their place in the larger networked information environment of the web. By the end of the second decade, what emerged as central to the value of digital libraries went beyond their collections or content, services or technologies to their efficacy for supporting their communities and their web-based, real-world practices in information seeking, learning, research, knowledge creation and dissemination, work, and play.

References to websites in Table 2.1

This list cites the data sources for the statistics reported about the sample of working digital libraries. Most of the statistics came from Alexa (www.alexa.com) and compete.com, which are well known providers of global or US web metrics for websites, as they were reported in April 2012. The following references are numbered in Table 2.1:

Table 2.1 A sample of digital libraries, their histories and funding. (Superior numerals in the table refer to the notes that follow.)

Type: National libraries	
Examples	**History, funding and notes**
National Library of Australia (NLA) **Trove** (www.trove.nla.gov.au) 'Find and get over 289,890,268 Australian and online resources: books, images, historic newspapers, maps, music, archives and more' (home page). Dates to 1999 and 'Picture Australia'; aggregates eight prior discovery services that had been organized by format (Cathro and Collier, 2010).	NLA funds Trove; some content comes from external contributors. 56% of the traffic to the National Library of Australia website goes to Trove. It is also a popular destination in the US with about 45,000 unique visitors per month.[1] It should be noted that a component of Trove is PANDORA—one of the first web archives created and managed by a national library (Cathro, 1999; Cathro, 2001; Cathro, Webb and Whiting, 2001). Chapter 10 discusses the significance of the Trove newspaper digitization project to the social web.
Bibliothèque nationale de France (BnF) **Gallica** (http://gallica.bnf.fr) First established 1997. One million books, manuscripts, maps, images, periodicals, sound recordings, scores (home page).	BnF funds Gallica and is assisted by a number of digitization partners. 51% of traffic to the BnF website goes to Gallica.[2]
US Library of Congress **American Memory** (www.memory.loc.gov) More than 9 million items in 100 collections. Includes access to written and spoken words, sound recordings, still and moving images, prints, maps, and sheet music. First introduced 1994.	The 1994 launch was supported by US$13 million in private sector donations. It was the flagship service of the National Digital Library Program. Now supported through a combination of private sponsors and the US Congress (see www.memory.loc.gov/ammem/about/sponsors.html). 19% of the traffic to the Library of Congress website goes to American Memory. The site attracts nearly 350,000 unique visitors a month in the US.[3]
Type: Discipline and subject-based digital libraries	
Examples	**History, funding and notes**
arXiv.org (www.arXiv.org) Open access service for pre-prints of articles in physics, mathematics, computer science, quantitative biology, quantitative finance and statistics. First started 1991 at Los Alamos National Laboratory (LANL). Over 700,000 articles; 60,000 annual submissions; 30 million downloads/year.	Funded by Cornell University since 2001 with some support from member institutions. Was supported from 1995 to 2000 by the US National Science Foundation, Los Alamos, and the US Dept of Energy. arXiv has been widely adopted by the physics, math and computer science communities, which it serves by providing rapid access to research findings and a platform for open peer review. arXiv ranks highly in the Cybermetrics Lab's 'Ranking Web of World Repositories' and attracts over 100,000 unique visitors a month in the US.[4]
Perseus (www.perseus.tufts.edu) Covers the history, literature and culture of the Greco-Roman world.	Under continuous development since 1987 (Marchionini, 2000) Perseus is hosted by Tufts University. Began with a grant of US$2.5 million from the Annenberg/CPB Projects; DLI-2 provided US$2.8 million in 1998 (National Science Foundation, 2007). Since then Perseus has received support in the form of grants from various federal agencies, the Mellon Foundation and individuals (www.perseus.tufts.edu/hopper/grants). 22% of the traffic to Tufts University goes to Perseus, which attracts about 65,000 unique visitors per month in the US.[5] *(Continued on next page.)*

Table 2.1 *(Continued)*

Type: Discipline and subject-based digital libraries   *(continued)*

Examples	History, funding and notes
ACM Digital Library (http://dl.acm.org) Access limited to subscribers. Published by the Association for Computing Machinery (ACM). Comprehensive collection covering computing and information technology. The full-text database includes the complete collection of ACM's publications, including journals, conference proceedings, magazines, newsletters, and multimedia titles. First introduced in 1997; significantly upgraded and reintroduced as the ACM Portal in 2001; reintroduced with new features in 2011 as the ACM Digital Library.	Funded by subscription fees and payments for downloading articles. ACM invested early in the move to online journals (Arms, 2000, 51) and was one of several Collaborating Publishing Partners associated with the CNRI-funded D-Lib Test Suite that followed DLI-1. The partners benefited from the transfer of technology from the Illinois testbed of the DeLIver system, which allowed for experimentation with the retrieval and display of full-text journal literature in an Internet environment (Mischo, 2002). 77% of the traffic to acm.org goes to the ACM Digital Library. It attracts about 93,000 unique visitors per month in the US.[6]

Type: Genre or format-based digital libraries

Examples	History, funding and notes
JSTOR (www.jstor.org for subscribers; see www.ithaka.org/our_work for brief information about JSTOR) Designed to substitute for back-issue files and serve as an archive of scholarly journals. Now 'an integral part of the global academic research infrastructure' (Carr, 2009, 67). Close to 44 million pages of content; over 7,000 participating institutions in 156 countries; journals come from 856 publishers.	Supported through JSTOR participant fees. It began with a grant from the Mellon Foundation to the University of Michigan, a participant in Elsevier's TULIP project, for software development and production costs (Kohler, 2009). JSTOR was established as an independent not-for-profit in 1995. Mellon awarded additional grants through the start-up period. JSTOR went live in 1997 with 190 libraries participating (Schonfeld, 2003). By the end of 1997 Mellon had invested US$5.2 million in developing JSTOR. JSTOR has been self-sustaining since 1999 (Kohler, 2009, 225–7). JSTOR is reported to have nearly 1.4 million unique visitors per month in the US.[7]
ScienceDirect (www.sciencedirect.com) Provided by Elsevier since 1997. Access limited to subscribers. Offers more than ten million articles primarily from e-journals; also includes some book chapters. Elsevier journals are known for including the leading research in the physical, life and social sciences. Half a million additions per year; backfiles reported to go back as far as 1823.	Funding comes from subscription fees, which many libraries consider too high (Van Orsdel and Born, 2009). Elsevier invested substantially in the early development of e-journals and online delivery systems. They organized the TULIP project in 1991 with nine US universities to test the networked desktop delivery of e-journals (Elsevier, 2012; Kluiters, 1997; Bonn et al., 1999). Concurrently they conducted an experiment with Tilburg University in the Netherlands (Collier, 2004). In 1995 Elsevier introduced EES (locally delivered e-journals) and also began developing the web-based service that became ScienceDirect, whose beta release was in 1997. The Koninklijke Bibliotheek (KB), national library of the Netherlands, archives all Elsevier journals. ScienceDirect is reported to have over one million unique visitors per month (US only).[8]
Papers Past (www.paperspast.natlib.govt.nz) Began in 2001. Contains more than two million pages of digitized New Zealand newspapers and periodicals from 1839 to 1945 and includes 70 publications from all regions of New Zealand.	Hosted and supported by the National Library of New Zealand. Began in 2001; relaunched in 2007 using Greenstone, a suite of open source, multilingual software for building digital libraries (NLNZ, 2007; Boddie et al., 2008; Thompson, Bainbridge and Suleman, 2011). Greenstone, an early and well known player in the digital library arena, developed its system as part of an international cooperative effort. 49% of the traffic to the website of the National Library of New Zealand goes to Papers Past.[9]

Table 2.1 *(Continued)*

Type: Genre or format-based digital libraries *(continued)*

Examples	History, funding and notes
NDLTD (www.ndltd.org) The Networked Digital Library of Theses and Dissertations (NDLTD) is an international organization that began in 1996 at Virginia Tech. Participating institutions grew from 20 in 1997 (Fox et al., 1997) to over 200 today. In 2010 the NDLTD Union Catalog contained one million electronic theses and dissertations (ETDs) from contributing institutions from over 25 countries on all continents.	Supported by membership fees from about 200 NDLTD members. The NDLTD Union Catalog runs on systems provided by Scirus and VTLS. With origins dating back to 1987, the initial 1996 funding from Virginia Tech for developing a working system was supplemented by a three-year grant from the US Dept of Education. Additional support came from public and private sector partners over the years. NDLTD was incorporated as a non-profit in 2003 (Hagen, Dobratz and Schirmbacher, 2003). It has become an important ETD program for developing nations. NDLTD, its annual ETD conference and its director Edward Fox have been key influencers in the development of digital libraries as a field of endeavor. The project and the conferences have given a major boost to the adoption of ETDs at universities worldwide.
British Library Sounds (http://sounds.bl.uk) Began in 1992 with 'Project Digitise.' Other projects followed, notably the Archival Sound Recordings Project from 2004-2009. A new version went live in January 2012 containing two levels of online access to 50,000 selected recordings of music, spoken word, and human and natural environments.	Supported out of the British Library Sound Archive, one of the world's largest collections of sounds, and from 2004–9 through the JISC Digitisation Programme, a set of large-scale projects with multiple phases. The British Library has set up innovative terms and conditions for online access to the recordings on the Sounds website; some of the content is freely available to all, and all 50,000 recordings are open to users from UK higher education institutions. Sounds.bl.uk is a popular destination on the British Library website.

Type: Mission and audience-directed digital libraries

Examples	History, funding and notes
Project Gutenberg (www.gutenberg.org) Begun in 1971 by founder Michael Hart with the goal of providing free access to literary works in the public domain. The first producer of ebooks and the oldest digital library. Offers over 40,000 free e-books. More e-books are available through affiliates.	Supported by volunteers and donations to the Project Gutenberg Literary Archive Foundation, a non-profit organization. After starting at the University of Illinois and transferring for a time to Carnegie Mellon, the Gutenberg system is now hosted by ibiblio, an online, public 'collection of collections' supported by the University of North Carolina at Chapel Hill. Gutenberg is estimated to have over 500,000 unique visitors a month in the US.[10]
Internet Archive (http://archive.org) Founded in 1995 by Brewster Kahle,[11] the Internet Archive (IA) is a mission-oriented digital library and archive of internet sites, texts, music, moving images, recordings and software. The IA is an active advocate for open, universal and free access to knowledge. The Wayback Machine provides access to archived versions of an estimated 220+ million websites. Three other popular digital library projects from IA are the Open Library (http://openlibrary.org), Archive-It (http://archive-it.org) and publicly available digital images from NASA (http://nasaimages.org).	IA is a non-profit organization. Funding for projects and services comes from the Kahle/Austin Foundation with support from other partners over the course of developing particular projects. IA also solicits donations. IA is reported to attract around *three million* unique visitors a month in the US alone; other web traffic analysis services place it among the top few hundred busiest sites worldwide. Traffic to the Wayback service is reported to account for over 75% of IA traffic.[12] The Open Library is reported to attract nearly 400,000 unique visitors a month,[13] while Archive-It attracts about 18,000 unique visitors a month[14] and NASA Images attracts about 12,000 unique visitors a month.[15] All estimates are for the US only.

(Continued on next page.)

Table 2.1 *(Continued)*

Type: Mission and audience-directed digital libraries	
Examples	**History, funding and notes**
SciELO (www.scielo.org) SciELO (Scientific Electronic Library Online) began in 1997 in Brazil (www.scielo.br) with the mission of enabling cooperative e-publishing in developing countries. The SciELO network (www.scielo.org) expanded and now includes eight national collections and two thematic collections in public health and the social sciences. Includes more than 500 Latin American open access journals and 191,000 articles.	Publicly funded by the State of São Paulo Research Foundation and BIREME (the Latin America and Caribbean Center on Health Sciences Information), an organization belonging to PAHO (the PanAmerican Health Organization) and to WHO (the World Health Organization) (Marcondes and Sayão, 2003). It was one of the first collections of open access journals in the world. SciELO has brought considerably greater impact to Brazilian and Latin American journals (Packer et al., 2010). Currently (2012) SciELO.br is ranked by the Cybermetrics Lab as the top portal in the world. Of the Cybermetrics Lab's top fifteen rankings of portals, six are SciELO sites.[16]
ICDL International Children's Digital Library (www.childrenslibrary.org) Available since 2002. A mobile application for iPhone and iPad has been available since 2008; a second mobile application (StoryKit) was released in 2009 (Bederson, Quinn and Druin, 2009; Quinn et al., 2009). ICDL's mission is to support the world's children by building a digital library of freely available, multilingual, online and outstanding children's books from around the world. Contains over 4,500 books in 61 languages. Visitors come from 228 countries.[17]	Administered by the International Children's Digital Library Foundation, a non-profit organization founded in 2006, with continuing support from NLF, IMLS, and the Library of Congress. Initial funding came from the US National Science Foundation and other publicly funded agencies; ICDL was one of the six-year projects funded under the DLI-2 initiative. Research and development started in 1999 at the University of Maryland with an interdisciplinary team led by the Human Computer Interaction Lab and the College of Information Studies. Initially the Internet Archive hosted the ICDL site. A high-impact result – beyond the creation of the digital library itself – was validating the importance of working with the primary user group (in this case, children) to design digital libraries and services (Druin et al., 2003; Druin, 2005). The ICDL attracts about 24,000 unique visitors a month from the US. No data is available for non-US visits to the site but it is an important destination outside the US.[18]

1 Site and web traffic information for the National Library of Australia, including Trove: www.alexa.com/siteinfo/nla.gov.au. Unique visitors from the US: http://siteanalytics.compete.com/trove.nla.gov.au/.

2 Site and web traffic information for the BnF, including Gallica: www.alexa.com/siteinfo/bnf.fr.

3 Site and web traffic information for the Library of Congress, including American Memory: www.alexa.com/siteinfo/loc.gov# and http://siteanalytics.compete.com/memory.loc.gov/.

4 Site and web traffic information for arXiv.org: Cybermetrics Lab ranking: http://repositories.webometrics.info/en and http://siteanalytics.compete.com/arxiv.org/.

5 Site and web traffic information for Tufts University, including Perseus: www.alexa.com/siteinfo/tufts.edu# [accessed 18 April 2012]. Perseus traffic

analysis: http://siteanalytics.compete.com/perseus.tufts.edu/.

6 Site and web traffic information for the Association for Computing Machinery, including the ACM Digital Library: www.alexa.com/siteinfo/acm.org# [accessed 18 April 2012]. ACM Digital Library traffic analysis: http://siteanalytics.compete.com/dl.acm.org/.

7 Site and web traffic information for JSTOR: http://siteanalytics.compete.com/jstor.org/.

8 Web traffic and ranking information for ScienceDirect: http://siteanalytics.compete.com/sciencedirect.com/.

9 Web traffic and ranking information for Papers Past: www.alexa.com/siteinfo/natlib.govt.nz#.

10 Web traffic and ranking information for Gutenberg.org: http://siteanalytics.compete.com/gutenberg.org/.

11 From the 'About' pages on the Internet Archive website: 'Since the mid-1980s, Kahle has focused on developing technologies for information discovery and digital libraries. In 1989 Kahle invented the internet's first publishing system, WAIS (Wide Area Information Server) system and in 1989, founded WAIS Inc., a pioneering electronic publishing company that was sold to America Online in 1995. In 1996, Kahle founded the Internet Archive which may be the largest digital library. At the same time, he co-founded Alexa Internet, which helps catalog the Web. Alexa was sold to Amazon.com in 1999. http://archive.org/about/bios.php.

12 Web traffic and ranking information for Internet Archive: http://siteanalytics.compete.com/archive.org/ and www.alexa.com/siteinfo/archive.org#.

13 Web traffic and ranking information for the Open Library: http://siteanalytics.compete.com/openlibrary.org/.

14 Web traffic information for Archive-It from Compete.com as of April 2012.

15 Web traffic information for NASA Images from Compete.com as of April 2012.

16 Information for SciELO: http://repositories.webometrics.info/en/top-portals.

17 Information in the 'About' and 'FastFacts' sections of the ICDL website: http://en.childrenslibrary.org/.

18 Web traffic information for ICDL from Compete.com as of April 2012.

CHAPTER 3

Key themes and challenges in digital libraries

Overview

This chapter provides a high-level view of the key themes, current position and challenges of digital libraries and their technologies, social aspects, collections and communities. It begins by identifying the key themes of the second decade (2002–12) of progress in the diverse, multidisciplinary, international field of digital libraries. A concept map visualizes the results of an analysis of second-decade digital library literature. The map provides new insights into this complex field by exposing thematic connections between technologies, collections, social forces and online community building. The chapter concludes with a consideration of key challenges facing digital libraries: interoperability, community engagement, intellectual property rights and sustainability.

The key themes of digital library work
Existing research to identify core topics

Jeffrey Pomerantz and colleagues (2006) produced a curriculum for digital library education that was aligned with the '5S framework' for digital libraries discussed in Chapter 1 (see also Yang et al., 2009). They validated their selection of curriculum module topics by manually classifying papers from 1996 to 2005 from two sources: (1) 543 papers in the proceedings of two renowned digital library conferences; and (2) 502 articles published in *D-Lib Magazine.*

Their analysis revealed concentrations from both sources in digital library services, architecture and interoperability, and metadata. The conference papers revealed an additional concentration on the topic of digital objects.

The *D-Lib* papers had additional concentrations around digital library collections, social issues and preservation.

Chern Li Liew (2009) provided a snapshot of the digital library literature from 1997 to 2007, focusing on articles about organizational and people issues. Liew was interested in digital libraries as 'socio-technical systems' that support not only information seeking and discovery but also community interaction and collaboration. The analysis drew from 577 articles on socio-technical topics published in peer-reviewed library and information science journals, with some exceptions (e.g., *D-Lib Magazine* is not a refereed journal). The methodology appears to have excluded conference papers. The findings indicated first, a trend toward more articles on socio-technical topics over time and second, the dominance of topics related to digital library use and usability plus organizational, economic and legal issues. Ethical and social/cultural issues were not well represented in the Liew sample articles.

Son Hoang Nguyen and Gobinda Chowdhury (2013) identified core research topics and subtopics and created a 'knowledge map' that offers a panoramic view of the digital library field over 20 years. Their work is the most up-to-date and comprehensive analysis of digital library research topics as of this writing. Their detailed analysis could serve multiple purposes: for example, to develop an updated digital library curriculum for LIS education.

Nguyen and Chowdhury focused on peer-reviewed publications from 1990 to 2010. Their initial topic list came from knowledgeable experts and from calls for conference papers. They refined this list using a formal knowledge organization approach. They then searched Scopus, a large abstract and citation database of research literature, for digital library publications and found 7905 records for conference papers and articles. They then used the records and the *Library and Information Science Abstracts* thesaurus to further refine and standardize the terminology for their core topics and subtopics. The result was 21 core topics and 1105 subtopics, which they present in a large table and as a series of charts. Three of the 21 core topics – architecture/infrastructure, digital library research and development, and information organization – produced 53% of the publications in the analysis (see their Figure 2).

A new concept map

This chapter builds on and extends these prior analyses by focusing on the work done in the second decade of digital library research and practice (2002-2012). My purposes in conducting the analysis included uncovering the key themes and core topics of the field in a way that would (1) suggest the nature of second-decade research and practice and (2) produce a conceptual frame for the rest of this book. The basis of the analysis was a manual evaluation of the roughly 440 full-length feature articles (articles, opinions and commentaries) published in *D-Lib Magazine* between 2002 and 2012. I considered *D-Lib* full-length features only and not its news items, conference reports or briefings.

History and impact of D-Lib

Founded early in the life of digital libraries (1995), *D-Lib Magazine* is freely available on the internet. It has tracked progress across participating disciplines and its articles include a range of both technical and professional perspectives. The primary intent is 'timely and efficient information exchange' (Wilson and Powell, 2005). *D-Lib's* founders and subsequent editors made a deliberate choice of quick turnaround from submission to publication in preference to the long timelines generally associated with publishing peer-reviewed articles.

In a tenth-anniversary feature article on *D-Lib*, Wilson and Powell noted that *D-Lib* articles have been widely cited; in 2005, the average citation rate was 117.5 cites of *D-Lib* articles per year, comparing favorably to the citation rates of journals in the fields of computer science and library and information science. The original funding for *D-Lib Magazine* came from DARPA and the NSF and was related to the DLI initiatives. From 2006 to the time of this writing, *D-Lib* has been produced by the Corporation for National Research Initiatives (CNRI) with assistance from the D-Lib Alliance and other contributors (www.dlib.org, under 'About D-Lib').

Other analyses of D-Lib Magazine

Others have evaluated the contents of *D-Lib Magazine*. Zhang, Mostafa and Tripathy (2002) used the contents of *D-Lib* articles from 1995 to 2002 to test their innovative information retrieval and visualization system, in the process automatically generating a set of concepts associated with these articles. Their process generated 69 concepts, which their system displayed visually in a number of ways (see their Figures 1–5). Bollen et al. (2005) completed an evaluation of ideas and concepts represented in *D-Lib* articles from 1995 to 2004 through the automatic detection of term co-occurrences. These two analyses used wholly quantitative methods. Park's bibliometric analysis

(2010) of *D-Lib* content from 1995 to 2008 produced information about *D-Lib*'s impact, authors and the number of citations per article, revealing its wide, global impact on multiple disciplines.

Methodology: evaluating the articles

The analysis of the 440 *D-Lib* articles involved both quantitative and qualitative methods. The first, qualitative steps of the analysis were to manually examine the articles, in the process assigning keywords or keyword phrases to each. Next, a quantitative analysis, using a word frequency macro, counted the occurrences of title words and keywords or keyword phrases. The frequency counts of title words, keywords and keyword phrases revealed patterns that suggest the comparative strength and evolution of themes in the 11-year span of articles. Table 3.1 summarizes the frequently occurring keywords or keyword phrases and their ranges of occurrences. A total of 77 keywords and keyword phrases (8.3% of all of the keywords and keyword phrases) occurred eight or more times each and accounted for a little over half (51.8%) of all occurrences of all keywords and keyword phrases in the dataset.

Table 3.1 Summary of frequently occurring keywords or keyword phrases	
Range of occurrences	**Sample of keywords or keyword phrases**
Between 34 and 90 times	Repositories, digital preservation, metadata, evaluation, open access, scholarly communication, OAI PMH, aggregation (this is the complete list, not a sample)
Between 27 and 33 times	Discovery, collaboration, standards, social web, federation, datasets, interoperability
Between 21 and 26 times	Education, registries, digitization, NSDL, national libraries, e-journals
Between 15 and 20 times	User studies, identifiers, data exchange, web services, portals, copyright
Between 8 and 14 times	OAIS, multimedia, automated metadata, web archives, Web 2.0 and libraries, METS, mass digitization, digital curation, user-centered design, re-use, newspapers, semantic web

The next phase of the analysis was to reflect on the patterns and themes that emerged from the keyword frequency data, develop an understanding of how the themes are connected, and then group related keywords and keyword phrases together (for example, 'mass digitization' and 'Google Books' were grouped with 'digitization'.

Methodology: constructing the map

The construction of the map came next. It involved a qualitative analysis to tease out interrelated themes and decide how to group them together visually.

This required choosing the map's x- and y-axes. The choice of axes was informed by the word frequency counts but not completely determined by them. After carefully reflecting on the patterns in the keyword frequency counts, I labeled the x-axis of the concept map to organize a continuum of themes and topics ranging from 'collections' to 'communities.' Similarly, the y-axis organizes a continuum of themes ranging from 'technology' to 'social and economic aspects.'

As I constructed the map, I added a few additional keywords and keyword phrases that occurred fewer than eight times, to aid the comprehensibility and completeness of the map. For example 'FRBR' (5 occurrences) and 'RDA' (4 occurrences) were added to the 'cataloging' cluster, and 'digital divide' (6 occurrences) was added as a social issue relevant to digital libraries. The last step of constructing the map was to select the themes for the two 'key challenges' boxes at the top and bottom of the map. The result of the evaluation of the articles and the construction of the map is Figure 3.1.

The map

Figure 3.1 places the concept 'Digital libraries' at the center, then presents and clusters the results of the word frequency analysis along the x- and y-axes. The relative type sizes of the text indicate how frequently a keyword or keyword phrase occurred. This concept map can be said to reveal significant themes in the 11-year span of articles, but not all themes. The overall intent is to organize the decade's themes and suggest one way to comprehend and explain them as a coherent conceptual whole.

The map suggests the nature and thematic structure of the past decade's digital library research and practice. It represents the principal themes and the relationships between key topics using the map's four cardinal directions and quadrants. The northern hemisphere represents a body of work focused on the enabling technologies of digital libraries and on addressing the field's key technological challenge: interoperability. The southern hemisphere clusters the body of work devoted to the social and economic aspects of digital libraries and to addressing the key challenges of community engagement, intellectual property rights and sustainability. The northwest and northeast quadrants of the map cluster work on the technological aspects of collection and community building, respectively. The southwest quadrant clusters the body of work on the social and economic aspects of digital library collections, while the southeast represents work on the social and economic aspects of building communities around digital libraries.

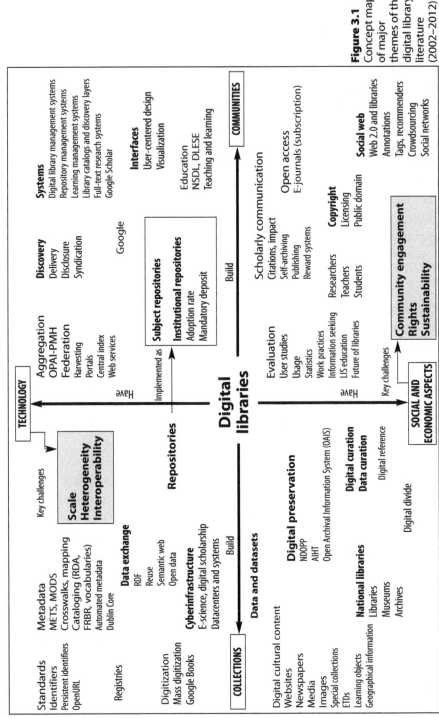

Figure 3.1
Concept map of major themes of the digital library literature (2002–2012)

The remainder of this chapter focuses on the 'key challenges' identified at the top and bottom of the map. Before continuing to those sections, however, it is important to write a few words about the limitations of this analysis of the second decade of digital library literature.

Limitations of the analysis

The analysis and concept map provide a snapshot but not a definitive evaluation of the digital library literature from 2002 to 2012. It focuses on what appeared in *D-Lib* alone, leading to the potential over-representation of some topics and the under-representation (or omission) of others. A more comprehensive analysis would examine the second-decade literature as represented in other forums, especially peer-reviewed journals and conference proceedings, and in languages other than English.

Key challenges

The next chapters of this book define and expand on the themes from the concept map in the context of the map's x-axis: *building collections* and *building communities*. Prior to those chapters' detailed discussions, this chapter describes and evaluates four key challenges to building collections and communities for digital libraries:

1 interoperability and its facets
2 community engagement
3 intellectual property rights
4 sustainability.

Key challenge 1: Interoperability

The information landscape can be said to be a highly distributed, heterogeneous one containing many islands of content. Interoperability became increasingly important as more and more content moved online and demand for unified access grew.

Many people perceive that Google – which grew out of Brin and Page's work on PageRank (discussed in Chapter 2) – and other general-purpose search engines have now solved the problem of interoperability. For many, whose needs are met by what search engines can achieve through the associative indexing of web documents, this is true. For the communities for whom digital libraries are or would be useful, it is not true. The next section discusses two of the reasons.

Hybrid libraries and the deep web

As described in Chapter 1, librarians have sought interoperability for hybrid library content. For the foreseeable future libraries will require ways to bring digital representations of their non-digital collections (printed books and journals, archives, primary sources, images, slides, maps, analog sound recordings, historical government documents, and more) into digital libraries.

Second, there is a part of the web called the 'deep,' 'hidden' or 'invisible' web that is not indexed by Google, Yahoo, etc. This means that searchers who rely only on results from search engines do not see and cannot reach deep web content. Bergman (2001) estimated the deep web is much larger than the 'surface' web that search engines crawl – in fact 400 to 500 times larger. Bergman's 2001 analysis further suggested that more than half of the deep web content resided in topic-specific databases (most publicly accessible) that weren't being crawled or indexed by the main search engines. In 2003, Lyman and Varian, using Bergman's results, estimated that the deep web contained up to 92,000 terabytes (more than 45 times the estimated contents of all US academic libraries at that time).

Research into deep web extraction has made progress (as described for example by Liu et al., 2010), and search engines are doing a better job finding and indexing deep web content than they were in 2003. However, Zillman (2013) estimates that the deep web still contains 'in the vicinity of one trillion plus pages of information located through the world wide web in various files and formats that the current search engines on the Internet either cannot find or have difficulty accessing.' Obviously, not all deep web content is of interest to the users of digital libraries, but a substantial portion of it is. Onaifo and Rasmussen (2013) investigated deep web indexing issues from a library perspective and found that (because it is in databases), a good deal of libraries' content is part of the deep web. They report strategies that libraries and subscription database vendors are taking to structure content in formats that common search engines can index (see Chapter 8's discussion of SEO and ASEO).

The problem of digital library interoperability is not solved

Carl Lagoze defines interoperability in terms of the user's experience: 'providing the user with a seamless experience as they use heterogeneous, distributed information services (discovery, access, browse, etc.)' (2010, 102). Search engines provide a degree of interoperability across the web of documents; a great deal of content can be discovered via the surface web or through the centralized indexes underlying tools like Google Scholar. But not all of it. And so, after 20 years of progress in the field of digital libraries, the challenge of interoperability remains.

The vision of researchers and digital library pioneers was to integrate 'tens of thousands of repositories of digital information that are autonomously managed yet integrated into what users view as a coherent digital library system' (Lynch and Garcia-Molina, 1995, under 'Executive Summary section III'). They could probably not have anticipated the scale and complexity of the ocean of content to be coherently integrated today. Digital libraries need to scale to a large amount of content; in addition they must be scalable in terms of efficiency and performance. This is made particularly difficult because the content of interest to the communities that digital libraries serve is heterogeneous, and so are the systems, software, and formats associated with that content.

Heterogeneity

Dictionary definitions of 'heterogeneity' suggest it describes a condition or quality 'lacking in uniformity,' 'diverse,' and 'composed of unrelated or differing elements.' In the field of digital libraries, heterogeneity refers on the one hand to diverse systems, interfaces and networks; and on the other to the greatly distributed, complex content that digital libraries seek to bring together for easy discovery and use. Besides being widely distributed on the web, content of interest is managed by many different organizations, and the formats of the digital objects are diverse: text, images, audio and video, other multimedia, geographical information, data and so on.

Many digital library experts' writings devote attention to the topic of interoperability, from the field's earliest days (see for example Lynch and Garcia-Molina, 1995; Paepcke et al., 1998; Arms, 2000, Chapter 11; Borgman, 2000, 212–13; Miller, 2000; Tedd and Large, 2005, Chapter 4; and Lagoze, 2010, under 'Technologies for interoperability'). Borgman (2000, 213) described interoperability in three dimensions:

- getting disparate systems to work together in real time
- enabling software to work on different systems
- supporting the exchange of content between systems.

A list of the aspects of interoperability ranges across user interfaces, naming and identification, formats for content and metadata, network protocols, search and retrieval protocols, authentication and security, and more (Arms, 2000, 70–2).

Early work on interoperability: Z39.50

This section extends the discussion of interoperability in Chapter 2 to discuss the contribution of an information retrieval protocol and International Standards Organization standard, ISO 23950, known as Z39.50. Z39.50, which pre-dates the web and has been used mainly by libraries, was the basis of early digital library efforts to achieve interoperability of distributed digital content stores. It performs broadcast searching in real time across a range of different information sources stored in different systems. Organizations can also set up their online resources (e.g., catalogs, databases, indexes) as Z39.50 targets – in other words, Z39.50 search services can gather records *from* them.

In some early digital library initiatives, Z39.50 was important for cross-searching and federating results in hybrid libraries; for example, from multiple catalogs, abstracting and indexing databases, and other kinds of resources of interest to libraries. Dempsey, Russell and Kirriemuir (1996) discussed its potential for building distributed information systems in Europe. NDLTD, which is one of the digital libraries described in Table 2.1, used it (Fox et al., 1997). Some UK projects funded under eLib or by JISC also relied on Z39.50 (Stubley, 1999; Gilby and Dunsire, 2004; Gilby, 2005). The European Library (TEL – www.theeuropeanlibrary.org), a portal and co-operative framework for 48 European national libraries and some research libraries, has used Z39.50 in particularly innovative ways and experimented with its descendants SRU/SRW (Woldering, 2004; Van Veen and Oldroyd, 2004). Chapter 5 contains an extensive discussion of portal projects, like TEL, and the use of Z39.50 as a protocol for metasearch.

Early digital library developers' experience using Z39.50 suggested the protocol's limitations for solving information retrieval and exchange problems outside the library domain. Many systems outside the library space are not Z39.50-compliant, and Z39.50 is a complex protocol, perceived by some developers as costly to implement. As Moen points out in his excellent conference paper on Z39.50 as a resource discovery tool, 'It is a standard that addresses important interoperability challenges but does so in a way, perceived as a library way, that may keep it a niche solution rather than as a broader solution to critical problems of networked information retrieval'

(Moen, 2000). Paepcke et al. (2000) noted that there has been a 'culture clash between the comprehensive, often complex approach of Z39.50, and the generally light-weight approaches typical in the design of Web related protocols.'

Other early work on interoperability

Chapter 2 discusses the Open Archives Initiative, OAI-PMH, reference linking and the importance of persistent identifiers. All are important outcomes of the first decade of digital library research and practice that continue to support digital library interoperability today.

Syntactic and semantic interoperability

In the same workshop discussed earlier in this chapter, Lynch and Garcia-Molina (1995), identified a continuum of interoperability with 'deep semantic interoperability' at one end, 'syntactic interoperability' in the middle, and 'superficial uniformity' at the other end. The word *semantic* relates to meaning in language or logic; the word *syntactic* relates to the proper arrangements of elements according to a structure and set of rules. Lynch and Garcia-Molina noted that syntactic interoperability can achieve common navigation, query and viewing interfaces as well as other functionality to support a degree of interoperability for digital library users. They saw deep semantic interoperability as holding the promise of enabling searchers to 'consistently and coherently' find and use autonomously managed, distributed information objects and services without being troubled by differences in the underlying systems and content.

Syntactic interoperability achieves coherence across systems based on common protocols, metadata formats, and digital object exchange standards. Tedd and Large (2005, Chapter 4) may provide the most comprehensive discussion of various aspects of standards and interoperability up to 2005. The best overview of the digital library community's development of syntactic interoperability may be that of Lagoze (2010, 102–114).

Interoperability and standards

The digital library community's approach to achieving interoperability has been to define, agree on and implement standards that ensure open systems and exchangeable data. This chapter applies the term 'standards' broadly to refer to established technical norms, requirements, specifications, processes or practices that can be officially ratified, proposed or in draft form, accepted, or recommended by international, regional or national organizations. Alternatively, there are *de facto* standards that are generally accepted and dominant in their communities. The purpose of standards is to support predictable, consistent results. When widely implemented they benefit the communities that use them and make co-operation and sharing easy and affordable across organizations.

The family of digital library standards

A large array of standards exists for the digital library field. Tedd and Large state that 'if standards and interoperability traditionally have been important in libraries, this importance is further emphasized in digital libraries' (2005, 85).

Relatively early on, Bill Arms recognized the potential challenges of an approach to interoperability based on large-scale community adoption of standards. He wrote 'an ideal approach would be to develop a comprehensive set of standards that all digital libraries would adopt' (2000, 207–209), but like other implementers, he quickly questioned the practicality of the ideal approach. He proposed a tempered approach to achieving interoperability – one that balances the costs (sometimes quite high) that organizations are willing to incur to implement standards against the degree of interoperability that adopting the standard will achieve. He later wrote 'if the cost of adopting a standard is high, it will be adopted only by those organizations that truly value the functionality provided. Conversely, when the cost is low, more organizations will be willing to adopt it, even if the functionality is limited.' Chapter 4 continues the discussion of the tension between standards and approaches developed or preferred by digital libraries and the less-constrained, low-barrier methods and simpler standards typically used by the larger web community.

Semantic interoperability

Digital library researchers and practitioners have been quite successful in advancing syntactic interoperability, but until recently, semantic interoperability has seemed to be a 'holy grail' (Lagoze et al., 2005). The web environment has considerably matured since the field of digital libraries emerged, and the principles of web architecture are clearer and better defined (see www.w3.org/standards/webarch and the documents linked from it). New developments have made it possible to renew the pursuit of the elusive 'holy grail of semantic interoperability.' How to deploy the semantic web and linked data to advance digital libraries is a new grand challenge for the digital library field. The following section, which provides a brief introduction to both, provides the background for this book's examination of the prospects of the semantic web in digital libraries (see Chapters 9 and 10).

The semantic web and linked data
The web of data

The first realization of the web has been called a 'web of documents' (www.w3.org/standards/semanticweb). Even though documents are marked up for use on the web, they are mainly intended for people to read, and it has been difficult to extract pieces of information from them in an automated, consistently generalizable way. A new vision of the web, the 'semantic web,' has been called a 'web of data.' The intent of the semantic web is to automatically bring together and disclose meaningful relationships between related resources stored in different places, as described by Hagedorn and Sattler:

> The problem of the inability of machines to interpret and process information published on web pages caused the development of a web of data, next to the web of documents. The idea is known as the 'semantic web', where links between information are established in a way that machines can understand and interpret.
>
> Hagedorn and Sattler, 2013

The semantic web does not replace the web of documents, but it has the potential to enable interoperability at a significantly higher and more useful level. The semantic web is important for many reasons. In the context of the progress of digital libraries:

1 The semantic web revives (and reshapes) the notion of a singular, 'universal digital library' that inspired the first digital library builders in the early 1990s. Bizer (2010), who manages DBPedia (www.dbpedia.org), has envisioned the semantic web as a 'single global information space', with hyperlinks connecting everything. The end goal is being able to

query the web as if it was one global database and get back useful results.
2 Semantic web applications offer new functionality and benefits for particular online communities (see Chapters 9 and 10).

From an individual's point of view, the semantic web has the potential to greatly facilitate information seeking. Instead of having to search and examine multiple websites and assemble needed information manually, many questions can be answered in one step. In addition, semantic web applications can disambiguate (identify separate meanings for) names that are the same, like Jerome the saint and Jerome the town in Arizona.

Computer and information scientists and librarians tend to articulate the benefits of semantic web approaches in different ways, but with equal enthusiasm. For example Keller (2011), university librarian at Stanford, explains why semantic web approaches are superior to current approaches to information discovery and access, which lock up pieces of information in silos and fail to comprehensively surface relevant information. Leading computer scientists Bizer, Heath and Berners-Lee (2009, 14) have made the point that semantic web approaches are superior to classic data integration systems as well as newer approaches using machine-to-machine data exchange based on web services, APIs and mashups (discussed in Chapter 4).

History of the semantic web

The idea of a semantic web is traced to Tim Berners-Lee, director of the World Wide Web Consortium (WC3), and the person widely acknowledged as the inventor of the web in 1989. In a set of slides from his plenary talk at the first International Conference on the World Wide Web in Geneva, he makes the point:

> To a user, [the world wide web] has become an exciting world, but there is very little machine-readable information there. The meaning of the documents is clear to those with a grasp of (normally) English, and the significance of the links is only evident from the context around the anchor. To a computer, then, the web is a flat, boring world devoid of meaning. This is a pity, as in fact documents on the web describe real objects and imaginary concepts, and give particular relationships between them.
>
> Berners-Lee, 1994

At that conference, Berners-Lee proposed 'adding semantics to the web,' and he and colleagues further elaborated on the idea in a book published in 1999. In 2001, *Scientific American* published Berners-Lee, Hendler and Lassila's article entitled 'The semantic web,' thus bringing the phrase into mainstream usage.

The Resource Description Framework (RDF)

RDF is a standard data model that supports data interchange and re-use on the web; it 'allows structured and semi-structured data to be mixed, exposed, and shared across different applications' (www.w3.org/RDF). RDF uses URIs (discussed next) as unique global identifiers to make simple statements about resources (entities) in terms of their properties and values. To make these statements machine-readable and interpretable, RDF uses an XML syntax. There is much to know about RDF; the *RDF Primer* (www.w3.org/TR/rdf-primer/), a W3C recommendation, is a good place to start. Chapter 2 mentions the history of RDF, which dates to 1998 and is associated with the sixth Dublin Core Workshop and, more broadly, the digital library field. It should be noted that not all advocates for the semantic web are advocates of RDF (Miličić, 2011 discusses this).

URIs, HTTP and RDF

The semantic web rests on a small number of web standards that serve as its foundation: URIs, HTTP and RDF.

- URIs (Uniform Resource Identifiers) are the technology for naming and addressing resources on the web (www.w3.org/Addressing); they consist of short strings identifying many types of resources, including documents, images, services, etc. A URI can identify an abstract or physical resource (Masinter, Berners-Lee and Fielding, 2005), and URIs are therefore more generic than URLs (Uniform Resource Locators), which point to web pages. URIs can point to any entity, including real-world objects like people. In the RDF, they both identify a resource and provide the means to express relationships to other resources.
- HTTP (Hypertext Transfer Protocol) is the data transfer protocol used on the web; it is a foundational standard of the web that has been in use since 1990. Expressing URIs using *http://* allows them to be looked up and retrieved on the web.

Linked data

Linked data provides the framework for publishing and consuming semantic web content. Heath and Bizer (2011) have written a highly readable book on linked data. Baker and colleagues (2011) make an important point about it: 'linked data is not about creating a different web, but rather about enhancing the web through the addition of structured data'. Briefly, linked data provides a 'set of best practices for publishing and connecting structured data on the web' (Bizer, Heath and Berners-Lee, 2009, 1). Linked data relies on structured data (URIs) in RDF format, and the notion of a uniquely identifiable resource that can be pointed to and retrieved on the web is fundamental. Berners-Lee (2006) introduced four principles for publishing linked data in accordance with the general architecture of the web:

1 Use URIs as names for things.
2 Use HTTP URIs so that people can look up those names.
3 When someone looks up a URI, provide useful information, using the standards (RDF; SPARQL).
4 Include links to other URIs, so that they can discover more things.

Building and using the web of data

Realizing the semantic web has required the creation of two things: a web of data and applications that make use of it. In 2007 the W3C and a number of partners began the Linking Open Data Project to encourage the building, publication and interlinking of open linked datasets (www.w3.org/wiki/SweoIG/TaskForces/CommunityProjects/LinkingOpenData). This active, community-based project began with nine interlinked datasets from DBPedia, GeoNames, MusicBrainz, the US Census, and others (Bizer et al., 2007). The links between datasets demonstrated the enormous potential for applications using semantic web data; for example, a single search result could combine information about a computer scientist represented in DBPedia (an extraction of structured data from Wikipedia) and her publications in the DBLP database (www.dblp.org; a computer science bibliography).

The number of open, interlinked datasets has grown many times over since then. In September 2011 (the latest count available at the time of this writing), there were 295 datasets containing billions of pieces of information and millions of links. The Linked Open Data (LOD) community has held annual workshops and periodically released a Linked Open Data Cloud diagram (www.lod-cloud.net/state), which shows continual rapid progress in the production of linked open data by many types of organizations. Currently, linked datasets can be found using the Data Hub (www.datahub.io), a community-run catalog. In June 2013, the Data Hub contained over 6500 open datasets; of these, 339 were identified as linked datasets. As will be discussed in Chapter 9, several national libraries, Europeana, and many other organizations related to the digital library field are taking part in the realization of the semantic web.

Applications for linked data

Linked data is increasingly being used to build innovative applications. Articles by Mendes, Jakob and Bizer (2012), Raimond et al. (2012) and Suchanek and Weikum (2013) discuss the uses that can be made of linked data, which include:

- providing a knowledgebase for disambiguating names
- automatically answering natural language questions (e.g., where was John Lennon born?)
- identifying related entities (e.g., titles that occur in multiple languages)
- expanding queries (e.g., suggesting other related searches)
- repurposing and representing web content created for one site in another context.

Heath and Bizer's book (2011) provides a section on deployed linked data applications (browsers, search engines and domain-specific applications) at the time of the book's publication. The W3C also hosts a list of use cases (www.w3.org/2001/sw/sweo/public/UseCases). Two highly visible linked data applications are the Google Knowledge Graph and the linked data applications of the BBC (Programmes, Music, Nature).

BBC applications of linked data

Since 2007 the BBC (British Broadcasting Corporation) has been using a semantic web approach to structuring information about its programs (www.bbc.co.uk/programmes) so that the data can be easily used in other contexts within the BBC. In effect, the BBC is using its own and other linked data on the web as its web content management system (Raimond et al., 2012). Since implementing BBC Programmes, the BBC has launched BBC Music (www.bbc.co.uk/music) and BBC Wildlife Finder (www.bbc.co.uk/nature/

wildlife). The BBC creates a web identifier (and an RDF representation of it) for each entity of interest (artist, species, habitat, etc.). BBC Music and Wildlife Finder are underpinned by other linked datasets (Musicbrainz and Wikipedia), plus data from other sources such as the World Wildlife Fund, Zoological Society of London and Animal Diversity Web. The linked data application repurposes the data and places it in a BBC context. For example, the BBC Music page for Bob Dylan brings together BBC features, a biography from Wikipedia, a list of similar artists from the Echo Nest, links to a number of Dylan tracks, information about Dylan's personal relationships, news, blog posts and other links. In addition the BBC makes data feeds available to others, and its editors contribute to MusicBrainz and Wikipedia, rather than internal systems.

The Google Knowledge Graph

The Google Knowledge Graph, introduced in 2012 (Singhal, 2012), is based predominantly on Freebase, a large, open linked dataset (Bollacker et al., 2008) that was acquired by Google in 2010 (Freebase, 2013). Google's Knowledge Graph also uses information from Wikipedia, the CIA World Fact Book, and other non-public sources that it has gathered based on its research into what people search for. Some have criticized Google because (as of this writing) access to the entire Knowledge Graph dataset is restricted. Some of the data is from closed datasets with terms that limit public redistribution (see Stewart, 2012; Torzec, 2012), and the linked data community highly values openness. In May 2013 at Google's annual I/O Conference for developers, Google developer Shawn Simister presented on open APIs for the core of Google's Knowledge Graph, Freebase (Simister, 2013).

Progress and prospects for semantic interoperability

Chapters 9 and 10 further discuss the semantic web and linked data with respect to their early adoption in digital libraries. Chapter 10 also discusses schema.org, a collection of schemas (HTML tags) that enable webmasters to provide structured metadata within web pages. The schema.org approach achieves greater visibility in search engines.

While the semantic web is growing rapidly and applications built upon it are beginning to appear, its evolution is still in early stages. Some have pointed out shortcomings and disappointment with progress; Robert Sanderson (2013) describes some of these in his recent presentation to the spring meeting of the Coalition for Networked Information. It must be admitted that at the time of this writing, the prospects for success remain unclear and unpredictable. Implementers have found that publishing and consuming linked data can be complex, and many practical and research challenges remain to be addressed (such as those described by Bizer, Heath and Berners-Lee, 2009, 15–22; Miličić, 2011).

Key challenge 2: Community engagement

In many ways, this book is about community engagement with digital libraries and the opportunities that digital libraries have to play stronger social roles. The digital library field has made enormous technical progress, and digital libraries have substantially improved the discoverability and accessibility of scholarly and cultural heritage content. But deep engagement with the communities that digital libraries are meant to serve has been uneven. A key challenge of the field is increasing digital libraries' value and engagement with the communities they serve. This book explores various aspects of increasing digital libraries' engagement with their communities, including:

- what sets thriving, long-lived digital libraries apart from those that attract only modest attention or have faded into memory; why some digital libraries have a distinctive impact on their communities, while others are more or less ignored
- the opportunity to embed digital libraries much more effectively in the web's discovery environments
- the opportunities afforded by the social web to greatly increase digital libraries' community engagement
- the opportunity to participate more fully in revitalizing the processes of scholarly communication in ways that will improve network-based scholarly collaboration, the speed of scientific discovery, and the progress and accessibility of knowledge
- the risk of continuing to emphasize the collections and information processes surrounding digital libraries over their societal or community-based roles
- the risk of continuing to conceive of digital libraries as ends in themselves, and not in the context of the enormous amount of online content that is useful to, and trusted by, the communities that digital libraries serve

- the opportunity to re-cast digital libraries in terms of their social roles and in ways that are better aligned with individuals' information needs, preferences and practices.

Key challenge 3: Intellectual property rights

The legal framework protecting intellectual property rights has been a key challenge for digital libraries. The digital world is here. With a massive amount of diverse content now online (text, images, audio and video and more), radical changes have occurred in how people and systems communicate, create, interact with, exchange and re-use, and link to content. This high-speed, dynamic, participatory online information environment benefits greatly from open systems and the easy, low-barrier sharing and exchange of digital content.

It remains essential to balance the values of openness with carefully protecting intellectual property rights. At the same time, the more open digital libraries are, the greater potential they have to play important social roles – for example, helping people everywhere gain access to high-quality content, benefit from the free flow of ideas, learn and make new discoveries, and advance knowledge and culture. The social roles of libraries have historically been supported by the legal framework. In many countries this takes the form of the principles of 'fair dealing', and in the US by the historic concept of 'fair use' and related exceptions and limitations of copyright. The following sections elaborate on these concepts.

In many countries, the legal framework protecting intellectual property is out of step with the new conditions of the digital world. The effect of not upgrading the copyright laws to reflect these new conditions has led to a poor climate for innovation, diminished public access and the limitation of some former provisions permitting the use, dissemination or long-term preservation of content by libraries. This section provides some basic information about the current situation and briefly lays out some ways in which digital libraries are responding.

Definition of intellectual property (IP)

The UK Intellectual Property Office introduces the concept of intellectual property in this way:

Intellectual Property (IP) results from the expression of an idea. So IP might be a brand, an invention, a design, a song or another intellectual creation. IP can be owned, bought and sold.

www.ipo.gov.uk

The UK IPO office goes on to define four main methods for legally protecting intellectual property: patents, trademarks, designs and copyright. The IP protection most relevant in the digital library domain is copyright, which is generally 'an automatic right which applies when the work is fixed, that is written or recorded in some way'. Most copyright systems require both this aspect ('fixity') in addition to 'originality' (and original work fixed in a tangible medium of expression).

Copyright

Copyright in the US is based on the Constitution, article 1, section 8. The pertinent part of the section, which lays out the powers of Congress to enact laws, reads:

To promote the Progress of Science and useful Arts, by securing for limited Times to Authors and Inventors the exclusive Right to their respective Writings and Discoveries.

Copyright prevents unauthorized copying of creators' work, performing it publicly, or developing derivative works of it. In the US, the objective is to grant creators exclusive rights for a period of time, after which their work enters the public domain (that is, copyright ends, though some rights may still apply). The purpose is to stimulate the creation and distribution of new original works, thereby benefiting the public. The incentive for creating new works is achieved by enabling creators to economically benefit from their works for a period of time. The purpose of copyright may differ in other countries; for example, to protect the moral rights of creators to control the use of their works. Hirtle, Hudson and Kenyon (2009) offer a comprehensive guide to US copyright law and its application to libraries, archives and museums. Cornish (2009) has provided guidance for UK libraries, archives and information services.

Adapting to the digital age

Copyright periods have been getting longer, and the copyright laws are not at this time well adapted to the digital era. There are deep concerns that the public domain is shrinking (Lessig, 2013). In the US, libraries have traditionally had certain exemptions as well as provisions for the 'fair use' of non-digital copyrighted works, including copying them without permission of the copyright owner and without the payment of a licensing fee (Hirtle, Hudson and Kenyon, 2009, Chapters 5 and 6). Attempts to adapt these permissions for the digital age have been only partially successful (for a US perspective, current as of this writing, see Brown, 2013).

Recent developments in the UK are encouraging. In 2010 the government commissioned the Hargreaves Review of IP and Growth, which produced recommendations for an IP framework better suited to 'supporting innovation and promoting economic growth in the digital age' (Hargreaves, 2011, 7). The report called out copyright law as being particularly in need of revision, especially to enable appropriate copying activities and certain types of text and data mining. The government broadly accepted the Hargreaves report's recommendations in August 2011 (www.ipo.gov.uk/types/hargreaves.htm) and efforts to implement them have begun.

Barriers for digital libraries

Digital libraries are by their nature open and they make the display, use and exchange of content easy. Furthermore, once content is digital and networked, many new innovations and applications become possible. The current state of copyright law – and its misalignment with the realities and opportunities of the digital era – has had significant impact on how digital libraries have developed. The influence of the current legal framework on digital library work is pervasive, affecting, for example, how digital content and metadata can be re-used and exchanged; what it is lawful to digitize or preserve; national legal deposit programs; the process and costs of licensing scholarly digital libraries, e-journals and e-books; and the complexity and costs of digital library development and implementation generally. The difficulties have driven digital library development in particular directions; Table 3.2 provides a brief guide to a number of the issues and some sources for further information.

Key challenge 4: Sustainability

The digital library field's knowledge of how to build digital libraries outpaces

Table 3.2 Issues associated with digital libraries and copyright

Issue: The public domain and orphan works	
Description	**Suggested sources**
Orphan works are copyrighted works whose owner is unknown or cannot be located. Certain categories of works whose copyrights have not been renewed are in the public domain. The problem is, it can be difficult and costly to determine whether copyright exists or has been renewed. The number of orphan works is vast. Orphan works are a problem for digitization and digital preservation projects because it is not clear what it is lawful to do with them and the rightsholder cannot be located to ask permission. Most large-scale projects do not have adequate funds to thoroughly investigate the copyright status of orphan works.	• JISC, 2009, *In From the Cold* • Hirtle, Hudson and Kenyon, 2009, Chapter 7 • European Commission, 2012a. Directive 2012/28/EU
Issue: Mass digitization	
Description	**Suggested sources**
Mass digitization generally alludes to the digitization of very large, whole collections of content, with no or minimal selection. Google Books is a mass digitization project of books, both copyrighted and public domain. Mass digitization projects can be done for other types of material under copyright besides texts (e.g., photographs). Library, museum and archive collections contain a massive number of orphan works. Both the Google Books project and HathiTrust have encountered legal difficulties. At least one case may be inching toward resolution: just before this book went to press, US circuit judge Denny Chin of New York dismissed a lawsuit by authors against Google Books, accepting Google's argument that its project constituted fair use under US copyright law. The European Commission announced a multinational mass digitization initiative in 2005, which has since been supported by research, development (e.g., the ARROW project), and implementation, as well as legal changes.	• Aaron, 2012 (HathiTrust) • Baksik, 2006 (Google Books lawsuit) • De La Durantaye, 2010 (European Union initiatives and Google Books) • Hahn, 2008 (preservation and Google Books) • Jockers, Sag and Schultz, 2012 (HathiTrust) • Ricolfi et al., 2008 (EU i2010 Digital Libraries) • Stratton, 2011 (ARROW) • *The Guardian*, 14 November 2013 (Google Books) • Travis, 2010 (Google Books) • Van Houweling, 2012 (photos) • Chapter 5 of this book
Issue: Digital preservation	
Description	**Suggested sources**
Digital preservation, which is important to economic growth and cultural memory, is the active management of digital information to ensure it remains accessible over time. Both digitized and born-digital content can be preserved. The amount of digital content that could be preserved is staggering. Traditionally, libraries have had the responsibility and legal rights to preserve the physical collections they own. National libraries have had the responsibility to collect and preserve publications through legal deposit programs. With the rise of massive online networked information, the responsibility and rights to preserve digital content have become diffuse and unclear.	• Saarti and Vattulainen, 2013 (legal deposit) • Waters, 2007 (preserving the scholarly record) • Preservation section of Chapter 6 of this book *(Continued on next page.)*

Table 3.2 *(Continued)*

Issue: Scholarly communications and open access

Description	Suggested sources
The open access movement is having an impact. The number of publishers requiring authors to transfer copyright is declining. Open access advocates have created 'author addenda' to publisher agreements and other means to help authors retain rights to their work, for example to make the work freely available under certain conditions. Scholars themselves exhibit a range of concern, confusion or indifference about copyright. Around the world, and especially in Europe, there is a policy shift toward open access to scholarly content produced as a result of public funding.	• Policy and legal frameworks section of Chapter 8 of this book • Hirtle, 2006 (author addenda) • Association of Learned and Professional Society Publishers, 2004 (recommended publisher practices)

Issue: A new library specialization, new enabling technologies

Description	Suggested sources
Instead of purchasing scholarly content as they did in the past, libraries now license access to its digital forms. Publishers restrict the rights to access, display and export most online scholarly content. These conditions have engendered a new field of library specialization and new enabling technologies to support licensing, renewals and payments; authenticating and authorizing access to licensed scholarly content; e-resource metadata management in catalogs and knowledgebases and on library websites; new systems and services for indexing, end-user discovery and use; and more.	• Chapter 5 of this book (hybrid libraries)

Issue: New ways to lawfully distribute digital content and data

Description	Suggested sources
The web, online information services and digital libraries are driving a shift to discovery and access models that rely on exchanging and linking digital content and metadata. Digital library implementers and others began searching for new ways to incorporate freer copying, distribution and re-use of content, while minimizing the potential for negative outcomes. Models supporting new lawful ways to distribute and exchange content and data have appeared. These new models (e.g., Creative Commons licensing) reserve a range of rights ('some rights reserved') or explicitly dedicate the content or data to the public domain ('no rights reserved').	• Creative Commons (www.creativecommons.org) • GNU Free Documentation License (www.gnu.org/licenses/licenses.html#FDL) • Open Data Commons (www.opendatacommons.org)

its understanding of how to sustain them. While the digital library builders aspire to offer free access to all, digital libraries are not free for their builders to create and maintain. These costs must be recovered somehow. Financial sustainability is critical.

Digital library sustainability has several aspects. Setting aside the technological aspects of sustainability for the moment, sustainability in digital libraries has economic, social and ethical characteristics (see Figure 3.2). Consider the following brief overview of these:

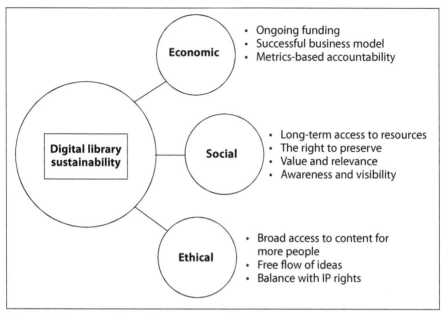

Figure 3.2 Aspects of digital library sustainability

- **Economic**: A sustainable digital library has ongoing funding and a workable business model for recovering its costs; its managers engage in ongoing business planning; it regularly gauges community needs, awareness and satisfaction with its services; it has clear accountability and evidence-based metrics to underpin strategic plans and investments in ongoing development.
- **Social:** A sustainable digital library is considered essential by the communities it serves (Hamilton, 2004, 393); it maintains its visibility and community awareness; it provides ongoing access to content and services that are highly valued by the communities it serves.
- **Ethical:** A sustainable digital library provides the broadest possible access to its content, and it supports open inquiry and the free flow of ideas while respecting the rights of content creators and producers.

Achieving and maintaining digital library sustainability is a challenge in a world dominated by the web, dynamic information-seeking expectations and practices, and transformed processes for scholarly communication. From an economic perspective, while funding is sometimes available for getting a digital library started, ongoing financial support can be difficult to find. Chapter 7 of this book provides further analysis of the current situation and the characteristics of sustainable digital libraries.

Conclusion

This chapter offers a new concept map derived from a qualitative and quantitative analysis of the digital library literature from 2002 to 2012. The map provides one framework for comprehending a large and diverse body of work as a set of interrelated key topics and challenges.

The second decade of digital library research and practice carried forward the first decade's emphasis on enabling technologies and on building collections. Three main areas of focus were building and aggregating repositories; technologies and models for digital preservation; and metadata. The key technological challenges continued to be scale, heterogeneity and interoperability; but over the course of the decade, the standards, processes and methods for achieving interoperability changed. Interest in the semantic web and linked data increased strongly from about 2007 forward. While the longer-term prospects for semantic web approaches remain unclear, impressive applications using these approaches have begun to demonstrate their potential. The long section on interoperability is intended to give readers a basic foundation for understanding subsequent chapters and other digital library literature.

Digital library research and practice evolved over the second decade, resulting in greater attention to social and economic issues, especially with respect to evaluating the use and users of digital libraries; advancing education and the processes of scholarly communication; and broadening access to high-quality digital content through open access. The continuing focus on digital collections is now paired with a new body of work that focuses on digital library communities. The second decade began to address key challenges related to engaging communities around digital libraries, coping with the barriers associated with a restrictive legal framework, and identifying success factors for sustaining digital libraries.

CHAPTER 4

Digital library collections: repositories

Overview

This chapter and the next discuss digital libraries and the web through the lens of collections and collection building. This chapter begins with an exploration of the parallel but separate developments of the web, digital library repositories and hybrid libraries. It then turns to an examination of digital library repositories. Topics include numbers, usage and discoverability of repositories; current position and roles; systems and software; federation and dissemination of repository content; next-generation repository systems; and cyberinfrastructure, data and e-research support. The next chapter moves on to the examination of hybrid libraries, then concludes with thoughts about advances, opportunities and challenges for both hybrid libraries and repositories.

The traditional library worldview

Over the course of the 19th and 20th centuries, conventional definitions of libraries and core assumptions of the general public have tended to emphasize their *collections* over their social roles. Services are sometimes mentioned, but the core assumptions are that libraries are collections of things (especially books) in fixed locations (buildings and later, online 'virtual' collections or repositories), and the role of libraries is to provide access and support for these collections on behalf of the communities they serve. In keeping with this set of core assumptions, library roles and services have tended to be defined through the collections lens: selecting, acquiring, organizing, preserving, managing, providing for access, answering questions and providing instruction about how to use collections. The result is that collections take center stage and dominate the current library worldview, or overall perspective from which people (including librarians) define libraries.

Carl Lagoze discusses the notion of library core assumptions as a 'meme' (a worldview) that has influenced digital library development. He contrasts the library meme with the web meme (2010, 48–71) and goes on to argue that over time, the library meme engendered digital library technical approaches and standards that did not play out well on the web as both the web and digital libraries evolved. Indeed, large-scale success for digital library researchers and practitioners has often depended on others being willing to adopt or accommodate digital library ways of doing things (as opposed to the ways things are typically done on the web). When digital library ways contrasted significantly with the less-constrained, low-barrier methods and simpler standards used by most web developers, digital library approaches were not widely adopted outside the digital library community.

Lagoze's insights into the library meme provide a partial explanation of how digital library repositories and hybrid library systems evolved separately from the web. Another explanation derives from the fact that at first, the simpler web-based approaches yielded inferior results (for example, early search engines were imprecise). These practical realities, combined with mindsets and backgrounds of early designers, does appear to have led to digital repositories modeled on library collections. This had implications later for how repositories evolved and how well or poorly they have been integrated into the larger web.

In the case of hybrid libraries, as much as core assumptions or worldview perhaps, the practical realities of supporting search and retrieval for both digital and non-digital collections produced special requirements and constrained libraries' options. Libraries manage production systems that their communities rely on daily, so it has been necessary to adapt and evolve library systems and migrate them as new possibilities emerged for production-ready environments. At the same time, library leaders knew it was imperative to address dramatic shifts in their communities' requirements. Consider the following:

- Until relatively recently, publishers, professional societies and indexing services did not allow their metadata to be harvested or crawled for inclusion in other systems. To provide for discovery and access to this content, libraries have needed to use a series of approaches that were compatible with what e-content providers and others made possible, what they could accomplish on their own, and what evolving library information systems could do.

- Most hybrid libraries' systems have been and continue to be dominated by bibliographic metadata describing non-digital (e.g., print) library collections. Libraries have understandably required systems that provide for reliable discovery and use of both online and non-digital content. This added complexity to developing and implementing systems.
- Open access repositories created new requirements for integration with library discovery environments.
- Digitization projects created new content that libraries wanted to reveal in their discovery systems.
- The need for frameworks to enable long-term preservation of content also brought special requirements.
- It became important for library systems to support not only the discovery and delivery of information for its communities, but also to be open to the exchange and disclosure of system contents to many other systems.

These factors have driven a number of related but essentially separate lines of systems development for digital repositories and hybrid libraries, described in this and the next chapter.

Repositories, libraries and the web
Repository architecture

A review of dictionary definitions of the word 'repository' indicates it is a place or container where things can be deposited for storage or safekeeping. Branin (2007) has provided a conceptual introduction to repositories from the library perspective. In digital library research and development, a repository has been a fundamental component of the Kahn-Wilensky architecture (introduced in Chapter 1). Kahn and Wilensky wrote their seminal paper in the early days of the web, at a time when the web was evolving in parallel with digital library research and practice. They were part of a community of computer science researchers leading digital library research initiatives at the time. Kahn and Wilensky's framework for building digital library collections grew out of their disciplines and was centered on digital objects and repositories.

Web crawling and indexing

The approach of Brin and Page (graduate students who worked on one of the DLI projects until they founded Google in 1998) was a major innovation that grew out of – and later defined – the parameters for the parallel universe in which the web was evolving. Their approach took advantage of the structure of hypertext (text with links) to crawl and index everything they could on the web. They did not begin with the notions of multiple repositories serving as collection points for particular kinds of well defined objects; their starting point was exploiting information already present in hypertext to build a very large-scale, universal information indexing and retrieval system. The Google repository component developed by Brin and Page contained not well described and managed digital objects, but compressed web pages that had been crawled with robots. The component they called the indexer then read and processed the repository's compressed pages to produce a number of outputs, resulting in an inverted index and PageRanks that supported user queries (Brin and Page, 1998 – see their Figure 1 and accompanying text).

The approach, which was completely automated, enabled very large stores of documents (the web) to be automatically crawled, indexed and searched at little cost and at great scale compared to other more formal approaches to information description and retrieval. Google's success kicked off an immense wave of further innovation and development on the web.

A multiverse of research and practice

A 'multiverse' is a set of parallel universes, each of which defines self-contained but co-existing realities. At the moment a multiverse of research and practice exists for organizing the world's information and making it discoverable. The evolution of the web played out in one parallel universe, which was populated with developers who were entrepreneurial, decentralized, relatively unbound by legacy systems or core assumptions, and minimally constrained by technical standards. It might be argued that this universe is now the only one that is highly visible to the information-seeking public.

Arms, in an essay on the tenth anniversary of *DLib Magazine*, recognized the separate evolutionary paths chosen by two other universes of research and practice when he noted 'computer scientists resisted the simple technology of the web; librarians disparaged the value of web search engines' (2005). Given their different starting points, histories and worldviews, the services and systems of the web, digital libraries, and libraries evolved at the same time but along largely separate paths.

While there are some trends suggesting eventual convergence, the parallel but separate realities of digital libraries and libraries persist. At least in US libraries, responsibility for digital library efforts has been widely distributed or organizationally isolated, and remains so (Maron and Pickle, 2013, 2–3). As already discussed, first-decade digital library projects in the US were most often managed out of computer or information science departments, and in the UK by librarians working on federally funded research and prototyping projects. What all digital library specialists had in common was their project-based work, which was generally undertaken outside the mainstream operations of libraries. Meanwhile, librarians had their own challenges adapting their collections, practices and systems to disruptive, constantly shifting requirements for the library's mainstream services and systems. Figure 4.1 offers a side-by-side view of three timelines that trace key events along these parallel paths. Subsequent sections of this chapter and the next describe these parallel but separate paths.

The evolution of digital library repositories
A key theme and focus for development
In the second decade of digital libraries, the topic of repositories dominated the attention of digital library researchers and practitioners more than any other. They were a key outcome of the first decade of digital library research and practice. There are two kinds: (1) subject-based repositories and (2) institutional repositories. Subject-based repositories collect and provide access to digital objects related to a subject or group of subjects; they are sometimes called discipline-based repositories. The International Network for the Availability of Scientific Publications (INASP) defines an institutional repository as 'an online locus for collecting, preserving, and disseminating, in digital form, the intellectual output of an institution.' The INASP site lists a number of registries of institutional repositories (www.inasp.info).

Emergence, numbers, costs
Emergence of repositories

Adamick and Reznik-Zellen's analyses of subject repositories (2010a; 2010b) indicate that four of the world's five highest-ranked subject-based repositories today – PubMed Central, RePEc, arXiv, and Social Science Research Network (SSRN) – were established in the first decade of digital library work (http://repositories.webometrics.info/en/world, July 2012). As discussed in

Repositories	Internet and web	Hybrid libraries
arXiv 1991, SSRN 1994, RePEC 1996 UK eLib Programme 1994 NDLTD (ETDs) 1996	**Amazon founded 1994** **Internet Archive founded 1996** **Google founded 1998**	First e-journal systems 1995–1997 First large digitization projects 1994–1999 First Z39.50 projects 1998–
	1999–2000	
Open Archives Initiative – Santa Fe 1999 OAI-PMH 2001	**Blogger founded 1999**	First MARC sets for e-resources produced 1999
		Serials Solutions founded 2000 (e-resource A to Z lists)
National Science Digital Library program 2000 Public Library of Science (PLoS) 2000		First deployment OpenURLs 2000
	2001–2002	
UVa and Cornell: FEDORA 2001 GNU ePrints and DSpace released 2002 OAIster begins 2002	**Wikipedia launched 2001** **Surface web triples in size 1999–2002; deep web defined**	ARL Scholars Portal project begins (metasearch portals; Z39.50) 2002
Open Access Declarations Budapest, Bethesda, Berlin 2002–2003		
	2003–2004	
ROAR and DOAJ 2003	**Delicious 2003 LinkedIn 2003**	Multiple portal services launched (metasearch) 2003–2005
BASE and DAREnet 2004	**Google Library Project 2004 Google Scholar 2004**	
OpenDOAR 2005		
SRU 1.1 (webservice) 2004		
	2005–2006	
OAI-ORE 2006	**O'Reilly 'What is Web 2.0?'**	84% of public starts research with a search engine 2005
SWORD protocol 2007	**Amazon cloud services 2006**	Multiple reports released crticizing traditional catalogs 2006
	Twitter 2006	
	2007–2008	Multiple next generation discovery services launched; the race to index e-content starts
US NIH requires grantees to post papers for public access 2008	**Google Books has scanned 7M books**	HathiTrust launched 2008
DRIVER in production 2008	**Facebook 100M users 2008**	Median ARL spends US$5.4M on e-content (53% of materials budget)
	2009–2010	
NIH VIVO project funded 2009	**Google Books releases 1M public domain e-books in EPUB format 2009**	Faculty preference for catalog declining; 79% prefer to start research with discipline- specific e-resource or search engine 2009
Evidence mounts – majority of repo traffic comes from Google		
US NSF requires grant documents to have data management plans 2010	**Amazon e-book sales top hardover sales 2010**	
	2011–2012	
NIH PubMed Central contains 2.2M articles; 20% are open access 2011	**2.3 billion people have internet access 2011**	Scholarly article growth 1.5 M articles/year, most e-format 2011
OA articles growing 30%/year	**One in five US adults owns a tablet or e-book reader 2012**	Several discovery services enable search for 4.6M HathiTrust digitized titles 2011
DuraCloud launched 2011		First cloud-based library services platforms in pilot or production 2012
First Hydra Project demonstrations		

Figure 4.1 Timelines for repositories, the internet and web, and hybrid libraries

Chapter 2, the international OpCit (Open Citation) project produced GNU EPrints, which was the first open source software available for building repositories. EPrints fueled a movement to build repositories at the *institutional* level.

The OAI framework

As discussed in Chapter 2, the Open Archives Initiative (OAI), which emerged from a meeting in Santa Fe in October 1999 to explore co-operation among already existing repositories, has sought to facilitate the distribution, sharing and discovery of scholarly research. The OAI's framework for supporting open scholarly communications, OAI-PMH, has facilitated scholarly collaboration and publication and a gradual shift away from increasingly less affordable models based on commercially published journals. The framers of OAI-PMH offered a fresh approach to building open systems that were capable of drawing together diverse resources in different locations into a single information service. OAI-PMH has contributed more than any other first-decade digital library innovation to the rapid growth of open access repositories around the world.

Growth of repositories

Other providers of open source software for building institutional repositories followed the release of GNU EPrints; specifics follow later in this chapter. Early adopters identified the necessary process and accompanying tools and standards for launching a repository. Once the process and infrastructure components had been identified, many organizations did launch repositories, either built locally or hosted by a third party. A number of forums and services exist to support implementers of repositories based on open source software. Some provide quantitative information, registry and tracking of repositories, guidance on management and policy matters, and other services. The Ranking Web of World Repositories (http://repositories.webometrics.info), a service of the Cybermetrics Lab, provides analysis and ranking of repositories.

Various directories support repositories; in their paper at IFLA, Oliver and Swain reported their research, which had identified 23 directories of open access repositories (2006). The two leading ones are:

- ROAR (Registry of Open Access Repositories; http://roar.eprints.org)
- OpenDOAR (Directory of Open Access Repositories; www.opendoar.org).

OpenDOAR and ROAR exist mainly to serve as a focal point for quantitative and statistical analysis and/or policy and standards development for the repository community. They also can be used as search portals to aggregated repository contents, although this is a secondary purpose. A report of a JISC-funded project on joint development of ROAR and OpenDOAR (Millington and Hubbard, 2010), explores a number of opportunities for further co-operation between the two.

As of this writing, 3429 repositories are registered in ROAR; 2322 are registered in OpenDOAR. The Cybermetrics Lab's ranking site currently tracks 1654 repositories. These registries are growing all the time, so these numbers will not be accurate for long. Using data from ROAR and OpenDOAR, Repository66 (http://maps.repository66.org) maps 2311 repositories, holding nearly 34 million items (Lewis, 2012). BASE, another large aggregation that provides search services across open access repositories, reports access to 40 million documents from 2400 sources that are harvested for BASE (www.base-search.net/about/en). These totals count both subject-based and institutional repositories plus other content indexed by BASE.

Not all repositories are registered, so the total numbers and holdings of repositories worldwide are unknown. As an indication of the difference between what the registries track and what exists, the example of DSpace may provide a guess. Currently available statistics from their web sites suggest that from two-thirds to 90% of DSpace repositories are registered in OpenDOAR and/or ROAR.

Costs

While open source software typically incurs no fees, building and running a repository is not free. A local installation incurs costs for hardware and labor among other costs. Estimates of the costs of implementing and running a repository vary widely; the OASIS site suggests labor costs of 1.5 to 3.0 FTE for set-up and 0.5 to 2.5 FTE for ongoing operations (Organization for the Advancement of Structured Information Standards, 2009). Grant funding supported the initial development of at least three of the top open source products – EPrints, DSpace, and Fedora – but the start-up and ongoing costs of those implementing these products at individual institutions are generally funded from an organization's operating budget. Burns et al. (2013) offer the most recent and comprehensive look at institutional repository costs, usage, and value as of this writing.

Current position and roles
Open access movement

The early digital library projects that enabled new repositories were important contributors to the international open access movement. Chapter 8 discusses the open access movement with a focus on its economic and social aspects.

Improving the discoverability and accessibility of scholarly information

Open access repositories have become increasingly important discovery and delivery mechanisms for the scholarly literature. At the time they first began being implemented, many if not most repositories could be crawled and indexed by search engines; most of the data stores of publishers and libraries could not. This made the research output available in open access repositories much more visible and publicly accessible. Even after publisher content began to be indexed by search engines, open access repositories have provided alternative access to copies of articles that are otherwise available only through purchase or subscribing libraries.

Over time, some repository managers have improved their abilities to configure their sites to optimize results for crawlers (see, for example, Suber, 2005). More recently, Arlitsch and O'Brien (2012) tested and reported on techniques for making repository contents more visible in search engines. They were able to identify and quantify ways to significantly improve repository indexing ratios in Google Scholar. These authors' research suggests that in 2012 the current indexing ratio of repositories (the number of URLs found in a search engine's index divided by the total number of URLs in a repository) may have averaged around 30%. Their tests indicate that a repository manager can improve a repository's indexing ratio in Google Scholar by adhering to Google Scholar's 'Inclusion Guidelines for Webmasters' (www.scholar. google.com/intl/en/scholar/inclusion.html). Following the publication of this influential article, Arltisch and O'Brien produced a book (2013) to provide additional guidance to repository managers on SEO (search engine optimization: practices by website owners to maximize the visibility of their content in search engine results). Chapters 8 and 10 further discuss SEO and other methods for extending repository reach and visibility.

Despite room for improvement, Google and Google Scholar already surface a good deal of content in open access repositories. Norris, Oppenheim and Rowland (2008) evaluated four search tools' utility for locating open access articles: Google, Google Scholar, OpenDOAR and OAIster. They searched a sample of a little more than 2500 articles from ecology, economics and sociology journals and found open access versions of 967 of them (38%). They then searched the titles of the open access articles using the different search tools. Google and Google Scholar performed the best for finding the open access articles, locating 76.84% of them. After discussing a number of reasons for the results, they concluded that those searching for open access articles are more likely to find them with Google or Google Scholar.

Centralized, easier access to previously hard-to-find content

Repositories also create workspace and centralized access for content that had previously been more scattered and difficult to find. They typically contain not only articles but pre- and post-prints, reports, theses and dissertations, conference and working papers, teaching materials, and presentations. Figure 4.2 provides a breakdown of the types of content that the repositories registered in OpenDOAR contained as of June 2013. The figure displays results for two subsets of OpenDOAR's registered repositories: subject-based repositories and institutional repositories. While it is clear that institutional repositories are more likely to contain theses and dissertations, and subject repositories are more likely to contain media and audiovisual materials, otherwise both kinds of repositories appear to hold similar types of content. From the perspective of the *number* of scholarly objects they contain, subject-based repositories do tend to contain more items than institutional repositories.

Reach, visibility and citation advantage

Open access repositories have had many positive impacts. They have already fostered greater discoverability and accessibility of the scholarly literature. Despite room for improvement, analyses suggest that Google and Google Scholar refer a great deal of traffic to open access repositories. Organ (2006) quantified the degree to which institutional repository content at the University of Wollongong (Australia) was downloaded as a result of referrals from search engines. Over the six-month period they studied, Google referrals were responsible for generating 95.8% of measurable full-text downloads from their repository.

Harnad and Brody's frequently cited paper (2004) makes the claim that open access articles have dramatic citation advantages and therefore greater impact on scholarship. Eysenbach's analysis (2006) suggested that open access articles 'are cited earlier and are, on average, cited more often' than non-open access articles. While these authors' findings about the 'citation advantage'

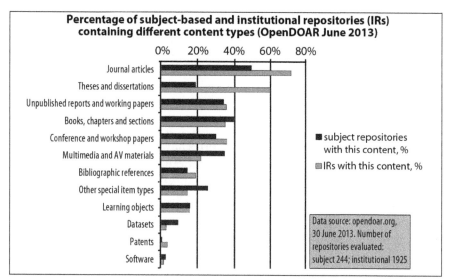

Figure 4.2 Contents of OpenDOAR repositories, mid-2013

have been debated, it does seem clear that open access articles reach a broader audience and are downloaded more often (Antelman, 2004; Davis, 2011; Gaulé and Maystre, 2011).

Proportion of annual scholarly output

For scholars in some disciplines, the subject-based repositories have succeeded in transforming the processes of scholarly communication and fostering worldwide collaboration in the disciplines they support. Deposit mandates (governmental or institutional requirements that researchers make their papers available in open access repositories) have also stimulated growth in the number of open access papers available. For example a new public access policy announced by the US National Institutes of Health (NIH) in 2008 required that papers from NIH-funded projects be submitted to PubMed Central and made publicly available within 12 months of publication (publicaccess.nih.gov). Chapter 8 discusses the benefits and challenges of deposit mandates.

The number of articles published in open access journals or available from open access repositories (both subject-based and institutional) or authors' web pages represents an increasing proportion of annual scholarly output. Björk and colleagues conducted a number of analyses (Björk, Roos, and Lauri, 2009; Björk et al., 2010; Laakso et al., 2011) and estimated that a little over 20% of the articles published in 2008 were openly available a year later. The results of the study that the team published in 2011 suggested that the number of open access journals has grown at an annual rate of 18% since 2000, and the number of open access articles has grown 30% a year.

Challenges of institutional repositories

While some of the subject-based repositories have been eagerly embraced by scholars as vehicles for facilitating collaboration and faster advances in knowledge, scholars have been comparatively slow to deposit their work in other repositories, especially institutionally based ones. Many authors have documented these low deposit rates by scholars. A study by van Westrienen and Lynch (2005) of institutional repositories in 13 countries suggested that most repositories contained only a few hundred items. The Netherlands was an exception, with an average of around 3000 full-text items each. In a census of institutional repositories in the US, Markey et al. (2007) found that respondents' repositories generally contained a few hundred documents; only a handful of reporting institutions had more than 5000 documents. The number of items deposited in institutional repositories that responded to a survey sponsored by the SURF Foundation for DRIVER (van Eijndhoven and van der Graaf, 2007) presented a slightly different picture: this survey found an average size per repository of almost 9000 items (the average was calculated based on responses from 114 institutions in 17 countries). Even so, finding a repository with more than 10,000 items continues to be the exception rather than the rule at the time of this writing.

How big should they be?

One might ask if a repository at a research university that has 10,000 items in it is small. The answer is yes, provided the repository is not brand new, or highly specialized with a small audience. Based on the rough estimates of Carr and Brody (2007), if all of the tenured academic research active staff at a UK university deposited all of their annual output (papers, presentations, learning materials, etc.) in the institutional repository, deposits would be in the range of 10,000 items per year. Even if this estimate is high it suggests that a repository of 10,000 items that has been in place five years or more is smaller than one would expect it to be, if faculty were depositing their work in it regularly.

Some repository managers responded to slow faculty adoption rates by batch-loading high-volume files into their institutional repositories, thereby growing their size substantially, as reported by Carr and Brody. Their research suggested that despite their larger size, the patterns of some of these repositories' deposits suggested they still had low faculty deposit rates and low engagement with individual faculty members.

Thomas and McDonald (2007) studied EPrints institutional repositories containing more than 500 deposits of scholarly papers; of 176 EPrints repositories registered at that time in OpenDOAR, only 11 repositories qualified by this measure, and the largest institutional repository they studied contained a little over 6000 scholarly papers. Despite the implementation of mandates on some campuses requiring researchers to deposit their papers in institutional repositories, small repository size and low researcher deposit rates continue to be central issues for institutional repositories.

Criticism of institutional repositories

Romary and Armbruster (2010) wrote a paper highly critical of the effectiveness of institutional repositories. One criticism had to do with size: 'there exist well over one thousand institutional repositories, the majority of which hold very little content.' Romary and Armbruster compare central research publication repositories like arXiv and SSRN with the global network of institutional repositories and argue the advantages of a more centralized solution (using PubMed Central as an example). Henty (2007) enumerates ten major issues for repositories in Australian universities, including engaging the community. Chapter 8 continues the discussion of the problems of recruiting content in the context of community engagement.

Repository systems and software

ROAR and OpenDOAR track repositories worldwide. They also track statistics for repositories by various categories, one of which is type of repository software or platform. The next three sections briefly discuss the two most wide-deployed types of repositories – EPrints and D-Space – plus Fedora. EPrints and DSpace are the only two types of repositories with more than 300 registered installations in ROAR and OpenDOAR. It should be mentioned that in the US, Digital Commons is another common choice of repository software; in a recent survey Mercer et al. (2011) found that the Digital Commons software is a distant second to the use of DSpace in ARL libraries.

As of this writing, repositories based on EPrints and DSpace make up over half of the registered repositories in ROAR and OpenDOAR. EPrints and DSpace were early, 'open source' (software for which the source code is freely available) packages that enabled building OAI-compliant repositories.

EPrints (www.eprints.org)

Chapter 2 and earlier parts of this chapter discuss the history of EPrints, which was a significant outcome of the eLib programme in the UK. EPrints 3, launched in 2007, is the current version, as of this writing (Millington and Nixon, 2007). It is maintained at the University of Southampton. Besides being deployed to run hundreds of repositories, EPrints supports a number of JISC projects including ROAR and SHERPA RoMEO (see Chapter 8). EPrints also offers a hosting and consulting service called EPrints Services, which generates an income stream for recovering costs. EPrints' principal contribution besides enabling the building of repositories is to provide support and advocacy for the open access movement. It is difficult to overstate the importance of EPrints' contributions in this regard.

DSpace (www.dspace.org) and DuraSpace (www.duraspace.org)

DSpace is currently the most-used repository software; its installations account for 40% of the repositories registered in DOAR and OpenDOAR at this time. Developed at MIT in a joint project with Hewlett Packard (HP), it was released as open source software in 2002, the same year as GNU EPrints. The MIT project, whose purpose was to enable the library to provide a repository for the digital research and educational material of the university, produced a system, tools and a platform that others could deploy for building repositories (Smith et al., 2003; Baudoin and Branschofsky, 2003).

MIT's intent from the beginning was to make the software open source and promote it as a new service of the MIT Libraries. A business planning process that began in 2001 concluded with DSpace's being funded initially through MIT (built into the Libraries' operating budget) with supplemental funding from cost-recovered premium services for other libraries (Barton and Harford Walker, 2002). A 'DSpace Federation' also provided an initial collaborative framework.

In 2007, with more than 200 projects worldwide using the software, HP and MIT established the DSpace Foundation (Hewlett Packard, 2007), a non-profit organization, to oversee DSpace using a community development model. In

2009, the DSpace Foundation and the Fedora Commons announced their intention to form a working collaboration (DuraSpace, 2009). With a planning grant from the Mellon Foundation, they designed a new support framework for both organizations called DuraSpace (www.duraspace.org). DuraSpace, a non-profit organization that develops and deploys open technologies for the purpose of promoting durable access to digital content, is funded through multiple sources (DuraSpace, 2012, 5). Funding sources noted in the annual report at that time included grants (75%), community sponsorships (20%) and revenue generating services (6%).

Fedora (www.fedora-commons.org)

Chapter 2 mentions Fedora (Flexible Extensible Digital Object and Repository Architecture), which started early in the new millennium as a collaborative digital libraries project of Cornell and the University of Virginia. Fedora is more an architecture or infrastructure that uses a modular approach and web services, rather than an out-of-the-box repository solution. The intent was to provide a new framework for interoperable, web-based digital libraries that integrate well with other systems (Lagoze et al., 2006). Fedora offers an open source solution for the foundation of many different types of digital library systems, not only repositories of textual content and metadata. Fedora-based systems support access and preservation for large and complex aggregations of historic and cultural images, artifacts, text, media, datasets, and documents. As part of their article on semantic registries, Powell, Black and Collins (2011) provide insight into the innovative approach to repositories and interoperability enabled by Fedora.

Subject-based repositories

As previously noted three of the most successful subject-based repositories were launched in the first decade of digital library research and practice (arXiv.org, RePEC, SSRN). Already mentioned in this chapter are Adamick and Reznik-Zellen's two analyses of subject repositories, which contain considerable detail about the state of subject repositories in 2010. They estimate there are 150–400 subject repositories worldwide. To supplement their information, Table 4.1 provides brief information compiled from OpenDOAR, ROAR, DRIVER, and other sources about some highly ranked subject-based repositories.

Table 4.1 Summary information: a sample of subject-based repositories worldwide

Name	Number of items (year reported)	Coverage	Software if known
Social Science Research Network (SSRN)	796,541 (2012)	Social sciences	
arXiv.org	776,811 (2012)	Physics, math, astronomy, computer science, quantitative biology	arXiv (See Table 2.2)
Research Papers in Economics (RePEc)	302,882 (2012)	Economics	
Europe PubMed Central	2.87 million (2012)	Biology, biochemistry, health, medicine. A mirror site for NIH PubMed Central; in addition contains output of UK researchers	PMC
SAO/NASA Astrophysics Data System (ADS)	Index entries for 9.7 million items in three databases (including arXiv.org)	Astronomy, astrophysics, physics, geophysics, and the contents of arXiv.org. Abstracts submitted by authors; access to full text when possible.	
CiteSeerX	716,772 (2006)	Computer and information science	
AgEcon Search	55,268 (2012)	Agriculture and applied economics	DSpace
E-LIS	13,564 (2012)	Library and information science	DSpace
Perseus Digital Library	1591 (2012)	Classics	Perseus (see Table 2.2)
Organic ePrints	12,887 (2012)	Organic agriculture	EPrints

Institutional repositories

Table 4.2 provides brief information compiled from OpenDOAR, ROAR, DRIVER, and other sources about institutional repositories with 10,000 or more items that were highly ranked by the Cybermetrics Lab in July 2012.

Common search services across distributed repositories

OAI-PMH harvesting and service providers

The 1999 meeting in Santa Fe (described in Chapter 2) was convened to work on facilitating interoperability across early e-print archives. The meeting generated several significant outcomes – the Open Archives Initiative and OAI-PMH – and led to the growth of OAI-compliant open access repositories. With the ensuing rapid growth in the number of repositories and digital collections generally, digital library researchers and practitioners were soon motivated to establish common search services across distributed repositories (the initial motivation for the 1999 Santa Fe meeting).

Table 4.2 Summary information: a sample of institutional repositories worldwide

Name	Number of records (year reported)	Software if known
CERN Document Server	1.2 million (mostly metadata) (2012)	Invenio
Universidade de São Paulo Biblioteca Digital de Teses e Dissertações	34,865 (2012)	
HAL Institut National de Recherche en Informatique et en Automatique Archive Ouverte (HAL-INRIA)	219,706 (2012)	HAL
Universitat Autònoma de Barcelona Dipòsit Digital de Documents	81,163 (2012)	Invenio
NASA Technical Reports Server	1,064,884 (2012)	
MIT DSpace	56,528 (2012)	DSpace
Universiteit Utrecht Igitur Archive	32,090 (2012)	DSpace
SIM University DSpace (Shanghai Institute of Microsystem and Information Technology, Chinese Academy of Sciences)	10,728 (2011)	DSpace
National Taiwan University Repository	184,572 (2012)	DSpace
HAL Sciences de l'Homme et de la Société (HAL-SHS)	39,192 (2012)	HAL

OAIster (www.oclc.org/oaister)

One early project to federate multiple repositories was OAIster, a project undertaken at the University of Michigan in 2001. The project was one of seven funded by the Mellon Foundation that year to study the use of the new OAI harvesting protocol for making catalogs and other valuable content of the deep web more accessible (Andrew W. Mellon Foundation, 2001, 28). Hagedorn (2003) provides a detailed description of the history, objectives, methodology and results of the OAIster project, which has been highly influential.

Bitter harvest

Implementers learned that metadata harvesting using OAI-PMH sometimes fell short of being the low-barrier, low-cost framework for interoperability that its creators envisioned. Nevertheless it was better than other approaches available within the digital library community at that time. Tennant, then at the California Digital Library (2004a), reported his shock at his 'bitter harvest' of metadata and provided an overview of the problems with OAI-PMH harvesting, most of which stemmed from a lack of common practices for creating harvest sets and applying metadata. Many problems were later alleviated through community work to define and adopt best practices, so that OAI-PMH is commonly used as a protocol for federating metadata from distributed repositories.

DAREnet and other projects

BASE (discussed in Chapter 5), early projects of the US National Science Digital Library (discussed in Chapters 7 and 8), DAREnet (see, for example, Dijk et al., 2006; Hogenaar and Steinhoff, 2008) and the China Digital Museum Project (Tansley, 2006) are or were among a number of services that brought distributed repository content together, using OAI-PMH by itself or as part of a larger framework for achieving interoperability.

New approaches to discovery

DRIVER (www.driver-repository.eu)

Peters and Lossau (2011) describe DRIVER, a project funded by the European Commission to build a sustainable global digital infrastructure for the networking of European open access repositories. With inspiration from the DARE project, the project team began work in 2005 and completed the first phase of DRIVER in 2007. DRIVER-II extends and builds upon its results (EC Framework Programme 7, 2007).

DRIVER has succeeded in delivering a common infrastructure and establishing a confederation of European digital repositories, called COAR, which has advocacy, policy and co-ordination roles (www.coar-repositories.org). As of June 2011 the DRIVER search portal provided access to 3.5 million publications from 295 repositories in 38 European countries (www.driver-repository.eu/PublicDocs/FACT_SHEET_I3_driver_ii.pdf). Manghi et al. (2010) discuss why DRIVER represents an important breakthrough in the evolution of repositories.

aDORe

The developers of aDORe were among many repository managers who, as the scale of digital content grew, faced

> the harsh reality that their solutions need to handle an amount of artifacts that is orders of magnitude higher than originally intended, and are reaching an understanding that approaches that work at the originally intended scale do not necessarily work at that next level
>
> Van de Sompel, Chute and Hochstenbach, 2008

A team at Los Alamos developed the aDORe federation architecture starting in 2003 to address three problems with their current design:

- Their approach was 'metadata-centric, treating descriptive metadata records as first class citizens and the actual digital assets as auxiliary items'.
- They stored tens of millions of digital assets as files in a filing system, resulting in 'a system administrator's nightmare'.
- Their design at that time tightly integrated content and the discovery application, preventing other applications from re-using the content.

Solutions were readily identified: use a compound object view instead of a metadata-centric view; put assets in storage containers instead of files; separate the repository from applications; and provide the needed machine interfaces. Implementing the solutions however, required multiple years of work. aDORe is one of several projects that signaled a trend to design repositories and interoperability mechanisms using approaches more closely aligned with those of web developers and the architecture of the web.

Building on and for the web: web services

Web services and web APIs are the currently dominant enabling technologies for supporting interoperability, in particular the exchange and re-use of content between sites. At this point a few sentences about web services and web APIs will be helpful for understanding how repositories and library systems have been changing and will continue to change as they adopt web-based approaches. This brief discussion begins with XML (Extensible Markup Language).

XML

XML was an important development on the web because it created a basis to exchange information in new, useful ways. XML was designed to support the encoding of structured data in a relatively simple and standardized way, to be usable over the web, thus facilitating the development of tools for automatic processing of this content and its use in applications and syndication (web feeds such as alerts).

Web services

Using XML to code and decode information and a protocol to transport the data over HTTP (Hypertext Transfer Protocol), web services take applications that run on the web and publish those applications in a machine-readable way. A directory or registry enables the registration and location of web service applications. These components, taken together, allow servers of different types and in different places to find and use each others' web services. Web services provide applications that can be called at any time, like a weather report or a converter that changes yards to meters, or they can be used to exchange data.

Web APIs

Web APIs (Application Programming Interfaces) are like web services except they have moved toward simpler communications methods. Web API requests and responses between systems are expressed in XML or a simpler alternative called JSON. Web APIs are what enable combining multiple services into new applications (called 'mashups').

It is important to remember that web services, Web APIs and mashups provide software-to-software interfaces and are not user interfaces. As discussed in Chapter 3, the semantic web and linked data may offer new approaches to interoperability and the exchange of digital content between sites.

Data re-use, disclosure and dissemination
Object Reuse and Exchange (ORE)

A seminal 2004 article about rethinking scholarly communications and 'building the system that scholars deserve' (Van de Sompel et al., 2004) brought to the fore changes in the nature of scholarly research, which by that time took place on the internet and was highly collaborative, international and data intensive. Citing opportunities to facilitate network-based collaboration and increase the speed of scientific discovery, the authors proposed a fundamental redesign to replace the increasingly problematic existing system. They made a case for a natively digital and interconnected set of services for capturing, making accessible, and preserving the scholarly record. Their envisioned system focused on 'units of communication' (text, datasets, simulations, software and more) moving through 'pathways' associated with the scholarly communications 'value chain': *registering* a new unit of communication; *certifying* it through peer review; generating *awareness* of the new unit; *archiving* it; and enabling *'rewards'* (e.g., being cited by others). The proposed system would bring many distributed services and players together and require the easy re-use and exchange of units of communication as well interconnections to support the flow of units through the system.

Two years later, Van de Sompel and his colleagues (2006) reported on work supported through the NSF Pathways project to investigate and prototype a natively digital, interconnected and interoperable scholarly communications system based on distributed repositories. Their prototype had three levels: repositories with internal data models and services for machine interaction; an interoperability layer; and a top layer consisting of registries for supporting shared infrastructure and loosely federating autonomous participating systems. In the prototype they experimented with building pathways for objects from arXiv, aDORe, DSpace and Fedora. They received funding from the Mellon Foundation to continue their work on a new OAI project called Object Re-use and Exchange, or OAI-ORE.

The ORE project has been influential. The team reported the results of the project – a set of specifications and user guides – in a paper that combined the characteristics of a technical report and a call to action (Lagoze et al., 2008). In keeping with the earlier work reported, the objective of the specifications and guides was to make it possible for many systems to use scholarly digital objects. The paper begins and ends with the reasons for the digital library community to embrace methods that are more integrated with web architecture and more accessible to web applications.

The principles of web architecture (www.w3.org/standards/webarch), the semantic web and linked data are the basis of the OAI-ORE specifications (Van de Sompel et al., 2009). A new publication by Lagoze et al. (2012) updates and expands on the earlier 2008 paper and discusses related work.

Lagoze and his colleagues, together with Tarrant et al. (2009) contrast the approach of ORE with the interoperability mechanisms of OAI-PMH, which harvests metadata from repositories. OAI-PMH was a first step toward repository interoperability; OAI-ORE, while not an extension or replacement for OAI-PMH, provides a model for expressing digital objects for exchange and re-use in many contexts.

Repository implementations of ORE

ORE offers a way to make the scholarly content in repositories easier to exchange and re-use across systems and services. It makes it possible to identify and interlink many types of scholarly resources – pre-prints and their corresponding refereed publications, software, e-research data, visualization, one or more presentations, etc. The ORE approach has numerous use cases in the domain of repositories. A couple of implementations described in the literature are:

- Tarrant et al. (2009) describe their award-winning demonstration of an application using ORE at the Open Repositories Conference 2008. Their demonstration combined OAI-ORE with the Fedora and EPrints repository platforms and transferred two live archives from one software to the other. Their work was completed under the aegis of the JISC-funded Preserv 2 project (http://preserv.eprints.org), which sought a way to replicate an entire repository across any repository platform. The ORE import and export plug-ins are available with the EPrints software.
- Maslov et al. (2010) report on their OAI-ORE project for the Texas Digital Library to add OAI-ORE support to the DSpace repository platform, enabling better data exchange between repositories.
- Foresite (http://foresite.cheshire3.org), a JISC-funded demonstration project that uses ORE to describe the compound digital objects that make up JSTOR (journals, issues, articles, pages), which can then be referenced by repositories (Witt, 2010). Foresite uses ORE with SWORD, described in the next section.
- In work related to OAI-ORE, Haslhofer and Schandl (2008 and 2010) describe the work they did to create the OAI2LOD Server, which exposes OAI-PMH metadata as linked data. Haslhofer was later active in work on the Europeana Data Model, discussed in Chapter 10.

ORE and e-research data

Research related to cyberinfrastructure (discussed in Chapter 8) has led to more attention for e-research data (Van de Sompel et al., 2009). An example of a project deploying ORE is the US National Virtual Observatory, which has the goal of enabling new ways of doing astronomy by combining astronomical data from telescopes worldwide. Librarians at Johns Hopkins, working with the American Astronomical Society, have contributed to the project by using ORE and SWORD to enable automatic capture of data related to an article as part of the article submission process (DiLauro, 2009).

Another use case for OAI-ORE is for modeling the many interrelated objects described in archives (Ferro and Silvello, 2013), in the process making them easier to find, link to and re-use on the larger web. Witt (2010) provides a readable and useful set of descriptions of ORE implementations in about a half a dozen projects in the US, UK, Belgium and Australia – some but not all related to repositories. Several of the projects use SWORD.

Simple publishing interface (SPI) and SWORD

The Simple Publishing Interface (SPI) was developed under the auspices of the European Committee for Standardization (see Ternier et al., 2010). Like ORE it was another development that made it easier to disseminate and re-use content and metadata in multiple systems and applications. SPI grew out of the e-learning community; it is a protocol used in combination with AtomPub, a format for web feeds commonly used by web developers. SPI is important because content and metadata can be created once and consumed directly in multiple applications. Ternier's paper provides a number of scenarios for using SPI and explains how it differs from SWORD.

SWORD, the Simple Web-service Offering Repository Deposit, was 'unapologetically built on and for the world wide web: in this it differs from many information exchange protocols arising out of the library/repository domain' (Duranceau and Rodgers, 2010). A UK working group, supported as part of JISC's Digital Repositories Programme, initially developed SWORD (www.ukoln.ac.uk/repositories/digirep/index/SWORD_Project). The working group was seeking a lightweight method for facilitating deposit in institutional repositories. Version 2 of SWORD was released in 2010. Duranceau and Rodgers describe an experiment in which MIT successfully used SWORD to enable automatic deposit of papers published by BioMed Central into DSpace@MIT, the institutional repository. Lewis, de Castro and Jones (2012) describe nine different scenarios to demonstrate the many ways in which SWORD can make it easier for faculty and repository managers to deposit new scholarly output in multiple locations. Some of the scenarios considered are:

- publisher to repository
- research information system to repository
- desktop to repository
- repository to repository.

As of this writing, arXiv, DSpace, EPrints, Fedora and a few other repositories are SWORD-compliant.

The semantic web and semantic interoperability

As discussed in Chapter 3, the semantic web and linked data have inspired excitement and much discussion in the field of digital libraries. Fedora and ORE, described earlier, use semantic web methods, as does VIVO, a researcher profiling system (see Chapter 9).

Next-generation repositories

Islandora and Hydra, described in the two sections that follow, are the outcomes of new thinking about repositories, their architectures and objectives and new approaches to achieving interoperability. They are not themselves repositories; rather they provided a layer on top of a repository that supports specific interactions with repository content: deposit, discovery, display, etc.

Islandora and Drupal

Islandora (www.islandora.ca) is an open source framework that combines Drupal (a web content manager) and Fedora Commons repository software in a digital asset management system. It was developed in 2006 at the University of Prince Edward Island (UPEI). Mark Leggott of the UPEI development team noted the choice of Fedora for its data models and ability to support diverse content types (Leggott, 2009). Islandora supports creating, editing, discovering, viewing and managing digital assets in a Fedora repository. It has been used to create 'Virtual Research Environments' or VREs. For a broader perspective and more background on VREs, De Roure, Goble and Stevens' highly cited paper (2009) makes the case for systems enabling shared scholarly workflows in a virtual research environment.

Scholar's Workbench and the Hydra Project

Green and Awre (2009) describe two JISC-funded projects undertaken at the University of Hull from 2005 to 2009 – RepoMMan and REMAP – that led to the Hydra Project. RepoMMan provides a browser-based interface and web services to support scholarly authoring and deposit processes. A second part of the project focused on publishing the scholar's content to a public-facing repository, in the process automatically generating metadata for the object. REMAP publishes and preserves the content. Green and Awre carried this work forward into a multi-institutional collaboration called the Hydra Project, whose initial stage ran through 2009 and involved three institutional partners. The project developed a Scholar's Workbench that provided a search and discovery interface and also enabled interactive workflows for pre- and post-publication. The word 'hydra' was chosen deliberately to convey the concept of one body and many heads, that is, one common Fedora repository with many purposes or applications. The point was to create a framework for integration and content re-use whose pieces could be deployed at multiple institutions.

The next stage of the Hydra Project ran from 2008 to 2011, included more partners and produced a framework that uses web architecture and web tools to support a range of uses and workflows. Awre et al. (2009) defined a number of use cases that a Hydra implementation might support, including accessioning digital content, managing a personal or institutional repository, and integrating content across systems or services. Awre and Cramer (2012) report on the project's most recent progress and new partners; the project wiki provides further information (http://wiki.duraspace.org/display/hydra).

Repositories in the cloud

Chapter 5 discusses cloud services in hybrid libraries. The potential for cloud services for repositories is a new area of investigation. In 2010 JISC and Eduserv organized an event to discuss 'Repositories and the Cloud,' a new area of investigation and experimentation. A JISC-sponsored project called 'Fedorazon' had looked into setting up a repository using Amazon cloud services (Flanders, 2008). Following a pilot program with the Library of Congress and a number of partners, in late 2011 DuraSpace began offering a service based on DuraCloud, a cloud-based platform for backing up, archiving and preserving repository content (www.duracloud.org). The 2011 DuraSpace annual report (2012) discusses the strategy and possible uses for DuraCloud.

Conclusion

Subject-based repositories appear to be on a firm footing. All repositories are contributing to the broader diffusion of knowledge to the public – an important social role of digital libraries, as discussed in Chapter 6. As for institutional repositories, a number of developments indicate they could get past current barriers, move to a new level, and take on broader roles in libraries, research institutions, on the web and in society. There is also the possibility that institutional repositories will evolve beyond their current forms. Chapters 8 and 9 further discuss the opportunities and challenges for repositories.

CHAPTER 5

·········

Hybrid libraries

Overview

This chapter continues the discussion of digital collections with a detailed look at the interplay between library users, hybrid library collections and enabling technologies for hybrid library systems and services. Hybrid library collections contain non-digital, digitized and born-digital resources. This chapter examines changing information-seeking behaviors and preferences, explores how they have fostered new collections strategies, and analyses the impact of both on discovery services and other enabling technologies for hybrid libraries. The chapter ends with some thoughts about the parallel but separate evolutionary paths of hybrid libraries, repositories and the web.

Changing information-seeking behaviors
Information moves online

The content of interest to those who use libraries is highly distributed across the web. Vast changes have occurred not only in the amount of information available but also where people prefer to look for what they need. Library collections exist alongside (and compete for attention with) many other choices for information seekers, including those for whom hybrid library collections are or would be useful.

Digital formats are beginning to dominate library collections, especially in academic libraries. Particularly with respect to the scholarly journal literature, library collections are already *digital* collections, and online formats are preferred. As discussed in Chapter 2, by 2001 a third of faculty and half of students reported they were relying exclusively or almost exclusively on online scholarly resources for their work (Friedlander,

2002). More than a decade later, preferences for web-based scholarly content are much stronger.

Research on information-seeking behaviors
Preferred sources of information

The attention of both the general public and academics has shifted rapidly to online networked content. Many people now prefer to look for information online, and most segments of the population place a high value on immediately available, convenient online sources, often preferring these sources over hybrid library collections. Much research has been focused on these trends, for example the following studies:

- **The American public.** According to a survey of people's perceptions of libraries and preferences for information discovery conducted by Harris Interactive on behalf of OCLC, 84% of surveyed Americans say they prefer to begin a search for information with a search engine. Furthermore, a majority (69%) of American respondents considered the information they find on the web to be as trustworthy as information from a library (De Rosa et al., 2011, 32, 40).
- **The British public.** Bob Usherwood reported on the results of a national survey to assess the value that the British public places on libraries, archives and museums as repositories of knowledge (Usherwood, Wilson and Bryson, 2005). His findings suggest that libraries are still valued for their role as trusted sources of information, but the findings also confirm the trend found in other studies: a preference for immediately accessible, convenient sources of information (the web, newspapers, television). Survey respondents also saw libraries' growing use of digitization and e-resources as positive steps for increasing what libraries can offer to an online world.
- **Undergraduates.** Head and Eisenberg (2010, 7) reported the results of their studies of the information-seeking behaviors of US undergraduates and the sources they consult for their coursework. Their study indicated that in 2010 the top three sources used by undergraduates for completing coursework were course readings (96%), search engines (92%), and online scholarly resources (88%). Students also frequently used Wikipedia to support their coursework (73%).
- **US and UK faculty.** An ITHAKA longitudinal study of US faculty members' preferences for starting their research suggests that most begin

with a discipline-specific e-resource (over 40%) or with a search engine (about 35%). Less than 20% begin with library online catalogs. These trends held up across respondents from the social sciences and sciences disciplines, with humanists showing roughly equal preference for starting research with discipline-specific e-resources, search engines and the online catalog (Schonfeld, Housewright and Wulfson, 2013, 21–2). The study was repeated in the UK; results indicated that 40% of UK faculty members begin their research with a search engine, 33% with a discipline-specific e-resource, and 15% each with an online or national/international library catalog (Housewright, Schonfeld and Wulfson, 2013, 21–2).

Web referral traffic and destinations

Web referral traffic comes from external websites and pages (these are called 'referrers') that lead web users to another site or page (these are called 'destinations,' in this context, digital library sites with specific URLs). In July 2010, one web technology analyst (Pozadzides, 2010) reported that the top referrers on the web as a whole were search engines (mainly Google), media sites (e.g., YouTube and Flickr) and social websites (especially Facebook).

Web referral traffic is extremely important in the library domain, although except for Google, the top referrers differ. Students are aware of and have continued to rely on online scholarly sources, but they are now discovering them more often through Google, Google Scholar and Google Books (Hampton-Reeves et al., 2009, 36). Now that the content of scholarly aggregations (like ScienceDirect and the content of open access repositories) is crawled and centrally indexed by Google, a huge amount of traffic to online scholarly content comes from Google (CIBER Research Ltd, 2009, 21; Hanson and Hessel, 2009).

The US and UK ITHAKA studies of 2012 suggest that for scholars, the most important role of the library is as a buyer/licensor of online content (US survey, 67–8; UK survey, 79–80). This is not to say that libraries' provision of online catalogs and library websites is no longer important – it is – but it is critical to understand the context in which library catalogs and websites function in the larger web environment. Hanson and Hessel (2009, 26–8), in their ground-breaking 'discoverability phase 1' report for the University of Minnesota Libraries, reported that 75% of the traffic to the libraries' reference linking service (enabling connections to library e-resources) originated from external referrers, specifically Google, PubMed and the websites of scholarly databases or indexes.

Changing use and engagement with hybrid libraries

Since about the 1990s, the position and comparative use of traditional library collections have changed dramatically. Hybrid library users are increasingly finding and engaging with library materials on the larger web, rather than visiting library sites as often as before. This section uses data for US public and academic libraries to illustrate these trends.

Comparative demand

The patterns of hybrid library collection use are different in academic and public libraries. There is a consistent downward trend from 2007 to 2011 in the circulation of the printed books and journals in ARL library collections (www.arlstatistics.org). Data from the US Public Library Data Services (Reid, 2012) indicates that circulation of public library collections (which contain high-demand popular materials) has shown an upward trend between 2007 and 2011 (Figure 5.1).

Academic libraries

Academics demonstrate what they want by what they use. The academic library circulation trends for the physical collections are directly related to

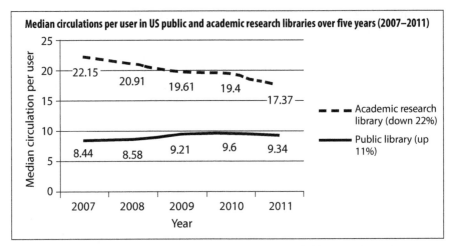

Figure 5.1 Trends in the use of public and academic research library traditional collections
(Sources: Public Library Data Service (Reid, 2012) and Association of Research Libraries (www.arlstatistics.org/analytics))

the findings of the user studies cited previously in this chapter. Academic research, teaching and learning increasingly rely on scholarly digital content and less on print.

Academic library print circulation trends are inversely correlated with the high traffic to the scholarly digital libraries like those in Table 2.1 (e.g., the ACM Digital Library, JSTOR, ScienceDirect). Tripathi and Jeevan (2013) offer an extensive literature review of the many aspects of the usage of e-resources in academic libraries: usage statistics, analytical methods, usage patterns across disciplines and institutions, information-seeking strategies and the growing importance of assessment.

Public libraries

US public libraries offer access to growing numbers of e-serials and scholarly databases, and state agencies typically purchase e-content licenses for the libraries in their states. Notwithstanding the provision of access to e-serials and databases, public library user demand is centered primarily on books, audiovisual materials and increasingly, e-books. Public libraries in the US collect materials largely for popular use and for children – circulation of children's materials accounts for a third of total circulation, according to the IMLS Public Library Surveys of 2009 and 2010. Books (which account for about 85% of public library collections) also account for most of what circulates (63%). However the 2009 and 2010 IMLS surveys reported that audiovisual materials and e-books are the fastest growing components of public library collections, and e-book demand is growing dramatically (Reid, 2012; Miller et al., 2011; Swan et al., 2013; Bowles and Hazzan, 2013; Hoffert, 2013; Price, 2013).

Demand for e-books

After a long foreground that featured debates about issues with reading online, whether publishers should or should not offer e-books, and other issues, the public's use of e-books and the ownership of e-book readers and tablets are finally taking off. The timelines in Figure 4.1 on p. 90 mark the points at which Google released a million public domain titles from the Google Books project in the EPUB e-book format (2009), Amazon e-book sales topped hardcover book sales (2010) and ownership of tablets and e-book readers reached 20% of US adults (2012). Rising e-book demand in US public libraries has already been mentioned. In US academic libraries, e-books are taking off more slowly. Restrictive licensing terms, resulting in trouble downloading files or printing more than a few pages, and other problems continue to slow acceptance and adoption rates (Walters, 2013a, 2013b).

Demand for digitized special collections

Chapter 2 and Table 2.1 (p. 53) discuss some of the early digital libraries of cultural heritage content that attracted considerable use by scholars, teachers and citizens. National library digitization programs in particular have attracted attention and high use by new types of audiences. These programs digitized books but also images, sound recordings, newspapers and more.

Libraries' response: changing hybrid library collections
Expenditures of materials budgets

Libraries tend to buy what their communities use. Hoffert (2013) explores changes in how US public libraries are spending their materials budgets based on the 2012 Library Materials Survey conducted by *Library Journal*. Survey results suggest that materials budgets are holding steady, and public libraries are spending 59% of their budgets on printed books, down from 68% in 2006. The difference appears to be going to media and e-books.

A combination of factors including rising demand for e-content and falling demand for print, combined with the economics of e-resource licensing (i.e., rising prices), has led to dramatic changes in how academic libraries spend their materials budgets. Based on median amounts, ARL libraries spent 42% of their materials budgets on e-serials in 2007, rising to 58% in 2011. For monographs, they spent a median of 21% of their materials budgets in 2007, dropping to 18% in 2011 (www.arlstatistics.org). Figure 5.2 provides another view of these expenditure trends over five years based on expenditures per student.

Managing physical collections in academic libraries

In the face of changing usage patterns for printed books and serials, academic library leaders began to ask serious questions about their low-use print collections, especially in light of the space that such collections take up in library buildings. Many libraries were crowded with people wanting different sorts of services (e.g., group study space, computers/information commons, space for library instruction, more seating in general). These questions took on new intensity after about 2009, when a large corpus of mass-digitized books had emerged.

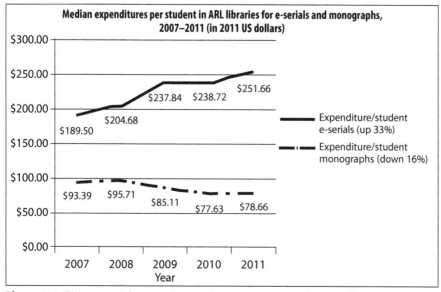

Figure 5.2 Rising e-serials expenditures, dropping monograph expenditures
Source: calculated from Association of Research Libraries data,
www.arlstatistics.org

Print collection management

David Block's article on the history of library collection storage notes that many US research libraries had reached their capacity for storing their collections by the 1980s (Block, 2000). High-density storage was the first type of solution sought (like the Harvard Depository, which dates from 1986). By 2005, there were 50 or more library storage facilities in the US and others in the planning stage. Most housed individual library collections but shared storage facilities were beginning to appear (Payne, 2005). Vattulainen (2004) reviewed the role of national or regional print repositories in Finland and several other European countries. In 2008 O'Connor and Jilovsky concluded their review of library collection storage solutions in a number of countries (UK, Australia, Finland, US, etc.) with a recommendation for a network of shared national or international print repositories. By about 2007 research library storage solutions had become a regular component of research library collection management strategy, and a component of preservation strategy as well (Rosenthal, 2010).

Conceptual, political or operational barriers

As the physicality of library collections has become less important, and digital content becomes more plentiful, rich and diverse, a trend of rethinking library collection strategies has begun. At the same time, research libraries have continued to be reluctant to undertake storage of large parts of their collections for conceptual, political or operational reasons.

Collections of e-books?

It remains an open question whether e-book licensing will substantially replace print book collecting, going forward. A major shift to e-books for providing access to current titles for academic libraries could happen, but many serious barriers remain (Walters, 2013a, 2013b). So far the tidal wave-like adoption of digital formats for databases, journals and articles that occurred in academic libraries between 2000 and 2005 has not been repeated with e-books. Meanwhile, a number of research libraries are experimenting with an innovative method for licensing e-books, called Patron-Driven Acquisitions, PDA, a model for licensing and purchasing e-books 'just in time,' based on library patron selections, rather than having librarians select and buy them 'just in case' they are needed (Nixon, Freeman and Ward, 2010; Hazen, 2011, 200; Fischer et al., 2012).

Rising priority of special collections and archives

As more scholarly content moves online and academic libraries license the same or similar e-content packages, individual libraries' online collections have become less distinctive. There is also considerable overlap in many legacy print collections (see section on mass digitization). Special collections and archives are what remain most distinctive about research library collections, and the results of cultural heritage digitization projects suggest that if such special collections were more discoverable online, they would attract new users and uses.

A number of reports recommend raising the priority of library efforts to enable the online discovery and use of special collections and archives (Loughborough University Library & Information Statistics Unit and Research Information Network, 2007; Association of Research Libraries, 2008; Dooley and Luce, 2010). Some research libraries have been able to digitize parts of these collections and produce new finding aids that make these archives more visible on the web, either through institutionally funded projects or through partnerships – see, for example, Hawkins and Gildart (2010) and Bingham (2010) on the partnership to digitize British historic newspapers 1600–1900. As of this writing, however, many important collections of primary sources continue to be hidden and inaccessible to discovery on the web.

Digitizing research library collections

Chapter 2 and Table 2.1 (p. 53) provide a number of examples of successful digital libraries that have their roots in the first decade of digital library work. These projects produced digitized library collections at small and large scales. One outcome of these early projects was to demonstrate the exciting potential, feasibility and value of digitization projects and techniques. The projects were characterized by careful selection of materials to be digitized and the development and use of digitization best practices. Preservation was an element of many if not most projects. In late 2004, Google introduced a new approach called 'mass digitization.' Mass digitization generally alludes to the digitization of very large, whole collections of content, with no or minimal selection.

The Google 5

In December 2004, Google announced agreements with five major research libraries (the New York Public Library and the libraries of Harvard, Michigan, Oxford, and Stanford universities) that enabled Google to digitize volumes from these libraries' printed book collections. These libraries were called the Google 5, and the project, which became known as the Google Books Library Project, now has more research library participants. The project has focused on indexing and access to book content and has no preservation component. The scale of the project and the speed with which it has progressed are unlike anything that came before it.

Lavoie, Connaway and Dempsey (2005) evaluated the Google 5's collections to estimate the proportion of the system-wide book collection that they represent. Their results suggested that the combined Google 5 collections could potentially be 10.5 million books, with the following characteristics:

- They would represent 33% of the system-wide book collection at that time.
- Half of the books would be in English, with another quarter of the remaining books in German, French and Spanish.
- 80% of the books would be in copyright.

Other US-based projects announced in 2005

In 2005 a second mass digitization project was announced, called the Open Content Alliance, with the goal of digitizing public domain books. The project had funding from Microsoft, Yahoo and others, and the scanning was done by the Internet Archive (Coyle, 2006; Hahn, 2008). That same year, Microsoft announced a mass digitization project called Live Search Books, another co-operative project with libraries; it ran from 2006 to 2008. The project's 750,000 digitized books are now part of the Internet Archive (Jones, 2010). Also that year the Librarian of Congress announced that Google had provided US$3 million to jumpstart the World Digital Library (see also www.wdl.org/en/contributors; Hahn, 2008).

Quand Google défie l'Europe

Jean-Noël Jeanneney, then President of the Bibliothèque nationale de France, responded about a month after Google's announcement with an editorial in *Le Monde*. It was called 'Quand Google défie l'Europe' ('When Google Challenges Europe'; Jeanneney, 2005). The editorial was later expanded into a book, *Google and the Myth of Universal Knowledge: a view from Europe* (Jeanneney, 2006).

In his 2006 analysis of the situation, David Bearman, a digital library leader and the founder of Archives and Museum Informatics, took the position that Jeanneney 'succeeded to a significant extent in motivating a movement to digitize European print heritage.' Bearman's article provides an overview of Jeanenney's compelling critique of Google and the Google Library Project.

i2010 Digital Libraries

In September 2005 the European Commission announced i2010 Digital Libraries, a plan to build a European digital library containing six million digitized books and other materials by 2010 (Forster, 2007). The initiative was intended to build on the organizational framework of TEL (The European Library), an initiative of CENL (Conference of European National Librarians).

The aims of the i2010 Digital Library Initiative were lofty: to provide for the digitization, online accessibility and preservation of Europe's cultural memory. The approach has been to work with publishers and libraries on the intellectual property rights aspects of the initiative (including how to manage orphan works). The European initiative also has preservation objectives.

Europeana

Europeana (www.europeana.eu) is the digital library that grew out of i2010 Digital Libraries. A preliminary version of Europeana went live in late 2008, followed by the first operational version in summer of 2010. That version provided access to over ten million digital objects from libraries, museums, archives and audiovisual archives from across Europe (Chambers and Schallier, 2010). At the time of this writing, Europeana provides access to 20 million digital objects. Chapter 10 discusses Europeana in more detail.

HathiTrust

Large-scale digitization has the potential to transform the library world. The launch of HathiTrust Digital Library (www.hathitrust.org) in October 2008 created new momentum for such transformation. It began as a partnership of the Committee on Institutional Cooperation (CIC; a consortium of 15 mostly midwestern US universities) and the University of California System. Many new partners have since joined HathiTrust, which uses a membership model to fund its operations and services. It is not a commercial or government-funded operation. HathiTrust's goals include creating a shared repository of digital collections for access and preservation and stimulating efforts for shared collection management strategies. The commitment to preservation is particularly strong.

Most of the HathiTrust repository consists of digitized content from libraries that participated in the Google Library Project. Other sources are digitized content from the former Microsoft Live Search Books project, the Internet Archive, and books digitized by the partners themselves (Christenson, 2011). The HathiTrust has many services, among them mechanisms for reviewing and documenting copyright, APIs, and metadata that libraries can load into their online catalogs. In June 2013, the Digital Public Library of America (DPLA) announced a partnership in which HathiTrust will share its public domain content, representing some 3.5 million volumes, with DPLA.

The lawsuit against HathiTrust

In September 2011 the Authors Guild and others brought a suit against HathiTrust alleging that HathiTrust's storage and search of full-text digital books is an infringement of copyright. A court within a particular circuit of the US federal system heard the case. The court provided a ruling in

November 2012 stating that HathiTrust's retention and use of digitized books for purposes of preservation, text search, and accessibility for the visually impaired are within the limits of the US laws regarding fair use (Crews, 2012). Since HathiTrust has not acted on its preliminary plans to make orphan works accessible, the judge did not comment on whether HathiTrust's plan would have been lawful. Chapter 3 briefly discusses the legal issues associated with Google Books and the HathiTrust Digital Library and Table 3.2 (p.81, under 'Mass digitization') provides some status information about the cases.

Implications for future collection management

At the time of this writing, the HathiTrust digital collections contained close to 11 million digitized volumes. Europeana provides access to 20 million digital objects (including books). Despite the open legal issues around mass digitization projects, when Europeana, HathiTrust and other initiatives are considered together, it seems clear that the content of academic library books is no longer limited to those with access to the physical collections held in academic library buildings; this content is now online and abundant.

In 2011 Constance Malpas reported on a Mellon-funded project to study managing print collections in a mass-digitized environment. With participation from OCLC Research, HathiTrust, the library of New York University and the Research Collections Access & Preservation (ReCAP) consortium, the project investigated the feasibility of radically different solutions for managing low-use print books using large-scale, shared print and digital repositories.

At current digitization rates, the HathiTrust Digital Library is expected to duplicate 60% of the retrospective collections of ARL libraries by June 2014 (Malpas, 2011, 10–11). If shared print and digital repositories were implemented, these research libraries could achieve significant efficiencies and repurpose thousands of square feet in their libraries for learning or information commons, media labs and other uses.

Shared print repositories and mass-digitized books

Robert Kieft and Lizanne Payne (2012) wrote an article that is cause for cautious optimism that new shared solutions are both practical and likely to emerge. They explore the concept of large-scale, regional and national co-operation for hybrid library collection management. They take as a given that the current legal obstacles around mass-digitized books will eventually be resolved through new legal models negotiated between libraries and publishers and new business models for compensating rights holders (Kieft and Payne, 140). The first part of the article lays out a detailed vision for the collective management of hybrid library collections in the 2020s. The second part provides examples of new models, and the article closes with a suggested research agenda for 'collective collecting.'

Changing technologies for hybrid libraries
Library management systems and business processes

By the late 1990s, the current generation of library management systems (also known as integrated library systems) were being implemented. These systems consist of integrated software applications generally based on relational databases. Library management systems support the business processes (activities that produce services or products) of libraries: selecting, acquiring, describing and managing, discovering, circulating/delivering/linking, and preserving library collections plus evaluation. They generally have two interfaces: one for staff use and one for end-users (the library online catalog).

These library management systems were initially developed at a time when library collections were still dominated by print. They have proved challenging to adapt to a world dominated by e-resources and new requirements for hybrid library collection building and management. This mismatch kicked off a technology replacement cycle that is still under way. At the time of this writing, my knowledge and evaluation of the landscape suggests that hybrid libraries are in a transitional period featuring many types of interim solutions.

Technology replacement: in transition

The enabling technologies of large academic libraries today are a complex, decentralized patchwork that stitches together various components. These components support hybrid library business processes on the one hand, and end-user discovery and access on the other. Achieving interoperability across this complex patchwork of enabling technologies is labor-intensive and costly, and for a variety of reasons some types of digital content (e.g., institutional repositories, local digital library content) are often not integrated in the mix at all (Menzies, Birrell and Dunsire, 2010).

Kress and Wisner (2013) offer an interesting model (based on supply chain management) for beginning to rethink and improve upon the current situation, but so far an overarching strategic framework for hybrid library enabling technologies – let alone an actual integrated solution – does not exist. Given the constant turbulence of the web environment, a new technical solution for managing hybrid library collections may not look much like library management systems up to now. Regardless, inter-operability is a key challenge in hybrid libraries now and it will continue to be a challenge going forward.

Types of enabling technologies and tools

Figure 5.3 illustrates the types of enabling technologies and tools now associated with the business processes of hybrid libraries. The business processes are listed along the top (select, acquire and pay, describe and manage, disclose and deliver, preserve), technologies and tools are in the text boxes below, and examples of evaluation processes are listed at the bottom of the figure. The figure labels the business processes as 'new' not because the processes themselves are new but because the technical requirements and tools for supporting them are new.

The reports of the second two phases of the University of Minnesota Libraries' 'discoverability' studies offer an interesting parallel to Figure 5.3's

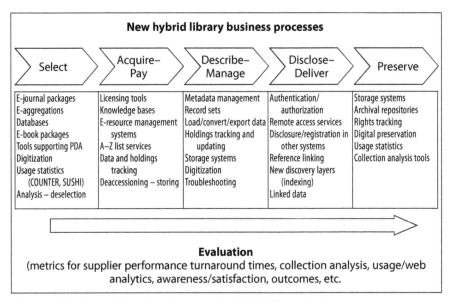

Figure 5.3 Technologies and tools supporting hybrid library business processes

visualization of transitional hybrid library technologies and tools. Hanson and colleagues (2012) articulate a vision for a new discovery environment that (1) integrates content and metadata from different sources, (2) exposes content and metadata to external systems and services, (3) indexes content from external sources (e.g., HathiTrust), (4) allows for personalization, and (5) provides evaluative information to support user-centered, evidence-based decision making.

The report of Fransen and colleagues (2012) on the third phase of the discoverability studies includes helpful thoughts about system requirements, a drawing of their technology 'ecosystem' as of 2011 and some comments on the cloud-based library management systems that are currently available.

It would take a whole separate book to describe all the technologies and tools in Figure 5.3 and how they help to achieve the purposes of hybrid libraries. In recent years, hybrid libraries have invested a great deal of attention into supporting the discovery of collections. The following sections describe this work, then turn to other efforts related to the progress of digital libraries.

Interoperability and the problem of discoverability

A key challenge for hybrid libraries is the same as the key challenge of digital libraries, discussed in Chapter 3: interoperability (see Chapter 3 for the full discussion of interoperability). An important objective of interoperability is discoverability, which involves integrating diverse digital content in a single system as well as making content discoverable in external systems and services. In the hybrid library context, discoverability has two dimensions:

1 **Disclosure and visibility of hybrid library collections on the network,** particularly on high-traffic sites. Study after study reported in this book and elsewhere provides strong evidence that for all types of people, information seeking and discovery begins on websites external to libraries. Individual hybrid library catalog data is generally not disclosed for crawling by search engines, and given the current redundant state of library catalogs, it would not make sense for search engines to crawl and index them. A better, network-level solution is needed for making library content discoverable in external systems and services, especially search engines. A later section returns to this topic.

2 **Institutionally or consortially based discovery services.** This type of discoverability has to do with integrating diverse content in a single site.

Libraries have accomplished a great deal of progress on this dimension of discoverability in recent years, as discussed in the following section.

Discovery services
E-resource discovery

Because library management systems of the late 1990s were ill-equipped to do so, librarians began to work on supplemental methods to enable discovery and delivery of e-resources (databases and indexes, numeric files, full text, etc.) Their first attempts using static web pages containing links and locally created descriptions, then searchable databases, quickly ran into problems of scale. Some early solutions featured 'A to Z lists' providing links to the titles of e-resources from the library's website; these are now common services offered by vendors.

The provision of metadata sets for loading e-resource descriptions into library online catalogs is also a commonly offered service today. These sets exemplify the shift from title-by-title bibliographic control to automated metadata management in hybrid libraries. Increasingly, this automated approach is used to support selection, acquisition and cataloging of many types of content, including e-books. This kind of approach is also used to disclose or register and maintain library holdings to external systems so that hybrid library collections can be more visible on the larger web.

Fragmented hybrid library interfaces

Another strong motivation to seek unifying discovery methods on hybrid libraries' destination sites was the proliferation of hybrid library interfaces: the library catalog, A to Z lists, static web pages, gateways, and more. Library users were obliged to know about these and search each interface separately (Calhoun, 2002, 149). Some of the separate interfaces continue to be needed, but libraries lacked one common user interface to everything – a single point of entry to their hybrid collections.

The promise of portals

The term 'portal' has a range of definitions, but from a functional perspective libraries wanted to simplify searching across and linking from and to diverse collections, and also make it easier to authenticate and authorize access to licensed resources.

Authentication and authorization

When libraries licensed only a few databases and e-resource packages, it was possible to keep track of individual logons and passwords for each of the interfaces. Once there were hundreds of these, an automated solution to authenticating users and authorizing access to all of the resources became essential. Authentication is the automated process of identifying a person (often based on a user name and password), and authorization is the automated process of providing the appropriate access rights.

Branding and a unifying interface

Portals were also intended to improve the library's ability to 'brand' itself as the provider of access to hybrid library content. Libraries wanted systems with a unifying interface that would federate searching of the distributed, heterogeneous content they licensed (e-content), wished to point to (publicly available websites) or owned locally (non-digital collections); and they wanted the system to present the results in a coherent way to searchers. They also wanted to offer their communities the ability to link from an information object in one resource (for example a citation database) to an object in another (for example the full article described in the citation). Librarians referred to these functionalities as 'metasearch' (also known as 'federated searching') and *reference linking* respectively.

The European Library (TEL)

At the beginning of the new millennium many new projects got under way in libraries to explore the possibilities of portals. In Europe, early work went back as far as 1995, when the British Library and the national libraries of Finland and the Netherlands launched the pilot project GABRIEL – Gateway and Bridge to Europe's National Libraries (Hakala, 1999). That pilot provided experience that eventually led to The European Library (TEL) – www. theeuropeanlibrary.org (Woldering, 2004; Van Veen and Oldroyd, 2004). TEL launched a new portal in 2005 and continues as a portal to collections as well as providing the channel for submissions of digital content to Europeana (discussed in Chapter 10).

Problems with metasearch and Z39.50

Other portal projects that tested metasearch were learning experiences that did not produce long-lasting services (see Feeney and Newby, 2005; see also the annotated bibliography of Freund, Nemmers and Ochoa, 2007, for further information about the problems of metasearch). By 2008, many early adopters of metasearch had replaced their implementations with other solutions (see Breeding, 2012a).

A new kind of library catalog: discovery services and centralized indexing

By 2005, it was clear that the traditional library online catalog was not going to be an adequate future discovery service (see, for example, Calhoun, 2006, 38). There were too many new requirements that the current generation of library management systems, online catalogs and supplemental tools could not meet. The centralized indexing approach used by popular search engines opened the market for new types of institutionally or consortially based discovery services.

The phrase 'discovery service' has meaning in several contexts, for example among web developers. This book defines the phrase in a library context, where discovery services refer to user interfaces that provide for unified, integrated search and retrieval based on a pre-harvested, centralized index to heterogeneous resources. Typically the discovery service indexes the library's licensed resources (e-journals, articles, e-books) and physical collections. Sometimes the index also points to external digital libraries (like HathiTrust). The service hosts the indexes centrally, and searchers get instantaneous results for their queries as the service links to and displays online full text. Discovery services are designed to meet the discovery and delivery requirements of hybrid library business processes (see Figure 5.3). They do not address requirements for other business processes. Discovery services co-exist with library management systems.

Early discovery services

Some institutions built discovery services early in the new millennium. A team at the libraries of Lund University in Sweden developed a discovery layer for e-content and launched it in late 2003 (Jørgensen et al., 2003; Mayfield et al., 2008). Bielefeld Academic Search Engine (BASE; www.base-search.net) anticipated the development of library vendors' discovery services by five years or more and it is still thriving (Lossau, 2004). As of this writing, BASE indexes over 48 million documents from more than 2600 sources. In 2004, North Carolina State University's librarians purchased Endeca's Information

Access Platform to create a new discovery layer and faceted search features for their library catalog (Antelman, Lynema and Pace, 2006).

AquaBrowser is an early service that offered a discovery layer based on visualization techniques and associative indexing. AquaBrowser was first launched in production in many public libraries in the Netherlands, and at the end of 2011 it had 250 installations (Breeding, 2012a). These early implementations significantly advanced the field's thinking about revitalizing the catalog through the introduction of discovery services (see for example Lindahl, Bowen, and Foster, 2007; Sadler, 2009; Emanuel, 2011). By late 2007, library service sector firms had introduced a number of discovery services (Sadeh, 2007; Wilson, 2007; Mayfield et al., 2008; The Library Corporation, 2008).

Evaluations of discovery services

The amount of content indexed in a discovery service may be the most important feature for libraries; they want to be sure that those who use their discovery services can get to all the content they have so expensively licensed on behalf of the communities they serve. The functionality of the discovery interface is another key consideration. The library literature is now full of reviews and evaluations from librarians who have implemented one of these services. Some are Asher, Duke and Wilson (2012); Fagan et al. (2012); Gross and Sheridan (2011); Holman et al. (2012); Stevenson et al. (2009); Stone (2010); Way (2010); Yang and Wagner (2010).

Next-generation hybrid library systems (the cloud)

Library management systems became less able to support the business processes of hybrid libraries as digital content moved to center stage. Cloud-based hybrid library systems may offer a better-integrated alternative to the current fragmented array of systems, tools and services that hybrid libraries must use. Breeding (2011, 2012a, 2012b, 2013a) provides highly readable information and annual updates on the emergence of cloud computing and cloud-based library systems.

By transitioning to cloud-based systems, libraries can replace their local library management systems with web-based applications that are accessed via common web browsers and whose infrastructure is supported 'in the cloud.' There is no software to install or update, no local servers to purchase or maintain, and local maintenance activities (like nightly backups) are managed externally by the service provider. At the time of this writing, cloud-based systems are just beginning to be implemented for managing hybrid library collections.

Licensing terms and conditions

As e-resources and digital collections became major elements of hybrid libraries, it became necessary to know much more about the legal issues of licensing and providing access to them. Chapter 3 discusses the key challenge of intellectual property rights in digital libraries and the difficulties surrounding copyright. These issues manifest themselves in particular ways in hybrid libraries. The following sections provide a brief introduction to a couple of aspects of this large field of inquiry.

Negotiating terms and conditions

Libraries now license and purchase access to digital content (articles, e-journals, e-books) instead of purchasing the content itself. Publishers and other online information service providers restrict the rights to access, display and export most online scholarly content. Open access journals and repositories provide an alternative to licensed content, and they are helping to mitigate the asymmetrical relationship between publishers and licensees like libraries, but so far there is not a critical mass of open access scholarly content (see Hazen, 2011, 198–200 for a discussion of this and other rights issues for research libraries). The problems are extremely complex and unlikely to yield to simple solutions. It is increasingly important for all librarians to have a basic grounding in the legal aspects of negotiating and adhering to the terms and conditions of digital content licenses. Those who manage licensing in large research libraries need additional training and experience.

Knowing about licenses is important because much is at stake in terms of the library budget. North American academic research libraries now spend more than half their materials budgets on e-resources; in 2011, the median expenditure for this type of content in an ARL library was US$7.3 million (www.arlstatistics.org). Most of the money (90% in 2011) is spent on costly bundles and packages of scholarly e-journals and articles. In 2012, ARL began tracking its members' expenditures on e-books; the median was US$626 thousand per library.

Licensing best practices

Rachel Miller (2007) provides an excellent introduction to e-resource licensing best practices, education and training for licensing, model licenses and checklists, and key licensing issues (of which there are many). She briefly discusses licensing negotiation, the importance of tracking licenses and renewals, consortial licensing, pricing and cancellation terms, defining the population of authorized users, standard uses and fair use (e.g., for interlibrary lending and reserves), securing perpetual access rights to content, content loading and retention rights, copying for preservation purposes, and resisting non-disclosure agreements.

Best practices for licensing e-books are in an earlier stage of development, but librarians are carrying forward what they have learned about licensing e-journal packages. Lowry and Blixrud (2012) write that ARL libraries 'did not want to repeat the license restrictions found in e-journal agreements that they are now trying to renegotiate.' For example, Horava (2013) explores a variety of options and license models in the context of consortial licensing of e-books in Ontario, Canada.

E-resource management, ERMs and e-resource usage metrics

E-resource management has emerged as a new specialization in hybrid libraries. The specialization matured quite quickly and now there are online discussion forums (e.g., LibLicense-L: http://liblicense.crl.edu), workshops and educational resources, occasional and annual conferences (e.g., Electronic Resources and Libraries, www.electroniclibrarian.com), and journals (e.g., *Electronic Library*). Enabling technologies and tools also emerged after about 2004 (Jewell et al., 2004; Ellingsen, 2004; Fons and Jewell, 2007), called 'e-resource management systems' or ERMs.

E-resource management relies on knowledgebases, which are digital registries (machine- or human-readable, usually both) that collect and organize metadata and content needed for specific functions, like managing e-resource holdings, licensing and rights information. Another important enabling technology in the domain of e-resource management has been the collection of comparative e-resource usage data to support evidence-based decision making in libraries (COUNTER, SUSHI; see Chandler and Jewell, 2006).

Remote access to licensed e-resources

Preference for remote access

Enabling technologies were needed to manage who could have access and who could not. The purpose of authentication and authorization mechanisms is to comply with the terms of licenses – but without requiring every user to log on for each session on each separate database or online full-text resource. For universities, often this was accomplished by giving the online content provider the institution's range of IP addresses, which identify the computers or devices on its network. But this method of providing access did not work for authorized users who were connecting to the e-content from their homes and offices (this is called 'remote access'). Hanson and Hessel (2009, 25) found in their study of usage patterns at the University of Minnesota Libraries that 65% of requests for library online content came from off-campus. The marked preference for using e-resources from off-campus emerged early and is well documented in the US (Troll Covey, 2003, 579).

Enabling remote access to licensed e-resources

The preference for remote access required another enabling technology to keep remote users' access from being blocked. In the US, hybrid libraries have provided for remote access largely with proxy servers or virtual private networks (VPNs). A proxy server intercepts remote users' requests and sends them to the server that delivers e-content. Remote users authenticate themselves by logging into the campus network. If authentication is successful the proxy server authorizes the remote user and passes along the request for content in a way that 'proxies' an acceptable IP address. Athens and Shibboleth are other popular authentication and authorization services used for managing remote access to e-resources. Even with these accommodations, troubleshooting e-resource remote access problems absorbs a great deal of the time and attention in libraries (Davis et al., 2012).

Disclosure and web visibility of hybrid library collections

Progress in institutionally or consortially based discovery services is impressive. Progress on the other dimension of discoverability – disclosure and visibility of hybrid library collections at the network level, on referring sites – is less noticeable. The evidence presented in this book suggests that a great deal of information-seeking for academic content has moved to search engines (especially Google), academic search engines like Google Scholar or discipline-specific databases and aggregations. Discovery happens on these sites. The discovery to delivery loop is completed when the referring site sends the request to the appropriate server for delivering the e-content.

Disclosure of e-resources in Google Scholar

In his thoughtful article considering the impact of the introduction of Google Scholar in late 2004, Marshall Breeding (2005) proposed a serious reconsideration of the library community's approach to searching online resources. Breeding predicted that Google Scholar might eventually become the default interface for finding scholarly information. The research reported in this book would suggest that it now has. For hybrid libraries, the success of Google Scholar implies that the disclosure and visibility of hybrid library collections in search engines and on other important referring sites is as important as the provision for institutionally or consortially based discovery of these collections.

Representing libraries' physical and digital collections on the web

Some cultural heritage digital libraries are reaching critical mass, gathering content from many contributors, so that they are popular destination sites on their own. For individual hybrid library sites, making their collections discoverable at the network level is crucial to their continuing value and relevance. Enabling technologies exist to allow disclosure and visibility of much scholarly e-content on top referring sites. More digital library managers are investing effort in improving the disclosure and visibility of repositories in academic search engines like Google Scholar.

The semantic web and linked data have promise for achieving greater disclosure of hybrid and digital library content, but at the time of this writing, few applications exist. Meanwhile, all the signs suggest that the technology associated with the discovery and reading of books is well into a new life cycle. Hybrid libraries need to make progress to heighten the discoverability of what they have to offer now. An encouraging development is the BIBFRAME project.

BIBFRAME

The Bibliographic Framework Initiative (www.loc.gov/bibframe) is a collaborative initiative of national libraries and other stakeholders, created and led by the Library of Congress since 2011, to examine the existing framework for bibliographic data and determine a transition path for MARC. The intent is to find ways to reap the benefits of newer technology like linked data. The project involves mapping the elements of MARC into a linked data structure. Zepheira, a firm with expertise in the standards of the semantic web, the principles of linked data and web architecture, has been supporting the effort. In November 2012, the Library of Congress announced a draft data model for web-based bibliographic description, a primer introducing the data model (Miller et al., 2012) and a project to test its feasibility. The data model is called BIBFRAME. The *BIBFRAME Primer* (Miller et al., 2012, 28–38) describes other linked data initiatives as well as several other projects that have informed the development of the BIBFRAME data model.

Knowledgebases and registries

An option is to move toward larger shared frameworks at the network level that would register many libraries' holdings and be able to feed this information to multiple providers on the web (Calhoun, 2012b, under 'Registries of library holdings'). The knowledgebases of cloud-based library management systems have the potential to provide the necessary metadata about holdings, etc. to such network-level registries, which would function to switch the user from discovery of content (on the network) to its delivery (from the appropriate library).

Some existing examples

Approaches to interoperability based on registries and knowledgebases are already widely used on the web and on social sites. E-journal 'A to Z' lists are produced from a knowledgebase that registers and keeps track of the e-journals to which a particular library has access. ARROW is another kind of registry; its purpose is to facilitate rights management across the many libraries' digitization projects that are associated with Europeana (Caroli et al., 2012).

Google Scholar can already function, in practice, as a 'registry' of library holdings for scholarly articles (given the relevant configuration data, Google Scholar switches user requests to connect to content to the appropriate institutional server). OCLC and Google Books have a partnership to provide a 'Find in a library' service from Google Books. The Find in a Library service relies on library holdings data associated with the WorldCat bibliographic database. A study of the success rate of switching users from Google Books to a university library catalog found that the quality of the data supporting linking and delivery of content is as important, if not more important, as the data elements supporting discovery (Calhoun, 2012a).

Engaging with the web

Through consensus and partnerships, libraries could feasibly move to registry-based systems and make substantial advances in the discoverability of hybrid library collections on the web. These registries would automatically direct a user from sites where content is discovered to what his or her library holds (or licenses, or points to). A recent article by Lorcan Dempsey (2012) elaborates on these and other ideas for improving the visibility and utility of libraries on major network-level hubs. I have made the case elsewhere that the time has come for libraries to fully engage with the global network infrastructure, deploying methods that are native to the internet and web. Open access repositories have potential for becoming key building blocks in this process (Calhoun, 2012b, under 'Building for the web' and 'Enlarged roles for open access repositories').

Conclusion
Substantial and important progress

Much of the output of scholarship is now online, and an increasing proportion of the books held in libraries are available in digital forms. Mass digitization projects have been incredibly productive, although legal barriers continue to block the full deployment of the digital content. The evidence presented in Chapter 4 demonstrates that open access repositories are contributing more every year to the diffusion of scholarly content to the public. E-books are taking off in terms of supply and demand. National library projects and international programs like Europeana are making many cultural heritage materials open to all. In short, immense progress has been made toward an abundance of digital content.

A new specialization and enabling technologies for e-resource management have emerged and continue to develop. Librarians are getting better at understanding and negotiating licensing agreements with digital content providers. Some are also working proactively to advance favorable licensing provisions, broaden fair use for scholarship and for preservation, or expand open access. New discovery services have greatly advanced the discoverability of hybrid library collections on library sites.

Challenges
Enabling technologies

While great progress has been made in enabling technologies supporting hybrid libraries, progress on the dimension of discoverability that relies on the adequate disclosure and visibility of hybrid library collections on the network is in its infancy. There is still no hybrid library management system that meets the requirements of hybrid library business processes (see Figure 5.3).

Awareness and relevance

Figure 3.2 (p. 83) suggests that sustainability has several dimensions in addition to the economic one. The social dimension of sustainability involves visibility, community awareness and perceived relevance. Digital library and hybrid library collections must operate and demonstrate value in the context of today's web. Increasingly, information seekers do not need libraries to find scholarly digital content, digital books and the many other types of content being created and consumed on the social web. Being a buyer or licensor of digital content is a tenuous claim to community relevance, subject to disruption by the next innovative business model for distributing this type of content.

The need for a collective strategy

The parallel but separate evolutionary paths of repositories, hybrid libraries and the global web (see Figure 4.1, p. 90) are a major challenge for libraries, going forward. Lavoie, Henry and Dempsey (2006) identified the risk posed by the lack of an overarching service framework for libraries some years ago and called for 'reusable, recombinant, and interoperable library services.' Reaching consensus about such a framework will require library co-operation and partnerships with a broad array of stakeholders.

A vision and examples of new shared solutions for managing hybrid library collections and mass-digitized books are beginning to emerge (e.g., Kieft and Payne, 2012). These ideas for shared solutions for physical collections might be tested for their applicability to establishing coherent, collective strategies for repositories, hidden special collections, digitization programs, hybrid libraries and network-level interoperability.

Demonstrating relevance and value

Information seekers have many alternatives for getting the content they need. Relevance and value require more than being the owner of collections, a purchaser of licensed e-content, a publisher of open access journals, a creator or provider of digitized copies of cultural heritage materials, or the host of an open access repository or aggregation. Collections are not ends in themselves; they matter to the degree that they effectively support what libraries do for their communities, both local and global. The next chapter discusses digital libraries' social roles and their value to the communities they serve.

·········

CHAPTER 6

Social roles of digital libraries

Overview

This chapter examines the social value of digital libraries. It begins by exploring past and present understandings of the value of libraries to their communities. Taking a well known framework that lays out libraries' social roles as a starting point, the chapter then suggests a possible new framework to describe the social roles of digital libraries. The remainder of the chapter explicates this potential framework, exploring aspects of each social role. The sections offer examples, consider benefits and challenges, and draw attention to key readings from digital library researchers and practitioners.

Introduction

This chapter treats aspects of the topic of the value of digital libraries to society. With respect to the concept map from Chapter 3 (Figure 3.1, p. 64), this chapter deals with the lower right quadrant – that is, the intersection of the communities that use digital libraries and their social and economic aspects. In a nutshell, the following sections center on social roles and how digital libraries might:

- support the free flow of ideas
- empower individuals
- support teaching, learning and the advancement of knowledge
- provide economic benefits
- preserve intellectual and cultural assets for future generations.

The approach to these questions can be informed by a brief look into how libraries' social roles have evolved in general. The leaders of the 18th-century French and American Revolutions, influenced as they were by classical ideals of free inquiry, the pursuit of enlightenment and the concepts of deism (as articulated, for example, in Thomas Paine's *Age of Reason*, 1794), tended to define libraries in terms of their social roles supporting knowledge, literacy and the principles of a free society. Olivier Fressard (2008) offers a French perspective on these issues.

The inscription quoting James Madison, the framer of the US Constitution and Bill of Rights, on the front entrance to the Library of Congress Madison Building is an example of their perspective: 'Knowledge will forever govern ignorance: and a people who mean to be their own governours must arm themselves with the power which knowledge gives.' These core assumptions about the societal roles of libraries were a factor in the development of strong public library systems, mission-driven national libraries and well funded college and university libraries in democratic societies around the world.

As discussed in previous chapters, for many years conventional thinking has tended to emphasize the *collections* of libraries over their societal or community-based roles. Many perceive libraries as collections of things (especially books), or tend to place information processes (selecting, collecting, organizing, preserving, providing access to information) at the center of how they define libraries. Yet when David Lankes and colleagues (Lankes, Silverstein and Nicholson, 2007) describe the library as a 'facilitator of conversations' they are bringing forward – and reframing for the digital age – equally important assumptions underlying the perception of libraries as trusted social institutions that are vital to democracies, open inquiry and the advancement of knowledge and culture.

McClure and Jaeger (2009, 15–17) have been studying the changing roles of public libraries in the US. They trace the development of the social position of the library as a 'marketplace of ideas' from the 1930s forward, when public libraries in the US began to consistently assert the importance of equal access to diverse information for all citizens. In the UK, Bob Usherwood, a leading library scholar, devoted much of his long career to research on the social roles of libraries and other cultural institutions (Corrall, 2013). In the process, Usherwood developed and applied innovative qualitative methods such as 'social audits' to get beyond the numbers and focus on the outcomes that public libraries produce (Usherwood, 2002b). Outcomes-based methods like Usherwood's are now being used to evaluate the impact of academic libraries in US higher education, in particular how libraries contribute to research, the advancement of knowledge and student success (see Oakleaf, 2010;

Association of College and Research Libraries, 2011).

Jaeger (2010) is one of many who have commented on the resurgence of attention to the societal value of public libraries that has been spurred by the economic crisis of recent years. Also recently, Bas Savenije (2011), director general of the national library of the Netherlands, has offered helpful detail on the societal role of libraries in that country.

In earlier work on the social roles of libraries, McClure (1987) laid out a framework, since updated several times in light of the internet's impact, describing US public libraries' community roles as:

- centers for activities, information, research, reference and independent learning
- providers of educational support
- providers of resources targeted to specific age groups or interests.

Usherwood's research results (2002a) suggest that UK public libraries have positive impacts on both individuals and communities in terms of:

- personal development and education
- social cohesion
- community empowerment
- local culture and identity
- imagination and creativity
- health and well-being.

McClure's framework and Usherwood's findings cast library roles in terms of direct social involvement in the community to be served. They capture what a library can accomplish, for whom, and for what community benefits. The outcomes-based approaches exemplified by McClure and Usherwood's work are extremely useful and liberating in that they shift attention away from an information-processing or collection-centric definition of libraries toward a community-centric definition. This shift of focus enables new ways to think about services, space, expectations and potential not just for libraries but also for digital libraries in the networked environment.

Taking the McClure framework as a jumping off point, I analysed the findings of digital library researchers and practitioners to tease out insights and results related to how digital libraries contribute, have contributed, or could contribute value to the communities they serve. The result was the construction of a potential service framework for digital libraries' social roles.

The remainder of this chapter describes the background and aspects of this potential framework.

Foundations of digital libraries' social roles

As has been noted earlier in this book, the initial US call for digital library proposals (DLI-1) focused mainly on achieving technological advances, extending existing information retrieval systems, and gathering digital content, with less attention accorded to the social, behavioral and economic aspects of digital libraries (National Science Foundation, 1993). Not-withstanding the call's technical focus, the source documents leading up to DLI-1 reveal many rich conversations and thoughtful deliberations around the potential social roles of digital libraries. This author perused and analysed the original white paper, several workshop summaries, and many participant observations in the 441-page *Source Book on Digital Libraries*, which contains various working papers from NSF-sponsored activities that led to the DLI-1 call for proposals (Fox, 1993b). The effort revealed some convergence around the notions that digital libraries would advance science, technology and education by creating an 'intellectual infrastructure' for:

- supporting rapid delivery and exchange of new research results and innovations (that is, establishing a scholarly 'marketplace of ideas' on the network)
- helping to make sense of the ever-increasing volume of information
- significantly increasing the productivity of scientists, engineers, educators, students and those working in the commercial sector
- providing easy recognition and re-use of earlier research results (thus reducing duplication of effort)
- underpinning further discoveries and innovations
- speeding technology transfer
- stimulating the development of computer-based training and distance learning
- supporting self-education
- improving scientific and engineering teaching and learning in general
- fostering and enhancing collaboration and partnerships among and across individuals, institutions, groups, and domains (education, research, commerce)
- broadening access to high quality information for all.

Given these hopes for the roles that digital libraries would play, and their resonance with several elements of McClure's framework for the social roles of libraries, it is perhaps not surprising that Fox's conclusion for the *Source Book* pairs his sketch of the purpose of a US national digital libraries initiative with a reference to Thomas Jefferson's ideals:

> Purpose: To advance US science and engineering efforts, particularly research, education and technology transfer, by improving the availability and supporting technology for access to useful information.
>
> Note: We launch this in 1993, the 250th anniversary of the birth of Thomas Jefferson, who insisted that the free and vigorous pursuit of knowledge was essential to a democracy.
>
> Fox, 1993b, 394

Social Aspects of Digital Libraries Workshop 1996

Pieces of the social agenda for digital libraries were taken up again in 1996, when the NSF funded an invitational 'Social Aspects of Digital Libraries Workshop' (Borgman, 1996). The workshop sought to uncover existing knowledge and propose a research agenda to develop new understandings of how digital libraries might support the professional, educational and recreational activities of diverse communities.

Christine Borgman, a key organizer and contributor to the 1996 NSF-funded workshop, has noted that the challenge for the information age will not be a choice between libraries and the internet, but 'how best to provide access to information and how best to support the marketplace of ideas' and an informed citizenry in democratic societies (2000, 169–70). Borgman wrote confidently of the potential of digital libraries to enhance access, support learning and promote the progress of knowledge, and with concern about balancing the broadest possible access with the rights of creators.

Digital divide

For the purpose of this book, the digital divide is the gap between those with and without access to digital information and ICT (information and communication technologies). Anaraki and Heidari (2010, 287–9, 304–5) examine the dimensions of the digital divide in developing countries and the potential role of digital libraries in diminishing it. Savenije (2010a) points out that the digital divide exists not just in developing countries, but within countries where only some privileged organizations have ready access to licensed scholarly content. Along these lines, Creaser comments on the difficulties of providing for access to scholarly outputs to external users of research libraries (2011, 59–64).

Countless writers have made their case for open access to digital libraries of all kinds as a means to bridge the digital divide. Craven (2011) focuses on the issues of providing equal access to information for all and points out that the EC has given high priority to 'e-inclusion' in its i2010 initiative. To a degree, the e-inclusion priority is driving EC investment in digitization, open access and digital preservation.

Noting that 'the "mobile library" of the future may in reality be a library service accessed by a mobile phone,' Harle and Tarrant (2011, 132) make a case for librarians to engage and contribute their expertise to developing new mobile and online information environments for the disadvantaged. Liew (2012, 99) identifies steps toward more socially inclusive digital libraries that can enrich and empower individuals and communities, but emphasizes that digital libraries 'will not do so by simply existing' and 'mere digitization . . . does not necessarily lead to social inclusion.' Liew's article, well worth consulting, lays out the special requirements for moving more people across the digital divide and enumerates a number of ways the digital library community can or has contributed to progress.

A possible framework of social roles

As of this writing, not many sources explicitly and directly frame digital libraries in terms of their social roles. When authors have considered the social aspects of digital libraries, often it is in the context of user-centered design, work practice studies, the social web and other topics related to specific projects or programs.

As Van House (2003, 271) has pointed out, a theoretical or conceptual base for the social aspects of digital libraries has been lacking. Lavoie, Henry and Dempsey (2006) have noted the lack of a shared view in librarianship and the absence of a unifying framework to stitch individual digital library projects into a meaningful whole. A notable exception is Tanner and Deegan's 2010 report for JISC on the value of digitized resources. This report includes a well argued case for digitization work, a wealth of useful and practical examples, a five-part model for digitization impact assessment and a helpful section on methods for approaching the evaluation of intangible assets like digitized cultural content (e.g., the balanced scorecard).

As the discipline and practice of digital libraries is still relatively young, it is understandable that relatively little material addresses digital libraries' value to society. There simply has not been time for a shared understanding or theory of digital libraries as socio-technical systems to evolve.

This section proposes a tentative framework of digital libraries' social roles based on an analysis of that portion of the digital library literature that frames digital libraries in terms of their societal value. The framework's purpose is to make some sense of the many separate and seemingly disjointed themes in the digital library literature. The framework is intended to cover digital libraries of two broad types: digital libraries of cultural heritage content and digital libraries that support scholarly knowledge work.

It is important to be clear up front that I make no claims that the world's digital libraries, taken as a whole, presently *deliver* these aspects of social value; what is offered is a possible *conceptual framework* for examining their social roles. The framework could be used to spur further discussion of the social roles of digital libraries; spark the development of a better framework; provide a tool for assessment; or provide a jumping off point for a variety of planning tasks such as analysing strategic options, considering priorities, or preparing targeted communications.

Figure 6.1 frames ten potential aspects of digital libraries' social value. The aspects are arranged in relation to one another and as a kind of flow or feedback loop. This arrangement is intended to illustrate how one social role can build on or reinforce another. There is nothing more intended in the way the social roles are arranged; other analysts may have ordered the roles differently than I did,

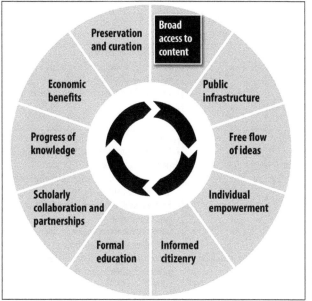

Figure 6.1
A framework of social roles of digital libraries

or for that matter altered the roles themselves. Table 6.1, provides some examples of each social role in context, in addition to some community benefits delivered as a result of this aspect of digital libraries' social roles. The subsections that follow the table offer a variety of perspectives on particular roles with the intent of further explicating what is meant by the content in the figure and table.

Table 6.1 Potential social contributions of digital libraries

Contributions	Examples of services to offer or engage with	Community benefits
Broad access to content	• International, national, regional, or local heritage digital libraries with historic content, images, maps, music, archives and more • Subject-based repositories • Institutional repositories • Digital libraries supporting teaching and learning for specific groups • Genre, format, or audience-based digital libraries	• Allow more content to be collected • Allow more access for more people in more places or contexts • Balance between open access for all and rights of creators and providers of content • Make information mobile • Enhance appreciation and engagement with culture • Enable full participation in a democratic society
Infrastructure component	• Machine-to-machine web services; linked data • Data-mining of openly accessible content • Syndication or linking of digital library content to high-traffic sites • Optimize indexing and referrals from search engines • Registries • Assignment and maintenance of persistent identifiers; metadata; advocacy/adherence to standards; support for disambiguation • Authentication and authorization • New models for licensing rights to digital content (e.g. Creative Commons) • 'Boundary objects' facilitating communication and exchange of content between different groups	• Fundamental component of the public information infrastructure by enabling the creation, deposit, dissemination and preservation of trusted information • Support information exchange and re-use (machine to machine and person to person) • Help to make sense of an increasing volume of information
Free flow of ideas	• Crowdsourcing • Annotations, tagging, ratings, recommendations, reviews • Citation managers • Alerts, social bookmarking • Blogs, wikis	• Be a locus of shared work • Provide virtual space for 'rational and enlightened discourse' • Facilitate interaction – content, creators, the public
Individual empowerment and an informed citizenry	• Virtual public libraries • Mobile interfaces • Citation management services • Aggregator of trusted content • Online archives • Online exhibits • Digital reference and chat • Online information literacy instruction/tutorials/games • Engagement with social networks and online personal profiling services	• Support self-education and self-improvement • Support construction and management of personal digital libraries • Increase knowledge about community, social and political issues • Enable pursuit of cultural, professional, and personal interests • Support information literacy and the development of critical thinking • Provide convenient access to and assistance with needed information for daily life and work

Table 6.1 (Continued)		
Contributions	**Examples of services to offer or engage with**	**Community benefits**
Formal education	• Educational digital libraries • Portals for teachers or students • Integration with learning management systems • Access to primary sources	• Improve teaching and learning • Support online teaching and learning environments
Progress of knowledge	• Virtual research environments • Self-archiving • Deposit incentives; mandatory deposit • Open access journals • Libraries as publishers • Digital libraries of theses and dissertations • Cross-repository services • Object re-use and exchange services • Workflow-based content creation and management • Data curation • Researcher profiling services	• Support knowledge work in a particular scholarly community • Support multidisciplinary knowledge work (across communities) • Enhance scholarly interactions • Open scholarly dialogue to a wider circle of readers and creators • Support the scholarly value chain: legitimize, disseminate, make accessible
Economic benefits	• Digital libraries that bring scattered technical content together, creating efficiencies and saving researcher time (e.g. see Kurtz et al., 2005, on NASA digital library) • Digital libraries of cultural heritage content (by attracting attention, spending and investment) • New products, processes, services and economic development spurred by access to digital libraries	• Support efficient and rapid access to intellectual and cultural assets • Provide rapid and easy recognition and re-use of previous results (reducing duplication of effort, raising quality) • Increase the productivity of researchers, scholars, and entrepreneurs • Foster new discoveries and innovations • Speed technology/knowledge transfer
Preservation and curation	• Preservation frameworks (models, standards, best practices) • Individual preservation-quality repositories • Community-based preservation frameworks, networks and shared repositories • National digital library and preservation frameworks • Web archives • Data archives • E-research infrastructure • Digital and data curation • Advocacy for the right to preserve, updating copyright and legal deposit laws for the digital age	• Preserve intellectual and cultural assets for future use • Provide education about preservation • Registration of content and data • Stewardship and long-term access

Broad access, infrastructure and the free flow of ideas

Those who have responsibility for leading or funding national or other large-scale digital library initiatives tend to speak more directly than other writers to why digital libraries matter to society and the reasons to invest in them. Dame Lynne Brindley of the British Library, for example, wrote of digital libraries' role in facilitating research, formal and informal education and the free flow of ideas (Brindley, 2009). She points to key challenges related to supporting long-term retention and re-use of a nation's intellectual assets; enabling collaboration; fostering information literacy and the development of critical thinking skills; enabling full participation in a democratic e-society; and balancing the values of open access with protecting intellectual property rights.

The National Library of Australia (NLA) is known for its success establishing unified national programs to support public education, contribute to culture, and preserve heritage. Warwick Cathro (1999, 2001, 2009a, 2009b) viewed the NLA's digital library as a key component of the national information infrastructure, vital to carrying out the national library's stewardship role. He worked to address a number of key digital library challenges: for example, to establish web archiving of selected Australian sites; to digitize and preserve national heritage content, especially newspapers; and to advocate extending legal deposit to digital publications and establishing reasonable access conditions for this content. Bas Savenije of the national library of the Netherlands has advocated tirelessly for open access, not only to cultural heritage materials in the public domain (Savenije and Beunen, 2012), but also for the purpose of breaking down access barriers to all types of content, including scholarly publications (Savenije, 2010a, 2010b, 2011). He has argued that open access to digital libraries of cultural and scholarly content is good economic and social policy for today's knowledge societies, enabling full cultural participation and providing indispensable support for national and international infrastructures for research and education.

Empowering and informing individuals

Simon Tanner (2009) remarks on the potential for digital libraries to empower individuals, inform citizens and narrow the digital divide. He contends that a major function of digital libraries is to enhance appreciation and engagement with culture and the information society in general. Noting that more people are becoming wirelessly connected, and devices are becoming more mobile, he argues for digital library designers and developers to focus new efforts on greater interaction with users in the 'ambient intelligent environment' that is emerging.

Digital libraries have demonstrated their value for empowering individuals in a number of ways. The evidence compiled by Davis (2011) suggests that open access publications reach more readers, especially readers outside the research community, thus increasing the diffusion of scientific knowledge to the public. Digital libraries can underpin not only independent learning, but also open community-based creation, contribution and aggregation of intellectual content. Aaron Krowne (2003), a co-founder of PlanetMath (www.planetmath.org), writes of digital libraries as actionable collections of knowledge, built by and for a grass-roots community of users (a 'commons').

Wikipedia and PlanetMath are similar in that they are community-sourced, open, socially shared knowledge spaces, but PlanetMath differs in that it was built using a digital library approach (and for a particular audience – those interested in mathematics, including all age groups and inside or outside professional or formal settings). Successful commons-based digital libraries like PlanetMath become even more visible when they are harvested into OAI-based aggregations, crawled by search engines or made available to the semantic web; in all these ways they become more discoverable by ordinary citizens as well as specialist groups.

Neil Beagrie (2005) was one of the first in the digital libraries field to write in detail on the trend to a 'more informal and increasingly empowered landscape of personal collection' on the web, along with a shift from passive digital information consumption to more active creation, customization and sharing of digital content. Personal digital libraries containing individual digital objects as well as external content are not uncommon and they can form part of an individual's public persona on the web. In parallel with this trend, a number of online services and collaborations have emerged that further empower individuals to create, interact with, manage and share digital content – sometimes for purely personal reasons and sometimes to contribute to say, citizen science initiatives. Chapters 9 and 10 discuss citizen science and Krowne's and Beagrie's ideas in the context of the social web.

Those building or maintaining digital libraries are increasingly responding to the personalization trend by embedding content in ways and where it can easily be consumed, shared, re-used and improved by individuals. 'The Commons' on www.flickr.com is one of the examples discussed in Chapter 10.

Supporting teaching and learning

The role of advancing formal education has been associated with digital libraries from the start. Fee-based digital libraries of articles and journals from well known scholarly publishers were quickly taken up by the academic community when they began becoming available in the 1990s. Cultural heritage digital libraries organized by national libraries, like American

Memory, Gallica and others, are well integrated into teaching and learning for all educational levels. Some subject, genre, or format-based digital libraries have become central to higher education in specific disciplines. Some broad-based digital libraries (the Internet Public Library, for example: www.ipl.org) are frequently used by primary and secondary school teachers and students. As noted by Tanner and Deegan (2010, 17), because a large body of the UK's cultural assets have been digitized, courses can be enriched and whole new topics can be studied.

The take-up of other educational digital libraries has been less straightforward. Once initiatives to build educational digital libraries for specific disciplines or learning communities got under way, it became obvious that being successful would involve more than pulling the appropriate digital collections together and making them searchable (as difficult as that could be). A number of early projects found that the principle of 'build it and they will come' is not a path to success. An important recognition has been that an educational digital library must be social – a meeting place or virtual lab for collaboration, overcoming isolation and engaging others; and it must be designed in alignment with teachers' or students' work practices and behaviors. Chapter 7 discusses these ideas further.

Scholarship, collaboration and the progress of knowledge

Nancy Van House (2003, 271) writes of the importance of digital libraries to cognitive or knowledge work. Digital libraries not only provide or aggregate widely distributed content critical to this work; they enable new frameworks for the social aspects of creating and certifying new knowledge. These aspects include collaborating and learning together across time and space, as well as the process of deciding what information, and which people and organizations, to trust.

Contending that digital libraries are boundary objects (entities that link different communities together), Van House (2003, 287) sees a digital library as 'a locus of shared work' for contributing content, using it, and participating in the digital library's creation and maintenance. She frames the digital library as 'a heterogeneous network of users, researchers, funders, operators, and other people; of documents, images, databases, thesauri, and other inform-ation artifacts; of practices and understandings; and of technology' (289–90). Along these lines, and as discussed in Chapter 1, the DELOS Digital Library Manifesto (Candela et al., 2006, 6) contains a collective vision of a digital library as 'a tool at the centre of intellectual activity.'

The complexities of the landscape of knowledge work are well documented by Harley et al. (2010), whose findings from 160 interviews of scholars from seven disciplines suggest that the current social and economic structures and reward systems underpinning scholarly communications are firmly entrenched and represent significant barriers to innovation. Nevertheless, Harley's findings suggest that open access repositories (both discipline and institutionally based) are having positive impact, when taken as a whole. Among their benefits, open access repositories can enable rapid recognition (and credit) for new findings and offer a place to deposit and build awareness for conference presentations or working papers. In addition, through openly available pre- and post-prints they substantially broaden access to high-quality scholarly papers to larger, cross-disciplinary audiences.

Economic benefits, innovations and technology transfer

The digital libraries discipline has produced little literature that directly addresses the economic value of digital libraries as a whole. A great deal has been written about sustainability. There are in addition a number of cost-benefit analyses of various types of digital libraries; many articles on business models, particularly with respect to open access; and articles on the economics of digital preservation. Discussions of some of this body of literature can be found in Chapter 7. This section has a different starting point: it briefly addresses the question of the *economic value of digital libraries to society*. It makes use of some perspectives from microeconomics in that it touches on topics like the sources of economic health, innovation, value chains and the nature of markets.

It is generally recognized that the global economy is a 'knowledge economy' or 'knowledge-based economy' (see Cooke and Leydesdorff, 2006, for a review of each phrase's development). In brief, a knowledge economy is driven by knowledge processes – the exploration, exploitation and examination of knowledge. In a knowledge economy, innovation and technology transfer are extremely important; these involve the efficient and effective transfer of new knowledge, technology or methods to those who can develop them into new products, processes or services, thus producing economic value. Castells (1996) is widely cited for his seminal work on how knowledge and networks spur innovation and economic growth. Within the library literature, Tanner and Deegan (2010) argue that the digital agenda and digital resources reduce the costs and quicken the pace of innovation, thereby increasing a nation's economic competitiveness.

Raym Crow's position paper (2002) for the Scholarly Publishing and Academic Resources Coalition (SPARC) is notable for its analysis of how scholarly knowledge markets work. He makes the claim that open access to scholarly content (enabled by repositories) will produce value for the knowledge economy by positively disrupting and rebalancing the current market (scholars, academic institutions and their libraries, publishers and readers). He argues for a new 'disaggregated' model for producing scholarly content – based on the existence of a global network of distributed, independent and open digital libraries of research materials – that 'unbundles the principal functions of scholarly communication, thus presenting the potential to realize market efficiencies.' These market efficiencies include:

- significantly expanding readership and availability of scholarly research (not just papers but also other types of content), thus reducing the digital divide
- improving operations and competition in the scholarly value chain (registration, certification, awareness, archiving, rewarding), thus reducing publisher monopoly power and increasing innovation
- increasing the likelihood that digital research material will be preserved for future generations.

Tanner and Deegan (2010) make a strong case for the economic and social benefits of digitizing cultural treasures. Carla De Laurentis (2006) offers a surprising and fresh assessment of digital cultural heritage content as a potential driver of innovation and economic value in networked knowledge economies. Arguing that digital content is among the underpinnings of successful knowledge economies, De Laurentis goes on to make a case for the economic value that can be generated by digital cultural heritage content from memory institutions (libraries, archives, museums) if it is appropriately used as a resource in a 'digital value chain'. The concept of a digital value chain is generally applied in an e-commerce context, describing how a digital resource of some kind is packaged and prepared for distribution and consumption on the web. In the context of De Laurentis' article, a digital value chain refers to a process that integrates and exploits digital cultural heritage content and, through a process in which many organizations participate, creates new value in new settings, such as e-learning, entertainment, media and business applications (e.g., supporting tourism).

De Laurentis argues that to produce this new economic value, memory institutions must shift from relatively passive roles as knowledge repositories to active participants in content production, in the process creatively collaborating with many kinds of partners (broadcasters and other media organizations, advertisers, educational institutions, etc.). Her ideas recall (and scale up) the previously discussed efforts by cultural heritage organizations to create new value by embedding digital content in new settings on the web (e.g., the Flickr 'Commons' discussed earlier). Similarly, her ideas are interesting to consider in light of Europeana's intention to contribute to economic growth in the EU through 'long tail' effects (Verwayen et al., 2008, 3–4).

Preservation of intellectual and cultural assets

'The preservation and re-use of digital data and information forms both the cornerstone of future economic growth and development, and the foundation for the future of memory.' Thus Seamus Ross, then a professor and digital curation specialist at the University of Glasgow, began his eloquent contribution to the large and substantial literature of digital preservation (Ross, 2000, 2). Yet the amount of networked-based content (which Ross labeled 'd-facts') is not only staggering; it also poses more challenges for preservation than content recorded in physical media ('artifacts'). D-facts are fragile, preservation requires active intervention, and unlike artifacts this type of content is unlikely to survive periods of neglect. Commitment to digital preservation is required so that new generations, like Isaac Newton in his time, can continue 'standing on the shoulders of giants.' Legislation like that founding the US National Digital Information Infrastructure and Preservation Program (NDIIPP) in 2000 was based on the realization that effective digital preservation could protect billions of dollars of investment in the nation's knowledge capital (National Digital Information Infrastructure and Pre- servation Program, 2011).

Digital libraries can and do contribute to ensuring the future of memory. However, inclusion in a digital library does not by itself preserve content. The extent to which digital libraries succeed in preserving content depends on how the organizations that manage them allocate resources to ongoing digital preservation practices, as suggested by Lavoie and Dempsey (2004). The following paragraphs offer a more detailed look at key social aspects of digital preservation of intellectual and cultural assets.

From collecting to preserving

Digital preservation is a subset of the endeavor known as 'digital curation,' which the UK's Digital Curation Centre describes as the active management and appraisal of digital information over its entire life cycle, from creation and active use to selection, transfer and preservation, access and re-use (Pennock, 2007; Higgins, 2008). Paul Conway (2010, 64–5) clarifies the distinction between collecting digital objects and preserving them: 'Digitization for preservation creates valuable new digital products, whereas digital preservation protects the value of those products, regardless of whether the original source is a tangible artifact or data that were born and live digitally.'

In the case of institutional and subject-based repositories, Hitchcock et al. (2007) have pointed out that relying on repository software for preservation is insufficient, as is merely storing content (which may become unusable as technologies advance). Yakel et al. (2008) report similar concerns. Instead, the claim to protect repository content over the long term must be backed up with formal programs and a preservation-quality technological framework. As an example, Shreeves et al. (2006) describe how the IDEALS repository at the University of Illinois (www.ideals.illinois.edu) is fully engaged in integrating digital preservation systems and practices.

Types of content

What follows is the briefest of introductions to an extremely large body of literature, beginning with a gloss on some of the types of content that have

Table 6.2 Some brief notes on digital preservation of selected types of content

Types	Examples (a combination of repositories and projects)	Selected references
E-journals	• LOCKSS, CLOCKSS • Portico • JSTOR	Seadle offers helpful analyses for licensed and open access journals (2010, 2011). Manz (2012) provides an overview of the current situation in a number of European countries.
Books in mass digitization projects	• HathiTrust • *Dutch National Platform for Digital Publications* (working name)	Rieger, 2008b; York, 2010; Christenson, 2011; Janssen, 2011 (Netherlands)
Web archiving	• Internet Archive Wayback Machine • PANDORA Archive • UK Web Archive	Niu, 2012 (overview of web archiving); Toyoda and Kitsuregawa, 2012 (covers Internet Archive, national and university web archives); Cathro, Webb and Whiting, 2001 (PANDORA); Bailey and Thompson, 2006; see also www.webarchive.org.uk.
Research data	• UK Data Archive • ICPSR (Inter-university Consortium for Political and Social Research) • National Space Science Data Center • DataCite	Gold (2007a, 2007b) provides an introduction to research data for libraries. Beagrie, Lavoie and Woollard's 2010 report for JISC includes a helpful taxonomy of the benefits of research data preservation. DataCite is a global registration agency for research data (Brase, 2009).

been the focus of digital preservation efforts, provided in Table 6.2. Each of these different types of content has a different preservation profile, requiring different action agendas and involving different players.

The right to preserve

Traditionally, libraries have had the responsibility and legal rights to preserve that part of the intellectual and cultural record that is represented in the physical collections they own. With the rise of massive networked information and an interlinked, online scholarly communications system underpinned by licensed content from publishers, responsibility for preservation has become diffuse, and the right to preserve has become unclear (Ayre and Muir, 2004). Ensuring against loss of network-based content for future users has come to require a great deal more action and collaboration across a diverse set of players and stakeholders who create, produce, select, manage, use and preserve content. A number of these players have the rights to preserve (such as commercial scholarly publishers that own or control content) but lack incentives to do so.

Community-based solutions

Don Waters (2007) analyses a number of approaches to dividing the labor among stakeholders and providing incentives for preserving the cultural and scholarly record 'on which future scholarship and education so clearly depend.' He offers insight into community-based solutions that not only generate the public good of preservation and produce savings, but also balance open access with the rights of creators and producers. The final report of the Blue Ribbon Task Force on Sustainable Digital Preservation and Access (Blue Ribbon Task Force and Rumsey, 2010) treats these issues in detail and offers a set of recommendations for sustainable preservation strategies across a diffuse set of stakeholders. This report clarifies a variety of stakeholder roles and offers action agendas for each group (BRTF, under their Table 5.1).

Roles for individual libraries

On behalf of ARL, Lars Meyer (2009) completed an analysis and report on how the networked digital environment is reshaping the core preservation functions of research libraries, both at the level of individual institutions and in the realm of collective action. Of particular interest to the managers of digital libraries is Meyer's illustration (2009, under Figure 1) of the potential range of a research library's preservation activities and commitments, from local to collaborative. There continue to be digital preservation roles for individual digital libraries (for a practical approach to defining them see Oehlerts and Liu, 2013). These roles require a heightened understanding of best practices for digitization and born digital content, what others are collecting and preserving, the rights to preserve, and the roles of partnerships within and outside their parent institutions. There are also many more opportunities for collective action to advance the digital preservation agenda. Walters et al. (2009) discuss a number of examples of collective initiatives, including the frequently mentioned MetaArchive Cooperative (www. metaarchive.org), a private LOCKSS network and an NDIIPP partner, that supports cultural heritage repositories at over 50 institutions.

Infrastructure

Efforts to establish a digital preservation infrastructure and best practices are progressing; a useful source is McGovern and Skinner's compilation (2012). The OAIS (Open Archival Information System) reference model is gaining recognition and use in the field (see Lee, 2010, for a brief introduction to OAIS). A growing number of important digital preservation programs are based on the OAIS model. TRAC (Trustworthy Repositories Audit & Certification), managed by the US Center for Research Libraries and OCLC, is a framework for certifying trusted digital repositories (Dryden, 2011, offers a succinct overview of TRAC and related standards and activities). Metadata specialists have added significantly to the store of knowledge required to capture the source of content and how it was created, how to open and read the content, terms of access, migration history and interrelationships with other software and records, and more (for more on digital preservation metadata see Guenther and Wolfe, 2009).

The public policy environment and legal frameworks

A number of national libraries are carrying out or facilitating ambitious programs to preserve their nations' digital assets (a small sample includes National Library of Australia, 2008; Archives New Zealand, 2009; Janssen, 2011; Ledoux, 2012). Part of this work involves fostering a public policy environment that promotes digital preservation and long-term access. Digital preservation faces significant legal obstacles due to current copyright laws and limitations on the legal deposit of digital content. A key finding of an NDIIPP study was that current legal frameworks 'discourage preservation best practices or even make them illegal' (National Digital Information Infrastructure and Preservation Program, 2011, 4).

Besek et al. (2008) describe the situation for copyright law and digital preservation around the world. Their study found that many national legal frameworks prevent digital preservation actions such as making multiple copies and migrating digital content to new technological formats and media. They conclude with joint recommendations for updating copyright and legal deposit laws for the digital era and in the public interest (Besek et al., 2008, 110–11). They also specify roles for 'preservation institutions' (libraries, archives and museums) that will enable them to carry forward past roles protecting intellectual and cultural assets for the future. In addition a number of writers have focused on how legal deposit for digital content can ensure long-term access to the greatest number while respecting intellectual property laws (see, for example, Stirling et al., 2012).

Conclusion

Descriptions and perceptions of digital libraries are most often centered on their collections. While collections are important, they are far from being the only way that libraries and digital libraries bring value to the communities they serve. This chapter offers a potential framework for examining and articulating digital library value across a range of social roles. The framework may assist digital library managers with:

- describing digital libraries to external audiences (for example parent institutions or funding bodies) in ways likely to resonate with them
- selecting strategic priorities and improving service to the communities that digital libraries serve
- defining desired social outcomes and assessing digital libraries based on their community impacts.

The pressure for greater accountability seems to be affecting all organizations that contribute to the welfare of the public; those building or maintaining libraries or digital libraries are not alone in this way. Fortunately, research and practice using outcomes-based assessment approaches in libraries are advancing. Usherwood was an early advocate and implementer of outcome-based approaches to evaluation (2002a; 2002b); other sources of ideas and methods are Oakleaf (2010; assessing social and financial impact in academic and other types of libraries); Lougee (2009; strategic impact); Koltay and Li (2010; impact measures); and Kaufman and Watstein (2008; return-on-investment, or ROI measures).

Greater clarity about the community value and positive impacts of digital libraries can also be achieved by looking into digital library success factors. What are the distinguishing characteristics of successful, sustainable digital libraries? How do digital libraries attract, build and support online communities? These are the subjects of the next chapter.

CHAPTER 7

Digital libraries and their communities

Overview

What sets thriving, long-lived digital libraries apart from those that attract only modest attention or have faded into memory? Why have some digital libraries had a distinctive impact on the communities they were built to serve, while others are more or less ignored? This chapter examines these issues. It builds on Table 2.1's descriptions of a sample of working digital libraries that have been successful since they began in the first decade of digital libraries (1991–2001). It also takes up themes from Chapter 6, which examines the ways that digital libraries produce, or could produce, value for the communities they serve.

Approach

This chapter uses the results of interviews with nine well known digital library experts (listed at the beginning of the book, p. xvi) to approach the question of what makes digital libraries successful in their communities. Interweaving the results of the interviews and the findings of other digital library researchers and practitioners, the chapter examines the distinguishing characteristics leading to long-term viability.

Successful, sustainable digital libraries

When digital libraries were beginning two decades ago, the web was characterized by fairly passive, read-only sites. As the web evolved into a more social space, users came to expect more interactive sites. It stands to reason that when users approach digital libraries, they bring their expectations and experiences from other sites with them. Accordingly, this chapter begins with an analysis from the domain of online communities, which, for the purpose of this discussion, are network-based spaces in which participants communicate and interact, share and contribute content, and build or maintain relationships.

The study of online communities

Alicia Iriberri and Gondy Leroy (2009) offer a life-cycle perspective on online community success. Their often-cited analysis focuses on the evolution of online communities and identifying success factors in each evolutionary stage: inception, creation, growth and maturity (or death). They take the characteristics of several types of online communities into account: support, interest-based, knowledge, gaming and transactions-based communities.

Iriberri and Leroy's life-cycle model is based upon a comprehensive review of research and practice in the emerging field of online communities – a body of literature that is highly multidisciplinary and growing fast. Unlike much of what has been written, their approach to modeling what attracts and maintains an online community is complex and contextual. Their model is a multilayered synthesis that interweaves social, behavioral, psychological, business, organizational, and technological elements. Iriberri and Leroy's article offers full explanations of the life-cycle stages and success factors for online communities, and a reading is well worth the time.

Figure 7.1 is an attempt to briefly summarize and tailor Iriberri and Leroy's life-cycle success factors to digital libraries. The quadrants of the circle contain the life-cycle stages (clockwise from the upper left quadrant) and the text boxes contain key success factors for that stage.

The purpose of presenting a figure adapted from Iriberri and Leroy's ideas is not to suggest that digital libraries are online communities (although some can be). Instead the life-cycle model can provide a frame for considering digital libraries in social environments.

Related work in the digital library domain

The idea of considering digital libraries in the context of social, community environments is not new. The report of an early NSF-sponsored workshop on the social aspects of digital libraries (Borgman, 1996) framed digital libraries in the context of social systems. Intriguingly, although it was written over 15

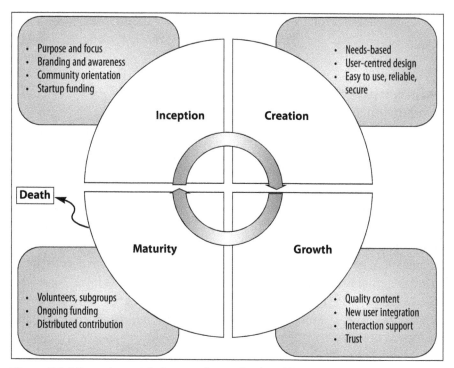

Figure 7.1 Life -cycle model of success factors for digital libraries in social environments

years ago, the report's illustration of the information life cycle in the art world (defined as a distributed community with myriad participants and groups playing different roles) seems quite familiar in today's context, in which the social web influences cross-community interactions, knowledge creation, communication and distribution. Along these lines and as discussed in Chapter 6, Van House (2003) has defined digital libraries as boundary objects (entities that link dispersed communities together).

What contributes to lasting digital libraries?

The first question in the interviews conducted with digital library experts had to do with the traits of successful, sustainable digital libraries. Interview responses resonated with many of the success factors included in Iriberri and Leroy's life-cycle model. The following sections focus on the success factors that were highly characteristic of interview responses. These were: purpose and focus; branding and awareness; community and needs orientation; user-centered design, ease of use and reliability; quality content; and funding and sustainability. Several of the success factors pertain to the inception stage, some to the creation stage, one to the growth stage, and one to the maturity stage.

Inception: purpose and focus
Commitment, engagement, mission

Responses from the interviews suggest that successful digital libraries grow out of the communities for which they are intended, based on a purpose or purposes articulated within that community. Digital libraries that thrive are backed by passionate, committed builders on the one hand, and enthusiastic, vested community participants on the other. Alignment and focus around a clear, compelling mission for the digital library appear to be significant indicators of future success. A mission is the task or purpose for which an organization, group, or initiative exists. For example, with respect to Table 2.1's five digital libraries built by national libraries (Trove, Gallica, American Memory, Papers Past and Sound Archive), there is a great deal of clarity, collaboration and commitment apparent around the mission, characteristic of national libraries, to:

- build and preserve a national collection reflecting cultural heritage and other fields
- make it available in the national interest to both current and future researchers, and
- carry forward this mandate in the digital age.

Needs assessment

Several interviewees also noted that the builders of successful digital libraries have tended to test and validate their assumptions about the purpose and focus of the digital library, including the:

- needs the digital library addresses
- appeal of its content, and
- characteristics, expectations and work practices of the intended audience(s).

One interviewee, speaking of the major end-user test that preceded the building of American Memory, noted that 'they initially thought the primary audience was professors and others in university settings. Actually, the audience turned out to be grade school and high school teachers.'

Just as needs and audiences can shift, the appeal of digital library content can change over time. Alternatives can appear for digital content that was unique at the inception of the digital library and naturally such changes in conditions have an impact on the ability to appropriately balance a digital library's audience, collections and technologies.

Community orientation

A few interviewees noted the importance of the builders' being members of the intended audience for the digital library. For example, Paul Ginsparg, the person who started arXiv.org, is a highly respected physicist, and physics is one of the disciplines served by the arXiv. The vision, determination and commitment of highly visible, credible leaders are important factors in the digital library's success.

Other examples include digital library founders Michael Hart (Project Gutenberg) and Brewster Kahle (Internet Archive). In Hart's case, he was an author and innovator, passionate about books and literacy, and an unstoppable man of the people, whose vision of freely available e-books was able to inspire volunteers and attract donations to make Gutenberg a success. Kahle was already an accomplished computer engineer and web entrepreneur when he founded the Internet Archive in 1996. Remarking on the Internet Archive, Carr (2009, 62) observes that 'the quantity of electronic information that Kahle has preserved in the last decade is mind-bogglingly large.' Like Hart and Kahle, numerous individuals provided remarkable leadership during the first decade of digital library research and practice.

Inception: branding and awareness

Interviewees noted that successfully communicating the identity, intent and nature of a digital library – in a way that resonates with its target audiences – increases the likelihood of the digital library's take-up and use. Although most digital library builders would not use the term, this activity is called 'branding.' Branding refers to the way intended audiences think about, identify and differentiate products, services, organizations and places. An example of successful branding is Starbucks, well known for its coffee and service.

The best brands capture and communicate the core values of the intended audiences. Keller (2000) provides a strong and readable introduction to product brands and branding; Berry (2000) explains service branding. Types of organizations and places can have brands too. Cathy De Rosa and her team determined, for example, that the library 'brand' is books (2011, 38–9). As for places, consider the association of Paris with the phrase 'city of light,' or the familiar expression 'I Love New York.'

Some digital library brands

Those who build and manage digital libraries do not tend to think of themselves as marketing or branding their collections or services. Nevertheless, in practice, successful digital library builders do describe their digital libraries in ways that attempt to capture their core value to the communities they serve. Not too many digital library builders brand their services. Among those who do, some examples are:

- Europeana 1914–1918: 'Your family history of World War One'
- Europeana: 'think culture'
- The British Library's EThOS: 'opening access to UK theses'
- FamilySearch: 'ancestors remembered'
- Internet Archive: 'universal access to all knowledge'
- Gallica: 'Une bibliothèque patrimoniale et encyclopédique' (heritage and encyclopedic library)
- HAL-INRIA: 'inventeurs du monde numériques' (inventors of the digital world)
- JSTOR: 'light up your mind. Scholarly journals, primary sources, and now books!'
- Mendeley: 'simplify your research workflow'
- Project Gutenberg: 'the first producer of free ebooks'.

Achieving awareness

Achieving high awareness of a digital library among its intended audiences is another success factor. Interviewees noted a number of paths to high awareness and usage:

- The builders are associated with a destination site that is recognized and well respected by its target audiences (for example, PubMed Central).
- The digital library is unique in some way and there are few or no substitutes for its content (for example, Perseus, www.perseus.tufts.edu).
- The digital library site's content is made highly visible through search

engine crawling (Google and/or Google Scholar), or by being embedded in or linked from other high traffic sites.

• The materials on the site are freely available to all (open access).

Discoverability

Being discoverable in major search engines and/or other high traffic sites on the web is an enormous boost to the visibility of a digital library and a major factor in determining how much it is used. Embedding or linking from high-traffic sites can also raise awareness and usage. Chapter 10 discusses the impressive results of embedding digital library images in 'The Commons' on Flickr. Several interviewees mentioned a new strategy for greatly increasing the awareness of valuable digital library content – linking from Wikipedia articles, as described by Proffitt and Snyder (2012). Snyder, who works in the Archives of American Art (www.aaa.si.edu) at the Smithsonian, reported that she and colleagues became interested in working with Wikipedia, which receives nearly half a million unique visitors a month, to help the Archives reach as many users as possible. Wikipedia has greatly boosted the visibility of some of the Archive's images, which were uploaded to the Wikimedia Commons. Wikipedia has also become the single biggest referrer of web traffic to the Archives of American Art.

Creation: community and needs orientation
The risks of 'push' initiatives

Interviewees also responded to the question of what makes digital libraries fail. Several mentioned projects characterized as 'push' initiatives. The builders moved through the inception and creation stages with a 'build it and they will come' attitude instead of a clear understanding of their intended audience(s) and the purposes with which these audiences would enthusiastically engage. Worse, the builders began with incorrect assumptions and a vague, untested value proposition (the benefits that users can expect to experience). Interviewees also pointed to the high risk of failure associated with digital library projects that were begun:

• with general frameworks (rather than defining a framework by working directly with the intended audience or audiences), or
• as academic exercises without a clear strategy or intent to build a lasting service.

Digital libraries as community centers

The results of the interviews suggest additional dimensions to successful digital libraries in their communities: the digital library is (1) valued and understood by the communities being served; (2) easy to use, with low barriers to getting started; and (3) in close alignment with those communities' needs and how they work or want to work (or play). Table 7.1 provides some examples of successfully building an active community around a digital library.

Table 7.1 Aligning digital libraries with community needs and practices: some examples	
National Library of Australia (Trove)	The NLA made a commitment 'to simplify the complex digital landscape and to ensure that the various services are interoperable' (Cathro, 2006, 5). The newspapers service is an iconic example of successful crowdsourcing (Holley, 2010a).
Bibliothèque nationale de France (Gallica)	The BnF developed a digital library of cultural heritage materials based on the needs of a remote public, a new kind of researcher (different from classical library users or professional researchers), and new ways of reading and understanding texts (Assadi et al., 2003).
International Children's Digital Library	The ICDL designed and tested its digital library through a process of remarkable collaboration with a team of children (Druin, 2005).
Social Science Research Network (www.ssrn.com)	SSRN, one of the world's top-ranked repositories (http://repositories.webometrics.info), was co-founded by Wayne Marr and Michael Jensen in 1994. Jensen, a former Harvard Business School professor, describes SSRN as a scholarly 'collaborative' providing services for both authors and readers, opportunities for peer interaction and participation, and early distribution of research results. SSRN contains a critical mass of highly discoverable papers on a trusted site widely perceived as dependable and highly beneficial to scholars (Ricciardi, 2007; Bray, Vizthum and Konsynski, 2008; Jensen, 2012).

A recent success in building an active community around a digital library is Europeana 1914–1918 (www.europeana1914-1918.eu), a highly interactive site where people can connect their stories and memorabilia with the holdings of libraries, museums and archives across Europe. Wilson (2012, 529–31) discusses Europeana 1914–1918 in his article on how new, more social methods for digital curation, which he calls digital 'co-curation,' can closely engage citizens with their countries' histories.

Whether community members directly contribute to a digital library or not, buy-in from, and engagement with, the community that gathers around the service is important. Cory Lampert and Jason Vaughan (2009, 123) gleaned the factors of a successful digitization program from a survey of ARL libraries that they administered. They learned that faculty collaboration, interest and faculty partnerships were among the top factors leading to successful digital library programs in the responding research libraries.

User-centered design

The NSF-funded National Science Digital Library (NSDL) offers a particularly focused window into what has worked for designing digital libraries for educational communities. The NSDL's aim has been to substantially contribute to science, mathematics, engineering and technology education. The program, which began in 2000 with US$13.5 million in grants for six projects, was intended to create openly accessible digital libraries serving the needs of learners from K-12 to higher education to life-long (Zia, 2000; Arms et al., 2002).

Educational digital libraries sometimes stand alone (for example matdl.org for the materials sciences); they are sometimes components of larger portals or social sites (for example Math Tools, part of mathforum.org at Drexel; or Teach the Earth, part of http://serc.carleton.edu, discussed below); and sometimes they are explicitly designed as 'landing pages' for searches referred from Google. A close partner of NSDL, the Digital Library for Earth Science Education (DLESE) provides a high-quality digital resource collection selected by geoscientists and educators working together (Marlino et al., 2001; Sumner, 2010). Educational digital libraries can also integrate or interoperate with learning management systems (for example, merlot.org, a digital library of peer-reviewed materials supporting online learning, is accessible from BlackBoard).

Understanding the context of use

Mimi Recker (Recker, Dorward and Nelson, 2004; Recker, 2006) participated in the NSDL projects and made a number of contributions to understanding how teachers find, access and use educational digital libraries and other learning resources, as did Mardis (2009) several years later. Writing of the early NSDL projects, Recker and colleagues noted 'missing . . . is a deep characterization and understanding of learning environments, and how digital learning resources may fit into such contexts' (2004, 94). Recker and her colleagues at Utah State University studied the needs and behaviors of teachers. What they learned echoes Iriberri and Leroy's findings on what makes online communities successful. Manduca and others (2005; 2006) wrote two key articles based on their experiences with another NSDL project, the Starting Point Digital Library, which is now part of the Science Education Resource Center at Carleton College (http://serc.carleton.edu). These articles are well worth consulting, as they document the breakthroughs in the team's understanding of how to build successful digital libraries in social environments.

The insights gained into the practices, behaviors and preferences of their audiences led NSDL researchers and implementers to extend their efforts beyond collections to fully support online communities of educators. Manduca and her team noted 'a successful digital library is as much a social process as a technical problem [that] . . . requires creation of a culture that fosters contribution to and use of the library' (2006, under 'Created by Partners'). As a result she and her team turned away from a traditional digital library interface, where the main service is distributed search across heterogeneous content. Instead they successfully introduced a social environment reflecting educator needs and the way that educators approach the site (from a variety of points on the network). Their digital library provides not just content, but a robust source of educator expertise. The new approach has been effective: as of the time of this writing, the Science Education Resource Center gets between 60,000 and 100,000 unique visitors per month (figures cover US only).

Moving targets

The NSDL was an ambitious national-level initiative with generous funding that spawned many projects, from which digital library researchers and practitioners learned a great deal about digital libraries and their communities. The massive disruption created over the last decade in the teaching and learning community by the rise of distance education, virtual learning environments (VLEs: web-based learning environments and systems that provide virtual access to classes, tests and other educational resources and enable interaction between teachers and students), and most recently, MOOCs (massive open online courses) has meant that digital library researchers and practitioners have been attempting to hit rapidly moving targets in the domain of web-based teaching and learning.

Digital Public Library of America (DPLA)

The Digital Public Library of America (DPLA) is a new initiative at the time of this writing. It launched in April 2013. The DPLA has a grand vision: to build 'a large-scale digital public library that will make the cultural and scientific record available to all' (Peek, 2012). As the DPLA rolls out over the next few years, it will be interesting to observe if its builders will take advantage of what the NSDL project teams learned about building active communities around digital libraries. The forecast is favorable: at the time of this writing, Dan

Cohen, a history professor, director of the Center for History and New Media (CHNM), and a leading digital humanities scholar, has just been appointed founding executive director of the DPLA (Cohen, 2013; Enis, 2013).

Creation: user-centered design, ease of use and reliability

Interviewees noted the importance to digital library success of ease of use, reliability and user-centered design (a philosophy and process for designing interactive systems in which the needs and practices of end-users receive extensive attention; sometimes called *human-centered design*). They pointed to failed projects plagued by technical problems; projects that took too long; and early digital libraries that were built in unhelpful or dead-end ways, requiring significant investment in upgrades – investment funds that are often not found, and so the digital library languishes and eventually fades away.

Usability and usefulness

From a life-cycle perspective, technological components take center stage during digital library creation, but they remain critical success factors throughout the growth and maturity stages of community-centered digital libraries. Iriberri and Leroy note that different technological features take priority depending on the online community's evolutionary stage: 'each stage requires different tools, features, mechanisms, technologies, and management activities. Developers have to identify the needs in each stage and add the right technology components' (Iriberri and Leroy, 2009, 15).

Studies of success factors in the digital library literature often examine ease of use, interface design and access issues. Buchanan and Salako (2009) point out that most digital library studies investigate usability. Jakob Nielsen, an expert in web interface design, defines 'usability' as 'a *quality attribute* that assesses how easy user interfaces are to use' (www.nngroup.com/articles/usability-101-introduction-to-usability). He points out that interfaces can be usable without being useful, and the best interface will not make up for the absence of features supporting what the user wants to accomplish. Buchanan and Salako cast their net beyond usability; they compile an integrated measurement framework based on an extensive review of the relevant literature on the topics of usability *and* usefulness. Table 7.2 summarizes these two key components in Buchanan and Salako's measurement framework. The table and text in their article contains considerably more detail, including definitions of each attribute.

Table 7.2 Key technological success factors	
Success factor	Attributes
Usability	Effectiveness, efficiency, aesthetic appearance, terminology, navigation, and learnability
Usefulness	Relevance, reliability, and currency

Community partnerships

As for user-centered design of digital libraries, Christine Borgman (2009, 46) crystallizes her two decades of experience with digital library and cyberinfrastructure research quite powerfully when she says 'community partnerships in design are essential'. While the application of user-centered design techniques in digital libraries dates back to the mid-1990s (Van House et al., 1996), experience suggests there were many projects in which the builders built, but the communities did not come. It is difficult to quantify how many, since the literature tends to be a poor source for learning about projects that failed.

Lage. Losoff and Maness (2011) report on their careful work to identify researchers on their campus who are receptive toward library involvement in data curation (the management and preservation of digital data over the long term). Their intent is to understand researcher work practices and preferences at the design (inception) stage, so that effective partnerships between the library and scientists can be strategically developed. Somerville and Brar (2009) provide a thorough analysis of involving students in the digital library inception and creation stages. They describe a user-centered design process that recalled interviewees' comments about digital libraries' needing to 'solve problems that users want solved' (rather than problems that builders think need to be solved).

Defining audiences

Chern Li Liew, in an article evaluating the people and organizational aspects of a decade of digital library literature, noted that user-centeredness and user needs assessment appear among the topics being dealt with more frequently in digital library research since 2005 (Liew, 2009, 253–4). Unfortunately, this trend appears to be weaker in ARL library special collections and digitization work: a key finding of an ITHAKA study published at the time of this writing was that 'investments in understanding the needs of the audience [for a digitized collection] are quite low' (Maron and Pickle, 2013, 2).

System performance and reliability

System stability, reliability, adequate performance, an effective access rights structure and (depending on the type of digital library), technical components supporting security and privacy are also essential success factors. In addition, across the various stages of a digital library's life, a number of other technical tools may become essential, such as machine-to-machine services, or (depending on the digital library) tools supporting user interaction or pers-onalization, recommending, commenting, user contribution, facilitation/moderation or volunteerism.

Growth: quality content

Interviewees pointed out that what seems to drive success is the distinctiveness of the digital library's content for a particular community; the digital library is perceived by its users as a hub for a certain type of content that is essential to their shared interests. What seems to matter is the presence of a critical mass of content for the target audience(s). A glance through the descriptions of the digital libraries in Table 2.1 reveals that the size of a digital library collection may not by itself be a primary factor for success: some are relatively large (e.g., Trove and the Internet Archive of websites) and some relatively small (e.g., the International Children's Digital Library and Project Gutenberg). Iriberri and Leroy's success factors for online communities include high-quality, up-to-date and legitimized content as critical during the growth stage; they also point to lack of quality content and infrequent contributions as symptoms of a dying community (Iriberri and Leroy, 2009, 11:21–11:25).

Maturity: funding and sustainability

With the brevity bred of long experience, William Arms remarked, 'financial sustainability is the Achilles heel of digital libraries' (Arms, Calimlim and Walle, 2009). It is perhaps not surprising, then, that the digital library experts interviewed for this chapter most frequently pointed to the lack of sustainable funding as the reason for digital library failure. They pointed to another reason, associated with the lack of ongoing funding: a lack of clarity around who has ongoing responsibility for a digital library.

Initial funding

Government, international agency, foundation, private sector, institutional, and individual funding sources all played a part in getting digital libraries started. In many cases, the funding was temporary (see, for example, Griffin, 2005). Many early projects were funded principally for research and prototype building – there was little or no intention to support large-scale implementations and ongoing services. Bill Arms and his co-authors, continuing their comments on the difficulties of financial sustainability for digital libraries, note 'while it is comparatively easy to raise money for innovation, few organizations have long-term funding to maintain expensive collections and services' (2009, under 'Lesson Two').

Challenges of ongoing funding

A digital library initiative can be successful in every other way, but still have difficulties with financial sustainability. The following cases illustrate this conundrum:

- Ricky Erway's white paper (2008) on the fate of the RLG Cultural Materials Alliance, which was discontinued, is an interesting case study of a digital library project's attempt to become financially self-sustaining in the real world of supply and demand on the web.
- DSpace has had a tremendous impact supporting open access repositories. MIT's final report to the Mellon Foundation, which with Hewlett Packard (HP) financed the initial development of DSpace (Barton and Harford Walker, 2002), provides a case study. The report illustrates the challenges of moving from start-up grant support to reliance on a *business model* that will continually cover the initiative's operating costs and also fund future development.
- If arXiv.org were assessed with this chapter's success factors, it would be deemed a thriving enterprise by nearly all measures (see Oya Rieger, 2011, under 'arXiv Sustainability Initiative'). The exception to its success is ongoing funding, which has been an issue for some years. 'Who is responsible for the arXiv?' became an increasingly pressing question for Cornell University Library, which has supported the arXiv since the end of federal grant funding in 2001. In 2010, Cornell invited pledges to an interim voluntary contribution model. Further planning (Rieger, 2012) led to the development of a new membership model, slated for launch in 2013.

Succeeding at sustainability

Maron, Smith and Loy (2009, 2–3), reporting on a set of ITHAKA case studies, list the following factors that contribute to digital library sustainability:

- dedicated and entrepreneurial leadership
- a clear value proposition
- minimizing direct costs (costs directly associated with providing the digital library as a service; an example would be labor costs)
- developing diverse sources of revenue
- clear accountability and metrics for financial and mission-related success.

The ITHAKA case studies can help digital library builders and managers understand the factors associated with various models for sustainability. The digital collections discussed in the 12 case studies represent work done in the UK, US, Germany, France and Egypt. The analysis uncovered a number of strategies for achieving sustainability, both financial and non-financial; Table 7.3 lists these.

The strategies laid out in Table 7.3 are further enriched by an article by Alma Swan, which includes a list of five operational models for sustaining

Table 7.3 Strategies for sustainability
Adapted from Maron, Smith and Loy, 2009

Strategy	Examples
Revenue generation	• Memberships and subscriptions • Content licensing • Advertising • Scholarships • Endowment income • Grants • Sponsorship • Government subsidies • Open access / author pays or subsidies • Premium services (combined with freely available ones) • Hybrids of one or more of these strategies
Non-financial support	• Volunteer labor • Partnerships (including public/private) • Support from host institution • Other in-kind contributions, e.g., free rent, technical support, server space, contributed staff time, non-billed overhead costs
Controlling and reducing costs	• Outsourcing • Sharing responsibility for some functions

digital repositories: institutional, public, community, subscription and commercial (Swan, 2008, Figure 2). Ricky Erway's profiles of seven highly successful subject-based repositories (2012, 16) provide another lens on how these types of digital libraries are financially sustained.

The findings of the 2009 ITHAKA study centered on the following points:

- Digital library builders and managers are using a mix of funding strategies; no consensus has emerged around best practices for funding.
- Virtually no initiatives earn enough revenue to survive without supplemental sources of funding.
- In-kind contributions from host institutions are extremely important, and these are rarely quantified, leading to 'fuzzy' accounting practices and an unclear picture of direct costs.
- Controlling and reducing costs are as important as identifying diverse sources of revenue.
- Open access to content can pose challenges to generating funds for cost recovery.

Public–private partnerships

With respect to the last bullet point above, Savenije and Beunen (2012) discuss public–private partnerships in the context of the tension between providing open access to content and achieving financial solvency. Such partnerships are a possibility, for example, when cultural heritage organizations are unable to raise the necessary funds for digitization. Savenije, however, points out the difficulties of insisting on open access to public domain content that was digitized by a private sector partner, who then has few options for recouping the investment it has made in scanning. Embargo periods, followed by open access to the content, have provided one way of dealing with this difficulty.

Business planning

In a paper prepared for the 2009 Nobel Symposium in Stockholm, Kevin Guthrie, president of ITHAKA, offered some additional insights into the results of the ITHAKA case studies (2011, 119–23):

- The ability to fund future development for maintaining value to users is unclear.

- A number of teams lacked business expertise and entrepreneurial skills or were heavily dependent on one or two individuals for these skills.

Mel Collier, Leuven University's chief librarian, has written and compiled a number of articles and case studies on business models and planning for sustaining digital libraries. In his overview essay, Collier lists the following planning questions for digital library builders and managers to explore (2010, 15):

- What benefits will the digital library generate for its intended audience(s)?
- What is the *unique selling point* (the particular qualities that differentiate the digital library from alternatives)?
- What is the target audience or audiences and what is its size?
- What are the enabling technologies?
- What are the risks?
- Who will fund the initiative now and over time, and how?

Collier introduces the elements of a business model (how a product, service or organization will generate income and/or cover costs). These include a statement of aims, vision and mission; what services are offered (or needs addressed); profile(s) of the target audience(s); nature of the enterprise (profit or non-profit, public or private, self-sustaining, combination); and nature and sources of income.

Business plans are not the same as business models: plans contain a different set of elements, although some elements overlap with those of business models. The particular set of elements vary from source to source (a 'how-to' book for business planning in libraries is Harriman, 2008, which includes sections describing the component parts of a business plan, 25 sample plans and a number of worksheets). Examples of digital library business plans can be hard to get (as they are often confidential); Collier's compilation (2010) includes numerous essays on the business planning aspects of digital libraries by sector (cultural heritage and higher education) and by type of content (e-journals, e-books, e-archives, web sites, repositories, etc.), as well as seven case studies.

Uncertainty and resourcefulness
Digital library builders and managers are often part of parent institutions that

are already funding a traditional set of services, and digital library costs make new demands on an already stretched budget. It is not uncommon for an ongoing digital library program to be running on various sources of external funds or with funds scraped together from otherwise uncommitted institutional funds of one kind or another. In other words, digital library programs have often been funded at the margins of the organization's budget (see also the 2013 ITHAKA study by Maron and Pickle). This is why digital library managers tend to learn how to be resourceful, from preparing grant proposals to being creative and entrepreneurial about funding strategies. It is also why digital library programs are increasingly creating pressure to restructure and reallocate budgets tied up in the provision of traditional library services – there is just not enough money to cover both the traditional services and the new initiatives. This pushes the search for sustainability in a number of new directions.

We don't know yet

The context in which digital library builders and managers are attempting to find successful models for sustainability is extremely challenging. Mike Lesk concluded a detailed examination of how to pay for digital libraries with the words 'we don't know yet' (2004, 50). While a great deal has changed since Lesk completed his analysis in 2004, the digital library field's knowledge of how to build digital libraries continues to outpace its understanding of how to sustain them.

Conclusion

Online communities have life cycles from inception through creation, growth and maturity. The life-cycle model can be used to examine what is likely to attract, grow and maintain a community around a digital library. It can also be used as a framework for providing insight into why some digital libraries are long-lived, while others fade into memory.

Successful digital libraries appear to have found the right mix of community engagement, quality collections, and technologies/methods supporting user-centered design, ease of use and reliable performance. A strong orientation to understanding the needs, goals and behaviors of the communities to be served appears to be a key success factor. The life-cycle model suggests that at maturity, successful digital libraries are trusted sites that engage a number of participating subgroups (contributors and consumers of content, individuals interacting with each other, volunteers and partners playing various roles, etc.). Securing sustainable funding continues to be a difficult challenge for many digital libraries.

The next chapter applies the life-cycle framework presented in this chapter to examine the prospects of open access repositories.

CHAPTER 8

The prospects of open access repositories

Overview

This chapter focuses on the potential of open access repositories for having a distinctive positive impact on scholarship and, more broadly, on their prospects for increasing the social and economic value of digital libraries. In addition to extending Chapter 4's discussion of open access repositories into new territory, it relates the frameworks presented in Chapters 6 and 7 to this particular type of digital library. Topics include subject-based and institutional repositories and their value; issues around recruiting repository content, including deposit mandates; legal frameworks, copyright and open access; discipline-specific norms, practices and reward systems; the discoverability of scholarly content; the sustainability of repositories; e-research data management; and prospects for the emergence of a global ecosystem of repositories.

Successful subject-based repositories

The most successful subject-based repositories have grown organically around the scholarly communities they serve (see the examples in Chapters 2, 4, 6 and 7), and they are woven into the way their disciplines communicate. As Erway (2012) notes in her review of several thriving subject repositories, 'the central repository for a researcher's field of study is where he goes for information, to see what's been published, and to look for collaborators. It's only natural that he would think of the same location when it comes time for him to deposit his work.' Due to their firm foundations within communities of research and practice, the successful subject repositories have tended to attract more submissions than institutional repositories.

Adamick and Resnik-Zellen wrote two articles about subject repositories (2010a; 2010b). The second article profiles ten selected subject repositories across nine metrics: year founded, subjects covered, software, content types, deposit policies, copyright policies, hosting, funding and governance. Overlaying Iriberri and Leroy's 2009 life-cycle model of online communities (Figure 7.1) on the profiles of these successful subject repositories, it is clear that the repositories have evolved through the life cycle, from a strong community orientation at inception to a high degree of trust and participation at maturity. As a result, while Google is an important referrer of searches to subject repositories, the most successful repositories can be said to be destination sites (sites that people visit by going directly to their URLs through typing or bookmarks). As discussed later, this has implications for repository interface design and development.

The value of institutional repositories

Several of the digital library experts interviewed for this book noted that some institutional repositories have been built without an understanding of research, teaching and learning practices. As a result, the articulated benefits of these repositories align and resonate poorly with the needs of contributors and the hosting institution. Along these lines Sefton and Dickinson (2011) note 'there is more work to be done to align the library-centric view of institutional repositories with their uses in other academic contexts.' These 'contexts' comprise the total package of value delivered to parent institutions, faculty and repository end-users.

The following analysis of the digital library literature supports interviewees' reservations about institutional repositories. Among the major barriers to the success of institutional repositories are:

- a lack of clarity around purpose and focus
- weak understandings of community needs and attitudes
- scholars' lack of awareness of the repository or its benefits
- recruiting content.

Iriberri and Leroy's analysis (see Chapter 7) indicates that if a network-based service's intended communities do not actively engage and participate, the service will die. The aims of this section are to offer ideas for making institutional repositories more successful by: (1) enumerating some priorities for aligning repositories around the communities to be served; and (2) better articulating the value of repositories.

Purpose, focus and community needs

Getting attention for an institutional repository is challenging, and understanding what the repository's stakeholders and target audiences want and need is even more difficult. Oya Rieger (2007), a digital library expert who provides oversight for a number of repositories, recommends gathering stakeholders and conducting a repository needs assessment to understand the organizational environment and existing workflows, identify common ground and use cases, and generate stakeholder awareness. Rieger is writing of the process of selecting a repository for an institution, but her advice around conducting a needs assessment is equally applicable when the repository is already in place and course corrections are needed. Unfortunately, in a census of institutional repositories, Markey et al. (2007, 31) found that systematic needs assessment has not been a significant factor in libraries' decisions to start or maintain institutional repositories.

Awareness and recognition

Raising awareness, recognition and branding of institutional repositories are priorities. The low level of faculty awareness of repositories has been reported for some time (for example Swan and Brown, 2004, 220; Rowlands and Nicholas, 2005; Watson, 2007; Morris and Thorn, 2009), so Gale Moore's 2011 report of low faculty awareness at the University of Toronto is not a surprise. In the Moore survey, less than half (43%) of faculty respondents were aware of the university's institutional repository, which had been in place for seven years at the time of the survey. Of those who had heard of it, only 15% had deposited work there. Further, over three-fourths of respondents were unaware of the university's open journal and book publishing services, and two-thirds were unaware of services related to hosting media and archiving data sets.

The problem of recruiting content

Institutional repository managers can be hard pressed to articulate the value to faculty and researchers persuasively enough to motivate the contribution of content. Consider one interviewee's remarks following a set of conversations recently conducted with faculty members:

> Faculty members think a repository and open access are good ideas and the right things to do. However, asked if they would deposit their work in the repository, they said no, they would not want to do this work.

Faculty perceptions

The digital library literature suggests that faculty and researchers are not only unwilling to do the work of depositing content in institutional repositories – many do not see sufficient reason to do so. One of the digital library experts interviewed for this chapter, who had recently been talking with faculty about institutional repositories, noted faculty members' prevalent belief (probably false) that the articles they write are already being found by all of those who are interested in them. Troll Covey's research (2011, 8) also indicates that some faculty may not believe that visibility and access to their work are problems, and thus there is little need to invest time in self-archiving. Looking at faculty attitudes from the perspective of scholars as readers (instead of as writers), Swan and Brown's results suggest nearly two-thirds of faculty believe they have easy access to most or all of the articles they need for their work (2005, 13). They found some variability in these results, with humanities scholars reporting somewhat more difficulty accessing what they need. Even when faculty and researchers do make open access copies of their published content available, a study by Kim (2010, 1914) found a preference for linking to open access copies from their personal web pages (66.7% of respondents), followed by research group and departmental websites, then subject and institutional repositories.

Value propositions

Another interviewee remarked 'libraries have not put forward adequate value propositions for the repositories they host.' Numerous studies, starting with one at the University of Rochester River Campus Libraries (Foster and Gibbons, 2005), have linked the problems with recruiting faculty content to the way that librarians talk with faculty about repositories. Issues with content recruitment have continued: six years after the Foster and Gibbons study, Wacha and Wisner (2011) studied 45 institutional repositories and found that only three contained the highest impact articles of faculty at their institutions. Chapter 4 presents the extensive evidence for low deposit rates in institutional repositories; the literature review of Lercher (2008) is also a good source of evidence for low deposit rates. The issue is what institutional repository builders and managers can do about it.

What follow are some solutions based on better articulating the value of institutional repositories for faculty and researchers. Conducting needs assessments – and then acting on what is learned – has already been mentioned. Formulating a crisp value proposition for faculty is also important. Two reports, noteworthy for their community-centered approaches, are particularly good sources of ideas. The report from the University of Toronto has already been mentioned (Moore, 2011, 130–1). The other is a Mellon-funded pilot study from Palmer, Teffeau and Newton (2008), which featured interviews with faculty, library liaisons and repository managers. While Moore's report looks into faculty attitudes and practices, Palmer's report focuses on what problems that institutional repositories might solve for faculty. Table 8.1 synthesizes the findings of the two reports into a potential value proposition for faculty.

Table 8.1 The value of institutional repositories to stakeholders and target audiences

Stakeholder or target audience	Value for this stakeholder or audience
Stakeholder: Hosting library	• Removing barriers and fostering open access to scholarship • Raising the profile of the library's curatorial and facilitation roles in scholarly communication processes • Raising the profile of the library's role in showcasing research at its parent institution • Demonstrating how the library contributes to advancing the institutional mission and goals
Stakeholder: Parent institution	• Showcasing the institution's intellectual output and raising prestige • Providing a source of metrics for institution-level scholarly outputs • Helping the institution to demonstrate its value to its communities and funders • Providing the means to publish and provide discovery and access for other types of intellectual and cultural assets produced at the institution (e.g., teaching materials, student honors work, working papers, presentations, conference proceedings, etc.)
Audience: The institution's end-users	• Finding out what research is being conducted locally • Collecting information related to institution-based dissertation topics and honors theses • Networking – finding people in different departments or potential collaborators • Getting to unpublished content not available elsewhere (data, video clips, learning materials, content related to events, etc.) • Finding institutionally relevant primary source documents for use in teaching and writing • Promoting research done within the institution to institutional colleagues
Audience: The institution's faculty and researchers	• Increasing exposure of an individual scholar's forthcoming and already published work (pre-prints and post-prints) • Providing exposure for a scholar's unpublished work (like working papers) • Solving specific information visibility, management or access problems (these vary by discipline) • Supporting specific faculty workflows for managing and disseminating digital content • Co-ordinating work with existing and emerging subject-based or funder repositories • Offering publishing services for a spectrum of the institution's intellectual output • Attracting audiences for content that is not easily discovered in the corpus of scholarship • Broadening dissemination of academic research to the public • Contributing to the open access movement
Stakeholder: Government agencies	• Supporting national research assessments • Demonstrating the societal benefits of publicly funded research • Supporting knowledge transfer and economic growth

Another source of ideas for securing commitment, recruiting content, and generally improving institutional repositories for a variety of audiences is Bell and Sarr (2010), who report how the University of Rochester's institutional repository was re-engineered. They added support for research and writing workflows, collaboration with peers, usage statistics and author profiles. In addition, the many reports and articles produced by the IMLS-funded MIRACLE project (Making Institutional Repositories A Collaborative Learning Environment: www.miracle.si.umich.edu) can guide repository managers' planning.

Articulating the value

Table 8.1 collects content from a number of sources that have reported evidence-based results suggesting the value of institutional repositories to different stakeholders and target audiences. Subsequent subsections discuss these sources. In particular, Alma Swan (2008) provides an in-depth, detailed analysis that articulates the value of digital repositories. She also defines a typology of business cases for them. In more recent work, Swan (2011) identifies the benefits of repositories to various audiences, including their value supporting national research assessments by providing a record of institutional research outputs.

Hosting libraries

Many institutional repository managers can articulate the value of repositories to their own libraries. Among other writers, Bankier and Smith (2010) and Markey et al. (2009) observe the benefits to hosting libraries; Table 8.1 lists these.

Addressing the serials crisis

An additional hoped-for benefit of institutional repositories for libraries has been to lower the costs of access to highly priced scholarly journals (in other words, to address what is called the 'serials crisis'). An early hope was that a robust system of open repositories would address spiraling journal costs in addition to delivering other benefits. Over the past ten years, that hope has been tested, and it remains unclear whether open access models (that is, open access journals and repositories) will reduce the costs of access to the scholarly literature (see Waaijers, 2008). Burns and others' consideration of the evidence suggests 'it is much too early to tell what kind of overall financial savings, if any, these entities [institutional repositories] have created' (Burns, Lana and Budd, 2013).

Parent institutions

Table 8.1's articulation of the benefits of an institutional repository to a library's parent institutions is drawn from Bankier and Smith's (2010) analysis.

The institution's end-users

As part of their work with the MIRACLE project, St Jean et al. (2011) examined the value of institutional repositories to end-users. There are at least three ways to approach a consideration of the value of institutional repositories to end-users. Chapter 4 of this book covers the high visibility and use of repository content by end-users around the world as a result of indexing by Google and Google Scholar. Chapter 6 covers the potential value of repositories to end-users as members of society. In contrast to these two perspectives on end-users, St Jean and her colleagues studied end-users who were deliberately using the institutional repository as a *local* resource and destination site. As they point out, not much research has been conducted on this particular end-user perspective. Their results suggest another avenue for aligning an institutionally based repository to benefit an institutionally based community. Table 8.1 lists the value of the institutional repository for this category of end-users, based on their end-user interviews.

The *personas* research of Maness, Miaskiewicz and Sumner (2008) at the University of Colorado at Boulder should also be mentioned in the context of the institutional repository's value for end-users. Personas are concrete but fictitious representations of a group of target users with common characteristics. A principal finding contradicted prior assumptions about target audiences' goals: the authors had expected a desire for a place to deposit pre- or post-prints of published work. Instead, their personas wanted the repository to be a place to share teaching and learning materials, identify potential collaborators, and promote their research to institutional colleagues. Maness and his colleagues' findings reinforce the results of St Jean and suggest a value proposition specifically targeted to the institutionally based, local community.

The institution's faculty

As already noted, the list in Table 8.1 is drawn from my analysis of studies by Moore (2011) and Palmer, Teffeau and Newton (2008), in addition to recent work by Swan (2011). With respect to the qualification of stressing open access in the value proposition to some but not all faculty and researchers, Palmer's study (26) found that while many faculty support open access, some have concerns (e.g., loss of control, timing, versioning, quality). In general the study found that gaining faculty engagement was more about explaining how the repository solves particular problems that faculty or researchers encounter in their daily work (22).

Government agencies

Increasingly, governments and international funding bodies are taking a keen interest in tracking and understanding the real-world societal benefits being produced by publicly funded research. Examples include the European Commission, the UK's Funding Councils and Research Councils UK; a following section discusses these.

The policy and legal frameworks
Open access and self-archiving
The open access movement

The open access movement has its roots in the first decade of digital library research and practice (see Chapter 2). As noted in Chapter 2, participants in the open access movement advocate making scholarly information publicly available in a way that is 'digital, online, free of charge, and free of most copyright and licensing restrictions' (Suber, 2004). Formal open access declarations that were made at meetings in Budapest (www.budapest openaccessinitiative.org), Bethesda (Suber, 2003) and Berlin (Max Planck Society, 2003) form the backbone of the movement's principles and objectives. Denicola (2006, 353–4) provides a brief summary of the beginnings of the open access movement.

Recent developments in Europe

As discussed later in this chapter's section on deposit mandates, the US National Institutes of Health (NIH), and many universities and funding agencies worldwide have issued policy statements requiring that papers produced with public funding be made openly available to the public. More generally, the UK's Finch Report (Finch and Jubb, 2012) and the endorsement of its recommendations by the UK government, UK Funding Councils and Research Councils UK and Research Excellence Framework will have the effect of placing great emphasis on open access to UK scholarly publications, especially after 2014 (Research Information Network, 2013). The European Commission's communication of new policies for open access to publications and research data (2012b), with its target for establishing open access policies in all member states by 2014, has further magnified the fresh momentum for open access to research that has been created around the world by the Finch Report. As this book was being completed, the US Open Government Initiative to make federal government information more open and accessible was gaining momentum.

Green and Gold open access

With respect to the processes of scholarly communication, the open access movement has evolved in two directions: 'Gold' and 'Green' open access. The literature that discusses open access is large, spirited and sometimes divisive, so much so that in October 2012 IFLA and the International Publishers Association issued a joint statement calling for a more nuanced, empirically based debate (www.ifla.org/publications/enhancing-the-debate-on-open-access).

Two articles, one by Stevan Harnad et al. (2004) and one by Jean-Claude Guédon (2008), provide frequently cited perspectives on Green and Gold open access. A more recent look at this ongoing debate is from Shieber (2009) and Gargouri et al. (2012). A report from the European Commission discussing new open access policies (2012b, 5, 7) provides definitions of the Green and Gold methods.

In brief, Gold open access is associated with publishing open access journals. Green open access is associated with self-archiving, which involves authors' depositing copies of their content on their own or group websites or in open access repositories, often after an embargo period (a delay before full text is openly available to all audiences). Self-archiving sits alongside the traditions of scholarly publishing. It is not a replacement for what publishers do. Because of its ties to the subject of this chapter – open access repositories – Green open access and self-archiving are the focus in this book (not Gold).

Copyright and repositories
Scholars' copyright concerns

In 2002, 90% of scholarly journal publishers required that authors transfer copyright to the publisher, according to a survey of 80 UK and US journal publishers (Gadd, Oppenheim and Probets, 2003). Since then the percentage of publishers requiring copyright transfer has been declining (Cox and Cox, 2008), and an increasing number of publishers now allow some form of self-archiving by authors. Nevertheless, many scholars continue to transfer the copyright in their content to publishers (or to believe that they have). It is not surprising then that scholars who are considering depositing their work in an open access repository are concerned about violating publisher copyright agreements (Swan and Brown, 2005; Watson, 2007).

Other studies suggest that scholars are concerned, confused or indifferent to copyright issues. Kim's (2010) and Troll Covey's (2011) results suggest that copyright concerns are significant barriers to faculty willingness to self-archive. Morris' (2009) and Moore's (2011) surveys found that many faculty members do not understand publisher contracts and copyright terms, and few have a clear picture of what rights they retain or could retain. In addition the Morris study found that authors overestimate their self-archiving rights for published PDFs and underestimate what publishers allow them to do with pre-prints and post-prints. Finally, it is possible that some scholars simply do not care much about copyright. Nine years ago, Rowlands, Nicholas and Huntington (2004, 265) found that 46% of surveyed authors 'took no interest at all' in copyright matters. These and other attitudes translate to major deterrents to self-archiving and thus to depositing content in open access repositories.

Copyright, authors' rights and self-archiving

Copyright law varies from country to country and is extremely complex. In brief, and acknowledging the possibility of variations in different university settings, academics who write scholarly articles are generally viewed as copyright holders, and they can frequently choose the terms under which articles are distributed or re-used (although scholarly tradition plays a role in what choices are truly actionable). Traditionally, in university settings, the author of a scholarly article has transferred his or her copyright to a publisher in exchange for what the publisher adds to the process: managing the peer review process, producing and disseminating the journals in which articles are published, and so on. Academic authors of scholarly articles in university settings still frequently sign copyright agreements that transfer their copyright to the publisher, but as of this writing it is not unusual for scholars to negotiate these agreements to either retain some rights or retain copyright but license some rights to the publisher. One possibility is for the author to grant the publisher the right to publish the article, but keep the right to make the article openly available under specific conditions, for example in an open access repository. Sometimes these agreements are subject to embargo periods.

In a survey of scholarly authors conducted in 2004, Swan and Brown (2005, 56–7) asked who held the copyright to the last article the author self-archived. Their results were that 35% of authors claimed to hold copyright themselves, 37% assigned copyright to the publisher, 22% didn't know who held the copyright, and 6% assigned copyright to some other party (e.g., employers). Asked if they were required to ask the publisher's permission to self-archive, 47% said no, 17% said yes, and 36% did not know. Asked if they did ask the publisher's permission to self-archive, 84% said no. In a 2008 study of thousands of self-archived articles on faculty web pages, Troll Covey (2009, 240) found that '38 percent are not aligned with [publisher] policy in terms of whether self-archiving on personal and departmental Web sites is allowed and whether publisher policy allows, prohibits, or requires self-archiving the publisher PDF. '

Sherpa RoMEO and copyright clearance

A number of organizations that advocate open access provide information for scholars who want to retain self-archiving and other rights (see for example the SPARC Author Rights Addendum, www.arl.org/sparc/author/addendum.shtm, and the Science Commons Scholar's Copyright Addendum, http://scholars.sciencecommons.org). Sherpa RoMEO (www.sherpa.ac.uk/romeo), based at the University of Nottingham in the UK, is a service that maintains a searchable directory of publishers' copyright conditions for self-archiving. The service tracks 'green' publishers and journals and other information needed by authors who wish to self-archive. Sherpa RoMEO has been a highly beneficial service to open access repository managers who help authors to deposit their work. Hanlon and Ramirez (2011) describe how repository managers use Sherpa RoMEO and other tools to support their copyright clearance activities. Unfortunately, faculty awareness of Sherpa RoMEO may be low, as reported in the results of the Troll Covey (2011) focus groups: not one of the hundred focus group participants had heard of Sherpa RoMEO.

Deposit mandates
Current situation

Policies requiring that researchers make their papers available via open access in a particular repository or repositories are known as 'deposit mandates.' Specific deposit mandate policy terms can vary, and there are a number of kinds of deposit mandates, with the main ones being those of funding agencies, institutions or groups of institutions, and university departments or other sub-units. An important practical influence on the current situation came in 2008, first when the US National Institutes of Health (NIH) announced a new public policy requiring that papers from NIH-funded projects be submitted to PubMed Central and made publicly available within 12 months of publication (http://publicaccess.nih.gov). That same year, the European Research Council announced it would require papers and monographs supported by Research Council funding to be made publicly available no later than six months after publication (for the latest version of the policy see http://erc.europa.eu/documents/open-access-policy-researchers-funded-erc). NIH and the European Research Council were not the first funding agencies to adopt such policies; for example, the deposit mandate of the Wellcome Trust in the UK had a major impact when it was implemented in October 2005 (see the timelines in the Open Access Directory, http://oad.simmons.edu/oadwiki/ Timeline). A number of other funding agencies and scholarly institutions followed suit. At the time of this writing, over 250 organizations worldwide have registered deposit mandates in ROARMAP (http://roarmap.eprints.org), which maintains a searchable list of these.

Peter Suber (2009), a leading open access advocate in the US, quickly placed the NIH and European Research Council's announcements in the context of other open access deposit mandates around the world. He also wrote of the mandates adopted in 2008 by Harvard University's Faculty of Arts and Sciences and the Harvard Law School. Both attracted a good deal of attention when faculty members voted unanimously to implement open access deposit mandates. Harvard was not the first university in the world to adopt mandates; 11 other universities already had deposit mandates at department or university-wide levels, with Queensland University of Technology taking the lead with its university-level mandate in September 2003 (see http://oad. simmons.edu/oadwiki/Timeline).

History of deposit mandates

Open access evangelist Stevan Harnad has vigorously argued the merits of open access deposit mandates. Stephen Pinfield (2005), another early advocate for deposit mandates, supports them on the grounds that they will accelerate the widespread adoption of open access, thereby improving the process of scholarly communication, increasing the impact of individual papers, and maximizing the free availability of large numbers of high quality scholarly content. In his study of seven Australian universities with institutional repositories, Arthur Sale (2006) found that mandatory deposit policies result in more self-archiving than voluntary deposit policies. In a later article, Sale (2007) recommended that repository managers pursue a 'patchwork' (department-level) mandate as a quicker route to growing institutional repository deposits.

Swan and Brown's report on author self-archiving is frequently cited for its finding that over four-fifths of authors would willingly comply with a deposit mandate (2005, 62–3). Carr et al. (2006) also urged institutions and funders to seriously consider mandating the practice of self-archiving. Thomas and McDonald's comparative analysis of voluntary- and mandatory-deposit repositories (2007) led them to suggest that deposit mandates might increase the number of papers deposited per author. More recently, a comparative study of two Australian universities by Mary Anne Kennan (2011) found that one of the universities' advocacy, education and support, combined with deposit mandates, did result in more repository deposits and deeper faculty engagement with the issues around open access publishing.

Mixed reviews of deposit mandates

There are other perspectives on deposit mandates, and whether a deposit mandate exists or not, self-archiving has been difficult to promote and manage. Compliance with the NIH and Wellcome Trust deposit mandates has developed slowly. Poynder (2012) reported that six years after putting its deposit mandate in effect, the Trust was achieving a 55% compliance rate, prompting the Trust to take new steps to enforce the mandate. Poynder's investigation suggested that the NIH mandate was getting better results, with a compliance rate of 75% after four years.

In an article formatted as a debate on the criticality of mandates to institutional repository success, with Harnad taking the affirmative and Nancy McGovern the negative (2009), McGovern pointed out issues with the expense and difficulty of promulgating and enforcing mandates. Arguing that incentives other than mandates (such as value-added services), peer pressure and evidence of positive outcomes might contribute more to institutional repository success, McGovern concluded 'mandates alone – or possibly at all – are not the determining factor in the success of institutional repositories.' The aggregated findings of a number of other studies support McGovern's conclusion:

- Kim's study (2010, 1916) of what motivates faculty to deposit their work in repositories suggests that the most powerful motivator is altruism: support for the spirit of open access to help others (that is, by implication, not mandates).
- Moore's results (2011, 4) confirm that faculty are generally in favor of the *principles* of open access, but her study also suggests that faculty understanding of open access *in practice* is limited, and strongly shaped by the norms of each discipline (again, by implication, not mandates).
- Results of a faculty survey and focus groups conducted by Creaser et al. (2010, 156) indicated mixed reactions to mandates and led to questions about their effectiveness for motivating faculty self-archiving.
- Palmer et al. (2008, 26–8) found faculty have mixed views about mandatory deposit in institutional repositories, with one faculty member noting 'there are lots of things that are mandated and don't happen on campus'.

Other incentives may help to drive self-archiving other than, or in addition to, mandates. Ferreira et al. (2008) discussed an original – and highly successful – approach that combined financial incentives for departments ('carrots') with the 'stick' of an institutional deposit mandate. Other authors point to incentives in the form of value-added services, better alignment with researcher workflows, help with copyright clearance, and more, as discussed in other sections of this chapter. Bankier and Smith (2010), while noting that some deposit mandates have been successful, also point out that such mandates continue to focus institutional repositories narrowly on pre- and post-prints, thereby ignoring opportunities for the repository to serve other purposes for other audiences. Table 8.1 lists these audiences and opportunities.

Other issues with self-archiving
Scholarly tradition and discipline-specific reward systems
In addition to copyright and other concerns, Kim's 2010 faculty survey also

identified the additional time and effort to deposit content as deterrents to faculty self-archiving. Others might add the traditions of academic reward systems to this list of barriers. In fact, faculty complaints about the additional time and effort required to self-archive in an institutional repository may to some degree be a presenting symptom of a deeper issue: faculty feel comfortable with their own disciplines' arrangements for disseminating new intellectual content and lack sufficient motivation to change.

In particular, when faculty members perceive a lack of discipline-based rewards (or worse, the possibility of risk) associated with depositing intellectual assets in the institutional repository, attempts to modify their behaviors and choices will be uphill battles. A variety of discipline-specific traditions and value systems exist, making this particular barrier even more complex to overcome, because the battle must be waged on multiple, discipline-specific fronts. While the processes of scholarly communications are changing, not all disciplines are changing at the same rate, and it is a mistake to underestimate the weight of discipline-specific norms, attitudes, fears or concerns. Moore's study found that faculty are willing to explore alternatives, but their choices of where and how to publish their work continue to be driven primarily by reputational factors such as peer review and journal readership/impact (2011, 4).

Oya Rieger's social constructivist analysis of institutional repositories is a highly recommended source for understanding how social and cultural factors can create a motivational gap between repository builders and faculty members:

> The library community has built a solution [institutional repositories] based on a perceived problem (scholarly communication crises); but because the academics do not perceive a problem that needs to be fixed, they are reluctant to adopt practices and policies imposed on them by others in the institution
>
> Rieger, 2008a, under section 2

Rieger concludes that most of the impediments to growing self-archived deposits in institutional repositories relate directly to the persistence of this gap. To make progress, institutional repository managers need to redouble their efforts to understand each discipline's value systems, research contexts and work practices. In this regard, library liaison outreach programs and work practice studies can guide repository developments and promotional programs.

Reducing time and effort
Mediated deposit

A comprehensive study suggests that two-thirds of self-archiving authors choose to do so using personal web pages, followed by research group or department web pages, then subject repositories, then institutional repositories (Kim, 2010, 1914). A number of studies indicate that in the US and UK a large percentage, if not the majority, of faculty deposits in institutional repositories are not truly *self*-archived but *mediated*, that is, undertaken by someone other than the creator of the work (Rieger, 2012; Hanlon and Ramirez, 2011; Armbruster, 2011; Darby et al., 2009). While mediated deposit may help to grow institutional repositories with content from faculty, taking on the task of mediating deposits is not without cost; offering a mediated deposit service has implications for institutional repository staffing. There is also the question of whether manually mediated deposit will successfully scale to a large number of deposits. In a study of time and costs associated with mediated deposit workflows in the Welsh Repository Network, Payne (2011) found a range between 12 and 15 minutes per deposit for workflows that did not include copyright clearance activities; her findings are roughly comparable to those of other studies she cites. For mediated deposit workflows that include copyright clearance activities, the time required per deposit would be greater, as described by Hanlon and Ramirez.

Automated deposit

Bulk deposits (large-scale uploads of repository content) and automated identification of objects for deposit are other techniques for reducing the time and effort needed to populate institutional repositories, for example as described by Shreeves (2009). Duranceau and Krieger's paper (2013) describes many implementations of automated deposit at different libraries, including some that use the new protocol SWORD (Simple Web-service Offering Repository Deposit). SWORD and SPI (Simple Publishing Interface) appear to be the way forward for making it easier to disseminate and re-use content and metadata in multiple systems and applications.

'Google has won'

A characteristic remark among the digital library experts who were interviewed for this book was something like 'Google has won the discovery game.' History and the evidence presented in this book support this perspective. Looking back, Sergey Brin and Larry Page founded Google in September 1998. It is highly unlikely that digital library pioneers at that time imagined how the Google search engine would transform where and how scholarly communities look for and get research-quality information.

The ITHAKA longitudinal study of faculty indicates that by 2009, 70% of faculty were often or occasionally using a common search engine to locate journal articles (Schonfeld and Housewright, 2010, Figure 5). A recent ITHAKA study of how academic historians go about their work found that their day-to-day research practices have been fundamentally changed by technology and the web, and that Google and Google Books have become singularly important to them:

> Interviewees use general Google searches to start the discovery process. For many of them, Google is the primary search tool in identifying archives that hold relevant materials . . . Google is recognized as a tool that has expanded the breadth of types of materials that an historian can access on a given topic, and introduce a researcher to collections that they were not aware of, even after years of working within a sub-field . . . Interviewees widely acknowledged Google Books . . . nearly all of them mentioned using it in some capacity.
>
> Rutner and Schonfeld, 2012, 18–19

SEO and ASEO

The librarians and archivists who began digitizing cultural heritage materials in the 1990s could not have predicted the eventual centrality of Google or Google Books to humanists' research practices. Similarly, the earliest repository managers would not have expected the majority of repository traffic to come from Google or Google Scholar, and they would likely have been surprised by Arlitsch and O'Brien's advice (2012) to optimize their metadata for academic search engine crawling (see the discussion in Chapter 4). Beel, Gipp and Wilde (2010, under section 2.1) describe ASEO (academic search engine optimization), which they define as 'the creation, publication, and modification of scholarly literature in a way that makes it easier for academic search engines to both crawl it and index it.' While Google Scholar is the undisputed leader among academic search engines at this time, Beel's article also identifies IEEE Explore, PubMed and SciPlore (www.sciplore.org) as academic search engines. Chapter 5 discusses the role of such sites as referrers to hybrid library collections.

Actively working with search engine optimization (SEO) techniques can be a controversial subject among librarians, as discussed by Onaifo and

Rasmussen (2013). At the same time, these authors found in their study of public library websites that SEO techniques do positively affect library website rankings and the degree to which they attract users. Arlitsch and O'Brien were able to significantly boost the findability and use of their institutional repository content through ASEO techniques. Chapter 10 returns to the discussion of SEO's role for digital libraries.

Web traffic analytics

If a key objective of repositories is to maximize access to research-quality content, repository managers need to not only collect data about the nature of their repository's online traffic, but also understand and emphasize SEO approaches to improving visibility and use. Finding time for this type of work can inform strategies for integrating repositories in real-world research, teaching and learning practices.

Destinations or content delivery sites?

While Google and Google Scholar are important referrers of searches to all repositories, the most successful repositories can be said to be destination sites as well (sites that people visit by going directly to their URLs through typing or bookmarks). At least with respect to discovery, the many remaining repositories function less as destination sites and more as content delivery mechanisms, responding to searches that originated elsewhere. The implications for repository interface design and development are discussed in a later section.

Making institutional repositories more valuable

This and other chapters have traced a variety of issues that can negatively affect the future prospects of institutional repositories. Table 8.2 brings together these barriers and offers possible service responses. While the table aggregates the points made across several chapters, it is important to understand that not all barriers and possible service responses apply to all audiences. Some service responses can be inappropriate in some contexts.

Understanding and identifying repository audiences

The starting point for using the table is to understand the specific needs of

Table 8.2 Barriers and possible service responses for institutional repositories

Barrier	Possible service response
Lack of clarity around repository's purpose and focus	• Conduct needs assessment(s) of audience(s) to be served • Involve intended audience(s) directly in setting mission/purpose and goals • Find champion(s) in audience(s) to be served • Validate assumptions about intended audience(s) needs, content, expectations • Agree upon shared mission
Lack of awareness	• Conduct needs assessment(s) of audience(s) to be served • Articulate audience-specific unique advantages (value propositions) • Communicate value through branding • Plan and carry out audience-specific communications programs • Build relationships: reach out directly to audience(s), e.g., through liaison librarians • Increase discoverability of content on the web
Lack of participation and engagement (low deposit rates)	• Conduct needs assessment(s) of audience(s) to be served • Articulate audience-specific unique advantages (value propositions) • Identify a problem an audience(s) wants solved, and solve it • Lower barriers to participation; easy to get started • Find partners in intended audience(s): undertake collaborations with them • Welcome new types of content • Engage audience(s) with content, e.g., crowdsourcing, social sharing • Provide incentives • Provide usage evidence and statistics • Offer mediated deposit (or deposit to multiple repositories) • Undertake automated deposit • Promote and support deposit mandates
Poor alignment with community work practices	• Study work practices; undertake user-centered design • Provide authoring support tools (virtual research environments; scholars' workbench concepts; version management; security/permissions) • Offer workspace for various types of content • Offer mediated and/or automated deposit alternatives
Complex legal framework	• Offer copyright advisory services and training • Provide information related to publishers and publication • Training
Traditions of scholarship	• Understand discipline-specific norms, peer review, reward systems, attitudes • Target efforts to those who are willing • Offer author information services • User-centered design: support disciplines' established workflows for depositing and credentialing new scholarly content; support collaboration with peers • Build relationships: reach out directly to audience(s), e.g., through liaison librarians
Discoverability	• Optimize discovery possibilities through ASEO and SEO best practices • Establish links from high-traffic sites (e.g., learning management systems) • Provide stable identifiers and URLs • Participate in registries and interoperability frameworks (e.g., repositories of repositories)
Sustainability	• Undertake business planning and establish metrics for success • Select one or more approaches to sustainability: institutional hosting/subsidies, sponsorship, partnerships, in-kind contributions, volunteers, etc.
Preservation	• Integrate digital preservation policies, systems and practices • Seek out partners • Participate in national or regional initiatives • Secure the right to preserve

the audience(s) that a specific repository might serve. The next step is the purposeful selection of which audience(s) to serve. The selection of audience(s), combined with an understanding of the needs of that audience or audiences, will reveal the most likely barriers and offer some possible service responses. No single repository enhancement is as important as deciding what audiences to serve and designing the repository with these audiences' needs and behaviors in mind. The aim is to establish a firm foundation for the repository within institution-specific communities of research and practice.

Implications for interface design and repository development

Selecting repository audience(s) and needs to be met has implications for interface design and overall development of the repository. To what extent will the repository serve as a content delivery or landing site for searches referred from elsewhere? Is the repository a destination site and if so, for which audience(s)? What local workflows will the interface support? Will the repository interoperate or provide content to other systems? These questions can only be answered in the context of how the repository is intended to support target audiences and specific needs.

The future of repositories

This and prior chapters have explored a number of questions related to where repositories will go from here. Two important questions have not yet been discussed:

1 In what ways will repositories support digital data management and 21st-century scholarly research infrastructure?
2 Today's thousands of repositories are more like a conglomerate (entities that can be conceptually grouped together but which remain distinct) than an ecosystem (a community of interconnected parts in an identifiable framework). To what extent are repositories likely to evolve into a sustainable, global ecosystem for capturing, making accessible, and preserving the scholarly record?

Brief discussions of these two questions conclude this chapter.

Cyberinfrastructure, e-research and data curation

Background

Since 2004, the NSF has issued a number of calls for grant proposals for research related to cyberinfrastructure and the stewardship of digital data (for details see Atkins et al., 2003). The term 'cyberinfrastructure' was first used by NSF and it refers to computing and data systems, repositories, instruments and high-speed networks that together frame scholarly research environments and enable advanced capabilities. In the UK, Hey and Trefethen (2003) previewed the anticipated 'data deluge' from e-science (computationally intensive science carried out through internet-enabled global collaborations). They argued for digital data libraries and curation (activities including selection, organization, preservation, maintenance and archiving) for scientific data. Later the e-science prefix 'e' was used to describe the same kinds of activities in the social sciences, humanities and so on. Current usage favors the more inclusive term 'e-research' (distributed, data- and information-intensive, collaborative research).

In her book on digital scholarship, Borgman (2007, xvii) stresses the point that 'data have become an important form of research capital.' Datasets supplement traditional scholarly publications, and they serve as important outputs of research and inputs to new research. At present it is not clear how data and scholarly publications can be linked together in scholarly information infrastructures. Nevertheless a growing number of developments have encouraged more systematic e-research data sharing, management and preservation.

E-research data sharing

Important policy changes have occurred for those submitting and working on research grants from public funds. In 2010, NSF announced a new requirement to incorporate data management plans (National Science Foundation, 2010) in grant documents. This development affirms the growing consensus reflected in the *OECD Principles and Guidelines for Access to Research Data from Public Funding* (Organization for Economic Cooperation and Development, 2007) that open access to research data is critical to the progress of science and optimizes the results of investing public funds in research projects.

In addition, a number of developments and activities to document and enable good practice in digital data collection, citation, federation and sharing have occurred. This section mentions only a few of many. For example,

DataOne (Michener et al., 2011) federates content from distributed repositories called member nodes, using an innovative scheme for using persistent identifiers (EZIDs) to manage and track digital objects across repositories. Crosas (2011) describes work at Harvard on the DataVerse Network (DVN). DVN supports individual researchers' data ownership and control, while at the same time enabling and incentivizing data sharing through a repository infrastructure for data identification, management, preservation, re-use, discovery and visibility. Brase (2009) discusses DataCite, an association that promotes and facilitates the use of persistent identifiers for datasets. Simons (2012) discusses a partnership with DataCite to mint DOIs for research data and provide them in a 'Cite My Data' service.

The literature around digital data management is large. Anna Gold's two-part 'cyberinfrastructure primer' provides a place to start (2007a; 2007b).

E-research data and repositories in Australia

A considerable amount of activity in Australia has explored the role of repositories for supporting data curation, for example Treloar, Groenwegen and Harboe-Ree (2007) at Monash University. Monash was a player in the development of the now-completed ARROW project (federating institutional repositories in Australia; not the same as the ARROW knowledgebase supporting rights management for Europeana). DART and ARCHER are two additional projects on researcher workflow and data management.

Wolski, Richardson and Rebello (2011) describe an initiative of Australian universities to develop a framework for feeding data into both a national research data service and university library discovery tools. Their infrastructure federates content created locally and makes it accessible for sharing in different systems, supporting different discovery environments. Two of these are the Australian Research Data Commons, which supports discovery in Research Data Australia (RDA), and LibrarySearch, which supports discovery of hybrid library resources (see Chapter 5 under 'A new kind of library catalog'). The work being done in Australia is encouraging to those who have hopes for a unified, large-scale service framework to interconnect e-research services, at least at the national level.

E-research, libraries and repositories

The conversation about e-research, digital data and data curation that began in 2003 has been taken up by both information scientists and academic librarians. In 2005 ARL obtained a grant from the NSF Office of Cyberinfrastructure (National Science Foundation, 2006) to convene experts and study new collaborative relationships between academic libraries and digital data producers. Their report (Friedlander and Adler, 2007) lays out the issues and proposes roles for libraries in e-science and data management that have been the subject of further collaborations and studies. A Research Information Network report in the UK (CIBER Research Ltd, 2010) describes the state of e-research support in four universities in the UK and concludes with recommendations, including a call for exploring expanded roles for information specialists to work with research teams. Much more inform-ation may be found in Bailey's bibliography on academic libraries and e-science (2011).

ARL reported the results of a survey of how US members are providing infrastructure or support services for research data and e-science (Soehner, Steeves and Ward, 2010). In an early report of work on a survey, Corrall, Kennan and Afzal (2013) investigated the bibliometrics and e-research data support services of 140 libraries in New Zealand, Australia, the UK and Ireland; a majority anticipated involvement in some aspect of e-research data support, with the primary areas of focus being technology infrastructure, data deposit services and policy development.

Corrall and her colleagues found that a major constraint on the development of e-research data services in libraries is the gaps in librarians' data management knowledge, skills and confidence. Others have also recognized this gap; Borgman's syllabus (2012) for her new course on data and data curation points to key topics and recommended readings for educating oneself in this emerging specialization for librarians, information scientists and digital library specialists.

While there are many encouraging signs that libraries and the repositories they host will have a role in supporting e-research and data curation, it is too soon to predict the outcome of current initiatives. One of the experts interviewed for this book cautioned:

> We really don't understand data management or digital libraries of data. Sharing, managing and making data sets more generally discoverable, accessible and reusable are very difficult problems requiring socio-technical advances and structural changes. Developing solutions will take a very long time.

It would be unfortunate for digital library history to repeat itself, with information scientists and librarians pursuing parallel but essentially separate paths. Looking at what has transpired so far, there is some troubling evidence that this could happen. More encouraging is the large-scale, NSF-funded project at Johns Hopkins, which is focused on building a technical framework on which an institution's data management and curation services can be layered (Mayernik et al., 2012). It is also encouraging that some groups are collaborating with the scholars for whom they are envisioning services (see Walters, 2009, describing a project at Georgia Tech).

The extensive literature review offered by Corrall, Kennan and Afzal (2013) also reveals some work to assess needs and develop campus partnerships. Many current initiatives are driven by worthy motives – but it must be admitted that few seem to be growing organically out of the needs and preferences of one or more specific scholarly audiences. A personas-based case study suggests that researcher receptivity to library-managed data curation is discipline-driven (Lage, Losoff and Maness, 2011). In keeping with lessons learned about institutional repositories, it appears that the success of university- or library-hosted data repositories will depend on understanding and engaging with specific communities of scholars in specific scholarly disciplines.

Future repositories: ecosystem or conglomerate?

The final section of this chapter explores the prospects for repositories' becoming key components of larger, more purposively co-ordinated research information environments of the future. From their recent survey of academic libraries with repositories, Burns and colleagues concluded:

> No one can predict the future of institutional repositories at this time and it remains to be seen if individual institutional management of a repository is the most efficient and effective means of operation. A question that should be asked of the users of repositories is whether their needs are met by the dispersed model of repositories that exists at the present time
>
> Burns, Lana and Budd, 2013

Burns' question is not new. Herbert Van de Sompel made the case some years ago for replacing the current scholarly communication system with 'an innately digital scholarly communication system that is able to capture the digital scholarly record, make it accessible, and preserve it over time' (Van de Sompel et al., 2004). He proposed a 'fundamental re-engineering to a network-based system that . . . provides interoperability across participating nodes.'

Ecosystem

Van de Sompel's 2004 call for a network-based system of loosely coupled, communicating services has been frequently cited. It led to a new set of web-compatible standards for aggregating resources (OAI-ORE) and a 're-mix and re-use culture' for sharing scholarly content (see for example Lagoze et al., 2012). Others around the world have been wrestling with the complex problem of better integrating heterogeneous content into dynamic research information environments. Starting in 2005, a number of JISC-supported reports appeared, referring to repositories as elements of an emerging 'ecosystem' or 'ecology' of scholarship, knowledge creation, discovery, use and transfer. Heery and Anderson (2005) called for an 'ecology of repositories' framed by common standards, protocols and interfaces that would support 'a distributed network of repositories interacting with national and international initiatives.' The following year, Heery and Powell (2006) provided a roadmap for the development of such a framework.

Various supporting mechanisms to underpin an ecosystem of repositories or digital libraries are present or emerging. OAI was an early breakthrough, enabling multiple repositories to be federated in aggregations like OAIster or DAREnet (see Chapter 4). OAI's evolution and the introduction of ORE have already been mentioned. In addition:

- DRIVER has demonstrated the feasibility of a common infrastructure for networking European digital repositories and federating their contents (Manghi et al., 2010; Peters and Lossau, 2011).
- National-level programs such as that of the Dutch national library have specified cross-domain aggregation and interoperability standards, enabling the wide discovery, use and re-use of Dutch digital content, including in Europeana (Janssen, 2011).
- The authors of the DELOS Reference Model and the DELOS Manifesto, now active in the EU co-funded D4Science-II project exploring e-infrastructures and Virtual Research Environments, have introduced the concept of a Knowledge Ecosystem model, which enables interoperability among multiple independent e-infrastructures (Candela, Castelli and Pagano, 2011, 14–15).
- Sefton and Dickinson (2011) describe how repositories are or could be a key component in an 'Academic Working Environment' or AWE, an evolving ecosystem supporting researcher workflows and services in Australia.

Conglomerate

Both 'ecosystem' and 'ecology' imply an environment, albeit complex and dynamic, with known or discoverable interrelationships and systematic interactions among the elements of the system. By contrast, a 'conglomerate' brings component parts together into a whole, but in and of themselves, the parts have no relationships and they remain distinct. Despite the progress toward a more purposively co-ordinated approach exemplified by the previous examples and advocated by so many in the digital library field, at present the world's repositories are for the most part isolated and dispersed. Taken as a group, they can be said to be a conglomerate – a conglomerate with a level of cross-repository search thanks to the effects of Google Scholar, other academic search engines and search engine crawling, which brings much repository content together for global discovery and use.

While some of the digital library experts interviewed for this book are optimistic that something like an organized ecology of worldwide repositories will emerge, others expressed doubts whether a well integrated, communicating set of services and systems is a likely scenario. The problems and issues they mentioned included:

1 The feasibility of large-scale collaboration among numerous and far-flung organizations; one interviewee commented 'we overestimate the usefulness of collaboration and underestimate the challenges'.
2 The difficulty of achieving sustainability; one interview wondered 'who would pay for an interconnected system?' There is a mismatch between the benefits of an interconnected ecosystem to scholarly endeavors, which are global, and the means by which repositories are commonly funded, which are usually local, sometimes consortial or national, and rarely international.
3 The likelihood of many diverse repository-hosting organizations' adopting digital library-specific standards requiring additional effort; one interviewee noted 'web companies have done well because they didn't ask contributors to do anything.'
4 The difficulty of achieving repository interoperability as originally conceived (i.e., through digital library standards-based cross-searching of many diverse collections at once); one interviewee noted 'it is easier to replicate content [in multiple repositories] than to integrate it with distributed search.'
5 The complexities of the legal framework governing access to scholarly content; one interviewee noted 'open access is not the silver bullet for

fixing scholarly communications that some claim it can be; a system with "shades of access" is more realistic.' In addition to the legal issues, managing authentication and authorization adds technical complexity.

6 The importance of discipline-specific solutions that arise from the community they are intended to serve; a generic solution around an organized ecology of repositories would represent a significant break with scholars' preferences for working within their own fields and in keeping with extant scholarly reward systems.

7 The fact that deposit in institutional repositories is at present haphazard; the lack of scholars' commitment to and engagement with most repositories.

8 The disruptive, rapidly changing socio-technical environment of which scholarly repositories are a part. It is difficult to know what will be the next innovation to break down former barriers and open up formerly inconceivable options. The prospects of the semantic web and linked data to create new solutions cannot be predicted at this point.

Force field analysis

Figure 8.1 is a force field analysis – a framework for evaluating the factors that could drive or restrain the emergence of a sustainable, global ecosystem of scholarly repositories. Driving forces are on the left, and restraining forces are on the right. The previous section discusses the restraining forces. Earlier sections have discussed the driving forces; in summary they include:

- the promise of a better, more economically and socially valuable system supporting scholarly communication that is global in scope and that supports the free flow of ideas, individual empowerment, teaching, learning and the advancement of knowledge now and for future generations
- the existence of successful regional, national and international programs
- the existence of *de facto* cross-repository search through common and academic search engines, Google Scholar (and/or its descendants)
- advocacy for maximizing the impact and utility of funded research, and the emergence of policies supporting open access to publicly funded research around the world
- advocacy for bridging digital divides not only in developing countries, but also within countries where only some have ready access to licensed scholarly content

- digital library practitioners' evolution toward building on and for the web, using low-barrier, lightweight standards, and away from more complex library/repository-specific standards; and new approaches for facilitating deposit and content re-use/exchange such as the SWORD protocol.

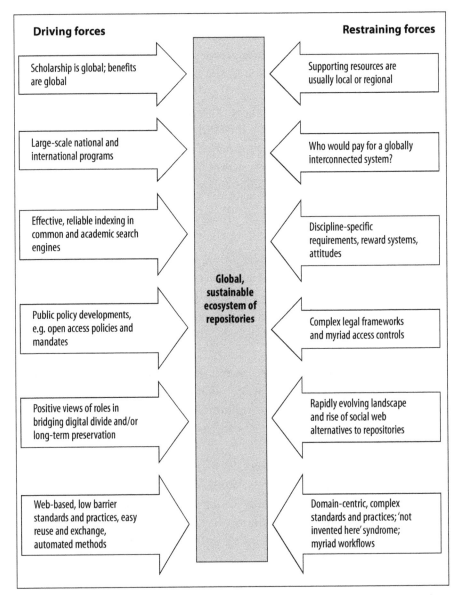

Figure 8.1 Force field analysis of the emergence of a sustainable, global ecosystem of repositories

Conclusion

Researchers disseminate their findings to make an impact on their field and for personal career progression. Both objectives are served by publishing in the peer-reviewed journals with the highest impact factors. Those repositories with a firm foundation in the scholarly communities that they serve have provided a needed service for sharing early results and establishing claims to new discoveries. Others, including most institutional repositories, have not yet achieved an integral role with scholars. On the other hand, taken as a whole, repositories have already contributed substantially to the achievement of a digital library social role – that of broadening access to the results of scholarship for a large number of people.

Depending how they evolve from this point, repositories have the potential to support other digital library social roles as well: enriching teaching and learning; providing enabling infrastructure; enabling multidisciplinary knowledge work and knowledge transfer; increasing scholarly productivity; preserving and curating intellectual assets for future use; and more. Overall the prospects of repositories are favorable, but much work needs to be done. The challenges mentioned in this chapter include:

- better understanding the needs and work practices of the communities to be served
- better understanding discipline-specific norms, peer review, reward systems and attitudes
- improving awareness and recognition; better articulating the value of repositories in ways that resonate and align with the needs of a variety of audiences
- increasing deposits
- assisting scholars with the complexities of open access and rights issues
- improving the productivity of scholars both individually and collectively
- aligning repository practices to optimize discoverability in search engines and academic search engines
- preserving and curating content; ensuring long-term access to intellectual assets
- achieving sustainability; undertaking business planning; establishing and achieving metrics for success.

To the degree that future repositories integrate well into the web and use web-based approaches, blend well into how their communities do things, attract attention to all kinds of collections, and provide the means to easily disclose, re-use and share content, they can be successful. Many of the pieces for assembling repositories into a useful global configuration are in place or emerging. Whether the pieces will in fact converge to produce a revitalized framework supporting scholarly communication is hard to say, but the potential exists. Much may be determined by the impending impact of the emergent (and presently chaotic) information space defined by e-research initiatives, scholarly social networks, repositories built around researchers (rather than their works), shifts in scholarly reward systems based on new metrics and the emergence of semantic web applications. This new information space is the subject of the next chapter.

·········

CHAPTER 9

Digital libraries and the social web: scholarship

Overview

This chapter is the first of two that consider the responses of digital libraries to the social web and to web-based practices for information seeking, learning, teaching, research, professional recognition, work, recreation and socializing. Both chapters elaborate on ideas introduced in Chapters 3–8. This chapter's first part examines the origins and chaotic, fast-moving nature of the social web, explores the possibility of digital libraries as social platforms and introduces a visual framework that attempts to bring some coherence to the many confusing elements of digital libraries' evolution toward the social web. The second part of the chapter turns to the branches of the visual framework that pertain to the social web's existing, emergent, or potential impacts on scholarship, research and researchers.

Introduction

As discussed in Chapter 6, the public library framework developed by McClure (1987) casts library roles in terms of direct involvement in the communities to be served. Their framework is liberating in that it shifts attention away from an information-processing or collection-centric definition of libraries toward a community-centric definition. In the same way, the advent of the social web provides an opportunity to shift the focus and core assumptions of digital libraries away from their collections and information processes (selecting, organizing, providing access, etc.) in favor of new ways of thinking about services, expectations and potential social roles. Before considering specific opportunities afforded by the social web, it is necessary to spend some time considering its background.

Background: Web 2.0 and Library 2.0

Tim O'Reilly dates the first use of the phrase 'Web 2.0' to a conversation he had with Dale Dougherty at a 2004 technology conference (O'Reilly, 2005). They intended the phrase to mark not just a turning point for the web following the dot-com collapse of 2001, but also to capture new notions of *the web as a platform for participation*, characterized by:

- machine-to-machine interactions (syndication, web services and mashups)
- significant user interface innovation
- a bias for two-way 'conversation' rather than one-way information dissemination
- radically democratized and collaborative content creation and exchange
- open, re-usable data.

While the phrase Web 2.0 became a buzzword for many, the concept captured enough meaning to fire both imaginations and actions that have transformed the web from a 'flat, read-only kaleidoscope' (Web 1.0) to a 'shared collaboratory' (Hammond, Hannay and Lund, 2004, characterizing Tim Berners-Lee's original conception of the web as a collaboration space).

Michael Casey, a librarian at Gwinnet County Public Library in Georgia, was one of those inspired by the concept of Web 2.0 and its implications for libraries. He launched the first 'Library 2.0' blog, called LibraryCrunch, in September 2005 (Casey and Savastinuk, 2007, xxi). Others quickly picked up and further developed the concept (among them Miller, 2005; Maness, 2006; Stephens, 2006; Habib, 2006; Blyberg, 2006; Levine, 2006; Abram, 2007). A professional debate emerged almost as quickly about the meaning and scope of Library 2.0. Did Library 2.0 simply refer to web-based technologies applied to library services and collections (e.g., tagging in the online catalog)? Or, as suggested by Blyberg (2006), was Library 2.0 inherently disruptive, fundamentally challenging the library assumptions and service models of the time? The debate was not resolved, and as of this writing, the use of the phrase 'Library 2.0' in the literature appears to be diminishing (a Google Scholar search for articles with 'library 2.0' in the title suggests the possibility that use of the phrase may have peaked in the period 2007–8). Nevertheless, as the societal impact of Web 2.0 has grown to a massive scale, many individuals have embraced the practices and values of this 'platform for participation' – and they bring their expectations with them when they visit libraries, including digital libraries.

What is the social web?

For the purpose of this book, the term 'social web' refers collectively to the websites, tools and services that facilitate interactions, collaboration, content creation and sharing, contribution and participation on the web. The distinguishing characteristic is human interaction: the social web supports many types of online communities, and not just those who participate in social networks. Their tools include e-mail, listservs, bookmarking, wikis and blogs, microblogs, photo- or video-sharing services, e-meeting rooms, review sites and more. Vickery and Wunsch-Vincent's extensive report for the OECD (Organization for Economic Cooperation and Development, 2007), worldwide in scope, documents and explains the participative web and its tools supporting user-created content at that time. Despite its age, the report remains informative for its definitions, data and multinational perspective.

It is worth interjecting a few words about wikis here, since the concept for them dates to 1994 ('History of Wikis', 2013) and they are so significant to the emergence of the social web and the importance of user-contributed content there. More than any other feature of the social web, perhaps, wikis exemplify the global shift to using the web as a platform for participation. Wikipedia (launched 2001) is of course the best-known example of a wiki. The definition of a 'wiki' is 'a website that allows users to add, remove or otherwise edit and change content collectively' (Vickery and Wunsch-Vincent, 2007, 33, 37).

In addition to the applications that are visible to users, a number of underlying machine-to-machine tools create the foundation for social web interactions, for example web services, APIs and mashups (discussed in Chapter 4). These allow servers in different places to exchange or combine services or content. This means that something that 'lives' in one place on the web (like a video, a calendar, or Twitter comments) can be dynamically shared, posted and updated in many places.

In addition to the many web services and APIs that support the social web, the large-scale take-up of mobile smartphones, tablets and other mobile devices has created a huge scope of opportunity for social web growth. The market for mobile application development (mobile apps) is large. As of this writing the latest Pew Internet Project reports indicated that 56% of American adults owned a smartphone; 34% owned a tablet; half reported having apps on their phones; and 82% had them on tablets (Anderson and Rainie, 2012; www.pewinternet. org, trends, device ownership, May 2013). In 2011 researchers began reporting that Americans spend more time using mobile apps than they do browsing the web using their mobile devices (Walsh, 2011). Chapter 10 returns to the discussion of mobile apps in the context of digital libraries.

Digital libraries and the social web

Chakraborty, in his overview of digital libraries and the social web, points out that despite the rise of personalized, interactive online environments, most digital libraries continue to operate from a traditional, collections-centered service model (2010, 127). Brusilovsky et al. (2010, 116) make the point that 'the social nature of the library is typically lost when the library goes digital'. Indeed, the first 15 years or so of digital library work produced mostly read-only ('Web 1.0') digital libraries, and a digital library that incorporates social software applications continues to be the exception rather than the rule. The typical digital library's service model aligns with the conventional, collections-centered library worldview discussed in Chapter 4.

Yet digital library users now expect more than rich collections. Hull, Pettifer and Kell (2008) describe scholarly digital libraries as 'cold, impersonal and isolated' as well as poorly integrated for human and machine interaction. They contrast such 'frozen' digital libraries with more social, interactive tools for scholars like Zotero, Mendeley, CiteULike and others, in which content moves fluidly between web applications. They make the case that such tools better support typical researcher workflows and methods for collaboration.

The social digital library?

Digital libraries are now faced with finding their place in the fast-moving, chaotic information space that is the social web. So far, digital libraries have not been displaced. However, at this point in digital library evolution it has become a pressing matter to not only adopt but embrace the social web's 'principles of participation,' as advocated by Lankes and colleagues for libraries in general (Lankes, Silverstein and Nicholson, 2007, 31). A number of digital library experts have also persistently called for aligning digital libraries with social web principles and practices. Notably, Candela et al. (2007, 6) of the DELOS Network of Excellence on Digital Libraries published its *Digital Library Manifesto*, which redefined the notion of a digital library as (emphasis added):

> a *tool at the center of intellectual activity* having no logical, conceptual, physical, temporal, or personal borders or barriers to information. Generally accepted conceptions have *shifted from a content-centric system* that merely supports the organization and provision of access to particular collections of data and information, *to a person-centric system*
>
> Candela et al., 2007, 6

Even before the DELOs Manifesto appeared, some digital library experts had begun to explore the feasibility and utility of Web 2.0 protocols and more participatory frameworks for digital libraries. Here it is worth mentioning the example of the Ockham Initiative (Morgan, Frumkin and Fox, 2004), an early digital library project that explored the possibilities of web-based registries, web services and social tools (e.g., annotating and reviewing) in a digital library environment. There are many other examples of early work: mining the digital library literature from 2003 forward produces a fair number of articles exploring social web concepts, attributes and tools. Subsequent sections of this chapter discuss a few of these articles.

Digital libraries as social platforms

Dan Cohen (2010), in a recorded lecture at Cambridge University on the social life of digital libraries, urged a transition from static repositories to social platforms that are active, open, modular, gregarious and 'chatty' with other software, servers, people and organizations. A number of digital library technologists, for example those working on the Hydra projects (www. projecthydra.org) discussed in Chapter 4, are exploring more open repository frameworks that could perhaps help with such a transition.

The nature of digital libraries is not incompatible with new roles as social systems. As discussed in Chapter 1, the Kahn-Wilensky architecture of digital libraries does not constrain them to being read-only repositories that support only search and retrieval services, nor does the architectural model exclude the incorporation of a variety of components and agents (see Altman, 2008, 154). In his analysis of digital libraries, Altman predicted the expansion of digital libraries' personalization and collaborative roles. There is nothing in the intrinsic nature of digital libraries blocking the way forward.

What may make the transition of digital libraries to social platforms difficult is the weight of libraries' long-successful traditions, core values and practices. One of the digital library experts interviewed for this book noted 'the values of the social web (for example, "everyone is a creator of content") are hard for librarians to integrate with their own values of authority and authenticity.' It is not that processes for vetting the credibility of sources are no longer respected or important; however, these approaches sit (at times uncomfortably) alongside the predominant values of the social web: engagement and participation.

The evolution of digital libraries' responses to the social web can be understood as a set of continuums with distinct extremes but many variations along the transition (Figure 9.1). Prior sections have already discussed the continuums from the focus on collections to the focus on networked communities, from repositories to social platforms, and from the values of authority and authentication to those of engagement and participation. Figure 9.1 proposes several others.

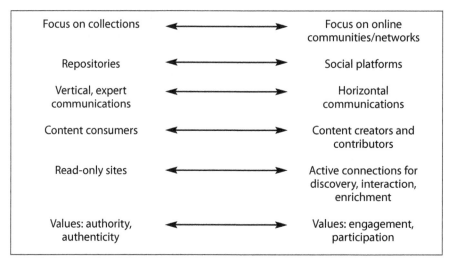

Figure 9.1 Transitions associated with the shift to social digital libraries

Librarianship is not the only profession affected by the shift to the social web's spirit of collaboration and personal self-efficacy; the impact on medicine and health care – where the use of relevant, credible sources is so critical – has perhaps been stronger. Gunther Eysenbach, a leading researcher in e-health, the internet and medicine, discusses the powerful impact of the social web on the medical and health care fields in his frequently cited article on 'Medicine 2.0' (Eysenbach, 2008). He describes how the social web has provided alternatives for patients to discover relevant, trustworthy information through a disintermediated process that taps into the collective wisdom of the social web, taking the form of shared bookmarks, recommender systems, wikis, social networks and other web tools.

Digital libraries' social evolution: a visual framework

Figure 9.2 is an attempt to visualize key drivers and components of the evolution of digital libraries toward new roles on the social web as the branches and roots of a tree. The left side of the map suggests the present situation for most digital libraries and other distinguishing characteristics of the current landscape. The right side of the map represents opportunities (some already realized) for a stronger social web presence and more robust community roles for digital libraries. The map places ideas related to the evolution of the scholarship as the upper branches of the tree. The middle branches represent innovations and opportunities for digital library collections to become more visible to and interactive with online communities. The roots of the tree illustrate the shifts in the core values and assumptions of digital libraries.

Scholarship

The second part of this chapter further explores the branches of Figure 9.2 that pertain to the social web's existing, emergent or potential impacts on

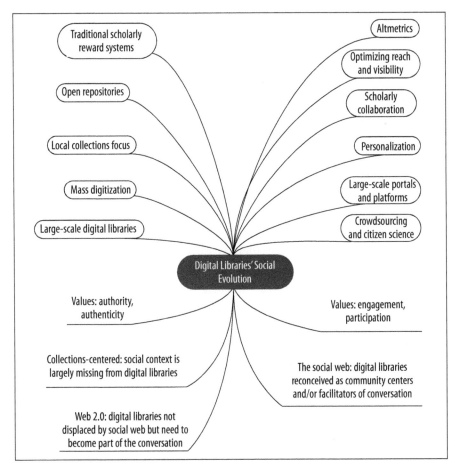

Figure 9.2 The evolution of digital libraries toward new roles on the social web

researchers and scholarship. Figure 9.3 visualizes a few examples, categories or opportunities associated with each of these branches. Individual sections then discuss each branch. The left side of Figure 9.3 visualizes the current situation; the right side visualizes innovations, experiments or possibilities.

The traditional scholarly reward system

It is obvious that the processes of scholarly communication have changed radically. But how much have scholars changed? Thinking back to the definition of 'scholarly communication' in Chapter 1, and aside from the radically changed *processes* they use, how much change has there been in scholars' values and preferences as writers, linkers, information disseminators and collaborators? This is not so clear. Oya Rieger's socio-cultural analyses of institutional repositories (2007; 2008a) suggest that the attitudes and preferences of faculty, researchers and graduate students are shaped by centuries-old scholarly practices and norms. The roles of commercial publishers and peer review in certifying the quality of new scholarly assets are deeply entrenched, and they provide the foundation for a scholar's promotion and tenure. Journal impact factors and citation counts can be expected to be at the heart of scholarly reward systems for the foreseeable future.

Rieger emphasizes that trying to move faculty and 'their deeply embedded value systems' directly to new technologies and forms of scholarly communication will fail. More recently, the latest ITHAKA longitudinal study of US faculty research behavior and preferences reveals the persistent importance of peer-reviewed journals with high impact factors to scholars' decisions of where to publish their work (Schonfeld, Housewright and Wulfson, 2013, 58–60). The study found little evidence for a decline in the importance of traditional, closed scholarly publishing practices in favor of more open and social dissemination of new research.

Chapter 8 discusses the fresh momentum for open access publication produced by the UK's Finch Report, the policies and targets announced by the European Commission in 2012 and new US federal initiatives. There may nevertheless be a gap between the policy-driven emphasis on open access and the current perspectives of many scholars. As an example, a UK study using the same methodology as the US ITHAKA study found that UK scholars, like US scholars, place high importance on reaching their academic peers using traditional methods involving peer review and high impact journals, and less importance on reaching the general public and making their work freely

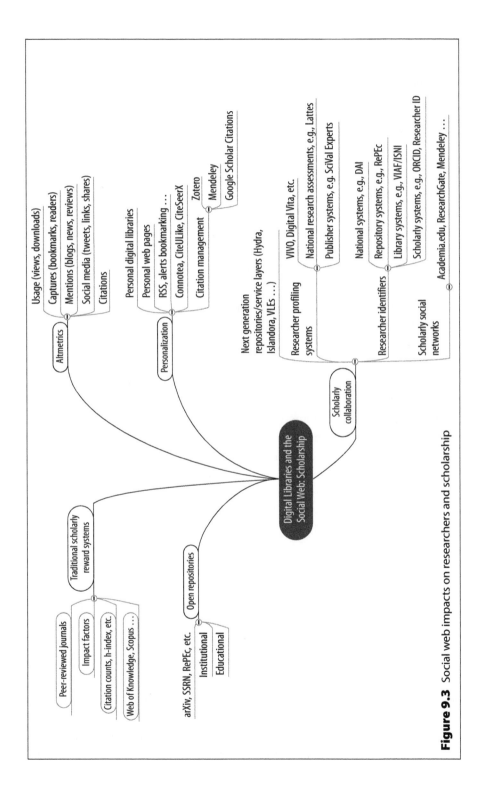

Figure 9.3 Social web impacts on researchers and scholarship

available on the internet (Housewright, Schonfeld and Wulfson, 2013, 8, 69–71).

At the same time, as in the fields of medicine and health care, the social web is providing valuable complements to traditional closed, hierarchical systems for pointing to trustworthy scholarly content. Like everyone else, scholars are participating in the social web and using its tools (such as blogs, shared bookmarking services, Twitter, Mendeley and more). As discussed in Chapter 4, open access repositories and search engine indexing are already disclosing an unprecedented amount of scholarly content to the public. It is becoming possible to take advantage of the collective wisdom represented by choices made using social web tools. In addition it is becoming possible to evaluate the credentials of scholars and researchers in new ways, for example using specialized social networks and researcher profiling systems (such as LinkedIn, Academia.edu, ResearchGate.net, Mendeley, Google Scholar Citations, VIVO, SciVal Experts and more). Scholarly outputs are also assessed using systems developed to support national research assessment exercises such as those discussed later in this chapter.

Altmetrics

A new subfield of bibliometrics (the quantitative analysis of scholarly communication) is emerging, called 'altmetrics' (new quantitative measures based on the social web; see Roemer and Borchardt, 2012, for an introduction to altmetrics). Jason Priem, who as of this writing is an information science PhD student, coined the term in a tweet in 2010 (Priem, Piwowar and Hemminger, 2012, reference 4). The intention is to use altmetrics alongside formal, acknowledged indicators of influence like citation counts. Priem et al.'s 2012 paper in arXiv.org reports their early results indicating the viability of altmetrics as a method for capturing the impact of papers. They studied social media tools and citation counts as sources of data related to over 24,000 articles in PLoS journals (their Table 1 lists the data sources, which included two shared bookmarking sites, Twitter, Wikipedia, Facebook, several blogs, downloads, citations, comments and rankings). They conclude that there is sufficient social web data to fuel the altmetrics approach; that with citation data, altmetrics can more fully describe scholarly impact; and that almetrics can provide insight into different types of impact on different audiences.

As of this writing there is a great deal of conversation and activity focused on altmetrics; however, it is early days to determine where the field will go from here. The value of altmetrics is being debated; for example Judy Luther's blog post on the subject (2012), which captured the main points of the controversy, attracted 40 comments, some forcefully stated. Richard Cave's presentation at a recent Charleston Conference (2012, slide 8) provides the typology of altmetrics data sources used in Figure 9.3.

Open repositories

While they are not social sites, the most successful subject-based repositories (arXiv, RePEc, SSRN, etc.) may be viewed as harbingers of the emergent online scholarly communities of the social web. As discussed in Chapter 8, the most successful subject-based repositories have grown organically around the scholarly communities they serve (see the examples in Chapters 2, 4, 6 and 7), and they are woven into the way their disciplines communicate. These repositories have evolved through the online community life cycle (described in Chapter 7), from a strong community orientation at inception to a high degree of trust and participation at maturity.

The progress of early educational digital libraries (for example, some of those spawned by the NSDL project, discussed in Chapter 7) illustrated some painful aspects of these repositories' social evolution, as some of their builders struggled to engage communities of teachers and learners. The evidence presented in multiple chapters makes it clear that institutional repositories continue to struggle to engage their intended communities. Well funded social web alternatives are beginning to emerge and attract participation by researchers (e.g., scholarly social networks). These developments increase the pressure on institutional repositories to find firmer footing among the services supporting the creation and dissemination of scholarship. Their most promising strategies (illustrated on the right side of Figure 9.3) appear to be evolution toward (1) next-generation repository platforms, as described in Chapter 4, and (2) better reach and visibility on high-traffic sites, including sites where the content can be not only discovered and consumed but also re-used, annotated, bookmarked and shared.

From personalization to collaboration
Personal digital libraries

Neil Beagrie, a digital preservation expert from the UK, had the foresight to recognize the immense impact that the trend toward individual digital creativity, coupled with the availability of large digital storage and computing power to individuals, would have on where digital content comes from, who collects it, and how it is stored and shared (Beagrie, 2005). Noting that 'people are able to create, capture and store an ever-increasing amount of digital information about or for themselves,' Beagrie articulated early the connection between web-based personalization and collaboration services and platforms. He argued that personal digital collections (such as e-mails, collected documents, alerts and bookmarks, personal webpages, blogs, portfolios of work, digital images, audio and video recordings and more) would engender new services for easily marking, tagging, annotating, editing, sharing and/or distributing them on the web and thereby 'reinforce informal social networks and mechanisms of communication.'

Tony Hammond and colleagues of the Nature Publishing Group recognized as early as 2004 the game-changing impact of content syndication tools like RSS (a web-based format for automated, immediate sharing and distribution of web content, like headlines or blog posts, to RSS feed subscribers to that site). The Nature Publishing Group and other science publishers began taking up RSS as a means of alerting interested readers to new content; the updates could be directed not only to desktops but to mobile devices (Hammond, Hannay and Lund, 2004).

RSS feeds and other innovations

RSS feeds joined a number of other innovations that had appeared by 2005 or 2006 to enable first, personalization and soon after, social web collaboration. Along with wikis, blogs and other tools, the means for social web collaboration included bookmarking, whose history predates search engines, as described by Hammond et al. (2005). The advantages to be had from collaboratively sharing bookmarks quickly spurred the introduction of various social bookmarking services, like delicious.com (founded in 2003), as well as a number of tools with an academic focus, like Connotea (Lund et al., 2005; in 2013 Baynes announced Connotea's retirement (Baynes, 2013)) or CiteULike.org (developed in 2004 and still highly popular today). CiteSeerX (http://citeseerx.ist.psu.edu) is an example of an early digital library/academic search engine – founded in 1998 and focused on the computer and information science literature – that has over the years developed a number of social bookmarking, citation management and networking features.

From citation management to networking

The rapid uptake of social bookmarking and tagging has led to a parallel evolution from still popular, but traditional bibliographic citation management tools like EndNote or RefWorks toward more social citation management tools like Zotero (launched in 2006) and Mendeley (first release 2008) that are better integrated with web-based research and writing practices. Fenner's brief article (2010) comparing several citation management tools offers a simple introduction from an end-user perspective; Cohen (2008) outlines the history, novel approach and significance of Zotero, while Puckett (2011) provides guidance on how to use it effectively. Zaugg et al. (2011) describe how Mendeley combines reference management with scholarly collaboration.

Citation management

Zotero is currently a popular tool supporting scholarly research, writing, citation and the personal organization or sharing of papers, reports, websites and blog posts, media and more. Its significance extends beyond its current functionality or user base. The principal achievement of the team that developed Zotero was to recognize and capitalize upon the inter-connectedness of the social web to facilitate how scholars and students work. In keeping with the goal of the Center for History and New Media (www.chnm.gmu.edu) to combine scholarship and technology, the builders of Zotero have created a cloud-based researcher's tool to connect and integrate a disparate applications, services, repositories and content in a novel way. Zotero brings content and functionality from many sources together in the browser and enables not only its organization and storage, but also the easy synchronization and exchange of references and content.

Mendeley's public launch in 2008 was significant because the cloud-based, online version combines citation management with social networking and sophisticated new approaches to managing data. Mendeley extracts meaning from researchers' personal digital libraries (of citations and content) and patterns associated with the use of this content to reveal either additional articles of possible relevance or colleagues with similar interests. Researchers can set up groups for collaboration, create professional profiles, and proactively connect and share content with other invited researchers. For some scholars, the impact of Mendeley has been powerful; one of the digital library experts interviewed for this book said using it has increased his productivity and 'changed much of my behavior.'

A blog post by political science professor Patrick Dunleavy (2012) captures some of the reasons for Mendeley's popularity among its estimated two million users (Henning 2012). Arguably, as of this writing Mendeley may be among the largest repositories of academic papers: its open catalog contains over 30 million papers, according to the Mendeley site (www.mendeley.com/how-we-help). It remains to be seen what the long-term impact of Mendeley's April 2013 acquisition by Elsevier will be; first reactions have varied (see for example Anderson, 2013; Dobbs, 2013; Howard, 2013).

Regardless of what the future holds for the individual services, Zotero and Mendeley considerably broadened, smoothed, and quickened the pace on the highway toward scholarly social networks. Their existence is an instance of a broad shift to systems and services that *focus on scholars themselves*, in addition to the content they create. The success of Google Scholar – and especially the introduction of citation counts and links to cited articles, followed by the introduction of Google Scholar Citations in 2011 (Ortega and Aguillo, 2012) – has further magnified the trend toward researcher-centered systems and online communities of scholars.

Scholarly collaboration on the social web
Researcher profiling systems

Scholarly researcher profiling systems increasingly use web-based tools to harvest information from disparate sources into expertise profiles for faculty, other researchers and even facilities like research labs. Some profiling systems are tied to national research assessment exercises (mentioned in the section on identifiers); others arose for other reasons.

VIVO

One early automated system dates to 2003, when a juxtaposition of disparate factors and opportunities at Cornell University led to the creation of VIVO (www.vivo.library.cornell.edu). VIVO was first implemented in 2004 as an online information service for providing an integrated view of the multidisciplinary, dispersed and disconnected life sciences community at Cornell (Devare et al., 2007; Corson-Rickert, 2009, 67–79). The Cornell system now covers all disciplines.

A major early influence on VIVO was the internationally supported Harmony Project, which brought fresh thinking to solving the complex interoperability problem of combining diverse metadata sets (Lagoze, Hunter and Brickley, 2000). Rather than building a self-contained repository of digital content, VIVO's implementers built an index that functions as an overarching, unifying layer that highlights researchers and their interconnections: their affiliations, courses taught, grants, publications and more.

In 2009 an agency of the US National Institutes of Health (NIH) granted US$12.2 million to build a new version of VIVO to support collaboration more broadly and enable scientists to network nationally (Gewin, 2009; Brynko, 2010; Krafft et al., 2010; Johnson, Buhler and Holmes, 2010). At the time of this writing, instances of VIVO had been launched or are being implemented at over 50 institutions in North and Central America, Europe, Asia and Australia/New Zealand (https://wiki.duraspace.org/display/VIVO/VIVO+Main+Page).

Irrespective of its current position and prospects, VIVO's initial development was significant because it foreshadowed or exemplified certain social and technological shifts:

- the social web's shift of focus to people, collaboration and connections
- the recognition that an array of factors (in addition to refereed publications) determine a scholar's impact and influence in his or her field
- a shift from theory to practice for services based on semantic web technologies – specifically, modeling resources (both digital objects and real-world objects like people) as entities and relationships in ways that greatly facilitate their discovery, citation, re-use and re-aggregation on the web
- the possibility to move digital libraries from self-contained file systems (traditionally conceived repositories) to service platforms for managing and providing access to diverse digital objects regardless of where they are stored
- automated harvesting as the preferred means of collecting or pointing to content
- the critical importance of open, re-usable and remixable data, not only for use within the site but also for disclosure to other sites.

Difficulties and prospects for researcher profiling systems

Creating web-based services that profile or recommend experts is a difficult technical problem that has pushed the limits of digital library practice. It is a problem space that has attracted researchers in computer science. For example, in one often-cited article, Tang and others (2008) describe their work at Tsinghua University to automatically extract researcher profiles from the web, integrate publication data, and use the results to create an academic social network called ArnetMiner. Another example is the work reported by Fazel-Zarandi et al. (2011). The authors, who note that the expert profiling process requires 'reasoning about multiple complex networks from heterogeneous sources,' report a new framework for constructing expert profiles and recommender services. Their paper concludes with their planned next steps – to test the framework with researchers in particular domains, VIVO (www.vivoweb.org) and SciVal (www.scival.com).

Prospects for researcher profiling systems

It is early days for researcher profiling systems; from a functional perspective, there are alternatives; and it is difficult to predict how such systems will develop from here. Quite a few of them now exist. The Wikipedia entry that discusses them ('Comparison of Research Networking Tools and Research Profiling Systems', 2013) compiles information on over a dozen open-source, commercial, and institutionally managed tools or systems, among them VIVO and Digital Vita, which grew out of research at the University of Pittsburgh (Schleyer et al., 2008). Prominent commercial offerings in the Wikipedia article list include ResearcherID from Thomson Reuters (further discussed below) and SciVal from Elsevier.

Despite the achievements of researchers and implementers so far, it is not clear how much value scholars themselves place on researcher profiling systems. One of the digital library experts interviewed for this book worried that while he is aware of the enthusiasm of university administrators and librarians for one such system, he has 'never heard a faculty member praise it'.

Marshak and Johnson (2010) conducted focus groups to look into faculty members' perceptions of the value of researcher profiling systems. The focus groups turned up a number of perceived benefits of researcher profiling systems, but also a set of issues – which will be familiar to institutional repository managers – that could lead to low faculty engagement (see Chapter 8). One (unsurprising) key finding was that faculty may be unwilling to keep their online profiles up to date. Another lesson for builders of academic profiling systems is that success may depend on a deep understanding and engagement with motivated, specific communities of scholars who have a stake in using the system for their own ends – and/or due to the requirements of national research assessment exercises, as discussed after the next section.

Scholarly social networks

Over the past three to five years, scholars have been adopting various tools associated with the social web. A number of studies have found that a majority of science and social science researchers report using non-academic social networks (Facebook), a growing number use services like LinkedIn, many are active on Twitter, and reading and commenting on academically oriented blogs is fairly common (see, for example, Nentwich, 2010; Giglia, 2011; Chenu-Abente et al., 2012; Gruzd and Goertzen, 2013). At the same time, traditional scholarly publishing and conferences continue to remain much more important to researchers than social networks and media like blogs; the latest ITHAKA studies of faculty preferences support this view, at least for US and UK researchers (Schonfeld, Housewright and Wulfson, 2013; Housewright, Schonfeld and Wulfson, 2013).

Existing networks

Nevertheless, the success of social networks generally has attracted investment in a number of social platforms designed explicitly for scholars. Menendez, de Angeli and Menestrina (2012, Figure 4.1) list 19 social networks for researchers and their number of users as of October 2011. The aims of these freely available, public, network-based platforms are to support researchers' efforts to find information and research partners, keep up to date, contact or follow colleagues, form or work in groups, share or locate papers, and establish an online presence in their fields. Generally these services require scholars to create a profile, fill in a publication list (or 'claim' their papers from a public database or databases), and identify their fields of interest.

Table 9.1 lays out summary information about the largest scholarly social networks as of early 2013: Academia.edu, ResearchGate, and Mendeley, which were all founded by web entrepreneurs who also have impressive credentials as scholars. Among these three, and as discussed previously, Mendeley is a kind of boundary object. It began as a citation management tool (similar to Zotero) and has been evolving into a highly successful social network for researchers.

Motivating factors for scholars

A question that is woven throughout this book also applies to these new social networks: what motivates or will motivate scholars to engage with them over the short and longer term? A study of social scientists' use of social sites

Table 9.1 Leading social networks specifically oriented to researchers, 2013
*Source: compete.com; latest statistics available are for the month of March 2013 and represent US traffic only

Name	Founded/ Location	CEO	Self-reported members/Date	US unique visitors/ Month*	Funding
Academia.edu	2008 San Francisco	Richard Price	3.1 million (May 2013)	500,000+	Venture capital
ResearchGate.net	2008 Berlin	Ijad Madisch	2.8 million (May 2013)	350,000+	Venture capital
Mendeley.com	2008 London	Victor Henning (now VP Strategy, Elsevier)	2.0 million (November 2012)	125,000	Venture capital initially (acquired by Elsevier, April 2013)

suggest that the most-sought benefits are following other researchers' work, keeping up to date, discovering new ideas or publications, making new contacts, and promoting their own work (Gruzd and Goertzen, 2013, 3338). The rapid growth of the three social networks discussed in this section suggests they are delivering these benefits and forming communities around their services.

At the same time, their claims of numbers of members are unconvincing. The UNESCO Institute for Statistics (2009) estimates there are around 7 million researchers worldwide; could 3.1 million of them (44%) have signed up for Academia.edu? It seems unlikely. Results of the 2011 survey of Academia.edu users by Menendez and others (Menendez, de Angeli and Menestrina, 2012, 54), extrapolated to the 3.1 million members reported on the Academia.edu home page as of this writing, suggests that well over half a million members are undergraduates, alumni, retired faculty, or hold other types of positions; 1.25 million are graduate students; and about 1.3 million are faculty, post-docs, and independent researchers (still an impressive number).

Engagement, participation, incentives

Some studies also suggest that while membership numbers may be high in these three social networks, members' actual engagement and activity levels may be quite low. For example, Menendez and colleagues' analysis of Academia found a low level of user interaction and engagement with the service, with almost half of the members never modifying their initial profiles (Menendez, de Angeli and Menestrina, 2012, 59). This is not a surprising finding; the challenge of getting users to actively participate in and contribute to online communities is not new. Despite their predominantly positive forecast for scholars' use of social media, Gruzd and Goertzen conclude that 'even though social media sites offer scholars a two-way form of communication and information exchange, scholars in the study tend to use social media in a one-directional mode' (2013, 3339).

Krichel and Zimmermann (2012), who have provided leadership for the RePEc open repository, discuss the critical importance of effective incentives to community engagement and participation (pointing in RePEc's case to its provision of an important author and institutional rankings service that is calculated from registration data). Government requirements related to national research assessments, research funding agency requirements and repository deposit mandates are *external* incentives that influence scholars' choices and behaviors. In looking ahead to the prospects of scholarly social networks, the possibility of external incentives needs to be considered in combination with *internal* ones related to the life cycle of online communities (described in Chapter 7). These include:

- how well scholarly social networks are able to align with the purposes and practices of multiple scholarly communities
- how successfully the builders can communicate and generate scholars' trust in their social network's value to scholarship
- how well aligned or embedded the social network is with other scholarly sites and requirements (for example, PubMed Central, arXiv, etc.; new requirements related to research assessments or researcher IDs, etc.)
- the perceived and actual benefits to visibility and prestige that they deliver
- how well they function (for example, how usable the sites are)
- how well they function as community centers across multiple disciplines
- what alternatives show up on the network over the next few years.

Researcher identifiers

In an ideal scholarly communication system there would be tools to browse, navigate, make recommendations and assess influence based on the complete graph of all actors (people, collaborations, institutions) and all communication artifacts (articles, comments, blog posts, usage data).

Warner et al., 2009

The source of this remark by Simeon Warner, a research associate at Cornell with ties to the library, arXiv.org and the information science department, is a paper he presented at the 2009 International Conference on Open Repositories. His presentation, which describes the linked data approach of arXiv's author identifiers, also discusses other author identifier systems and the reasons they are important. One is that unambiguously identifying authors and associating them accurately with their works may be the keystone of next-generation, global-scale collaboration for researchers on the social web.

Many have stressed the importance of developing author identifiers, often making the same points made decades ago for developing persistent identifiers for objects. For books, think of the benefits of an ISBN (International Standard Book Number); for articles, think of a DOI (Digital Object Identifier). Both exist to:

- unambiguously and persistently identify these entities
- make entities and objects related to them straightforward for machines and people to find and retrieve (see also the discussion of the Handle System in Chapter 2).

Discoverability of researchers

Anyone who participates in the social web knows that it is can be far from straightforward to find and link to a single researcher, if the only way to search is that person's name. It is much harder to unambiguously identify people than other types of entities. Consider just a few aspects of the problem: many researchers have the same name (like Smith or Wang); the same individual's name can appear in various forms (e.g., with or without initials); and transliterations of non-Roman names yield variant spellings and word order. These types of problems are massively augmented in a global network environment in which millions of researchers' names are indexed.

In the context of scholarship's shift to the network, the challenges of accurately identifying particular scholars and attributing the results of scholarship to the right individual have become monumental. Julia Lane of the US National Science Foundation, writing for *Nature*, notes 'on an international level, the issue of a unique researcher identification system is one that needs urgent attention' (Lane, 2010, 488). Rotenberg and Kushmerick (2011), whose article provides background on the author identification challenge, point to several factors driving the need for new solutions for scholarly name disambiguation, among them:

- the expansion of research output globally
- the rise of global collaborations and data sharing
- increasing government or institutionally based requirements to track research outcomes
- large-scale growth in the number of researchers with Asian names, whose Roman transliterations are challenging to disambiguate (data from the UNESCO Institute for Statistics, 2009 suggests that 38% of the world's estimated seven million researchers worldwide are in Asia, with half of these in China).

Library-based systems and VIAF

Libraries have a long tradition of community-wide systems (generally at the national level) for disambiguating names based on name authority control (the process of establishing the authoritative form of a name and linking variant forms as references, for the overall purposes of bringing the works related to that name together in the catalog, in turn facilitating search and retrieval). Niu (2013) describes name authority control in libraries, placing these practices in the context of recent initiatives inside and outside the library domain, and forecasting future directions for name authority control in libraries.

The most important recent library authority control-related developments in name identifiers include VIAF (the Virtual International Authority File; www.viaf.org), which leverages the investments in name authority control made by libraries all over the world. In 2009 VIAF became available as linked data, creating a new opportunity for the work of libraries to contribute to services that use semantic web approaches (Hickey, 2010). A 2013 update on VIAF indicates it now brings together 27 national level authority files (Hickey 2013).

With respect to its contribution to author identification, VIAF links together different countries' authoritative forms of names, then assigns identifiers to the resulting clusters. These identifiers have subsequently been deployed as ISNIs (ISNIs are discussed below; see also Hickey, 2011, and MacEwan, Angjeli and Gatenby, 2013).

Will a single researcher identification system emerge?

Many individuals and types of organizations have a stake in unambiguously identifying authors and relating them to his or her scholarly contributions, collaborations or activities. Authors themselves have a stake, as do other researchers who are searching for related work, centers of expertise or potential collaborators. Libraries, funding agencies, research administrators, publishers and other aggregators of scholarly information have keen interest in attributing scholarly outcomes to the correct individuals.

Considering the social web, the deployment of a lightweight infrastructure to disambiguate names would make cross-domain searching, alerts, social bookmarking, citing and sharing content, social networking and researcher profiling services work more effectively and efficiently. Liu and colleagues (2012), who articulate a future-oriented perspective in their proposal for a research social network approach for analysing local collaboration networks, would certainly be aided by reliable automated methods for unambiguously identifying authors and their works. There are excellent reasons to embrace and implement a unifying web-enabled system for uniquely and persistently identifying authors and reliably associating them with their work.

The use of author identifiers is still not common. The emergence of a single system for identifying authors is an unknown at the time of this writing. For now, many different author identifier systems co-exist. Further, the most likely scenario is each author's having multiple identifiers. The rest of this section discusses a few of the better known alternatives that have been taken up in or across various communities. Martin Fenner's relatively brief overview of the author identification landscape (2011) is another source to consult.

Table 9.2 provides high-level summary data about the researcher identification services that are further discussed in the following subsections. The table lists only the better-known services and is not intended to be comprehensive.

General systems for identifying persons

ISNIs (International Standard Name Identifiers), which consist of 16 digits, are intended to disambiguate the identities by which individuals, characters and organizations are publicly known. ISNI is a certified global standard of the International Standards Organization (ISO) for 'the unique identification of public identities across all fields of creative activity,' including 'the millions of contributors to creative works and those active in their distribution,

Table 9.2 Selected researcher identification services

Name	Began	Type/Audience
VIAF (Virtual International Authority File)	2009	Library-based initiative, global in scope
ISNI (International Standard Name Identifier)	2010	Creators/contributors, producers, publishers ... ISO standard Global in scope
OpenID	2005	Authentication
DAI (Dutch Author Identifier)	2008	Dutch researchers
Lattes Platform	1999	Brazilian researchers
MIMAS Names Project	2007	UK researchers
ResearcherID	2007	Researchers worldwide
Scopus Author ID	2006	Researchers worldwide
arXiv Author ID	2005	Researchers in physics, math, computer science and several other disciplines
RePEc Author Service	1999	Researchers in economics and related sciences
AuthorClaim	2008	Researchers worldwide (based on RePEc's service)
ORCID (Open Contributor and Researcher ID)	2009	Researchers worldwide

including writers, artists, creators, performers, researchers, producers, publishers, aggregators, and more' (www.isni.org/about). ISNIs, which function as a bridge to other name identification services and systems, form part of the family of identifiers that include the DOI and ISBN. The ISNI database contains or uses information drawn from a variety of data sources including VIAF, as noted previously (see also www.isni.org/how-isni-works). ISNI and ORCID (mentioned again later in this section) are complementary but distinct organizations. ORCID is focused on research and researchers and relies on researcher self-registration, while ISNI ingests, compiles and establishes identifiers from existing data sources across a number of domains.

OpenID (www.openid.net) is another standards-based, general-purpose system to unambiguously identify persons for the purpose of internet authentication. It is mentioned here for the purpose of clarification; OpenIDs do not have researcher profiling information associated with them; they are simply mechanisms for authentication. First developed by Brad Fitzpatrick (2005), OpenID enables users to sign on to the thousands of websites that accept OpenID authentication. The OpenID Foundation, an international non-profit membership organization established in 2007, is governed by sustaining, corporate and community members including among others Google, Facebook, Microsoft and PayPal (Thibeau, 2011).

National systems and research evaluation

Some countries require the establishment of author profiles in support of national-level research evaluation and the showcasing of national research outputs (one example is Australia; see www.arc.gov.au). The following list briefly highlights the researcher identification systems associated directly with national research evaluation programs in four countries:

- Dutch Author Identifier (DAI) is a unique identifier for each researcher in the Netherlands, linked to researcher profile pages (Jippes, Steinhoff and Dijk, 2010).
- The government-supported, major source of information on Brazilian researchers, the Lattes Platform (www.lattes.cnpq.br), contains unique identifiers assigned by the CNPq system so that people with similar names are credited correctly. In 2010 Lattes contained data on about 1.6 million Brazilian researchers and students (Lane, 2010; Hill, 2011). It is the best example in the world of a mature and successful national system.
- National researcher identification systems are also well established in Norway (www.cristin.no/english) and Japan (http://rns.nii.ac.jp/html_us/help_en.html).

The UK agency JISC is investigating the possibilities for a national researcher identification system. The MIMAS Names Project (http://names.mimas.ac.uk), a collaboration of the University of Manchester and the British Library funded by JISC, explored and prototyped a service for UK repositories for uniquely identifying researchers. The project ran from 2007 to late 2011 (Cross et al., 2011) and delivered about 45,000 identifiers for top UK researchers who were part of the national Research Assessment Exercise in 2008. Among other efforts, the project experimented with assigning ISNIs through machine matching, and it produced a plug-in for the EPrints repository software to help unambiguously associate researcher names with their work.

In a separate effort commissioned by JISC, Amanda Hill, the UK Names project manager, evaluated existing national researcher identifier systems (2011). She found that national systems tying the completion of researcher profiles to eligibility for research funding were the most successful at becoming integral parts of a nation's research infrastructure. Hill later presented on possibilities for future work (2012). She places the UK Names Project and the JISC Researcher Identifier evaluation in the context of other national systems and international initiatives such as ISNI and ORCID.

Publisher or repository-based systems

Leading scholarly publishers also provide identification systems. For instance, ResearcherID from Thomson Reuters is a freely available author identification service that functions at a global level (across national, publisher, institutional, research funding and disciplinary boundaries). While the service is associated with Thomson Reuters' Web of Science and Web of Knowledge, ResearcherID operates independently of them. Rotenberg and Kushmerick (2011) reported that there were 127,000 ResearcherID profiles as of July 2011. An interactive map on the ResearcherID site suggests that the service is currently most deployed in the US, China, Brazil and Australia, and across Europe. Elsevier also provides a researcher identification service called Scopus Author identifier, and ProQuest assigns researcher identifiers in connection with its large searchable database of faculty profiles, Scholar Universe.

A number of leading open repositories have author identification systems, with the most prominent being the arXiv author ID and the RePEc Author Service (http://authors.repec.org), which in mid-2012, registered 32,000 authors representing 85– 90% of the top economists worldwide (Krichel and Zimmermann, 2012). The code for the RePEc Author Service has been used to generate AuthorClaim (http://authorclaim.org), an author profiling and identification service with much broader scope across all disciplines.

Open Contributor and Researcher ID (ORCID)

CrossRef (www.crossref.org), an official DOI registration agency for scholarly publications, has been a strong advocate for a global, centralized author identification system. CrossRef convened an 'AuthorID' meeting in early 2007 to discuss the possibilities for a registry and standard identification numbers for authors (Fenner, 2009). Representatives from commercial and open access publishers, national libraries and library co-operatives and scholarly societies attended (www.crossref.org/CrossTech/2007/02/crossref_author_id_meeting. html), among them Jim Pringle of Thomson Reuters, who spoke at the CrossRef meeting about ResearcherID (the code for ResearcherID was later licensed by ORCID).

The ORCID initiative started in 2009 following the first Name Identifier Summit convened by Nature Publishing Group and Thomson Reuters (CrossRef and KnowledgeSpeak, 2009; Ratner, 2012). ORCID, an open, non-proprietary and independent registry, went into operation in October 2012 (Open Contributor and Researcher ID, 2012). As of May 2013, there were

130,161 ORCID IDs (http://support.orcid.org/knowledgebase/articles/150557-number-of-orcid-ids). If ORCID succeeds in promoting the large scale uptake of identifiers by scholars and in making the many disparate researcher identification systems around the world more interoperable, it will be a massive force for advancing scholarly social networking in ways that will alter how scholars are identified, how they collaborate, how they are associated with their work, and how they are assessed.

The ORCID initiative has gained momentum across organizations, disciplines and countries in the past two years (Ratner, 2011 and 2012; Haak et al., 2012). It is the most prominent current initiative, with a growing membership (www.orcid.org/about/community/members) providing financial support. The ORCID team has made a concerted effort to engage with the other organizations and initiatives discussed in this section (Ratner, 2011, slides 28 and 29), with several represented on its board, as launch partners or on working groups.

ORCID is intended to bridge to and from other identification systems, supporting data exchange with ResearcherID, Scopus, RePEc, arXiv and others (Ratner, 2012, slide 27). CrossRef, an ORCID launch partner, has continued to be a strong supporter of the initiative (www.crossref.org/10quarterly/quarterly.html), encouraging publishers to integrate ORCID IDs into their systems. ORCID IDs and ISNIs are interoperable 16-digit numbers, formatted to be compliant with the ISNI ISO standard. ORCID is using a block of numbers reserved for it by ISNI (Haak, 2013). Infrastructure and organizational partnerships appear to be falling into place, but it remains to be seen if researchers themselves will be motivated to participate.

Conclusion

New notions of the web as a platform for participation have multiplied the possibilities for social digital libraries. When individuals who use social sites and tools approach digital libraries, they bring their social web expectations with them. The digital libraries that continue to operate from a traditional, collections-centered service model (that is, nearly all of them) are now faced with finding their place in the fast-moving, chaotic information space of the social web. There is nothing in the intrinsic nature of digital libraries blocking the way forward; most of the barriers arise from libraries' long-successful core values and assumptions. These values and assumptions sit somewhat uncomfortably beside the social web's core values: engagement and participation.

This chapter makes an attempt to visualize the key drivers and components of the evolution of digital libraries toward new roles on the social web. The chapter then turns to the consideration of the existing, emergent and possible impacts of the social web on researchers, scholarly tradition and scholarly practices. The social web is providing valuable complements to traditional methods for assessment, the identification of scholars and their works, and scholarly networking. A range of new social tools and services are now available to support research, keep up to date, learn about other scholars, track research outputs and more.

This chapter's analysis suggests that the social web offers many opportunities and benefits for scholars, but the transition may be slow or uneven due to motivational issues and scholarship's centuries-old, deeply entrenched traditions. Required participation in research assessments and other mandates aside, what will motivate scholars to engage with the new tools and social networks over the short and longer term is an open question. Motivational factors have been a persistent barrier to the uptake of open repositories.

At the same time, open repositories are having a large impact on moving scholarship online in a way that makes it freely available to all. The publisher-provided scholarly literature has been online since 2008: a study by Cox and Cox (2008) reported that over 95% of science, technology and medicine and 85% of arts, humanities and social science journal titles were available in digital format. So, while almost all scholarly *literature* is online, so far the social web has not been a magnet for online *scholarly practice*.

The next and final chapter continues the consideration of digital libraries' evolution to the social web, this time in the context of new opportunities for digital library collections. That chapter concludes with some thoughts about what digital libraries can do for a society that is now so dominated by the social web.

CHAPTER 10

Digital libraries and the social web: collections and platforms

Overview

This chapter continues the consideration of digital libraries' responses to the social web. It builds on the visual framework introduced in Chapter 9 to consider the transition of digital collections to platforms that align well with how people find information, work and play on the social web; are highly visible and invite interaction; and re-mix and re-use data from other sources. The chapter closes with some thoughts about future digital libraries and libraries' digital future.

Visualizing the shift from collections to platforms

The starting point for this chapter is Figure 9.2 (p. 215), specifically the branches that pertain to the shift of digital libraries from collections to platforms. Figure 10.1 offers a closer look at these branches and individual sections of this chapter discuss each branch. The left side of Figure 10.1 visualizes the current situation; the right side visualizes some innovations, experiments or possibilities.

The dilemma of the national or local collections focus
The dilemma

The builders and maintainers of real-world digital libraries face a dilemma that comes from two sources:

- core assumptions about digital libraries as destination sites, complete in themselves
- the tension between who uses digital libraries and who pays for them.

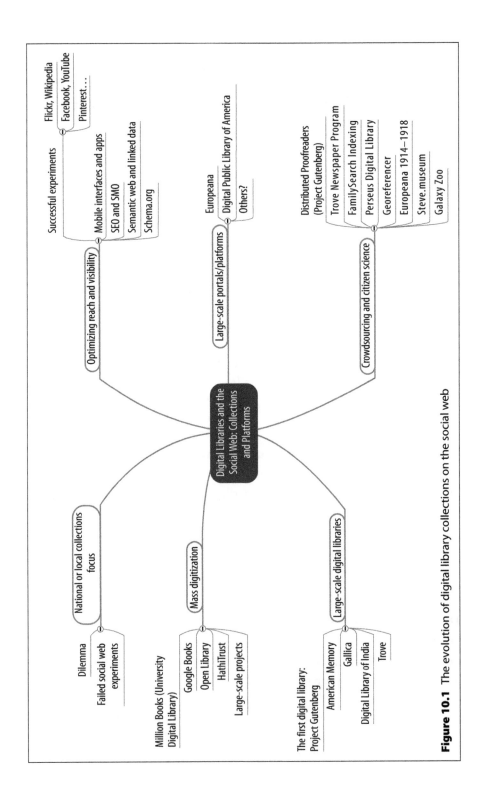

Figure 10.1 The evolution of digital library collections on the social web

Digital library builders constructed the first wave of digital libraries at national or local institutional levels, or scholarly publishers built them to move their content online. As the web grew up around them, second-wave initiatives and technologies to give digital libraries web interfaces and to make them more interoperable with each other developed (like metasearch or OAI-PMH). Nevertheless, a core assumption was that the communities for whom the digital library was built would visit the digital library at its own URL (that is, the digital library would be a destination site).

The third wave (where the field is now) is integrating digital libraries more fully with the web and web technologies. Much of that work is described in this book. A key realization of digital library builders has been that most digital libraries are not destination sites, and even ones that are need to be discoverable on the larger web, not only by people but also by machines (i.e., via web services and APIs). Lorcan Dempsey has been making these points for years on his blog; his post after reading Tim O'Reilly's now famous essay on Web 2.0 is particularly interesting in this regard (O'Reilly, 2005; Dempsey, 2005; see also Dempsey, 2006b).

The fourth wave began as the social web grew up around third-wave initiatives. As the social web's impact is felt, the goals of making digital libraries more compatible with web technologies, more interoperable with each other and more visible in search engines are shifting again. The fourth wave is about fully responding to how different communities of people work and play on the web – how they learn and get things done, how they look for other people and information (using search engines and social sites), how they share what they create or find, how information shows up in diverse contexts on the social web, and more. This fourth wave requires an even higher commitment to disclosing digital library content and services in external contexts and for global audiences that the builders never see. This new wave is a disruptive and destabilizing force, but transition is necessary if digital libraries are to continue to thrive.

At the same time, library collections are usually funded at local, regional or national levels, and their funding is intended to support communities at local, regional or national levels. Even before digital libraries began to evolve toward the social web, traditional library funding models (from local or national parent bodies, for local or national communities) did not work well for open digital libraries, which from the beginning transcended the boundaries of place and attracted global audiences. But the global audience for an open digital library does not fund it; the funding body does. As Cliff Lynch pointed out ten years ago in his insightful piece on political and economic aspects of digital library development (2003), tension around the design, development and continuous improvement of open digital libraries arises when there is a mismatch between who benefits from the digital library and who pays for it.

The tension created by this mismatch can be considerable, but it can be reduced through careful work with a digital library's political and economic stakeholders. New business models for open digital libraries can also help; the story of moving to a community-based model to fund arXiv.org is a case in point (Rieger, 2011). Calling for a collaborative sustainability strategy, Rieger notes[1] 'as scholars worldwide depend on the stable operation and continued development of arXiv, sustainability is best assured by aligning revenue sources with [the institutions whose scholars] . . . realize value from their use of ArXiv'.

Failed social web experiments

Digital libraries have tended to offer simple information access; along the continuums depicted in Figure 9.1, many if not most digital libraries today belong at the left (focus on collections and expert communications; read-only or authorized contributions only). As such, they do not offer a favorable 'habitat' for successful implementations of social web tools, which arose from quite different conditions (active online communities). This has led to a number of failed experiments introducing social web tools to digital libraries. Derek Law, in an essay about future digital developments for libraries, characterizes some library attempts to apply social web tools as well intentioned attempts to use new information spaces to deliver old information. He writes:

> librarians have engaged in almost every fad . . . without perhaps considering how service philosophy should change . . . the [key definers of social networks] need to underpin any decision to use the tools . . . or else we run the risk of further littering the web with inactive library blogs, lifeless virtual library communities and out-of-date Facebook pages
>
> Law, 2011, 367

The social web is not simply a new fashion; it represents a new way of thinking and doing things. Applied superficially, social web tools will lead to results like those reported by Gerolimos (2011), whose review of the literature about libraries on Facebook and his own study led him to conclude that library Facebook pages are unlikely to stimulate significant interaction between libraries and their communities. Another study by Gerolimos and

Konsta (2011) suggested that except for RSS, academic library imple-mentations of social media tools generated low levels of use and participation.

A source of this failure is that some implementers have used social web tools to merely promote what they are doing, instead of using them to establish and maintain relationships or help their communities do what *they* want to do. Schrier (2011) emphasizes that a successful social media strategy for digital libraries involves becoming 'intertwined with the knowledge creation processes relevant to their collections.' This approach differs from learning how to use a few social media tools and then adding them to a web interface. Schrier offers a set of five general principles (listening, participation, transparency, policy, and strategy) for planning digital library strategic options and becoming 'facilitators of conversations' on the social web. Digital library experiments with social media tools can also benefit from studying what has made social web tools successful in other settings. Such an approach is likely to uncover not only a solid strategy and receptive audience(s) for digital library experiments, but also any technical or organizational barriers to overcome. Gazan, for example, constructed a decision model for examining the prospects of introducing digital library annotation tools (2008).

Being successful on the social web will also require digital library builders to understand, innovate and continue responding to how their communities look for people and information using search engines and social sites, how they share what they create or find, and how information shows up in diverse contexts on the social web. Among other things this involves optimizing the reach and visibility of digital library content.

Optimizing the reach and visibility of digital libraries
Some successful experiments

Digital library managers have successfully experimented with social web techniques to make their collections easier to find and use in an environment where even well known digital libraries must compete for the attention of online communities. Two of the numerous examples of early experiments involved Flickr and Wikipedia.

Flickr

In 2007 a small team at the Library of Congress began a low-cost pilot project to test ways to increase awareness of historic photographs from the collection. Other project objectives were to gain experience and understanding of the social web, tagging and community interaction. The team chose Flickr (www.flickr.com: a popular photosharing site) for the experiment (Springer et al., 2008). Their sharing of two collections of 4615 digitized photographs beginning in January 2008 met with overwhelming positive response. A few months later, the photos had been viewed over 10 million times; 79% had been added to Flickr members' personal collections; over 67,000 tags had been added; thousands of comments had been left; and average monthly visits to the LC's own photographs site had risen 20%. Subsequent evaluations demonstrated sustained high community interaction (Bray et al., 2011). The Library learned it could reach new audiences and demonstrate its value to the public using social web approaches.

Conversations between the Library and Flickr also led to the launch of the Flickr Commons (www.flickr.com/commons), where many cultural heritage institutions now share public photo collections, including the Smithsonian (Kalfatovic et al., 2008). Bray et al. (2011) provide information about the highly positive outcomes achieved by several other participants in the Flickr Commons.

Wikipedia

Motivated by a well known survey (De Rosa, 2005) indicating low use of library websites for starting research, the University of Washington (UW) Libraries initiated a project in early 2006 to have students insert links about the libraries' digital collections into Wikipedia (Lally and Dunford, 2007). The objectives were to test this new way to reach out to users and determine if it would drive new traffic to UW websites. The team chose Wikipedia because it was already a top referrer to the collections. Analysis of their server statistics over the ensuing months indicated that the added links drove a sustained upward climb of traffic from Wikipedia to UW digital libraries. They concluded that Wikipedia is an essential, low-cost tool for making digital library content highly visible outside the library's web pages. Proffitt and Snyder's more recent findings (2012) confirmed that links and images added to Wikipedia can help to build a digital library's reach and visibility.

Other experiments

Libraries and museums have also reported successful experiments with tagging, Facebook, Twitter, YouTube and Pinterest (just a few of the available analyses are Trant, 2009a; Thornton, 2012; King, 2012). These types of experiments by individual libraries have continued in parallel with the emergence of new, large-scale methods and technologies for reaching new audiences and making digital library content more visible in search engines and in many contexts on the social web.

Mobile apps and interfaces

The use of mobile devices is becoming ubiquitous around the world and increasingly there is an expectation that services will provide mobile applications (apps) and interfaces (Purcell, 2010). Trends reported in Pew Internet reports suggest that 56% of American adults owned a smartphone, 34% owned a tablet, half reported having apps on their phones and 82% had them on their tablets (Anderson and Rainie, 2012; pewinternet.org trend data, device ownership, May 2013). Seeking for online news and information increasingly relies on portable devices (Purcell, 2010, slide 66). Mobile is linked to the social web, too: a global web research firm reported that mobile is the main factor driving the use of social platforms across all markets (GlobalWebIndex, 2013).

Lippincott (2010) examined the implications of increasing ownership of mobile devices for academic libraries and concluded there are both opportunities and challenges for academic libraries that develop mobile applications. Since then, libraries have begun to go mobile: Thomas (2012) reported continued growth in the implementation of mobile services by American public and academic libraries from the baseline captured in 2010, when 34% of American public libraries and 44% of academic libraries reported providing some type of mobile service.

Mobile access to digital libraries

Mitchell and Suchy (2012) examine mobile access to *digital libraries* based on four case studies and found that developing mobile access to digital collections remains in early stages at the time of this writing. Using the EPrints software, Adewumi (2013) built a repository for Covenant University in Nigeria and tested its usability on various mobile devices. Noting that only the Greenstone platform provided a mobile interface to digital repositories at the time, Rosa et al. (2012) presented their design process for a mechanism for making DSpace repositories accessible on mobile phones. The intent was to meet a need in regions of the world where widespread access to the internet is not common but use of cell phones is. The paper is well worth consulting, as the design process featured the use of surveys and the development of personas to learn the characteristics, needs and expectations of intended users of the mobile interface. A mobile interface was added to the DSpace 3.0 code this year (Tzoc, 2013).

A quick literature review of work on mobile interfaces and apps for digital libraries suggests only nascent development in this area. However, given that social media use and information seeking preferences are shifting strongly in the direction of mobile devices, it seems inevitable that digital libraries will eventually want to be able to reach their communities through mobile devices.

SEO and SMO

SEO (search engine optimization) is important on the social web because the more frequently a site is included on the first few pages of search result lists, the more visitors it will receive. The more visitors a site receives, the greater the likelihood that selected content will be tweeted, tagged, bookmarked, shared on a social network, and linked to. This cycle of activity also works in reverse: findings of a number of the experiments discussed in an earlier section of this chapter demonstrated a positive correlation between sharing selected digital library content on social media sites and increased visits to the digital libraries' web sites. Onaifo and Rasmussen's analysis (2013) found that the amount of traffic that a site receives is a factor driving its ranking by search engines, which in turn is a factor driving where information indexed from that site appears in search engine results.

Most digital library managers do not have an SEO strategy for improving the reach and visibility of their digital libraries. The literature about SEO in any library context is quite small. As discussed in Chapter 8, Beel, Gipp and Wilde (2010) and Arlitsch and O'Brien (2013) provide information on how to utilize SEO techniques to increase the visibility of digital library content in academic search engines. Onaifo and Rasmussen offer the most thorough recent analysis of SEO and the findability of library web pages. Through an evaluation of the findings of a study of Ontario public library web sites, most of which were poorly ranked in search engine results, they identified which website characteristics are positively correlated with increased findability and ranking by search engines.

The Onaifo and Rasmussen article also contains a reference to a new set of techniques – social media optimization or SMO, a phrase first introduced in 2006 by Bhargava (2010) – that libraries can use to increase their linkability from social media sites. Onaifo and Rasmussen remark 'it is insufficient to use social media simply as a store front, as many libraries do, if the goal is to attract users to the library's website. It is also a good SMO strategy to make it easier for others to tag and bookmark library content, as well as engage with library content through such means as comments and content sharing (within copyright limits).' An updated list of Bhargava's five rules for SMO follow:

1 Create shareable content
2 Make sharing easy
3 Reward engagement
4 Proactively share content
5 Encourage the mashup.

It will be an important step in the evolution of digital libraries on the social web for digital library managers to begin to apply SEO and SMO best practices to digital library sites and content.

The semantic web and linked data

Chapter 1 examines the compelling vision that led to the emergence of digital libraries. One section quotes J. C. R. Licklider, an internet pioneer who foresaw the power of human interaction with the body of knowledge 'conceived of as a dynamic process involving repeated examinations and intercomparisons of very many small and scattered parts' (1965, 5). The semantic web and linked data have the potential to realize this aspect of Licklider's vision for libraries of the future. Chapter 3 introduces the semantic web and linked data and explains why these 'very many small and scattered parts' could be important to the advancement of knowledge and culture themselves. Chapter 4 discusses the history and current situation for OAI-ORE, a relatively new standard that uses a semantic web approach for describing and exchanging aggregations of web resources (usually scholarly resources). Chapter 5 provides an introduction to library linked data that describes traditional library collections (rather than digital libraries). How to deploy these new technologies and standards in digital libraries is a new grand challenge to the field.

Erik Mitchell (2012) explains why the semantic web and linked data are important to the digital libraries built and maintained by libraries, archives and museums. The semantic web and linked data are important to the social web because they produce open, re-usable bits of data that facilitate machine-to-machine interactions, in turn enabling better integration and interoperability of digital library information in other contexts.

Scholarly research and linked data

The semantic web and linked data offer the possibility of 'a more data-centric, semantically-linked, and social network-embedded scholarly communication model that resembles the profound changes in social, political, and economic discourse characteristic of Web 2.0' (Van de Sompel et al., 2009). Put another way, the semantic web and linked data offer new opportunities for scholars to share the results of their work in more dynamic, interactive ways.

An examination of the Data Hub (www.datahub.io) for linked datasets representing scholarly content suggests that scholarly linked data has begun to be available to re-mix and re-use, especially in the following areas:

- computer and information science and engineering – examples include linked datasets representing DBLP and ACM publications and IEEE papers and e-research data; the contents of the ECS (Electronics and Computer Science) Southampton repository are also available as linked data
- life sciences – the prominent example is PubMed
- repositories – examples include the linked datasets representing the contents of EPrints Southampton and several institutional repositories at the Open University in the UK.

In addition, Data Hub searches reveal quite a number of e-research datasets, particularly in the areas of the life sciences, chemistry and environmental science, although only a small subset are structured as linked data.

Identifiers, interlinking and linked data

Identifiers are an essential component of the Kahn-Wilensky architecture of digital libraries. Key outcomes of the first decade of digital libraries were a keen understanding of the role of identifiers and their importance for reliably linking between and across web resources and sites (think of DOIs).

The new vision of the web as a semantic, global web of data has renewed attention to URIs (Uniform Resource Identifiers) for both persistently identifying a resource and providing the means to express relationships and link to other resources. The digital library field has continued to contribute substantially to the work to build linked datasets and to further develop the utility of a range of identifiers in linked data. Some examples of this work include:

- CrossRef DOI Resolver – a linked dataset that contains URIs for every DOI that CrossRef manages. This supports the use of DOIs in linked data applications.
- Medline – a linked data implementation of 19 million Medline articles, linked to their DOI URIs and journal identifiers.
- VIAF – a representation as linked data that includes URIs for VIAF IDs in the dataset. These URIs link to the clusters of multilingual forms of names in multiple cultural heritage institutions' name authority files (e.g., consider the many ways in which different nations express the name of the playwright Anton Chekhov).
- The British National Bibliography (BNB), LIBRIS (Swedish academic library union catalog), and several other national library catalogs – the linked data representations of these link to URIs in VIAF.

Digital library linked data

Linked datasets have been seen as a way to make library metadata – not just resource descriptions, but vocabularies and metadata schemas – more relevant and interoperable on the web. Digital library linked data is important on the social web because it has the potential to surface digital library content – and its relationships to other content – much more easily on social sites, as well as to support new social web services. So far this potential has not been realized, but the first step is to make digital library linked data available to be used in applications.

There are some linked datasets that represent library-managed digital libraries; one example is Chronicling America (http://chroniclingamerica.loc. gov). At the time of this writing the most prominent of the digital libraries represented by linked data is Europeana (www.europeana.eu). Other leaders in the deployment of semantic web and linked data approaches in digital libraries include the Bibliothèque nationale de France (for its Gallica and Data Digital Libraries; see Edelstein et al., 2013) and the University of Alicante in Spain (for its Biblioteca Virtual Miguel de Cervantes). These digital library initiatives were honored with 2013 Stanford Prizes for Innovation in Research Libraries (Zaino, 2013).

Europeana and linked data

Europeana, the European Union's flagship digital library project, provides a portal to discover cultural heritage materials held in libraries, museums, archives and audiovisual collections across Europe. In early 2013 Europeana was providing discovery services for 26 million objects in cultural heritage institutions in 28 countries (Cousins, 2013; Europeana Foundation, 2013, 8–9). The Europeana Data Model (EDM) is a framework for ingesting, managing and publishing metadata from its contributing organizations (Isaac, 2012). Its basis is in OAI-ORE and the principles of linked data. The EDM is designed so that it can be used by other organizations to structure their metadata. The Digital Public Library of America's model builds on the experience of EDM (Digital Public Library of America, 2013).

Following their work on the EDM specification, the Europeana team soon mounted a project to represent Europeana metadata using the EDM and make the results available as linked data (Haslhofer and Isaac, 2011). In 2012 Europeana released the restructured metadata as open linked data, first in a pilot. Later the same year, Europeana released all Europeana metadata as open linked data; at the time of the initial release the dataset contained metadata on 20 million objects (Europeana Foundation, 2013). This means there is now a substantial and significant body of linked data about European digital library collections to be re-used and re-mixed in other contexts, including social web sites.

Rights issues and digital library linked data

The semantic web has been conceived as a public data commons, open to anyone. Linked datasets function most effectively if they are open and available for re-use with no or minimal restrictions. 'Europeana Terms for User Contributions' (www.europeana.eu/portal/rights/terms-for-user-contributions.html) specifies that Europeana will make organizations' contributed metadata available under the terms of the Creative Commons CC0 1.0 Universal Public Domain Dedication (CC0; www.creativecommons.org/publicdomain/zero/1.0). This means that the contributor is dedicating the metadata to the public domain and waiving all rights to it. The legal issues related to aggregating, exchanging and re-using data from cultural heritage institutions can be complex, especially in an international context. Rights to metadata may be restricted, terms for re-use and exchange may be unclear, or the metadata might be an organization's key business asset (Baker et al., 2011, under 3.3).

Digital library contributions to the semantic web

There is ample reason for digital library researchers and builders to be inspired by the prospects of the semantic web and linked data, and good progress is being made. As noted in Chapter 4, next-generation repositories and projects related to OAI-ORE are using semantic web approaches. Tools for publishing metadata as RDF are readily available (Byrne and Goddard, 2010, Appendix). At this time, however, digital library specialists are contributing more to the development of the semantic web by publishing linked datasets than by building applications that use linked data. It will take time for developers inside and outside the digital library space to build applications that consume linked data.

Schema.org

Schema.org (www.schema.org) is an organization formed in June 2011 through a joint effort of search engine leaders Bing, Google and Yahoo. It offers a collection of metadata element sets that enable webmasters to take advantage of semantic web approaches to structuring data and then use them for SEO and other purposes. A simple explanation of schema.org is that it provides a vocabulary of types of things (movies, books, events, etc.) and uses *microdata* (a mechanism for embedding structured machine-readable data in HTML documents). For example, the schema.org vocabulary, combined with properties defined by microdata, can alert a search engine that the marked-up section of a web page communicates the name of a person, and what that name is. In that sense schema.org is a *semantic* web approach (that is, it is based on the machine encoding of *meaning*). The major search engines (Google, Bing and Yahoo) 'understand' and deploy this structured data to assess relevance and augment the display of search engine results.

Semantic web approaches based on schema.org and microdata are increasingly being used in e-commerce (Hepp, 2012). Li, Wald and Wills (2012) describe how these techniques are being used in multimedia applications to expose the inside content of multimedia resources ('media fragments') for indexing by search engines. Examples are part of a YouTube video or part of a music recording.

In the digital library domain, Ronallo (2012) offers an overview, tutorial and examples of schema.org and microdata used to mark up web pages for digital objects in the North Carolina State University Libraries Digital Collections. Ronallo also explains some current limitations of these techniques for the cultural heritage sector. In the library space in general, OCLC is experimenting with embedding structured metadata in each WorldCat.org record based on schema.org (Miller et al., 2012, 34; Breeding, 2013b) to promote better discovery of library materials in schema.org participating search engines. The prospects for more digital library applications of schema.org seem good, but at the time of this writing, it is early days for these techniques.

Mass digitization and digital libraries

Chapter 5 discusses mass digitization and a number of other large-scale digitization projects for book collections. There are now millions and millions of digitized books around the world. What does it mean for digital libraries? No one knows. At the time of this writing, except for public domain books, and despite Google Books' most recent victory in the courts (*The Guardian*, 2013) the legal challenges and publisher resistance are preventing the entire impact of the Google Library Project and other initiatives from rolling out. But mass digitization of widely held materials in libraries has already had a good deal of influence on the digital library landscape for individual libraries.

For many reasons, the role and primacy of huge legacy book collections held by academic research libraries are changing. Special collections and archives are now widely perceived as key assets of research collections, because they are what make research library collections distinctive. Unfortunately, small special collections budgets and other problems constrain the possibilities to pursue high-cost strategies around them (see for example Education Advisory Board, 2011, xiii, 78; Maron and Pickle, 2013, 2–3). If fresh new approaches to mounting and sustaining projects could be found, given how many of these collections remain hidden (see for example Dooley and Luce, 2010), there is the potential for many new digital library initiatives.

Not just new investment, but social web, participatory approaches could help to add new and enhance existing digital libraries, make these collections visible on the web, preserve more unique materials for future generations, and spawn outreach programs to make this digital content accessible in new contexts and to many communities. Whether this actually happens or not remains unpredictable. Continued pressure on library budgets is a hindering factor, but the possibilities of partnerships and increasing public and research interest in digital representations of cultural heritage content, driven by large initiatives such as those in the Netherlands and France and by Europeana and DPLA, are driving factors.

Large-scale digital libraries, portals and platforms

Chapter 2 discusses a sample of 15 working digital libraries that have endured since the start of digital libraries. The oldest is Project Gutenberg (www.gutenberg.org), which is not only the first digital library, dating from 1971, but also the project that has exemplified strong connections to a community of participants from the beginning (Lebert, 2008).

Another one of the sample projects from the first decade of digital libraries is Trove (www.trove.nla.gov.au; Holley, 2010b), which developed a strong community around its digitized newspaper content, whose OCR text accuracy was a concern for the NLA (National Library of Australia). The decision was made to expose the raw OCR text to the public for correction, starting in December 2007. The public's response was immediate and positive beyond any expectation (Holley, 2009; 2010a). The project is now famous for crowdsourcing work on a large-scale digitization project. Crowdsourcing, discussed in the next section, is a massive collaboration technique that enables individuals, working as a virtual group, to collectively accomplish a shared, large and significant goal.

The implementers of two other early projects, Gallica, from the Bibliothèque nationale de France (http://gallica.bnf.fr) and American Memory, the flagship service of the US National Digital Library Program (www.memory.loc.gov), launched traditional read-only digital libraries but made unanticipated discoveries about the communities that engaged deeply with their content and services. The BnF's 2002 BibUsages project studied the usage and users of Gallica and concluded that 'digital libraries, far from being simple digital versions of library holdings, are now attracting a new type of public, bringing about new, unique and original ways for reading and understanding texts' (Assadi et al., 2003). In the course of the interviews I conducted for this book, I learned that American Memory was initially targeted at professors and others in university settings; a pre-test revealed the true primary audience to be grade school and high school teachers. An interviewee for this book recounted her insight that, thanks to the end-user test, 'teachers developed curricular ideas and shared them. As a result, many years later, many digital resources continue to be used, discussed and remembered.'

Europeana (www.europeana.eu) has begun experimenting with projects to engage ordinary citizens, scholars, teachers and children with its massive, cross-cultural and multilingual digital library. In March 2011 it launched the highly interactive Europeana 1914–1918 (www.europeana1914-1918.eu/en), which allows people to connect their stories and memorabilia to Europeana. The online social features are supplemented with road shows; the ones in

Germany alone resulted in 25,000 artifacts being scanned (Charlton, 2012) and added to the collection. Another community engagement project, in partnership with the Digital Public Library of America (DPLA), focuses on Europeans immigrating to America (Berkman Center, 2011).

Europeana's leaders have conceived the program's public mission in the context of the social web. In a 2012 interview, Jill Cousins, executive director of Europeana, said 'The whole Europeana concept is not about creating a destination site in Europeana.eu but about distributing the aggregated data into other systems, mobile applications and so forth so that the content can be used in many different ways and sustain different ways of looking at the material – e.g. in higher education and schools' (Cranfield, 2012).

The Digital Public Library of America, or DPLA (www.dp.la) is intended to be 'a digital library in service of the American public' (Cranfield, 2012) bringing digital content from many sources together in one platform. DPLA launched in April 2013, having recently hired Dan Cohen, an historian and well known leader of social web-inspired initiatives at the Center for History and New Media, as DPLA's founding Executive Director. In an interview shortly after the hiring was announced, Cohen remarked that 'successful digital projects mainly involve getting diverse people working together towards an ideal.' Cohen envisions DPLA as a portal that 'will bring entirely new audiences to formerly scattered collections' and 'a large open storehouse for classroom use and scholarly investigation' (Enis, 2013).

Crowdsourcing and citizen science
Crowdsourcing background

This section is a brief treatment of a large and significant subject; it offers some background, some sources for further study, and a few examples. William Safire (2009), the well known columnist, explored the origins of the word 'crowdsourcing' in a piece for the *New York Times Magazine*. He reported that Jeff Howe of *Wired* magazine had coined the term in 2005 and wrote about it in 2006 (Howe, 2006). An examination of these sources and several others reveals that crowdsourcing arose in the business sector as an innovative way to outsource work to ordinary people instead of employees or contractors.

Daren Brabham, a researcher who wrote his dissertation on crowdsourcing and the collective intelligence of online communities, explains why crowdsourcing has had so much success in the business community. He concludes that crowdsourcing is 'a model [enabled by the web] capable of aggregating talent, leveraging ingenuity while reducing the costs and time formerly needed to solve problems' (Brabham, 2008, 87). Brabham's dissertation (2010) treats the topic of crowdsourcing much more broadly and thoroughly. Many other types of organizations outside the business world rapidly embraced crowdsourcing. Of course, Wikipedia is the epitome of crowdsourcing and the power of the social web (and it predates the coining of both terms).

Digital library crowdsourcing

In the digital library space, the promising results of Europeana 1914–1918 have already been mentioned as well as the digital program for historic newspapers of the National Library of Australia's Trove service. Another noted experiment is the steve.museum project, which found crowdsourcing to be successful for enhancing access (through tagging) and creating alternative vocabulary to museum documentation (Trant, 2009b).

Holley's article on crowdsourcing (2010a) discusses several other organizations' successful experiments with the technique. Two of the six projects that she covers are FamilySearch Indexing and Distributed Proofreaders. FamilySearch Indexing (https://familysearch.org/volunteer/indexing) crowdsources the indexing of family history records and makes the results freely available. Volunteers had indexed over a billion family history records as of the time of this writing. Project Gutenberg, the first digital library, fittingly inspired one of the earliest crowdsourcing projects, which dates from 2000 and is called Distributed Proofreaders (www.pgdp.net/c/). As of this writing, Distributed Proofreader volunteers had helped convert nearly 26,000 public domain titles into freely available e-books.

Using amateurs to address large-scale professional or technical challenges was once considered to have no chance of succeeding. In the digital library arena, Gregory Crane of the Perseus Digital Library has documented the challenges of extracting geospatial data from a very large number of unstructured historical textual sources (2004). The Perseus Digital Library recently began experimenting with crowdsourcing (Davis, 2012). Fleet, Kowal and Přidal (2012) describe other crowdsourcing efforts related to digitized historical maps – an online initiative to crowdsource the georeferencing of historical map images using the Georeferencer application. Five institutions had implemented projects as of late 2012: the Moravian Library (Brno), the Nationaal Archief (The Hague), the National Library of Scotland (Edinburgh), the British Library (London), and the Institut Cartografic de Catalunya (Barcelona). At each location, the public's online participation significantly increased the number of historical maps that were georeferenced. At the Institut Cartografic de Catalunya, for example, 1000 early printed and manuscript maps and aerial photographs were all georeferenced in 24 days by 88 volunteers.

Citizen science

Experiences with crowdsourcing have contributed to the rapid development of citizen science initiatives. Andrea Wiggins and Kevin Crowston have been reporting on the impressive work being done at the Syracuse University School of Information Studies to study and understand citizen science, which they define as a form of research collaboration involving members of the public in scientific research projects that address real-world problems.

Wiggins and Crowston (2011, 2012) present their analyses and categorization of citizen science initiatives, concluding 'under the right circumstances, citizen science can work on a massive scale, generating high quality data that lead to reliable, valid scientific outcomes as well as unexpected insights and innovation' (2012, 3426). They particularly note the efficacy of virtual (web-based) citizen science, such as the well known Galaxy Zoo (www.galaxyzoo.org) project, which crowdsources the classification of images of galaxies. Over three years in the project's life, more than 250,000 volunteers participated in the classification of over 56 million galaxies (2011, 7).

Crowdsourcing and citizen science may be the most important social web phenomena for digital library specialists to watch, as there are many potential ideas and applications that would be worth considering as digital libraries move into the future.

Conclusion

The social web is an emergent, highly chaotic space. Social web initiatives related to the digital library field are equally chaotic, representing the convergence of many overlapping, parallel or directly competing efforts. More contenders for the attention of a digital library researcher or professional seem to enter this confusing new space every week. One of the digital library leaders interviewed for this book said 'this space is a mess at the moment. Many projects will fail. It is hard to predict which ones will succeed.'

In the evolution of digital libraries toward new roles on the social web, existing conventions and supporting systems are already undergoing significant disruption, and while the disruption is painful, it also presents new opportunities for digital libraries to go beyond what they have achieved in their first two decades. While these achievements are impressive, they will not guarantee future success, especially in the fast-moving world of the social web. The best way to honor digital libraries' past is to participate in creating their future.

Chapter 5 of this book makes a case for merging hybrid library and digital library strategic agendas; it simply makes no sense to continue separate, parallel lines of development. Chapter 6 makes a case for evolving digital library research and practice by shifting the primary focus toward digital libraries' social roles, in particular how they might empower individuals and support the progress of knowledge, learning, the free flow of ideas and an informed citizenry. Marilyn Deegan and Simon Tanner (2002, 216–17), in an eloquent passage in their book *Digital Futures*, write 'librarians should redefine the profession, not in terms of the collections we hold, but in terms of the skills, abilities and value we bring to our communities . . . the time has come for us not to be defined by infrastructure'. Infrastructure can be buildings, collections, or enabling technologies. Libraries' and librarians' social roles and communities are more likely to abide over time; collections and enabling technologies are more likely to shift.

Derek Law, writing of digital developments in the library landscape, speaks of the urgent need for an 'overarching philosophical redefinition of what libraries should be' (2011, 374). To emphasize his point about the trouble that libraries are having staying relevant and viable in a world dominated by the web, Law rewords quotes from Clay Shirky's famous blog post on the demise of the newspaper industry (Shirky, 2009). Law's version replaces some of Shirky's words with words related to libraries (362–3). I have followed Law's lead but supplied some of my own rewording:

> Society doesn't need ~~newspapers~~ libraries. What we need is ~~journalism~~ knowledge and understanding . . . When we shift our attention from "save ~~newspapers~~ libraries" to "save society," the imperative changes from "preserve the current institutions" to "do whatever works." And what works today isn't the same as what used to work . . . No one experiment is going to replace what we are now losing with the demise of ~~news on paper~~ libraries as they have been, but over time, the collection of new experiments that do work might give us the ~~journalism~~ libraries and librarians we need.

R. David Lankes has written and spoken widely on the importance of a new worldview that is free of assumptions carried forward from libraries' past successes and librarians' traditional roles. He is well known for his conceptualization of 'participatory librarianship' and for his emphasis of librarians' societal roles:

> The mission of librarians is to improve society through facilitating knowledge creation in their communities
>
> Lankes, 2011

Lankes has provided new conceptual models not only for librarianship, but also for libraries as community platforms. While the models are intended for redefining libraries generally, they are equally useful for defining the next steps for digital libraries' participation in the social web.

Most digital libraries continue to operate from a traditional, collections-centered service model. Change will be difficult, especially in the realm of scholarly practices and norms, where the roots of tradition are deep. Lankes and Law offer clear-eyed appraisals of current prospects and new models for rethinking what libraries and digital libraries should and can do for a society that is now so dominated by the social web. Their work and that of the hundreds of other people cited in this book provide ample reason for optimism.

Internet pioneer J. C. R. Licklider predicted long ago that the 'libraries of the future' may not resemble libraries as they have been. Digital libraries are moving to the mainstream, but for them too, the future may not look much like the past. The social web opens the door to new possibilities, but experimenting superficially with social media will not increase libraries' or digital libraries' value in a globally networked world. Community-centered strategies, aligned with the large changes shaping the web and society, are required.

The first grand vision of digital libraries inspired two decades of digital library research and practice that have been, and continue to be, a powerful force for advancing the pursuit of knowledge and culture. Emulating the creativity and pioneering spirit of digital libraries' first 20 years is the starting point for creating the next grand vision for libraries' digital future.

········

References

This list contains references to the content that I have cited in the chapters. It does not contain references to other work.

Aaron, James (2012) The Authors Guild V. Hathitrust: A Way Forward for Digital Access to Neglected Works in Libraries. *Lewis & Clark Law Review* 16 (4). http://papers.ssrn.com/sol3/papers.cfm?abstract_id=2205374.

Abram, Stephen (2007) Web 2.0, Library 2.0, and Librarian 2.0: Preparing for the 2.0 World. In *Online International Conference Proceedings*. http://stephenslighthouse.com/files/OnlineIntrenationalProceedings1.pdf.

Adamick, Jessica, and Rebecca Reznik-Zellen (2010a) Representation and Recognition of Subject Repositories. *D-Lib Magazine* 16 (9/10). doi:10.1045/september2010-adamick.

Adamick, Jessica, and Rebecca Reznik-Zellen (2010b) Trends in Large-Scale Subject Repositories. *D-Lib Magazine* 16 (11/12). doi:10.1045/november2010-adamick.

Adewumi, Adewole Oluwasegun (2013) Deployment and Usability Evaluation of Mobile Access to Institutional Repository. Master's thesis, Covenant University. http://dspace.covenantuniversity.edu.ng/handle/123456789/39.

Altman, Micah (2008) Digital Libraries. In *Handbook of Research On Public Information Technology*: 152–62. Hershey, PA: Information Science Reference.

Anaraki, Leila Nemati, and Azadeh Heidari (2010) Bridging the Digital Divide. In *Developing Sustainable Digital Libraries*: 286–310. IGI Global.

Anderson, Janna Quitney, and Lee Rainie (2012) *The Future of Apps and Web*. Pew Research Center Internet & American Life Project. www.pewinternet.org/Reports/2012/Future-of-Apps-and-Web.aspx.

Anderson, Kent (2013) A Matter of Perspective – Elsevier Acquires Mendeley . . . or, Mendeley Sells Itself to Elsevier. *The Scholarly Kitchen*. April 8.

http://scholarlykitchen.sspnet.org/2013/04/08/a-matter-of-perspective-elsevier-acquires-mendeley-or-mendeley-sells-itself-to-elsevier/.

Andrew W. Mellon Foundation (2001) *Annual Report*. Mellon Foundation. www.mellon.org/news_publications/annual-reports-essays/annual-reports/content2001.pdf.

Antelman, Kristin (2004) Do Open-Access Articles Have a Greater Research Impact? *College & Research Libraries* 65 (5) (September): 372–82.

Antelman, Kristin, E. Lynema, and A. K. Pace (2006) Toward a 21st Century Library Catalog. *Information Technology and Libraries* (September).

Archives New Zealand (2009) *Digital Continuity Action Plan: Managing Information for Public Sector Efficiency*. Wellington NZ. http://archives.govt.nz/download-digital-continuity-action-plan.

Arlitsch, Kenning, and Patrick S. O'Brien (2012) Invisible Institutional Repositories: Addressing the Low Indexing Ratios of IRs in Google Scholar. *Library Hi Tech* 30 (1): 60–81. doi:10.1108/07378831211213210.

Arlitsch, Kenning, and Patrick S. O'Brien (2013) *Improving the Visibility and Use of Digital Repositories through SEO*. LITA Guides. ALA Editions.

Armbruster, Chris (2011) Open Access Policy Implementation: First Results Compared. *Learned Publishing* 24(4): 311–24.

Arms, William Y. (1995) Key Concepts in the Architecture of the Digital Library. *D-Lib Magazine* 1 (1).

Arms, William Y. (2000) *Digital Libraries*. MIT Press.

Arms, William Y. (2005) A Viewpoint Analysis of the Digital Library. *D-Lib Magazine* 11 (07/08). doi:10.1045/july2005-arms.

Arms, William Y. (2012) The 1990s: The Formative Years of Digital Libraries. *Library Hi Tech* 30 (4): 579–91.

Arms, William Y., C. Blanchi, and E. A. Overly (1997) An Architecture for Information in Digital Libraries. *D-Lib Magazine* 3 (2).

Arms, William Y., Manuel Calimlin, and Lucia Walle (2009) EScience in Practice. *D-Lib Magazine* 15 (5/6) (May). dpi:10.1045/may2009-arms.

Arms, William Y., Diane Hillmann, Carl Lagoze, Dean Krafft, Richard Marisa, John Saylor, Carol Terrizzi, and Herbert Van de Sompel (2002) A Spectrum of Interoperability. *D-Lib Magazine* 8 (1) (January). doi:10.1045/january2002-arms.

Asher, Andrew D., Lynda M. Duke, and Suzanne Wilson (2012) Paths of Discovery: Comparing the Search Effectiveness of EBSCO Discovery Service, Summon, Google Scholar, and Conventional Library Resources. *College & Research Libraries* (May 17). http://crl.acrl.org/content/early/2012/05/07/crl-374.

Assadi, H., T. Beauvisage, C. Lupovici, and T. Cloarec (2003) Users and Uses of Online Digital Libraries in France. *Research and Advanced Technology for Digital*

Libraries: 1–12.

Association for Information Science and Technology (ASIS&T) (2013) ASIS&T Announces Management Partnership with DCMI. June. www.asis.org/news/DCMI_announcement.html.

Association of College and Research Libraries (ACRL) (2011) *Standards for Libraries in Higher Education*. www.ala.org/acrl/standards/standardslibraries.

Association of Learned and Professional Society Publishers (ALPSP) (2004) *ALPSP Principles of Scholarship-friendly Journal Publishing Practice*. www.library.arizona.edu/documents/dlist/SFpub210104.pdf.

Association of Research Libraries (ARL) (2008) *Special Collections Task Force Final Status Report, 2006*. www.arl.org/rtl/speccoll/spcolltf/status0706.shtml.

Atkins, Daniel, Kelvin K. Droegemeier, Stuart I. Feldman, Hector Garcia-Molina, Michael L. Klein, David G. Messerschmitt, Paul Messina, Jeremiah P. Ostriker, and Margaret H. Wright (2003) *Revolutionizing Science and Engineering Through Cyberinfrastructure*. National Science Foundation Blue-Ribbon Advisory Panel on Cyberinfrastructure. http://arizona.openrepository.com/arizona/handle/10150/106224.

Avram, Henriette D. (1969) *The MARC Pilot Project: Final Report on a Project Sponsored by the Council on Library Resources, Inc*. Library of Congress.

Awre, C. and T. Cramer (2012) Building the Hydra Together: Enhancing Repository Provision through Multi-institution Collaboration. *Journal of Digital Information* 13 (1). https://journals.tdl.org/jodi/article/download/5879/5923.

Awre, C., T. Cramer, R. Green, L. McRae, B. Sadler, T. Sigmon, T. Staples, and R. Wayland (2009) Project Hydra: Designing & Building a Reusable Framework for Multipurpose, Multifunction, Multi-institutional Repository-powered Solutions presented at the 4th International Conference on Open Repositories, May 20. http://smartech.gatech.edu/handle/1853/28496.

Ayre, Catherine, and Adrienne Muir (2004) The Right to Preserve. *D-Lib Magazine* 10 (3) (March). doi:10.1045/march2004-ayre. www.dlib.org/dlib/march04/ayre/03ayre.html.

Bailey, Charles W. (2011) E-science and Academic Libraries Bibliography. Digital Scholarship. http://digital-scholarship.org/ealb/ealb.htm.

Bailey, Charles W., K. Coombs, J. Emery, A. Mitchell, C. Morris, S. Simons, and R. Wright (2006) *Spec Kit 292 Institutional Repositories*. Association of Research Libraries.

Bailey, Steve, and Dave Thompson (2006) UKWAC: Building the UKs First Public Web Archive. *D-Lib Magazine* 12 (1) (January). doi:10.1045/january2006-thompson.

Baker, Thomas, Emmanuelle Bermès, Karen Coyle, Gordon Dunsire, Antoine Isaac,

Peter Murray, Michael Panzer et al. (2011) Library Linked Data Incubator Group Final Report. W3C Library Linked Data Incubator Group. www.w3.org/2005/Incubator/lld/XGR-lld-20111025/.

Baker, Thomas, and Makx Dekkers (2003) Identifying Metadata Elements with URIs. *D-Lib Magazine* 9 (7/8) (July). doi:10.1045/july2003-baker.

Baksik, Corinna (2006) Fair Use or Exploitation? The Google Book Search Controversy. *Portal: Libraries and the Academy* 6 (4): 399–415.

Bankier, Jean-Gabriel, and Courtney Smith (2010) Digital Repositories at a Crossroads: Achieving Sustainable Success through Campus-wide Engagement. *VALA2010 Conference Proceedings*. http://works.bepress.com/jean_gabriel_bankier/8.

Barton, Mary, and J. Harford Walker (2002) *MIT Libraries DSpace Business Plan Project Final Report to the Andrew W. Mellon Foundation.* Massachusetts Institute of Technology.

Baudoin, P., and M. Branschofsky (2003) Implementing an Institutional Repository: The DSpace Experience at MIT. *Science & Technology Libraries* 24 (1/2).

Baynes, Grace (2013) Connotea to Discontinue Service. *Of Schemes and Memes Blog.* January 24. http://blogs.nature.com/ofschemesandmemes/2013/01/24/connotea-to-discontinue-service.

Beagrie, Neil (2005) Plenty of Room at the Bottom? Personal Digital Libraries and Collections. *D-Lib Magazine* 11 (06) (June). doi:10.1045/june2005-beagrie.

Beagrie, Neil., B. Lavoie, and M. Woollard (2010) *Keeping Research Data Safe 2.* HEFCE. www.prestocentre.org/system/files/library/resource/keepingresearchdatasafe2.pdf.

Bearman, David (2006) Jean-Noël Jeanneney's Critique of Google. *D-Lib Magazine* 12 (12). doi:10.1045/december2006-bearman.

Bearman, David (2007) Digital Libraries. *Annual Review of Information Science and Technology* 41 (1): 223–72.

Bederson, B. B., A. Quinn, and A. Druin (2009) Designing the Reading Experience for Scanned Multi-lingual Picture Books on Mobile Phones. In *Proceedings of the 9th ACM/IEEE-CS Joint Conference on Digital Libraries*: 305–8.

Beel, Jöran, Bela Gipp and Erik Wilde (2010) Academic Search Engine Optimization (ASEO). *Journal of Scholarly Publishing* 41 (2): 176–90.

Bell, Suzanne, and Nathan Sarr (2010) Case Study: Re-Engineering an Institutional Repository to Engage Users. *New Review of Academic Librarianship* 16 (sup1): 77–89. doi:10.1080/13614533.2010.509517.

Bergman, Michael K. (2001) White Paper: The Deep Web: Surfacing Hidden Value. *Journal of Electronic Publishing* 7 (1). http://quod.lib.umich.edu/cgi/t/text/text-idx?c=jep;view=text;rgn=main;idno=3336451.0007.104.

Berkman Center for Internet and Society. Harvard University (2011) Digital Public Library of America and Europeana Announce Collaboration. October 21. http://cyber.law.harvard.edu/node/7159.

Bermès, Emmanuelle (2006) Persistent Identifiers for Digital Resources: The Experience of the National Library of France. *International Preservation News* 40 (December): 22–6.

Berners-Lee, Tim (1994) Plenary Talk by Tim BL at WWWF94: Overview. www.w3.org/Talks/WWW94Tim.

Berners-Lee, Tim (2006) Linked Data – Design Issues. July 27. www.w3.org/DesignIssues/LinkedData.html.

Berners-Lee, Tim, James Hendler, and Ora Lassila (2001) The Semantic Web. *Scientific American* 284 (5): 28–37.

Berry, Leonard L. (2000) Cultivating Service Brand Equity. *Journal of the Academy of Marketing Science* 28 (1): 128–37. doi:10.1177/0092070300281012.

Besek, June M., Jessica Coates, Brian Fitzgerald, Wilma Mossink, William G. LeFurgy, Adrienne Muir, Mary Rasenberger, and Christopher D. Weston (2008) Digital Preservation and Copyright: An International Study. *International Journal of Digital Curation* 3 (2) (December 2). doi:10.2218/ijdc.v3i2.61.

Bhargava, Rohit (2010) The 5 NEW Rules of Social Media Optimization (SMO). *Influential Marketing Blog*. August 10. www.rohitbhargava.com/2010/08/the-5-new-rules-of-social-media-optimization-smo.html.

Bingham, Adrian (2010) The Digitization of Newspaper Archives: Opportunities and Challenges for Historians. *Twentieth Century British History* 21 (2) (June): 225–31. doi:10.1093/tcbh/hwq007.

Bishop, Ann P., N. A. Van House, and Barbara Pfeil Buttenfield (2003) *Digital Library Use: Social Practice in Design and Evaluation*. MIT Press.

Bizer, Christian (2010) Linked Data: Introduction to the Semantic Web – Invited Tutorial at ISWC 2010 presented at the ISWC 2010, November 7, Shanghai. http://people.csail.mit.edu/pcm/Bizer.pdf.

Bizer, Christian, Tom Heath, Danny Ayers, and Yves Raimond (2007) Interlinking Open Data on the Web. In *Demonstrations Track, 4th European Semantic Web Conference, Innsbruck, Austria*. http://skua.googlecode.com/svn/trunk/docs/presentations/20080218-SemAst-TL/LinkingOpenData.pdf.

Bizer, Christian, Tom Heath, and Tim Berners-Lee (2009) Linked Data – The Story So Far. *International Journal on Semantic Web and Information Systems (IJSWIS)* 5 (3) (July 1): 1–22. doi:10.4018/jswis.2009081901.

Björk, Bo-Christer, A. Roos, and M. Lauri (2009) Scientific Journal Publishing–Yearly Volume and Open Access Availability. *Information Research* 14 (1).

Björk, Bo-Christer, Patrik Welling, Mikael Laakso, Peter Majlender, Turid Hedlund, and Guðni Guðnason (2010) Open Access to the Scientific Journal Literature: Situation 2009. *PloS One* 5 (6): e11273.

Blake, M. (2002) Implementation of the OpenURL and the SFX Architecture in the Production Environment of a Digital Library. In *11th Biennial Conference of the Victorian Association for Library Automation, Melbourne, Australia.*

Block, David (2000) Remote Storage in Research Libraries. *Library Resources & Technical Services* 44 (4): 184–9.

Blue Ribbon Task Force on Sustainable Digital Preservation and Access and A. S. Rumsey (2010) *Sustainable Economics for a Digital Planet: Ensuring Long-term Access to Digital Information: Final Report.*
http://brtf.sdsc.edu/biblio/BRTF_Final_Report.pdf.

Blyberg, John (2006) 11 Reasons Why Library 2.0 Exists and Matters. *Blyberg.net.* January 9.
www.blyberg.net/2006/01/09/11-reasons-why-library-20-exists-and-matters/.

Boddie, S., J. Thompson, D. Bainbridge, and I. H Witten (2008) Coping with Very Large Digital Collections Using Greenstone. In *Proceedings of the ECDL Workshop on Very Large Digital Libraries (September 2008).*

Bohn, R. E., and J. E. Short (2009) How Much Information?: 2009 Report on American Consumers. Global Information Industry Center, University of California, San Diego.
http://jedgar.nist.gov/refs/HMI_2009_ConsumerReport_Dec9_2009.pdf.

Bollacker, Kurt, Colin Evans, Praveen Paritosh, Tim Sturge, and Jamie Taylor (2008) Freebase: a Collaboratively Created Graph Database for Structuring Human Knowledge. In *Proceedings of the 2008 ACM SIGMOD International Conference on Management of Data*: 1247–50.

Bollen, Johan, Michael L. Nelson, Giridhar Manepalli, Giridhar Nandigam, and Suchitra Manepalli (2005) Trend Analysis of the Digital Library Community. *D-Lib Magazine* 11 (01). doi:10.1045/january2005-bollen.

Bonn, Maria S., Wendy P. Lougee, Jeffrey K. MacKie-Mason, and Juan F. Riveros (1999) A Report on the PEAK Experiment. *D-Lib Magazine* 5 (6) (June). doi:10.1045/june99-bonn.

Borgman, Christine L. (1993) NEL Workshop Report. In *Source Book on Digital Libraries: Prepared for and Sponsored by the National Science Foundation*: 121–42. Virginia Tech. http://eprints.cs.vt.edu/archive/00000377/01/TR-93-35.pdf.

Borgman, Christine L. (1996) *UCLA-NSF Social Aspects of Digital Libraries Workshop: Final Report.* UCLA.
http://is.gseis.ucla.edu/research/dig_libraries/UCLA_DL_Report.html.

Borgman, Christine L. (1999) What Are Digital Libraries? Competing Visions. *Information Processing and Management* 35 (3): 227–43.

Borgman, Christine L. (2000) *From Gutenberg to the Global Information Infrastructure. Digital Libraries and Electronic Publishing.* MIT Press.

Borgman, Christine L. (2007) *Scholarship in the Digital Age.* MIT Press.

Borgman, Christine L. (2009) Digital Libraries: Now Here, or Nowhere? (Keynote). Presented at the Joint Conference on Digital Libraries 2009, Austin, TX. http://works.bepress.com/borgman/213.

Borgman, Christine L. (2012) Syllabus for Data, Data Practices, and Data Curation Part 1; Winter 2012. http://works.bepress.com/borgman/262.

Borgman, Christine L., and Jonathan Furner (2002) Scholarly Communication and Bibliometrics. *Annual Review of Information Science and Technology* 36 (1): 2–72. doi:10.1002/aris.1440360102.

Bowles, Vickery, and Linda Hazzan (2013) Balancing Patron Demand for All Formats. *Public Libraries Online.* http://publiclibrariesonline.org/2013/04/balancing-patron-demand-for-all-formats/.

Brabham, Daren C. (2008) Crowdsourcing as a Model for Problem Solving: An Introduction and Cases. *Convergence: The International Journal of Research into New Media Technologies* 14 (1) (February 1): 75–90. doi:10.1177/1354856507084420.

Brabham, Daren C. (2010) *Crowdsourcing as a Model for Problem Solving: Leveraging the Collective Intelligence of Online Communities for Public Good.* PhD dissertation, University of Utah. http://content.lib.utah.edu/cdm/ref/collection/etd2/id/1190.

Branin, Joseph (2003) Institutional Repositories: A Pre-publication Draft Article Submitted to the *Encyclopedia of Library and Information Science,* Summer. http://hdl.handle.net/1811/441.

Brase, J. (2009) DataCite-A Global Registration Agency for Research Data. In *Fourth International Conference on Cooperation and Promotion of Information Resources in Science and Technology, 2009. COINFO09:* 257–61.

Bray, David A., Sascha Vitzthum, and Benn Konsynski (2008) SSRN as an Initial Revolution in Academic Knowledge Aggregation and Dissemination. SSRN Scholarly Paper ID 1081478. Rochester, NY: Social Science Research Network. http://papers.ssrn.com/abstract=1081478.

Bray, Paula, Sebastian Chan, Joseph Dalton, Dianne Dietrich, Effie Kapsalis, Michelle Springer, and Helena Zinkham (2011) Rethinking Evaluation Metrics in Light of Flickr Commons. In *Museums and the Web 2011.* Toronto: Archives and Museum Informatics. www.museumsandtheweb.com/mw2011/papers/rethinking_evaluation_metrics_in_light_of_flic.

Breeding, Marshall (2005) Plotting a New Course for Metasearch. *Computers in Libraries* 25 (2): 27–9.

Breeding, Marshall (2011) A Cloudy Forecast for Libraries. *Computers in Libraries* 31 (7): 32–4.

Breeding, Marshall (2012a) Automation Marketplace 2012: Agents of Change. *Digital Shift*. March 29. www.thedigitalshift.com/2012/03/ils/automation-marketplace-2012-agents-of-change.

Breeding, Marshall (2012b) *Cloud Computing for Libraries*. American Library Association.

Breeding, Marshall (2013a) Automation Marketplace 2013: The Rush to Innovate. *Digital Shift*. April 2. www.thedigitalshift.com/2013/04/ils/automation-marketplace-2013-the-rush-to-innovate/.

Breeding, Marshall (2013b) Linked Data: The Next Big Wave or Another Tech Fad? *Computers in Libraries* 33 (3) (April). www.infotoday.com/cilmag/apr13/Breeding--Linked-Data--The%20Next-Big-Wave-or-Another-Tech-Fad.shtml.

Brin, S., and L. Page (1998) The Anatomy of a Large-scale Hypertextual Web Search Engine. *Computer Networks and ISDN Systems* 30 (1–7): 107–117.

Brindley, Lynne J. (1988) Online Versus Print Versus CD-ROM. *Serials: The Journal for the Serials Community* 1 (2): 21–4.

Brindley, Lynne J. (1989) *The Electronic Campus: An Information Strategy*. British Library. www.opengrey.eu/item/display/10068/496014.

Brindley, Lynne J. (2009) Introduction. In *Digital Library Economics: An Academic Perspective*. Chandos.

Brown, Melissa A. (2013) Copyright Exceptions for Libraries in the Digital Age: US Copyright Office Considers Reform of Section 108, Highlights of the Symposium. *College & Research Libraries News* 74 (4): 199–214.

Brusilovsky, P., L. Cassel, L. Delcambre, E. Fox, R. Furuta, D. Garcia, F. Shipman, P. Bogen and M. Yudelson (2010) Enhancing Digital Libraries with Social Navigation: The Case of Ensemble. *Research and Advanced Technology for Digital Libraries*: 116–23.

Brynko, Barbara (2010) VIVO: Connecting the .Docs. *Information Today* 27 (3) (March). www.infotoday.com/it/mar10/Brynko.shtml.

Buchanan, Steven, and Adeola Salako (2009) Evaluating the Usability *and* Usefulness of a Digital Library. *Library Review* 58 (9) (October 9): 638–51. doi:10.1108/00242530910997928.

Burns, C. Sean, Amy Lana, and John M. Budd (2013) Institutional Repositories: Exploration of Costs and Value. *D-Lib Magazine* 19 (1/2). doi:10.1045/january2013-burns.

Burrows, Toby (1999) Electronic Texts, Digital Libraries, and the Humanities in Australia. *Library Hi Tech* 17 (3) (September): 248–56. doi:10.1108/07378839910289330.

Bush, Vannevar (1945) As We May Think. *Atlantic Magazine* 176 (1): 101–8. www.theatlantic.com/magazine/archive/1945/07/as-we-may-think/3881.

Byrne, Gillian, and Lisa Goddard (2010) The Strongest Link: Libraries and Linked Data. *D-Lib Magazine* 16 (11/12) (November). doi:10.1045/november2010-byrne.

Calhoun, Karen (1994) A Microeconomic Analysis of the Online Information Industry. Unpublished report.

Calhoun, Karen (2002) From Information Gateway to Digital Library Management System: a Case Analysis. *Library Collections, Acquisitions, and Technical Services* 26 (2): 141–50. doi:10.1016/S1464-9055(02)00226-9.

Calhoun, Karen (2003) Technology, Productivity and Change in Library Technical Services. *Library Collections, Acquisitions, and Technical Services* 27 (3): 281–9.

Calhoun, Karen (2006) *The Changing Nature of the Catalog and Its Integration with Other Discovery Tools.* Library of Congress. www.loc.gov/catdir/calhoun-report-final.pdf.

Calhoun, Karen (2007) Being a Librarian: Metadata and Metadata Specialists in the Twenty-first Century. *Library Hi Tech* 25 (2): 174–87.

Calhoun, Karen (2012a) Data Quality and the End-user's Experience. University of Pittsburgh Library. www.slideshare.net/amarintha/data-qualty-and-the-users-experience-feb-2012-pitt.

Calhoun, Karen (2012b) Supporting Digital Scholarship: Bibliographic Control, Library Cooperatives and Open Access Repositories. In *Catalogue 2.0.* Facet Publishing. http://d-scholarship.pitt.edu/16084.

Candela, L., D. Castelli, Y. Ioannidis, G. Koutrika, P. Pagano, S. Ross, H. J. Schek, and H. Schuldt (2006) The *Digital Library Manifesto.* DELOS Network of Excellence on Digital Libraries. www.citeulike.org/group/890/article/1137192.

Candela, Leonardo, Donatella Castelli, and Pasquale Pagano (2011) History, Evolution, and Impact of Digital Libraries. In *E-Publishing and Digital Libraries: Legal and Organizational Issues*: 1–30. Hershey, PA: Information Science Reference.

Candela, L., D. Castelli, P. Pagano, C. Thano, Y. Ioannidis, G. Koutrika, S. Ross, H. J Schek, and H. Schuldt (2007) Setting the Foundations of Digital Libraries: The Delos Manifesto. *D-Lib Magazine* 13 (3): 4.

Caplan, P., and W. Y. Arms (1999) Reference Linking for Journal Articles. *D-Lib Magazine* 5 (7/8). doi:10.1045/july99-caplan.

Caroli, Cinzia, Gabriella Scipione, Elda Rrapi, and Giuseppe Trotta (2012) ARROW: Accessible Registries of Rights Information and Orphan Works Towards Europeana. *D-Lib Magazine* 18 (1/2) (January). doi:10.1045/january2012-caroli.

Carr, Leslie, and Tim Brody (2007) Size Isn't Everything. *D-Lib Magazine* 13 (7/8). doi:10.1045/july2007-carr.

Carr, L., A. Swan, A. Sale, C. Oppenheim, T. Brody, S. Hitchcock, C. Hajjem, and S. Harnad (2006) Repositories for Institutional Open Access: Mandated Deposit Policies. http://eprints.ecs.soton.ac.uk/13099.

Carr, R. (2002) Towards the Academic Digital Library in the UK: a National Perspective. *Nordinfo Publikation* 48: 221–33.

Carr, R. (2009) A History of Digital Library Economics. In *Digital Library Economics: An Academic Perspective*: 57–70. Chandos.

Casey, Michael E., and Laura C. Savastinuk (2007) *Library 2.0: A Guide to Participatory Library Service*. Information Today, Inc.

Castells, Manuel (1996) *The Rise of the Network Society*. Blackwell Publishers.

Cathro, Warwick (1999) Digital Libraries: a National Library Perspective. *National Library of Australia Staff Papers*. www.nla.gov.au/openpublish/index.php/nlasp/article/view/1112.

Cathro, Warwick (2001) Visions for Fundamental Change in Libraries and Librarianship for Asia Pacific. *National Library of Australia Staff Papers*. www.nla.gov.au/openpublish/index.php/nlasp/article/view/1317.

Cathro, Warwick (2006) The Role of a National Library in Supporting Research Information Infrastructure. In *72nd IFLA General Conference and Council*. Seoul, Korea.

Cathro, Warwick (2009a) Collaboration Strategies for Digital Collections: The Australian Experience. *National Library of Australia Staff Papers*. www.nla.gov.au/openpublish/index.php/nlasp/article/view/1433/1738

Cathro, Warwick (2009b) Digital Library Economics: The Australian Perspective. In *Digital Library Economics: An Academic Perspective*: 119–30. Chandos.

Cathro, Warwick and S. Collier (2010) Developing Trove: The Policy and Technical Challenges. *National Library of Australia Staff Papers*. www.nla.gov.au/openpublish/index.php/nlasp/article/viewArticle/1666.

Cathro, Warwick., C. Webb, and J. Whiting (2001) Archiving the Web: The PANDORA Archive at the National Library Australia. In *Preserving the Present for the Future Web Archiving Conference, Copenhagen, 18–19 June 2001*. www.nla.gov.au/openpublish/index.php/nlasp/article/viewArticle/1314.

Cave, Richard (2012) Overview of the Altmetrics Landscape presented at the Charleston Conference, November 9. www.slideshare.net/rcave/overview-of-the-altmetrics-landscape.

Chakraborty, Arun Kumar (2010) Web 2.0 and Social Web Approaches to Digital Libraries. In *Developing Sustainable Digital Libraries*: 108–32. IGI Global.

Chambers, Sally, and Wouter Schallier (2010) Bringing Research Libraries into Europeana: Establishing a Library-Domain Aggregator. *Liber Quarterly* 20 (1): 105–18.

Chandler, Adam (2009) *Results of L'Année Philologique Online OpenURL Quality Investigation: Mellon Planning Grant Final Report*. Cornell University Library.

Chandler, Adam, and Tim Jewell (2006) Standards–Libraries, Data Providers, and

SUSHI: The Standardized Usage Statistics Harvesting Initiative. *Against the Grain* 18 (2): 82–3.

Chapman, Stephen, and Anne R. Kenney (1996) Digital Conversion of Library Research Materials: a Case for Full Informational Capture. *D-Lib Magazine* (October). http://dlib.org/dlib/october96/cornell/10chapman.html.

Charlton, John (2012) New Collection Gathers World War I Artifacts. *Information Today* 29 (5): 16+.

Chenu-Abente, R., M. Menendez, F. Giunchiglia, and A. De Angeli (2012) An Entity-based Platform for the Integration of Social and Scientific Services. In *8th International Conference on Collaborative Computing: Networking, Applications and Worksharing (CollaborateCom)*: 165–74. Pittsburgh PA.

Chowdhury, Gobinda G., and Sudatta Chowdhury (2003) *Introduction to Digital Libraries*. Facet Publishing.

Chowdhury, Gobinda G., and Schubert Foo (2012) *Digital Libraries and Information Access: Research Perspectives*. Facet Publishing.

Christenson, Heather (2011) HathiTrust. *Library Resources & Technical Services* 55 (2): 93–102.

CIBER Research Ltd (2009) *E-Journals: Their Use, Value and Impact: a Research Information Network Report*. Research Information Network. www.rin.ac.uk/system/files/attachments/E-journals-report.pdf.

CIBER Research Ltd (2010) *Research Support Services in UK Universities*. London: Research Information Network. www.ciber-research.eu/download/20101116-RSS-report.pdf.

Clapp, Verner W. (1965) Foreword. In *Libraries of the Future*, v–ix. MIT Press.

Cohen, Daniel (2008) Creating Scholarly Tools and Resources for the Digital Ecosystem: Building Connections in the Zotero Project. *First Monday* 13 (8) (August). http://firstmonday.org/htbin/cgiwrap/bin/ojs/index.php/fm/article/view/2233.

Cohen, Dan (2010) *The Social Life of Digital Libraries*. The Arcadia Programme, University Library, University of Cambridge. www.dspace.cam.ac.uk/handle/1810/226651.

Cohen, Dan (2013) The Digital Public Library of America, Me, and You. *Dan Cohen's Digital Humanities Blog*. March 5. www.dancohen.org/category/dpla/.

Collier, Mel (2004) After the Digital Library Decade: Where Are the Next Frontiers for Library Innovation? In *Digital Libraries: Policy, Planning, and Practice*, 229–37. Ashgate Publishing.

Collier, Mel (2010) *Business Planning for Digital Libraries: International Approaches*. Leuven University Press.

Collier, Mel, Anne Ramsden, and Dian Zhao (1995) Networking and Licensing Texts for Electronic Libraries: De Montfort University's Experience. *Interlending & Document Supply* 23 (4) (December): 3–13. doi:10.1108/02641619510155068.

Comparison of Research Networking Tools and Research Profiling Systems (2013) *Wikipedia, the Free Encyclopedia.* April 22.

Conway, Paul (2010) Preservation in the Age of Google: Digitization, Digital Preservation, and Dilemmas 1. *Library Quarterly* 80 (1): 61–79.

Cooke, Philip, and Loet Leydesdorf (2006) Regional Development in the Knowledge-Based Economy: The Construction of Advantage. *Journal of Technology Transfer* 31 (1) (November 30): 5–15. doi:10.1007/s10961-005-5009-3.

Coordination of European Picture Agencies Stock, Press and Heritage (CEPIC) (2011) BnF Signs New Deal with Jouve-Safig-Diadéis Partnership for Digitization of Its Print Collections. *CEPIC – Centre of the Picture Industry.* April 24. www.cepic.org/news/industry_press_releases/2011/04/bnf_signs_new_deal_jouv e_safig_diad%C3%A9_partnership_digitization.

Copeland, Peter (1994) Project Digitise: An Initiative for Access. *Playback* (8): 5–7.

Cornish, Graham P. (2009) *Copyright: Interpreting the Law for Libraries, Archives and Information Services.* Facet Publishing.

Corrall, Sheila (2011) Professional Education for a Digital World. In *University Libraries and Digital Learning Environments*, 49–68. Ashgate Publishing.

Corrall, Sheila (2013) Getting Research into Policy and Practice: A Review of the Work of Bob Usherwood. *Library Trends* 61 (3): 735–50. doi:10.1353/lib.2013.0000.

Corrall, Sheila, Mary Anne Kennan, and Waseem Afzal (2013) Bibliometrics and Research Data Management Services: Emerging Trends in Library Support for Research. *Library Trends* 61 (3): 636–74.

Corson-Rikert, Jon (2009) New Approaches for Mainstreaming Metadata In Digital Library Project Development and Management. In *Metadata and Digital Collections*, 54–81. Cornell University Library. http://cip.cornell.edu/cul.pub/1238609300.

Cousins, Jill (2013) Creating the Backbone. In *Digital Public Spaces*, 12–13. FutureEverything.

Cox, John, and Laura Cox (2008) *Scholarly Publishing Practice: Academic Journal Publishers' Policies and Practices in Online Publishing.* Association of Learned and Professional Society Publishers.

Coyle, Karen (2006) Mass Digitization of Books. *Journal of Academic Librarianship* 32 (6): 641–45.

Crane, Gregory (1996) Building a Digital Library: The Perseus Project as a Case Study in the Humanities. In *Proceedings of the First ACM International Conference on Digital Libraries*: 3–10.

Crane, Gregory (2004) Georeferencing in Historical Collections. *D-Lib Magazine*

10 (5) (May). http://dlib.org/dlib/may04/crane/05crane.html.

Crane, Gregory, Bridget Almas, Alison Babeu, Lisa Cerrato, Matthew Harrington, David Bamman, and Harry Diakoff (2012) Student Researchers, Citizen Scholars and the Trillion Word Library. In *Proceedings of the 12th ACM/IEEE-CS Joint Conference on Digital Libraries*, 213–22.

Cranfield, Andrew (2012) EUROPEANA – Groundbreaking Collaboration (interview with Jill Cousins) *Revy* 35 (4) (July 4): s. 14–15. http://cjas.dk/index.php/revy/article/view/3595.

Craven, Jenny (2011) Widening Access to Information: The Haves and the Have Nots? In *Libraries and Society: Role, Responsibility and Future in an Age of Change*, 101–18. Oxford, UK: Chandos.

Creaser, Claire (2011) Scholarly Communication and Access to Research Outputs. In *Libraries and Society: Role, Responsibility and Future in an Age of Change*: 53–66. Chandos.

Creaser, Claire, J. Fry, H. Greenwood, C. Oppenheim, S. Probets, V. Spezi, and S. White (2010) Authors' Awareness and Attitudes Toward Open Access Repositories. *New Review of Academic Librarianship* 16 (S1): 145–61.

Crews, Kenneth D. (2012) Court Rules on HathiTrust and Fair Use. *Columbia Copyright Advisory Office*. November 8. http://copyright.columbia.edu/copyright/2012/10/11/court-rules-on-hathitrust-and-fair-use.

Crosas, Mercè (2011) The Dataverse Network®: An Open-Source Application for Sharing, Discovering and Preserving Data. *D-Lib Magazine* 17 (1/2) (January). doi:10.1045/january2011-crosas.

Cross, Philip, Alan Danskin, Amanda Hill, and Daniel Needham (2011) Names Project, Phase Two. MIMAS. University of Manchester. http://names.mimas.ac.uk/files/Final_Report_Names_Phase_Two_September_2011.pdf.

CrossRef and KnowledgeSpeak (2009) Research Community Members Seek to Resolve Author Name Ambiguity Issue. *CrossRef Blog*. December 7. www.crossref.org/crweblog/2009/12.

Crow, Raym (2002) The Case for Institutional Repositories: a SPARC Position Paper. *ARL Bimonthly Report 223*. http://works.bepress.com/cgi/viewcontent.cgi?article=1006&context=ir_research.

Darby, R. M., C. M. Jones, L. D. Gilbert, and S. C. Lambert (2009) Increasing the Productivity of Interactions between Subject and Institutional Repositories. *New Review of Information Networking* 14(2): 117–35.

Das, Anup Kumar, B. K. Sen, and Chaitali Dutta (2010) Collaborative Digital Library Development in India: A Network Analysis. In *Developing Sustainable Digital Libraries*: 206–22. IGI Global.

Davis, Philip M. (2011) Open Access, Readership, Citations: a Randomized Controlled Trial of Scientific Journal Publishing. *The FASEB Journal* 25 (7): 2129–34. doi:10.1096/fj.11-183988.

Davis, Rebecca (2012) Crowdsourcing, Undergraduates, and Digital Humanities Projects. *Rebecca Frost Davis*. September 3. http://rebeccafrostdavis.wordpress.com/2012/09/03/crowdsourcing-undergraduates-and-digital-humanities-projects.

Davis, Susan, Teresa Malinowski, Eve Davis, Dustin MacIver, Tina Currado, and Lisa Spagnolo (2012) Who Ya Gonna Call? Troubleshooting Strategies for E-resources Access Problems. *Serials Librarian* 62 (1–4): 24–32.

De La Durantaye, Katharina (2010) H Is for Harmonization: The Google Book Search Settlement and Orphan Works Legislation in the European Union. *New York Law School Law Review* 55: 157–73.

De Laurentis, Carla (2006) Digital Knowledge Exploitation: ICT, Memory Institutions and Innovation from Cultural Assets. *Journal of Technology Transfer* 31 (1) (January 1): 77–89. doi:10.1007/s10961-005-5014-6.

De Rosa, Cathy (2005) *Perceptions of Libraries and Information Resources: a Report to the OCLC Membership*. OCLC. www.oclc.org/reports/2005perceptions.en.html.

De Rosa, Cathy, Joanne Cantrell, Matthew Carlson, and Peggy Gallagher (2011) *Perceptions of Libraries, 2010: Context and Community*. OCLC. www.oclc.org/reports/2010perceptions.htm.

De Roure, David, Carole Goble, and Robert Stevens (2009) The Design and Realisation of the Virtual Research Environment for Social Sharing of Workflows. *Future Generation Computer Systems* 25 (5): 561–7. doi:10.1016/j.future.2008.06.010.

De Sutter, Bjorn, and Aäron Van Den Oord (2012) To Be or Not to Be Cited in Computer Science. *Communications of the ACM* 55 (8): 69–75.

Deegan, Marilyn, Emil Steinvel, and Edmund King (2002) Digitising Historical Newspapers: Progress and Prospects. *RLG Diginews* 6 (4) (August).

Deegan, Marilyn, and Simon Tanner (2002) *Digital Futures: Strategies for the Information Age*. New York; London: Neal-Schuman Publishers; Library Association Publishing.

Delorme, Bruno (2011) Digitization at the Bibliothèque Nationale de France, Including an Interview. *Serials: The Journal for the Serials Community* 24 (3) (November 1): 261–5. doi:10.1629/24261.

Dempsey, Lorcan (1994) Network Resource Discovery: a European Library Perspective. In *Libraries, Networks and Europe: a European Networking Study*. LIR Series 101. London: British Library Research and Development Department. ftp://ftp.funet.fi/pub/doc/library/europe.rtf.

Dempsey, Lorcan (1995) The UK, Networking and the European Libraries

Programme. *Library & Information Briefings* (57) (February): 15. http://opus.bath.ac.uk/23730.

Dempsey, Lorcan (2005) Making Data Work – Web 2.0 and Catalogs. *Lorcan Dempsey's Weblog*. October 4. http://orweblog.oclc.org/archives/000815.html.

Dempsey, Lorcan (2006a) Ariadne. *Lorcan Dempsey's Weblog*. January 16. http://orweblog.oclc.org/archives/000921.html.

Dempsey, Lorcan (2006b) The (Digital) Library Environment: Ten Years After. *Ariadne* (46). www.ariadne.ac.uk/issue46/dempsey.

Dempsey, Lorcan (2012) Thirteen Ways of Looking at Libraries, Discovery, and the Catalog: Scale, Workflow, Attention. *EDUCAUSE Review* (December). www.educause.edu/ero/article/thirteen-ways-looking-libraries-discovery-and-catalog-scale-workflow-attention.

Dempsey, Lorcan, Rosemary Russell, and John Kirriemuir (1996) Towards Distributed Library Systems: Z39. 50 in a European Context. *Program: Electronic Library and Information Systems* 30 (1): 1–22.

Dempsey, Lorcan, and Stuart Weibel (1996) The Warwick Metadata Workshop. *D-Lib Magazine*. http://webdoc.sub.gwdg.de/edoc/aw/d-lib/dlib/july96/07weibel.html.

Denicola, R. C. (2006) Copyright and Open Access: Reconsidering University Ownership of Faculty Research. *Nebraska Law Review* 85: 351.

Devare, Medha, Jon Corson-Rikert, Brian Caruso, Brian Lowe, Kathy Chiang, and Janet McCue (2007) VIVO: Connecting People, Creating a Virtual Life Sciences Community. *D-Lib Magazine* 13 (7/8) (July). doi:10.1045/july2007-devare. http://dlib.org/dlib/july07/devare/07devare.html.

Digital Public Library of America (2013) *Digital Public Library of America: Metadata Application Profile, Version 3.* http://dp.la/info/wp-content/uploads/2013/04/DPLAMetadataApplicationProfileV3.pdf.

Dijk, E., C. Baars, A. Hogenaar, and M. Meel (2006) NARCIS: The Gateway to Dutch Scientific Information. Paper presented at the ELPUB Conference, Bansko, Bulgaria. http://depot.knaw.nl/5631.

DiLauro, Tim (2009) CERN Workshop on Innovations in Scholarly Communication presented at the CERN Workshop on Innovations in Scholarly Communication, June 17, University of Geneva. http://indico.cern.ch/contributionDisplay.py?contribId=9&sessionId=3&confId=48321.

Dobbs, David (2013) When the Rebel Alliance Sells Out. *Elements: The New Yorker*. April 12. www.newyorker.com/online/blogs/elements/2013/04/elsevier-mendeley-journals-science-software.html.

Dooley, Jackie M., and Katherine Luce (2010) *Taking Our Pulse: The OCLC Research Survey of Special Collections and Archives.* Dublin, Ohio: OCLC Research. www.oclc.org/research/publications/library/2010/2010-11.pdf.

Dougan, Kirstin (2010) Music to Our Eyes: Google Books, Google Scholar, and the Open Content Alliance. *Portal: Libraries and the Academy* 10 (1): 75–93. doi:10.1353/pla.0.0088.

Druin, A. (2005) What Children Can Teach Us: Developing Digital Libraries for Children with Children. *The Library Quarterly* 75 (1).

Druin, A., Benjamin B. Bederson, Ann Weeks, Allison Farber, Jesse Grosjean, Mona Leigh Guha, Juan Pablo Hourcade et al. (2003) The International Children's Digital Library. *First Monday* (May 5). 1996–2003. http://firstmonday.org/htbin/cgiwrap/bin/ojs/index.php/fm/article/viewArticle/1050/970.

Dryden, Jean (2011) Measuring Trust: Standards for Trusted Digital Repositories. *Journal of Archival Organization* 9 (2): 127–30. doi:10.1080/15332748.2011.590744.

Dunleavy, Patrick (2012) Organizing Your Personal Research Library and Compiling Bibliographies: I Was an EndNote Refusenik, but Now I'm a Mendeley Convert. *LSE Impact of Social Sciences.* August 20. http://blogs.lse.ac.uk/impactofsocialsciences/2012/08/20/organisation-research-library-mendeley-convert.

Duranceau, Ellen Finnie, and Sue Kriegsman (2013) Implementing Open Access Policies Using Institutional Repositories. In *The Institutional Repository: Benefits and Challenges*: 75–97. American Library Association. Association for Library Collections and Technical Services. www.ala.org/alcts/sites/ala.org.alcts/files/content/resources/papers/ir_ch05.pdf.

Duranceau, Ellen Finnie, and Richard Rodgers (2010) Automated IR Deposit via the SWORD Protocol: An MIT/BioMed Central Experiment. *Serials: The Journal for the Serials Community* 23 (3) (January 1): 212–14. doi:10.1629/23212.

DuraSpace (2009) DSpace Foundation and Fedora Commons Receive Grant from the Mellon Foundation for DuraSpace. http://duraspace.org/node/639.

DuraSpace (2012) *DuraSpace Annual Report 2011.* DuraSpace. www.duraspace.org/sites/default/files/u6/DuraSpaceAnnualReport2011.pdf.

EC Framework Programme 7 (2007) DRIVER-II: Digital Repositories Infrastructure Vision for European Research. www.driver-repository.eu/PublicDocs/FACT_SHEET_I3_driver_ii.pdf.

Edelstein, Jeff, Lola Galla, Carolyn Li-Madeo, Julia Marden, Alison Rhonemus, and Noreen Whysel (2013) *Linked Open Data for Cultural Heritage: Evolution of an Information Technology.* Noreen Y. Whysel. www.whysel.com/papers/LIS670-Linked-Open-Data-for-Cultural-Heritage.pdf.

Education Advisory Board (2011) Redefining the Academic Library: Managing the Migration to Digital Information Services. 23634. Washington DC.

Ellingsen, Mark (2004) Electronic Resource Management Systems. *LIBER Quarterly* 14 (3/4). www.religionandgender.org/index.php/lq/article/view/7782/7894.

Elsevier (2012) E-journals at Elsevier: Over Two Decades of Experimentation and

Development. *Elsevier Company News*. www.elsevier.com/wps/find/authored_ newsitem.cws_home/companynews05_00021.

Emanuel, J. (2011) Usability of the VuFind Next-generation Online Catalog. *Information Technology and Libraries* 30 (1): 44.

Enis, Matt (2013) Q&A with Dan Cohen, DPLA Founding Executive Director. *The Digital Shift*. March 12. www.thedigitalshift.com/2013/03/digital-libraries/qa-dan-cohen-on-his-role-as-the-founding-executive-director-of-dpla.

Erway, Ricky (2008) *Seeking Sustainability*. OCLC Programs and Research.

Erway, Ricky (2012) *Lasting Impact Sustainability of Disciplinary Repositories*. OCLC Research. www.oclc.org/research/publications/library/2012/2012-03.pdf.

European Commission (2012a) Orphan Works: Directive 2012/28/EU. http://ec.europa.eu/internal_market/copyright/orphan_works/index_en.htm.

European Commission (2012b) *Towards Better Access to Scientific Information: Boosting the Benefits of Public Investments in Research*. Brussels: European Commission. http://ec.europa.eu/research/science-society/document_library/pdf_06/era-communication-towards-better-access-to-scientific-information_en.pdf.

Europeana Foundation (2013) *Europeana Annual Report and Accounts 2012*. http://pro.europeana.eu/documents/858566/99cea5ba-46ce-4037-a913-a9c81080079b.

Eysenbach, G. (2006) Citation Advantage of Open Access Articles. *PLoS Biology* 4 (5): 0692-0698. doi:10.1371/journal.pbio.0040157.

Eysenbach, Gunther (2008) Medicine 2.0: Social Networking, Collaboration, Participation, Apomediation, and Openness. *Journal of Medical Internet Research* 10 (3) (August 25). doi:10.2196/jmir.1030. www.ncbi.nlm.nih.gov/pmc/articles/PMC2626430/.

Fagan, J. C., M. A. Mandernach, C. S. Nelson, J. R. Paulo, and G. Saunders (2012) Usability Test Results for a Discovery Tool in an Academic Library. *Information Technology and Libraries* 31 (1): 83–112.

Fazel-Zarandi, Maryam, Hugh J. Devlin, Yun Huang, and Noshir Contractor (2011) Expert Recommendation Based on Social Drivers, Social Network Analysis, and Semantic Data Representation. In *Proceedings of the 2nd International Workshop on Information Heterogeneity and Fusion in Recommender Systems*: 41–8. HetRec '11. ACM. doi:10.1145/2039320.2039326.

Feeney, M., and J. Newby (2005) Model for Presenting Resources in Scholar's Portal. *Portal-Libraries and the Academy* 5 (2): 195.

Fenner, Martin (2009) Interview with Geoffrey Bilder. *Gobbledygook*. February 17. http://blogs.plos.org/mfenner/2009/02/17/interview_with_geoffrey_bilder.

Fenner, Martin (2010) Reference Management Meets Web 2.0. *Cell Therapy and Transplantation* 2 (6): 1–3.

Fenner, Martin (2011) Author Identifier Overview. *Gobbledygook*. January 2.
http://blogs.plos.org/mfenner/author-identifier-overview.

Ferreira, Miguel, Eloy Rodrigues, Ana Alice Baptista, and Ricardo Saraiva (2008)
Carrots and Sticks. *D-Lib Magazine* 14 (1/2) (January).
doi:10.1045/january2008-ferreira.

Ferro, Nicola, and Gianmaria Silvello (2013) Modeling Archives by Means of OAI-
ORE. In *Digital Libraries and Archives*: 216–27. Communications in Computer and
Information Science 354. Springer Berlin Heidelberg.

Finch, Janet, and Michael Jubb (2012) *Accessibility, Sustainability, Excellence: How to
Expand Access to Research Publications*. Research Information Network.
www.researchinfonet.org/wp-content/uploads/2012/06/Finch-Group-report-
FINAL-VERSION.pdf.

Fischer, Karen S., Michael Wright, Kathleen Clatanoff, Hope Barton and Edward
Shreeves (2012) Give'Em What They Want: A One-year Study of Unmediated
Patron-driven Acquisition of E-books. *College & Research Libraries* 73 (5): 469–92.

Fitzpatrick, Brad (2005) Distributed Identity: Yadis. *LiveJournal*. May 16.
http://lj-dev.livejournal.com/683939.html.

Flanders, David (2008) *Fedorazon – Cloud Repository: Final Report*. JISC.
http://ie-repository.jisc.ac.uk/426.

Fleet, Christopher, Kimberly C. Kowal, and Petr Přidal (2012) Georeferencer:
Crowdsourced Georeferencing for Map Library Collections. *D-Lib Magazine*
18 (11/12) (November). doi:10.1045/november2012-fleet.

Follett, B., Higher Education Funding Council for England, N. Ireland, S.H.E.F
Council, and Higher Education Funding Council for Wales (1993) *Joint Funding
Councils' Libraries Review Group: Report, December 1993*. Higher Education
Funding Council for England.

Fons, Theodore A., and Timothy D. Jewell (2007) Envisioning the Future of ERM
Systems. *The Serials Librarian* 52 (1–2): 151–66.

Forster, Horst (2007) The I2010 Digital Libraries Initiative: Europe's Cultural and
Scientific Information at the Click of a Mouse. *Information Services and Use* 27 (4):
155–9.

Foster, Nancy Fried, and Susan Gibbons (2005) Understanding Faculty to Improve
Content Recruitment for Institutional Repositories. *D-Lib Magazine* 11 (01)
(January). doi:10.1045/january2005-foster.

Fox, E. A. (1993a) Digital Libraries. *Computer* 26 (11): 79–81.

Fox, E. A. (1993b) *Source Book on Digital Libraries*. Virginia Tech.
http://eprints.cs.vt.edu/archive/00000377/01/TR-93-35.pdf.

Fox, E. A., R. M. Akscyn, R. K. Furuta, and J. J. Leggett (1995) Digital Libraries.
Communications of the ACM 38 (4): 22–8.

Fox, E. A., J. L. Eaton, G. McMillan, N. A. Kipp, P. Mather, W. Schweiker, and B. DeVane (1997) Networked Digital Library of Theses and Dissertations: An International Effort Unlocking University Resources. *D-Lib Magazine* (September). http://dlib.org/dlib/september97/theses/09fox.html.

Fox, E. A., and O. Sornil (2003) Digital Libraries. In *Encyclopedia of Computer Science.*

Fransen, Janet, Lara Friedman-Shedlov, Nicole Theis-Mahon, and Stacie Traill (2012) Setting a Direction for Discovery: a Phased Approach. In *Planning and Implementing Resource Discovery Tools in Academic Libraries*, 174–93. Information Science Reference.

Freebase (2013) *Wikipedia, the Free Encyclopedia.* May 25. http://en.wikipedia.org/w/index.php?title=Freebase&oldid=556663704.

Fressard, Olivier (2008) The Digital Spirit: Digital Libraries and Democracy. In *Digital Libraries*, 61–82. John Wiley & Sons.

Freund, Leilani, John R. Nemmers, and Marilyn N. Ochoa (2007) Metasearching. *Internet Reference Services Quarterly* 12 (3–4) (September 20): 411–30. doi:10.1300/J136v12n03_11.

Friedlander, Amy (2002) *Dimensions and Use of the Scholarly Information Environment: Introduction to a Data Set.* Digital Library Federation.

Friedlander, Amy, and Prudence Adler (2007) *To Stand the Test of Time: Long-term Stewardship of Digital Data Sets in Science and Engineering.* Association of Research Libraries.

Gadd, E., C. Oppenheim, and S. Probets (2003) RoMEO Studies 4: An Analysis of Journal Publishers' Copyright Agreements. *Learned Publishing* 16 (4): 293–308.

Gargouri, Yassine, Vincent Larivière, Yves Gingras, Les Carr, and Stevan Harnad (2012) Green and Gold Open Access Percentages and Growth, by Discipline. ArXiv e-print 1206.3664. http://arxiv.org/abs/1206.3664.

Gaulé, Patrick, and Nicolas Maystre (2011) Getting Cited: Does Open Access Help? *Research Policy* 40 (10): 1332–8.

Gazan, Rich (2008) Social Annotations in Digital Library Collections. *D-Lib Magazine* 14 (11/12) (November). doi:10.1045/november2008-gazan.

Geleijnse, Hans (1999) The Tilburg Digital Library. *IFLA Publications* 88: 141–58.

Gerolimos, Michalis (2011) Academic Libraries on Facebook: An Analysis of Users' Comments. *D-Lib Magazine* 17 (11/12) (November). doi:10.1045/november2011-gerolimos.

Gerolimos, Michalis, and Rania Konsta (2011) Services for Academic Libraries in the New Era. *D-Lib Magazine* 17 (7/8) (July). doi:10.1045/july2011-gerolimos.

Gewin, Virginia (2009) Networking in VIVO. *Nature* 462 (7269) (November 5) doi:10.1038/nj7269-123a.

Giglia, Elena (2011) Academic Social Networks: It's Time to Change the Way We Do

Research. *European Journal of Physical and Rehabilitation Medicine* 47 (2) (June): 345–49.

Gilby, J. (2005) *Hyper Clumps, Mini Clumps and National Catalogues: Resource Discovery for the 21st Century*. UKOLN.

Gilby, J., and Gordon Dunsire (2004) COPAC/Clumps Continuing Technical Cooperation Project: Final Report. https://pure.strath.ac.uk/portal/files/341252/strathprints014104.pdf.

Ginsparg, Paul (2011) It Was Twenty Years Ago Today . . . *arXiv:1108.2700* (August 14). http://arxiv.org/abs/1108.2700.

GlobalWebIndex (2013) Stream Social Q1 2013: Facebook Active Usage Booms. GlobalWebIndex. www.globalwebindex.net/Stream-Social.

Gold, Anna (2007a) Cyberinfrastructure, Data, and Libraries, Part 1: A Cyberinfrastructure Primer for Librarians. *D-Lib Magazine* 13 (9/10). http://dlib.org/dlib/september07/gold/09gold-pt1.html.

Gold, Anna (2007b) Cyberinfrastructure, Data, and Libraries, Part 2: Libraries and the Data Challenge: Roles and Actions for Libraries. *D-Lib Magazine* 13 (9/10). http://dlib.org/dlib/september07/gold/09gold-pt2.html.

Gonçalves, Marcos André (2004) Streams, Structures, Spaces, Scenarios, and Societies (5S): A Formal Digital Library Framework and Its Applications. Ph.D., Blacksburg, VA: Virginia Polytechnic Institute and State University. www.csdl.tamu.edu/DL94/paper/fox.html.

Google (2012) Our History in Depth – Company – Google. www.google.com/intl/en/about/company/history/#1995-1997.

Green, Richard, and Chris Awre (2009) Towards a Repository-enabled Scholar's Workbench. *D-Lib Magazine* 15 (5/6) (May). doi:10.1045/may2009-green.

Greenstein, D., and Suzanne Thorin (2002) *The Digital Library: A Biography*. Digital Library Federation, Council on Library and Information Resources. http://isnet.hbi.ir/web/files/elib/pages/docs/article/biography.pdf.

Griffin, S. M. (1999) Digital Libraries Initiative – Phase 2: Fiscal Year 1999 Awards. *D-Lib Magazine* 5 (7/8). http://dlib.org/dlib/july99/07griffin.html.

Griffin, S. M. (2005) Funding for Digital Libraries Research. *D-Lib Magazine* 11 (07/08). doi:10.1045/july2005-griffin. www.dlib.org/dlib/july05/griffin/07griffin.html.

Gross, Julia, and Lutie Sheridan (2011) Web Scale Discovery: The User Experience. *New Library World* 112 (5/6) (May 17): 236–47. doi:10.1108/03074801111136275.

Gruzd, Anatoliy, and Melissa Goertzen (2013) Wired Academia: Why Social Science Scholars Are Using Social Media. In *46th Hawaii International Conference on System Sciences (HICSS)*, 3332–41. doi:10.1109/HICSS.2013.614.

Guédon, Jean-Claude (2008) Mixing and Matching the Green and Gold Roads to

Open Access – Take 2. *Serials Review* 34 (1) (March): 41–51. doi:10.1016/j.serrev.2007.12.008.

Guenther, Rebecca, and Jacqueline Radebaugh (2004) *Understanding Metadata*. NISO Press. www.niso.org/publications/press/UnderstandingMetadata.pdf.

Guenther, Rebecca, and Robert Wolfe (2009) Integrating Metadata Standards to Support Long-Term Preservation of Digital Assets: Developing Best Practices for Expressing Preservation Metadata in a Container Format. In *iPRES 2009: Sixth International Conference on the Preservation of Digital Objects*. California Digital Library. http://escholarship.org/uc/item/0s38n5w4.

Guthrie, Kevin (1997) JSTOR: From Project to Independent Organization. *D-Lib Magazine* 3 (7/8). www.dlib.org/dlib/july97/07guthrie.html.

Guthrie, Kevin (2001) Archiving in the Digital Age. *Educause Review* 36 (6): 56–62.

Guthrie, Kevin (2011) Opportunity and Challenge: Sustaining Platforms for Knowledge Dissemination in the Digital Age. In *Going Digital*, 106–26. Nobel Symposium 147. Nobel Foundation.

Haak, L. (2013) ORCID and ISNI Issue Joint Statement on Interoperation, April 2013. Laurel Haak's blog, 22 April. https://orcid.org/blog/2013/04/22/orcid-and-isni-issue-joint-statement-interoperation-april-2013.

Haak, Laurel L., Martin Fenner, Laura Paglione, Ed Pentz, and Howard Ratner (2012) ORCID: a System to Uniquely Identify Researchers. *Learned Publishing* 25 (4): 259–64. doi:10.1087/20120404.

Habib, Michael C. (2006) Toward Academic Library 2.0: Development and Application of a Library 2.0 Methodology. University of North Carolina at Chapel Hill. School of Information and Library Science. http://ils.unc.edu/MSpapers/3219.pdf.

Hagedorn, K. (2003) OAIster: A 'no Dead Ends' OAI Service Provider. *Library Hi Tech* 21 (2): 170–81.

Hagedorn, Stefan, and Kai-Uwe Sattler (2013) Discovery Querying in Linked Open Data. In *Proceedings of the Joint EDBT/ICDT 2013 Workshops*, 38–44. EDBT '13. ACM. doi:10.1145/2457317.2457324.

Hagen, John H., Susanne Dobratz, and Peter Schirmbacher (2003) Electronic Theses and Dissertations Worldwide: Highlights of the ETD 2003 Symposium. *D-Lib Magazine* 9 (7/8). www.dlib.org/dlib/july03/hagen/07hagen.html.

Hahn, Trudi Bellardo (2008) Mass Digitization. *Library Resources & Technical Services* 52 (1): 18–26.

Hakala, Juha (1999) Gabriel – Gateway to Europe's National Libraries. *Tietolinja News* (January). www.kansalliskirjasto.fi/extra/tietolinja/0199/gabriel.html.

Hamilton, Val (2004) Sustainability for Digital Libraries. *Library Review* 53 (8): 392–95. doi:10.1108/00242530410556210.

Hammond, Tony, Timo Hannay, and Ben Lund (2004) The Role of RSS in Science Publishing. *D-Lib Magazine* 10 (12) (December). doi:10.1045/december2004-hammond.

Hammond, Tony, Timo Hannay, Ben Lund, and Joanna Scott (2005) Social Bookmarking Tools (I). *D-Lib Magazine* 11 (04) (April). doi:10.1045/april2005-hammond.

Hampton-Reeves, S., C. Mashiter, J. Westaway, P. Lumsden, H. Day, and H. Hewertson (2009) *Students' Use of Research Content in Teaching and Learning: a Report for the Joint Information Systems Council*. University of Central Lancashire, Centre for Research-Informed Teaching. http://ie-repository.jisc.ac.uk/407/1/Students_Use_of_Research_Content.pdf.

Hanlon, A., and M. Ramirez (2011) Asking for Permission: A Survey of Copyright Workflows for Institutional Repositories. *Portal: Libraries and the Academy* 11 (2): 683–702.

Hanson, Cody, and Heather Hessel (2009) *Discoverability: Phase 1 Final Report*. University of Minnesota Libraries. http://conservancy.umn.edu/bitstream/48258/3/DiscoverabilityPhase1Report.pdf.

Hanson, Cody, Heather Hessel, Deborah Boudewyns, Janet Fransen, Lara Friedman-Shedlov, Stephen Hearn, Nancy Herther, Nicole Theis-Mahon, Darlene Morris, and Stacie Traill (2012) *Discoverability*. http://conservancy.umn.edu/bitstream/99734/3/DiscoverabilityPhase2ReportFull.pdf.

Hargreaves, Ian (2011) Digital Opportunity: A Review of Intellectual Property and Growth. UK Intellectual Property Office. www.ipo.gov.uk/ipreview.htm.

Harle, Jonathan, and John Tarrant (2011) Tackling Inequalities Around the Globe: The Challenge for Libraries. In *Libraries and Society: Role, Responsibility and Future in an Age of Change*: 119–39. Chandos.

Harley, D., S. K. Acord, S. Earl-Novell, S. Lawrence, and C. J. King (2010) *Assessing the Future Landscape of Scholarly Communication: An Exploration of Faculty Values and Needs in Seven Disciplines*. Center for Studies in Higher Education. http://escholarship.org/uc/item/15x7385g.pdf.

Harnad, Stevan (1990) Scholarly Skywriting and the Prepublication Continuum of Scientific Inquiry. *Psychological Science* 1 (6): 342–4.

Harnad, Stevan (1999) Integrating and Navigating ePrint Archives through Citation-Linking. University of Southampton. www.cogsci.soton.ac.uk/~harnad/citation.html.

Harnad, Stevan, and Tim Brody (2004) Comparing the Impact of Open Access (OA) vs. Non-OA Articles in the Same Journals. *D-Lib Magazine* 10 (6). doi:10.1045/june2004-harnad.

Harnad, Stevan., T. Brody, F. Vallières, L. Carr, S. Hitchcock, Y. Gingras,

C. Oppenheim, H. Stamerjohanns, and E. R. Hilf (2004) The Access/impact Problem and the Green and Gold Roads to Open Access. *Serials Review* 30 (4): 310–14.

Harnad, Stevan, and Nancy McGovern (2009) Topic 4: Institutional Repository Success Is Dependent Upon Mandates. *Bulletin of the American Society for Information Science and Technology* 35 (4): 27–31.

Harriman, J. H. P (2008) *Creating Your Library's Business Plan: a How-to-do-it Manual with Samples on CD-ROM*. Neal-Schuman Publishers.

Hart, Michael (1992) History and Philosophy of Project Gutenberg. *Project Gutenberg* 3. www.gutenberg.org/wiki/Gutenberg:The_History_and_Philosophy_of_Project_Gutenberg_by_Michael_Hart.

Harzing, Anne-Wil (2012) A Longitudinal Study of Google Scholar Coverage Between 2012 and 2013. *Scientometrics*: 1–11.

Harzing, Anne-Wil (2013) A Preliminary Test of Google Scholar as a Source for Citation Data: a Longitudinal Study of Nobel Prize Winners. *Scientometrics* 94 (3): 1057–75.

Haslhofer, Bernhard, and Antoine Isaac (2011) data.europeana.eu: The Europeana Linked Open Data Pilot. In *International Conference on Dublin Core and Metadata Applications*, 94–104. http://dcpapers.dublincore.org/index.php/pubs/article/view/3625.

Haslhofer, Bernhard, and Bernhard Schandl (2008) The OAI2LOD Server: Exposing OAI-PMH Metadata as Linked Data. In *International Workshop on Linked Data on the Web (LDOW2008), Co-located with WWW 2008*. Beijing. http://events.linkeddata.org/ldow2008/papers/03-haslhofer-schandl-oai2lod-server.pdf.

Haslhofer, Bernhard, and Bernhard Schandl (2010) Interweaving OAI-PMH Data Sources with the Linked Data Cloud. *International Journal of Metadata, Semantics and Ontologies* 1 (5) (March): 17–31.

Hawkins, R. A., and K. Gildart (2010) *Promoting the Digital Literacy of Historians at the University of Wolverhampton Using Nineteenth Century British Library Newspapers Online*. Higher Education Academy.

Hazen, Dan (2011) Lost in the Cloud. *Library Resources & Technical Services* 55 (4): 195–204.

Head, Alison J., and Michael B. Eisenberg (2010) *How College Students Evaluate and Use Information in the Digital Age*. Information School, University of Washington. http://web20kmg.pbworks.com/f/How+College+Students+evaluate+information+Digital+Age+2010.pdf.

Heath, Tom, and Christian Bizer (2011) Linked Data: Evolving the Web into a Global Data Space. *Synthesis Lectures on the Semantic Web: Theory and Technology* 1 (1) (February 9): 1–136. http://linkeddatabook.com/editions/1.0/.

Heery, Rachel, and Sheila Anderson (2005) *Digital Repositories Review.* JISC. http://opus.bath.ac.uk/23566/2/digital-repositories-review-2005.pdf.

Heery, Rachel, and Andy Powell (2006) Digital Repositories Roadmap: Looking Forward. Joint Information Systems Committee. http://opus.bath.ac.uk/23564/1/reproadmap.pdf.

Henning, Victor (2012) Mendeley Has Two Million Users! To Celebrate, We're Releasing the Global Research Report. *Mendeley Blog.* November 1. http://blog.mendeley.com/academic-life/mendeley-has-two-million-users-to-celebrate-were-releasing-the-global-research-report/.

Henty, Margaret (2007) Ten Major Issues in Providing a Repository Service in Australian Universities. *D-Lib Magazine* 13 (5/6). doi:10.1045/may2007-henty.

Hepp, Martin (2012) The Web of Data for E-Commerce in Brief. In *Web Engineering,* edited by Marco Brambilla, Takehiro Tokuda, and Robert Tolksdorf: 510–11. Lecture Notes in Computer Science 7387. Springer Berlin Heidelberg. http://link.springer.com.pitt.idm.oclc.org/chapter/10.1007/978-3-642-31753-8_58.

Hewlett Packard (2007) HP Press Release: HP and MIT Create Non-profit Organization to Support Growing Community of DSpace Users. July 17. www.hp.com/hpinfo/newsroom/press/2007/070717a.html.

Hey, T., and A. Trefethen (2003) The Data Deluge: An e-Science Perspective. In *Grid Computing,* 809–24. http://onlinelibrary.wiley.com/doi/10.1002/0470867167.ch36/summary.

Hickey, Thom (2010) Using VIAF for Semantic Enrichment presented at the Europeana v1.0 WP3 Meeting, October, Amsterdam. http://pro.europeana.eu/documents/866205/331925/EuV1_WP3_Amsterdam_October_2010_14_Hickey_VIAF.pdf.

Hickey, Thom (2011) VIAF and Other IDs. *Outgoing.* July 11. http://outgoing.typepad.com/outgoing/2011/07/viaf-and-other-ids.html.

Hickey, Thom (2013) VIAF Update presented at the OCLC EMEA Regional Council Meeting, February 25, Strasbourg, France. www.slideshare.net/oclcr/viaf-update.

Higgins, S. (2008) The DCC Curation Lifecycle Model. *International Journal of Digital Curation* 3 (1): 134–40.

Hill, Amanda (2011) *Report on National Approaches to Researcher Identification Systems.* JISC.

Hill, Amanda (2012) National Researcher Identifier Services: Names Project presented at the GrandIR Technical Session on Author Identifiers, September 6, Barcelona. http://openaccess.uoc.edu/webapps/o2/handle/10609/16342.

Hirtle, Peter (2006) Author Addenda. *D-Lib Magazine* 12 (11) (November). doi:10.1045/november2006-hirtle.

Hirtle, Peter B., Emily Hudson, and Andrew T. Kenyon (2009) *Copyright and Cultural*

Institutions: Guidelines for US Libraries, Archives, and Museums. Cornell University Library. https://ecommons.library.cornell.edu/handle/1813/14142.

History of Wikis (2013) Wikipedia, May 15. http://en.wikipedia.org/w/index.php?title=History_of_wikis&oldid=555260811.

Hitchcock, Steve, Donna Bergmark, Tim Brody, Christopher Gutteridge, Les Carr, Wendy Hall, Carl Lagoze, and Stevan Harnad (2002) Open Citation Linking. *D-Lib Magazine* 8 (10). doi:10.1045/october2002-hitchcock.

Hitchcock, Steve, Tim Brody, Jessie M. N. Hey, and Leslie Carr (2007) Digital Preservation Service Provider Models for Institutional Repositories. *D-Lib Magazine* 13 (5/6) (May). doi:10.1045/may2007-hitchcock.

Hitchcock, Steve, Les Carr, Wendy Hall, and Steve Harris (1998) Linking Electronic Journals: Lessons from the Open Journal Project. *D-Lib Magazine* (December). www.dlib.org/dlib/december98/12hitchcock.html.

Hoffert, Barbara (2013) Materials Mix: Investigating Trends in Materials Budgets and Circulation. *Library Journal.* February 19. http://lj.libraryjournal.com/2013/02/publishing/materials-mix-investigating-trends-in-materials-budgets-and-circulation/.

Hogenaar, A., and W. Steinhoff (2008) Toward a Dutch Academic Information Domain. In *CRIS 2008.* Maribor, Slovenia. http://depot.knaw.nl/5629/1/Dutch_AID.pdf.

Holley, Rose (2009) How Good Can It Get? *D-Lib Magazine* 15 (3/4) (March). doi:10.1045/march2009-holley.

Holley, Rose (2010a) Crowdsourcing: How and Why Should Libraries Do It? *D-Lib Magazine* 16 (3/4) (March). doi:10.1045/march2010-holley.

Holley, Rose (2010b) Trove: Innovation in Access to Information in Australia. *Ariadne.* http://eprints.rclis.org/handle/10760/15515.

Holman, L., E. Darraj, J. Glaser, A. Hom, H. Mathieson, D. Nettles, and A. Waller (2012) How Users Approach Discovery Tools. In *Planning and Implementing Resource Discovery Tools in Academic Libraries*: 252–67. IGI Global.

Horava, Tony (2013) Today and in Perpetuity: A Canadian Consortial Strategy for Owning and Hosting Ebooks. *Journal of Academic Librarianship* (in press).

Housewright, Ross, Roger C. Schonfeld, and Kate Wulfson (2013) *ITHAKA S+R, JISC, RLUK UK Survey of Academics 2012.* ITHAKA S+R. http://repository.jisc.ac.uk/5209/1/UK_Survey_of_Academics_2012_FINAL.pdf.

Howard, Jennifer (2013) Sale to Elsevier Casts Doubt on Mendeley's Openness. *Chronicle of Higher Education,* April 9, sec. Research. http://chronicle.com/article/In-Sale-to-Elsevier-Mendeley/138449.

Howe, Jeff (2006) The Rise of Crowdsourcing. *Wired Magazine* 14 (6): 1–4. www.wired.com/wired/archive/14.06/crowds_pr.html.

Hull, D., S. R. Pettifer, and D. B. Kell (2008) Defrosting the Digital Library: Bibliographic Tools for the Next Generation Web. *PLoS Computational Biology* 4 (10): e1000204.

Humphreys, Betsy L. (2000) Electronic Health Record Meets Digital Library A New Environment for Achieving an Old Goal. *Journal of the American Medical Informatics Association* 7 (5) (September): 444–52. doi:10.1136/jamia.2000.0070444.

Ide, Nancy M., and Christopher Michael Sperberg-McQueen (1995) The TEI: History, Goals, and Future. In *Text Encoding Initiative*, 5–15. Springer.

International DOI Foundation (2012) DOI System Factsheet. www.doi.org/factsheets/DOIKeyFacts.html.

Iriberri, Alicia, and Gondy Leroy (2009) A Life-cycle Perspective on Online Community Success. *ACM Computing Survey* 41 (2) (February): 11:1–11:29. doi:10.1145/1459352.1459356.

Isaac, Antoine (2012) The Europeana Data Model. http://pro.europeana.eu/documents/900548/40262c74-d4a3-44d4-95ea-2f4146b50c92.

Jaeger, P. T. (2010) Looking at Newness and Seeing Crisis? Library Discourse and Reactions to Change. *The Library* 80 (3).

Janssen, Olaf D. (2011) Digitizing All Dutch Books, Newspapers and Magazines – 730 Million Pages in 20 Years – Storing It, and Getting It Out There. In *Research and Advanced Technology for Digital Libraries*: 473–6. Berlin, Heidelberg: Springer Berlin Heidelberg.

Jeanneney, Jean-Noël (2005) Quand Google Défie l'Europe. *Le Monde*, January 23.

Jeanneney, Jean-Noël (2006) *Google and the Myth of Universal Knowledge: A View from Europe*. University of Chicago Press.

Jensen, Michael C. (2012) ABOUT SSRN: From The Desk of Michael C. Jensen, Chairman. February 2. www.ssrn.com/update/general/mjensen-20th.html.

Jewell, Timothy D., Ivy Anderson, Adam Chandler, Sharon Farb, Kimberly Parker, Angela Riggio, and Nathan D. M. Robertson (2004) *Electronic Resource Management: Final Report of the DLF Initiative*. Digital Library Federation. http://citeseerx.ist.psu.edu/viewdoc/download?doi=10.1.1.203.49268&rep=rep1&type=pdf..

Jippes, Arnoud, Wilko Steinhoff, and Elly Dijk (2010) NARCIS: Research Information Services on a National Scale. In *The 5th International Conference on Open Repositories (OR2010)*, 6–9. Madrid: Universitat Bielefeld eCollections. http://or2010.fecyt.es/Resources/documentos/GSabstracts/NARCIS.pdf.

Jockers, Matthew, Matthew Sag, and Jason Schultz (2012) Brief of Digital Humanities and Law Scholars as Amici Curiae in Authors Guild, Inc. Et Al V. Hathitrust Et Al. *Et Al V. Hathitrust Et Al.(July 7, 2012)*. http://papers.ssrn.com/sol3/papers.cfm?abstract_id=2102542.

Johnson, Margeaux, Amy Buhler, and Kristi L. Holmes (2010) Enabling a Network of Scientists: 2010 VIVO Conference. *Library Hi Tech News* 27 (9/10) (February 11): 1–4. doi:10.1108/07419051011110577.

Joint Information Systems Committee (JISC) (2007) *The JISC Digitisation Programme.* www.jisc.ac.uk/media/documents/programmes/digitisation/digitisation_brochure_v2_final.pdf.

Joint Information Systems Committee (JISC) (2009) *In From the Cold: An Assessment of the Scope of 'Orphan Works' and Its Impact on the Delivery of Services to the Public.* http://sca.jiscinvolve.org/wp/files/2009/06/sca_colltrust_orphan_works_v1-final.pdf.

Jones, E. (2010) Google Books as a General Research Collection. *Library Resources & Technical Services* 54 (2): 77–89.

Jørgensen, Lotte, Anna Alwerud, Ingegerd Rabow, Salam Shanawa, and Lars Bjørnshauge (2003) Electronic Information Resources: Integration – Integration – Integration. *Serials: The Journal for the Serials Community* 16 (3) (November 1): 313–17.

Kahn, R., and R. Wilensky (1995) *A Framework for Distributed Digital Object Services, May 1995.* Corporation for National Research Initiatives.

Kahn, R., and R. Wilensky (2006) A Framework for Distributed Digital Object Services. *International Journal on Digital Libraries* 6 (2): 115–23. doi:10.1007/s00799-005-0128-x.

Kalfatovic, Martin R., Effie Kapsalis, Katherine P. Spiess, Anne Van Camp, and Michael Edson (2008) Smithsonian Team Flickr: A Library, Archives, and Museums Collaboration in Web 2.0 Space. *Archival Science* 8 (4): 267–77.

Kaufman, Paula, and Sarah Barbara Watstein (2008) Library Value (return on Investment, ROI) and the Challenge of Placing a Value on Public Services. *Reference Services Review* 36 (3): 226–31.

Keller, K. L. (2000) The Brand Report Card. *Harvard Business Review* 78 (1): 147–58.

Keller, Michael A. (2011) Linked Data: A Way Out of the Information Chaos and Toward the Semantic Web. *EDUCAUSE Review* 46 (4). www.educause.edu/ero/article/linked-data-way-out-information-chaos-and-toward-semantic-web.

Kennan, Mary Anne (2011) Learning to Share: Mandates and Open Access. *Library Management* 32 (4/5) (May 17): 302–18. doi:10.1108/01435121111132301.

Kieft, Robert H., and Lizanne Payne (2012) Collective Collection, Collective Action. *Collection Management* 37 (3–4): 137–52. doi:10.1080/01462679.2012.685411.

Kilgour, F. G. (1969) Initial System Design for the Ohio College Library Center: a Case History. In *Proceedings of the 1968 Clinic on Library Applications of Data Processing,* 79–88. Urbana, IL: University of Illinois. Graduate School of Library Science. www.ideals.illinois.edu/handle/2142/827.

Kim, J. (2010) Faculty Self-archiving: Motivations and Barriers. *Journal of the American Society for Information Science and Technology* 61 (9): 1909–22.

King, David Lee (2012) Social Media. *Library Technology Reports* 48 (6): 23–6.

King, Edmund (2005) Digitisation of Newspapers at the British Library. *Serials Librarian* 49 (1– 2): 165–81.

Kirriemuir, John (1996) eLib Starts to Deliver. *Ariadne: Web Magazine for Information Professionals* (1) (January). www.ariadne.ac.uk/issue1/elib.

Kluiters, Chris C. P. (1997) Delivering 'Building Blocks' for Digital Libraries: First Experiences with Elsevier Electronic Subscriptions and Digital Libraries in Europe. *Library Acquisitions: Practice & Theory* 21 (3): 273–9. doi:10.1016/S0364-6408(97)00041-0.

Kohler, Scott (2009) Case 78: JSTOR. In *Casebook for The Foundation*: 225–7. PublicAffairs.

Koltay, Zsuzsa, and Xin Li (2010) *SPEC Kit 318: Impact Measures in Research Libraries*. Association of Research Libraries.

Krafft, Dean B., Nicholas A. Cappadona, Brian Caruso, Jon Corson-Rikert, Medha Devare, Brian J. Lowe, and VIVO Collaboration (2010) Vivo: Enabling National Networking of Scientists. http://journal.webscience.org/316.

Kress, Nancy, and Joel Wisner (2013) A Supply Chain Model for Library Quality and Service Improvement. *Journal of Operations and Supply Chain Management* 5 (2).

Krichel, Thomas, and Christian Zimmermann (2012) Author Identification in Economics . . . and Beyond. SSRN Scholarly Paper ID 2096422. Rochester, NY: Social Science Research Network. http://papers.ssrn.com/abstract=2096422.

Krowne, Aaron (2003) Building a Digital Library the Commons-based Peer Production Way. *D-Lib Magazine* 9 (10) (October). doi:10.1045/october2003-krowne.

Kumar, Bharat (2010) Digital Library and Repositories: An Indian Initiative. In *Developing Sustainable Digital Libraries*, 184–205. IGI Global.

Kurtz, M. J., G. Eichhorn, A. Accomazzi, C. Grant, M. Demleitner, and S.S. Murray (2005) Worldwide Use and Impact of the NASA Astrophysics Data System Digital Library. *Journal of the American Society for Information Science and Technology* 56 (1): 36–45.

Laakso, Mikael, Patrik Welling, Helena Bukvova, Linus Nyman, Bo-Christer Björk, and Turid Hedlund (2011) The Development of Open Access Journal Publishing from 1993 to 2009. *PLoS ONE* 6 (6): e20961. doi:10.1371/journal.pone.0020961.

Lage, Kathryn, Barbara Losoff, and Jack Maness (2011) Receptivity to Library Involvement in Scientific Data Curation: A Case Study at the University of Colorado Boulder. *Portal: Libraries and the Academy* 11 (4): 915–37. doi:10.1353/pla.2011.0049.

Lagoze, Carl (2010) *Lost Identity: The Assimilation of Digital Libraries into the Web.* PhD dissertation, Cornell University.

Lagoze, Carl, Jane Hunter, and Dan Brickley (2000) An Event-aware Model for Metadata Interoperability. In *Research and Advanced Technology for Digital Libraries*: 103–16. Springer. http://link.springer.com/chapter/10.1007/3-540-45268-0_10.

Lagoze, Carl, D. B. Krafft, S. Payette, and S. Jesuroga (2005) What Is a Digital Library Anymore, Anyway. *D-Lib Magazine* 11 (11). doi:10.1045/november2005-lagoze.

Lagoze, Carl, Clifford A. Lynch, and Ron Daniel (1996) The Warwick Framework: A Container Architecture for Aggregating Sets of Metadata. Cornell University. https://ecommons.library.cornell.edu/handle/1813/7248.

Lagoze, Carl, S. Payette, E. Shin, and C. Wilper (2006) Fedora: An Architecture for Complex Objects and Their Relationships. *International Journal on Digital Libraries* 6 (2): 124–38.

Lagoze, Carl, and H. Van de Sompel (2001) The Open Archives Initiative: Building a Low-barrier Interoperability Framework. In *Proceedings of the 1st ACM/IEEE-CS Joint Conference on Digital Libraries*: 54–62.

Lagoze, Carl, Herbert Van de Sompel, Michael Nelson, and Simeon Warner (2002) *Open Archives Initiative – Protocol for Metadata Harvesting – V.2.0.* Open Archives Initiative. www.openarchives.org/OAI/2.0/openarchivesprotocol.htm.

Lagoze, Carl, Herbert Van de Sompel, Michael L. Nelson, Simeon Warner, Robert Sanderson, and Pete Johnston (2008) Object Re-use & Exchange: A Resource-Centric Approach. *arXiv:0804.2273* (April 14). http://arxiv.org/abs/0804.2273.

Lagoze, Carl, Herbert Van de Sompel, Michael Nelson, Simeon Warner, Robert Sanderson, and Pete Johnston (2012) A Web-based Resource Model for Scholarship 2.0: Object Reuse & Exchange. *Concurrency and Computation: Practice and Experience* 24 (18): 2221–40. doi:10.1002/cpe.1594.

Lally, Ann M., and Carolyn E. Dunford (2007) Using Wikipedia to Extend Digital Collections. *D-Lib Magazine* 13 (5/6) (May). doi:10.1045/may2007-lally.

Lampert, C. K., and J. Vaughan (2009) Success Factors and Strategic Planning: Rebuilding an Academic Library Digitization Program. *Information Technology and Libraries* 28 (3): 116–36.

Lane, Julia (2010) Let's Make Science Metrics More Scientific. *Nature* 464 (7288): 488–9.

Lankes, R. David (2011) *The Atlas of New Librarianship.* MIT Press.

Lankes, R. David, Joanne Silverstein, and Scott Nicholson (2007) Participatory Networks: The Library As Conversation. *Information Technology and Libraries* 26 (4) (December 1): 17.

Larsen, Ronald L., Howard D. Wactlar, and Amy Friedlander (2003) Knowledge Lost in Information: Report of the NSF Workshop on Research Directions for

Digital Libraries. School of Information Science, University of Pittsburgh. www.sis.pitt.edu/~dlwkshop/report.pdf.

Lavoie, Brian, Lynn Silipigni Connaway, and Lorcan Dempsey (2005) Anatomy of Aggregate Collections. *D-Lib Magazine* 11 (9).

Lavoie, Brian, and Lorcan Dempsey (2004) Thirteen Ways of Looking at . . . Digital Preservation. *D-Lib Magazine* 10 (7/8) (July). doi:10.1045/july2004-lavoie.

Lavoie, Brian, Geneva Henry, and Lorcan Dempsey (2006) A Service Framework for Libraries. *D-Lib Magazine* 12 (7/8) (July). doi:10.1045/july2006-lavoie.

Law, Derek (1988) The State of Retroconversion in the United Kingdom: a Review. *Journal of Librarianship and Information Science* 20 (2): 81–93. doi:10.1177/096100068802000201.

Law, Derek (2011) Library Landscapes: Digital Developments. In *Libraries and Society: Role, Responsibility and Future in an Age of Change: 361–77.* Oxford, UK: Chandos. http://strathprints.strath.ac.uk/31320.

Lebert, Marie (2008) *Project Gutenberg (1971–2008).* Project Gutenberg. www.enebooks.com/data/JK82mxJBHsrAsdHqQvsK/2010-01-17/1263695736.pdf.

Ledoux, Thomas (2012) Digital Repository at the National Library of France (BnF): Long-term Access and Preservation. In *International Conference 2012: Trusted Digital Repositories and Trusted Professionals, 11-12 December.* Florence: Fondazione Rinascimento Digitale. http://93.63.166.138:8080/dspace/handle/2012/101.

Lee, Christopher A. (2010) Open Archival Information System (OAIS) Reference Model. *Encyclopedia of Library and Information Sciences:* 4020–30.

Leggott, M. A. (2009) Islandora: a Drupal/Fedora Repository System. Presented at the 4th International Conference on Open Repositories. http://smartech.gatech.edu/handle/1853/28495.

Lercher, Aaron (2008) A Survey of Attitudes About Digital Repositories Among Faculty at Louisiana State University at Baton Rouge. *Journal of Academic Librarianship* 34 (5) (September): 408–15. doi:10.1016/j.acalib.2008.06.008.

Lesk, Michael (1997) *Practical Digital Libraries: Books, Bytes, and Bucks.* Morgan Kaufmann.

Lesk, Michael (2004) *Understanding Digital Libraries.* Elsevier.

Lesk, Michael, E. A. Fox and Michael McGill (1993) A National Electronic Science, Engineering and Technology Library. In *Source Book on Digital Libraries: Prepared for and Sponsored by the National Science Foundation,* 4–24. Virginia Tech. http://eprints.cs.vt.edu/archive/00000377/01/TR-93-35.pdf.

Lessig, Lawrence (2013) Re-crafting a Public Domain. *Yale Journal of Law & the Humanities* 18 (3) (May 8). http://digitalcommons.law.yale.edu/yjlh/vol18/iss3/4.

Levine, Jenny (2006) 3 . . . 2 . . . 1 . . . ALA Library 2.0 Course Launch. *The Shifted Librarian.* May 3. www.theshiftedlibrarian.com/archives/2006/05/03/

321_ala_library_20_course_launch.html.

Levy, David M., and Catherine C. Marshall (1995) Going Digital: a Look at Assumptions Underlying Digital Libraries. *Communications of the ACM* 38 (4) (April): 77–84. doi:10.1145/205323.205346.

Lewis, Stuart (2012) Repository Maps. January 19. http://maps.repository66.org/.

Lewis, Stuart, Pablo de Castro, and Richard Jones (2012) SWORD: Facilitating Deposit Scenarios. *D-Lib Magazine* 18 (1/2) (January). doi:10.1045/january2012-lewis.

Li, Yunjia, Mike Wald, and Gary Wills (2012) Let Google Index Your Media Fragments. In *WWW2012 Developer Track*. Lyon, France. http://eprints.soton.ac.uk/336529/.

Licklider, J. C. R. (1965) *Libraries of the Future*. MIT. Press.

Liew, Chern Li (2009) Digital Library Research 1997–2007: Organisational and People Issues. *Journal of Documentation* 65 (2): 245–66.

Liew, Chern Li (2012) Towards Socially Inclusive Digital Libraries. In *Digital Libraries and Information Access: Research Perspectives*: 97–111. Facet Publishing.

Lindahl, D., J. Bowen, and N. F. Foster (2007) *University of Rochester eXtensible Catalog Phase 1: Final Report*. Mellon Foundation. http://docushare.lib.rochester.edu/docushare/dsweb/Get/Document-27534/XC%20Phase%201%20Final%20Report%20public%20version.pdf.

Linke, Erica C. (2003) Million Book Project. In *Encyclopedia of Library and Information Science*, 1889–. CRC Press.

Lippincott, J. K. (2010) A Mobile Future for Academic Libraries. *Reference Services Review* 38 (2): 205–13.

Liu, Xiaoyan, Zhiling Guo, Zhenjiang Lin, and Jian Ma (2012) A Local Social Network Approach for Research Management. *Decision Support Systems*. doi:10.1016/j.dss.2012.10.055.

Liu, Wei, Xiaofeng Meng, and Weiyi Meng (2010) ViDE: A Vision-Based Approach for Deep Web Data Extraction. *IEEE Transactions on Knowledge and Data Engineering* 22 (3): 447–60. doi:10.1109/TKDE.2009.109.

Liu, Yan Quan (2004) Is the Education on Digital Libraries Adequate? *New Library World* 105 (1/2): 60–8.

Lossau, Norbert (2004) Search Engine Technology and Digital Libraries: Libraries Need to Discover the Academic Internet. *D-Lib Magazine* 10 (6) (June).

Lougee, Wendy (2009) The Diffuse Library Revisited: Aligning the Library as Strategic Asset. *Library Hi Tech* 27 (4) (November 20): 610–23. doi:10.1108/07378830911007718.

Loughborough University Library & Information Statistics Unit and Research Information Network (2007) *Uncovering Hidden Resources: Progress in Extending the*

Coverage of Online Catalogues: Report of a Study Undertaken for the Research Information Network. Research Information Network.

Lowry, Charles, and Julia Blixrud (2012) E-Book Licensing and Research Libraries: Negotiating Principles and Price in an Emerging Market. *Research Library Issues* (280) (September): 11.

Lucier, Richard E., and Peter Brantley (1995) Red Sage Project: Experimental Digital Journal Library for Health Sciences. *D-Lib Magazine* (August). www.dlib.org/dlib/august95/lucier/08lucier.html.

Lund, Ben, Tony Hammond, Martin Flack, and Timo Hannay (2005) Social Bookmarking Tools (II). *D-Lib Magazine* 11 (04) (April). doi:10.1045/april2005-lund.

Luther, Judy (2012) Altmetrics – Trying to Fill the Gap. *Scholarly Kitchen*. July 15. http://scholarlykitchen.sspnet.org/2012/07/25/altmetrics-trying-to-fill-the-gap.

Lyman, Peter (1996) What Is a Digital Library? Technology, Intellectual Property, and the Public Interest. *Daedalus* 125 (4): 1–33.

Lyman, Peter, and Hal R. Varian (2003) How Much Information? 2003. UC Berkeley. School of Information Management and Systems. www2.sims. berkeley.edu/research/projects/how-much-info-2003/printable_report.pdf.

Lynch, Clifford (2000) From Automation to Transformation. *Educause Review* 35 (1): 60–8.

Lynch, Clifford A. (2003) Colliding with the Real World: Heresies and Unexplored Questions About Audience, Economics, and Control of Digital Libraries. In *Digital Library Use: Social Practice in Design and Evaluation*: 191–216. MIT Press.

Lynch, Clifford (2005) Where Do We Go From Here? *D-Lib Magazine* (July). doi:10.1045/july2005-lynch.

Lynch, Clifford, and Hector Garcia-Molina (1995) *Interoperability, Scaling, and the Digital Libraries Research Agenda*. IITA Working Group. www.sis.pitt.edu/~repwkshop/papers/DL1995.pdf.

Ma, Yongqing, Warwick Clegg, and Ann O'Brien (2009) A Review of Progress in Digital Library Education. In *Handbook of Research on Digital Libraries: Design, Development, and Impact*, 533–42. Information Science Reference.

MacEwan, Andrew, Anila Angjeli, and Janifer Gatenby (2013) The International Standard Name Identifier (ISNI): The Evolving Future of Name Authority Control. *Cataloging & Classification Quarterly* 51 (1–3): 55–71. doi:10.1080/01639374.2012.730601.

Malpas, Constance (2011) *Cloud-sourcing Research Collections: Managing Print in the Mass-digitized Library Environment*. OCLC.

Manduca, Cathryn A., Sean Fox, and Ellen R. Iverson (2006) Digital Library as Network and Community Center. *D-Lib Magazine* 12 (12) (December).

doi:10.1045/december2006-manduca.

Manduca, Cathryn A., Ellen R. Iverson, Sean Fox, and Flora McMartin (2005) Influencing User Behavior through Digital Library Design. *D-Lib Magazine* 11 (05) (May). doi:10.1045/may2005-fox.

Maness, Jack M. (2006) Library 2.0 Theory: Web 2.0 and Its Implications for Libraries. *Webology* 3 (2) (June). www.webology.org/2006/v3n2/a25.html.

Maness, Jack M., T. Miaskiewicz, and T. Sumner (2008) Using Personas to Understand the Needs and Goals of Institutional Repository Users. *D-Lib Magazine* 14 (9/10).

Manghi, Paolo, Marko Mikulicic, Leonardo Candela, Donatella Castelli, and Pasquale Pagano (2010) Realizing and Maintaining Aggregative Digital Library Systems: D-NET Software Toolkit and OAIster System. *D-Lib Magazine* 16 (3/4). doi:10.1045/march2010-manghi.

Manz, Susanne (2012) Ensuring Perpetual Access to Licensed Content: Introduction to the Main Issues presented at the Symposium of the Consortium of Swiss Academic Libraries, June 5, Bern. http://e-collection.library.ethz.ch/view/eth:5613.

Marchionini, G. (2000) Evaluating Digital Libraries: A Longitudinal and Multifaceted View. *Library Trends* 49 (2): 304–33.

Marcondes, C. H., and L. F. Sayão (2003) The SciELO Brazilian Scientific Journal Gateway and Open Archives. *D-Lib Magazine* 9 (3). doi:10.1045/march2003-marcondes.

Mardis, Marcia A. (2009) Classroom Information Needs. *D-Lib Magazine* 15 (1/2) (January). doi:10.1045/january2009-mardis. www.dlib.org/dlib/january09/mardis/01mardis.html.

Markey, Karen, Soo Young Rieh, Beth St Jean, Jihyun Kim, and Elizabeth Yakel (2007) *Census of Institutional Repositories in the United States*. Council on Library and Information Resources. http://clir.org/pubs/reports/pub140/pub140.pdf.

Markey, K., S. Y. Rieh, B. St Jean, E. Yakel, and X. Yao (2009) Secrets of Success: Identifying Success Factors in Institutional Repositories. In *4th International Conference on Open Repositories*. Atlanta, GA. http://smartech.gatech.edu/handle/1853/28419.

Marlino, Mary, Tamara Sumner, David Fulker, Cathryn Manduca, and David Mogk (2001) The Digital Library for Earth System Education: Building Community, Building the Library. *Communications of the ACM* 44 (5) (May): 80–1. doi:10.1145/374308.374356.

Maron, Nancy, and Sarah Pickle (2013) *Appraising Our Digital Investment: Sustainability of Digitized Special Collections in ARL Libraries*. ITHAKA S+R and Association for Research Libraries. www.arl.org/bm~doc/digitizing-special-collections-report-21feb13.pdf.

Maron, Nancy, K. K. Smith, and M. Loy (2009) *Sustaining Digital Resources: An On-the-ground View of Projects Today: ITHAKA Case Studies in Sustainability.* ITHAKA S+ R. http://sca.jiscinvolve.org/files/2009/11/sca_ithaka_ sustainingdigitalresources_executivesummary_uk_lr.pdf.

Marshak, David W., and Todd R. Johnson (2010) What Faculty Members Want From a Research Information System. Presented at the 1st Annual VIVO National Conference, New York NY. www.vivoweb.org/files/FacultyWant.pdf.

Masinter, Larry, Tim Berners-Lee, and Roy T. Fielding (2005) Uniform Resource Identifier (URI): Generic Syntax. January. http://tools.ietf.org/html/rfc3986.

Maslov, Alexey, James Creel, Adam Mikeal, Scott Phillips, John Leggett, and Mark McFarland (2010) Adding OAI-ORE Support to Repository Platforms. *Journal of Digital Information* 11 (1).

Mayernik, Matthew S., G. Sayeed Choudhury, Tim DiLauro, Elliot Metsger, Barbara Pralle, Mike Rippin, and Ruth Duerr (2012) The Data Conservancy Instance: Infrastructure and Organizational Services for Research Data Curation. *D-Lib Magazine* 18 (9/10).
http://dlib.org/dlib/september12/mayernik/09mayernik.print.html.

Mayfield, I., L. Humphreys, S. Shadle, and M. Watson (2008) Next-generation Library Catalogues: Reviews of ELIN, WorldCat Local and Aquabrowser. *Serials* 21 (3): 224–30.

Max Planck Society (2003) Berlin Declaration. October. http://oa.mpg.de/lang/en-uk/berlin-prozess/berliner-erklarung.

McClure, Charles R. (1987) *Planning and Role Setting for Public Libraries: a Manual of Options and Procedures.* American Library Association.

McClure, Charles R., and Paul T. Jaeger (2009) *Public Libraries and Internet Service Roles: Measuring and Maximizing Internet Services.* ALA Editions.

McGovern, Nancy Y., and Katherine Skinner (2012) *Aligning National Approaches to Digital Preservation.* Educopia Institute Publications.
www.educopia.org/sites/default/files/ANADP_Educopia_2012.pdf.

Meho, Lokman I., and Kiduk Yang (2007) Impact of Data Sources on Citation Counts and Rankings of LIS Faculty: Web of Science Versus Scopus and Google Scholar. *Journal of the American Society for Information Science and Technology* 58 (13): 2105–25. doi:10.1002/asi.20677.

Mendes, Pablo N., Max Jakob, and Christian Bizer (2012) DBpedia: A Multilingual Cross-Domain Knowledgebase. In *Proceedings of the Eight International Conference on Language Resources and Evaluation (LREC'12), European Language Resources Association (ELRA), Istanbul, Turkey.*
www.lrec-conf.org/proceedings/lrec2012/pdf/570_Paper.pdf.

Menendez, Maria, Antonella de Angeli, and Zeno Menestrina (2012) Exploring the

Virtual Space of Academia. In *From Research to Practice in the Design of Cooperative Systems: Results and Open Challenges*: 49–63. Springer London.

Menzies, Kathleen, Duncan Birrell, and Gordon Dunsire (2010) New Evidence on the Interoperability of Information Systems Within UK Universities. In *Research and Advanced Technology for Digital Libraries*: 104–15. Lecture Notes in Computer Science 6273. Springer Berlin Heidelberg.

Mercer, Holly, Jay Koenig, Robert B. McGeachin, and Sandra L. Tucker (2011) Structure, Features, and Faculty Content in ARL Member Repositories. *Journal of Academic Librarianship* 37 (4): 333–42. doi:10.1016/j.acalib.2011.04.008.

Meyer, L. (2009) *Safeguarding Collections at the Dawn of the 21st Century: Describing Roles & Measuring Contemporary Preservation Activities in ARL Libraries.* Association of Research Libraries.

Michener, William, Dave Vieglais, Todd Vision, John Kunze, Patricia Cruse, and Greg Janée (2011) DataONE: Data Observation Network for Earth – Preserving Data and Enabling Innovation in the Biological and Environmental Sciences. *D-Lib Magazine* 17 (1/2) (January). doi:10.1045/january2011-michener.

Miličić, Vuk (2011) Problems of Linked Data (1/4): Identity. *Bew Citnames*. July 26. http://milicicvuk.com/blog/2011/07/26/problems-of-linked-data-14-identity.

Miller, Eric, Uche Ogbuji, Victoria Mueller, and Kathy MacDougall (2012) *Bibliographic Framework as a Web of Data: Linked Data Model and Supporting Services.* Library of Congress. www.loc.gov/bibframe/pdf/marcld-report-11-21-2012.pdf.

Miller, K., D. Swan, T. Craig, S. Dorinski, M. Freeman, N. Isaac, P. O'Shea, P. Schilling, and J. Scotto (2011) *Public Libraries Survey: Fiscal Year 2009*. Institute of Museum and Library Services. www.imls.gov/assets/1/News/PLS2009.pdf.

Miller, Paul (2000) Interoperability: What Is It and Why Should I Want It? *Ariadne* (24). www.ariadne.ac.uk/issue24/interoperability.

Miller, Paul (2005) Web 2.0: Building the New Library. *Ariadne* (45) (October). www.ariadne.ac.uk/issue45/miller.

Miller, Rachel (2007) Acts of Vision: The Practice of Licensing. *Collection Management* 32 (1–2): 173–190. doi:10.1300/J105v32n01_12.

Millington, Peter, and Bill Hubbard (2010) *OpenDOAR & ROAR Joint Development Project: April 2008–December 2009 Final Report*. JISC. http://ie-repository.jisc.ac.uk/482/1/OpenDOARfinalreport.pdf.

Millington, Peter, and W. Nixon (2007) Take a Peek Beneath the EPrints V3 Wrappers. *Ariadne* (50). www.ariadne.ac.uk/issue50/eprints-v3-rpt.

Mischo, William (2002) *D-Lib Test Suite Project (1999–2001): Final Report Submitted to Corporation for National Research Initiatives (CNRI)*. University of Illinois at Urbana-Champaign. http://dli.grainger.uiuc.edu/idli/progress_reports/final_report.htm.

Mischo, William (2004) United States Federal Support for Digital Library Research and Its Implications for Digital Library Development. In *Digital Libraries: Policy, Planning, and Practice*: 5–18. Ashgate Publishing.

Mitchell, Carmen, and Daniel Suchy (2012) Developing Mobile Access to Digital Collections. *D-Lib Magazine* 18 (1/2) (January). doi:10.1045/january2012-mitchell.

Mitchell, Erik T. (2012) Why Digital Data Collections Are Important. *Journal of Web Librarianship* 6 (3): 213–16.

Mitchell, Joan S., and Diane Vizine-Goetz (2009) Dewey Decimal Classification. *Encyclopedia of Library and Information Science*. CRC Press.

Miyazawa, Akira (2005) *Japanese Journal Digitization and Portal Service GeNii: National Institute of Informatics (Japan)*. ALA. International Relations Committee. http://citeseerx.ist.psu.edu/viewdoc/download?doi= 10.1.1.94.5131&rep=rep1&type=pdf.

Moen, W. E. (2000) Resource Discovery Using Z39.50: Promise and Reality. In *Bicentennial Conference on Bibliographic Control for the New Millennium: Confronting the Challenges of Networked Resources and the Web*.

Molyneux, R. E. (1994) What Did Rider Do? An Inquiry into the Methodology of Fremont Rider's 'The Scholar and the Future of the Research Library'. *Libraries & Culture*: 297–325.

Moore, Gale (2011) *Survey of University of Toronto Faculty Awareness, Attitudes, and Practices Regarding Scholarly Communication: A Preliminary Report* (March 3). https://tspace.library.utoronto.ca/handle/1807/26446.

Morgan, Eric Lease, Jeremy Frumkin, and Edward A. Fox (2004) The OCKHAM Initiative – Building Component-based Digital Library Services and Collections. *D-Lib Magazine*, November. www.dlib.org/dlib/november04/11inbrief.html.

Morris, Sally (2009) Journal Authors' Rights: Perception and Reality. Publishing Research Consortium. http://web.archive.org./web/201108251521/ http://www.publishingresearch.net/documents/JournalAuthorsRights.pdf.

Morris, Sally, and Sue Thorn (2009) Learned Society Members and Open Access. *Learned Publishing* 22 (3): 221–39. doi:10.1087/2009308.

Mugridge, Rebecca L. (2006) *SPEC Kit 294: Managing Digitization Activities*. Association of Research Libraries.

National Digital Information Infrastructure and Preservation Program (US) (2011) *Preserving Our Digital Heritage: The National Digital Information Infrastructure and Preservation Program 2010 Report*. Library of Congress. www.digitalpreservation. gov/multimedia/documents/NDIIPP2010Report_Post.pdf.

National Library of Australia (2008) Digital Preservation Directions Statement 2008 to 2012. www.nla.gov.au/digital-preservation-directions-statement-2008-to-2012.

National Library of New Zealand (2007) Papers Past Relaunched on Greenstone.

LibraryTechNZ. http://librarytechnz.natlib.govt.nz/2007/09/papers-past-relaunched-on-greenstone.html.

National Science Foundation (1993) *NSF 93-141 – Research on Digital Libraries*. www.nsf.gov/pubs/stis1993/nsf93141/nsf93141.txt.

National Science Foundation (1998a) *Digital Libraries Initiative Phase 2: NSF 98-63*. www.nsf.gov/pubs/1998/nsf9863/nsf9863.htm.

National Science Foundation (1998b) *Award#9411306 – The Stanford Integrated Digital Library Project*. www.nsf.gov/awardsearch/showAward.do?AwardNumber=9411306.

National Science Foundation (2001) *Award#9907892 – DLI-International: Integrating and Navigating Eprint Archives Through Citation-Linking*. www.nsf.gov/awardsearch/showAward.do?AwardNumber=9907892.

National Science Foundation (2006) *Award#0638866 – Workshop: New Collaborative Relationships: Academic Libraries in the Digital Data Universe*. www.nsf.gov/awardsearch/showAward.do?AwardNumber=0638866.

National Science Foundation (2007) *Award#9817484 – DLI Phase 2: A Digital Library for the Humanities*. www.nsf.gov/awardsearch/showAward.do?AwardNumber=9817484.

National Science Foundation (2010) Dissemination and Sharing of Research Results. www.nsf.gov/bfa/dias/policy/dmp.jsp.

Nelson, Michael, and B. Danette Allen (2002) Object Persistence and Availability in Digital Libraries. *D-Lib Magazine* 8 (1) (January). www.dlib.org/dlib/january02/nelson/01nelson.html.

Nentwich, Michael (2010) Web 2.0 and Academia. In *Proceedings of the 9th Annual IAS-STS Conference, Critical Issues in Science and Technology Studies*, 66–78. www.researchgate.net/publication/49579798_Web_2.0_and_academia/file/9fcfd505755e3366b0.pdf.

Nguyen, Son Hoang (2011) Digital Library Research (1990–2010): A Knowledge Map of Core Topics and Subtopics. Pre-print of a paper for the 2011 International Conference on Asia-Pacific Digital Libraries. www.slis.tsukuba.ac.jp/digitalarchive/WIS2011/Papers2011.10.24/SH-Nguyen.pdf.

Nguyen, Son Hoang, and Gobinda Chowdhury (2013) Interpreting the Knowledge Map of Digital Library Research (1990–2010). *Journal of the American Society for Information Science and Technology*. doi:10.1002/asi.22830.

Niu, Jinfang (2012) An Overview of Web Archiving. *D-Lib Magazine* 18 (3/4) (March). doi:10.1045/march2012-niu1.

Niu, Jinfang (2013) Evolving Landscape in Name Authority Control. *Cataloging & Classification Quarterly* 51 (4): 404–19. doi:10.1080/01639374.2012.756843.

Nixon, Judith M., Robert S. Freeman, and Suzanne M. Ward (2010) Patron-driven

Acquisitions: An Introduction and Literature Review. *Collection Management* 35 (3–4): 119–24.

Norris, M., C. Oppenheim, and F. Rowland (2008) Finding Open Access Articles Using Google, Google Scholar, OAIster and OpenDOAR. *Online Information Review* 32 (6): 709–15.

Oakleaf, Megan (2010) *The Value of Academic Libraries: A Comprehensive Research Review and Report*. American Library Association. Association of College and Research Libraries. www.citeulike.org/group/4576/article/7847697.

OCLC Research (1996) OCLC Makes PURL Software Available Free of Charge. June 21. www.oclc.org/research/news/1996/06-21.html.

OCLC Research (2007) OCLC and Zepheira to Redesign PURLs. July 11. www.oclc.org/research/news/2007/07-11.html.

OCLC Research (2009) Dublin Core Metadata Initiative. June 11. www.oclc.org/research/activities/dublincore.html.

O'Connor, Steve, and Cathie Jilovsky (2008) Approaches to the Storage of Low Use and Last Copy Research Materials. *Library Collections, Acquisitions and Technical Services* 32 (3): 121–6.

Oehlerts, Beth, and Shu Liu (2013) Digital Preservation Strategies at Colorado State University Libraries. *Library Management* 34 (1/2) (January 11): 83–95. doi:10.1108/01435121311298298.

O'Leary, Mick (1993) Dialog and Data-Star Look to Online's Future. *Online* 17 (4): 14–19.

Oliver, K. B., and R. Swain (2006) Directories of Institutional Repositories: Research Results & Recommendations. In *72nd IFLA General Conference and Council*, 20–4. http://citeseerx.ist.psu.edu/viewdoc/download?doi=10.1.1.127.8372&rep= rep1&type=pdf..

Oltmans, Erik, and Adriaan Lemmen (2006) The e-Depot at the National Library of the Netherlands. *Serials: The Journal for the Serials Community* 19 (1): 61–7.

Onaifo, Daniel, and Diane Rasmussen (2013) Increasing Libraries' Content Findability on the Web with Search Engine Optimization. *Library Hi Tech* 31 (1): 87–108.

Open Contributor and Researcher ID (ORCID) (2012) ORCID Launches Registry. October 16. http://orcid.org/news/2012/10/16/orcid-launches-registry.

O'Reilly, Tim (2005) What Is Web 2.0: Design Patterns and Business Models for the Next Generation of Software. *O'Reilly*. September 30. http://oreilly.com/web2/archive/what-is-web-20.html.

Organ, Michael (2006) Download Statistics – What Do They Tell Us? *D-Lib Magazine* 12 (11). doi:10.1045/november2006-organ.

Organization for Economic Cooperation and Development (OECD) (2007) OECD

Principles and Guidelines for Access to Research Data from Public Funding. Paris: OECD. www.oecd.org/science/scienceandtechnologypolicy/38500813.pdf.

Organization for the Advancement of Structured Information Standards (OASIS) (2009) Business Models, Costs and ROI. *OASIS Open Access Scholarly Information Sourcebook.* www.openoasis.org/index.php?option=com_content&view=article&id=166&Itemid=357.

Ortega, José Luis, and Isidro F. Aguillo (2012) Science Is All in the Eye of the Beholder: Keyword Maps in Google Scholar Citations. *Journal of the American Society for Information Science and Technology* 63 (12): 2370–7. doi:10.1002/asi.22761.

Ostrow, Stephen E. (1998) *Digitizing Historical Pictorial Collections for the Internet.* CLIR Report 71. Council on Library and Information Resources. www.clir.org/pubs/reports/ostrow/reports/ostrow/pub71.html.

Packer, A. L., R. Meneghini, S. M. Santos, F. M. Lapido, and A. Luccisano (2010) SciELO Program Publishes More Than 500 Latin-American Open Access Journals. *Towards Open Access Scholarship*: 51.

Paepcke, Andreas, R. Brandriff, G. Janee, R. Larson, B. Ludaescher, S. Melnik, and S. Raghavan (2000) Search Middleware and the Simple Digital Library Interoperability Protocol. *D-Lib Magazine* 6 (3).

Paepcke, Andreas, C. C. K. Chang, T. Winograd, and H. García-Molina (1998) Interoperability for Digital Libraries Worldwide. *Communications of the ACM* 41 (4): 33–42.

Paepcke, Andreas, Hector Garcia-Molina and Rebecca Wesley (2005) Dewey Meets Turing. *D-Lib Magazine* 11 (07/08) (July). doi:10.1045/july2005-paepcke.

Page, L., S. Brin, R. Motwani, and T. Winograd (1999) *The PageRank Citation Ranking: Bringing Order to the Web.* Technical report. Stanford InfoLab.

Paine, Thomas (1794) *The Age of Reason.* Paris: Barrois.

Palmer, C. L., L. C. Teffeau, and M. P. Newton (2008) *Identifying Factors of Success in CIC Institutional Repository Development-final Report.* Urbana, IL: Center for Informatics Research in Science and Scholarship. www.ideals.illinois.edu/handle/2142/8981.

Park, Taemin Kim (2010) D-Lib Magazine: Its First 13 Years. *D-Lib Magazine* 16 (1/2). doi:10.1045/january2010-park.

Payette, S., and T. Staples (2002) The Mellon Fedora Project Digital Library Architecture Meets XML and Web Services. *Research and Advanced Technology for Digital Libraries*: 87–106.

Payne, Hannah (2011) Time and Cost Analysis for Repository Deposit: The Welsh Repository Network Mediated Deposit Bureau. *ALISS Quarterly* 6 (3) (April): 10–13.

Payne, Lizanne (2005) Depositories and Repositories: Changing Models of Library Storage in the US. *Library Management* 26 (1/2): 10–17.

Peek, Robin (2012) Digital Public Library of America. *Information Today* 29 (2) (February).

Pennock, M. (2007) Digital Curation: a Life-cycle Approach to Managing and Preserving Usable Digital Information. *Library and Archives Journal* 1. www.ukoln. ac.uk/ukoln/staff/m.pennock/publications/docs/lib-arch_curation.pdf.

Peters, D., and N. Lossau (2011) DRIVER: Building a Sustainable Infrastructure for Global Repositories. *Electronic Library* 29 (2): 249–60.

Pinfield, S. (2004) eLib in Retrospect: a National Strategy for Digital Library Development in the 1990s. In *Digital Libraries: Policy, Planning, and Practice*, 19–36. Ashgate Publishing.

Pinfield, S. (2005) A Mandate to Self Archive? The Role of Open Access Institutional Repositories. *Serials: The Journal for the Serials Community* 18 (1): 30–4.

Pitti, Daniel (1997) Encoded Archival Description: The Development of an Encoding Standard for Archival Finding Aids. *American Archivist* 60 (3) (July 1): 268–83.

Pomerantz, Jeffrey, Barbara M. Wildemuth, Seungwon Yang, and Edward A. Fox (2006) Curriculum Development for Digital Libraries. In *Proceedings of the 6th ACM/IEEE-CS Joint Conference on Digital Libraries*: 175–84. New York: ACM Press.

Powell, James E., Krista Black, and Linn Marks Collins (2011) A Semantic Registry for Digital Library Collections and Services. *D-Lib Magazine* 17 (11/12). doi:10.1045/november2011-powell.

Poynder, Richard (2012) Open Access Mandates: Ensuring Compliance. *Open and Shut?* May 8. http://poynder.blogspot.com/2012/05/open-access-mandates-ensuring.html.

Pozadzides, John (2010) Analysis: What Are the Web's Top Sources of Referral Traffic? July 28. *ReadWrite*. http://readwrite.com/2010/07/28/analysis_what_are_the_webs_top_sources_of_referral_traffic#awesm=~oaDtE8RpDLQS3t.

Price, Gary (2013) New Statistics Available: IMLS Releases New 'Public Library Report' (FY 2010). *LJ INFOdocket*. January 22. www.infodocket.com/2013/01/22/new-statistics-available-imls-releases-new-public-library-report-fy-2010/.

Priem, Jason, Heather A. Piwowar, and Bradley M. Hemminger (2012) Altmetrics in the Wild: Using Social Media to Explore Scholarly Impact. *arXiv Preprint arXiv:1203.4745*. http://arxiv.org/abs/1203.4745.

Proffitt, Merrilee, and Sara Snyder (2012) Wikipedia, Libraries & Archives What's the Connection? presented at the Coalition for Networked Information Fall Membership Meeting, December 11, Washington DC.

Puckett, Jason (2011) *Zotero: a Guide for Librarians, Researchers and Educators*. Association of College and Research Libraries.

Purcell, Kristen (2010) *My Digital Library: Leveraging Today's Mobile and Participatory*

Information Ecosystem. Pew Research Center Internet & American Life Project. http://libraries.pewinternet.org/2010/07/29/my-digital-library-leveraging-todays-mobile-and-participatory-information-ecosystem.

Quinn, A. J., B. B. Bederson, E. M. Bonsignore, and A. Druin (2009) *StoryKit: Designing a Mobile Application for Story Creation by Children and Older Adults*. Technical Report. Human Computer Interaction Lab, University of Maryland.

Raimond, Yves, Tom Scott, Patrick Sinclair, Libby Miller, Stephen Betts, and Frances McNamara (2012) Case Study: Use of Semantic Web Technologies on the BBC Web Sites. January 7. www.w3.org/2001/sw/sweo/public/UseCases/BBC/.

Ratner, Howard (2011) ORCID Update & Other Researcher Identifiers. Presented at the CrossRef Annual Members Meeting, November 15. www.slideshare.net/CrossRef/orcid-howard-ratner.

Ratner, Howard (2012) ORCID: Getting to Launch presented at the ORCID Outreach Meeting, October 17, Berlin. www.slideshare.net/ORCIDSlides/2-ratner-orcid-getting-to-launch-v5.

Recker, Mimi (2006) Perspectives on Teachers as Digital Library Users. *D-Lib Magazine* 12 (9) (September). doi:10.1045/september2006-recker.

Recker, Mimi, J. Dorward, and L. M. Nelson (2004) Discovery and Use of Online Learning Resources: Case Study Findings. *Journal of Educational Technology and Society* 7: 93–104.

Reid, Ian (2012) *The Public Library Data Service 2012 Statistical Report: Characteristics and Trends*. Public Library Data Service. http://publiclibrariesonline.org/2012/12/the-public-library-data-service-2012-statistical-report-characteristics-and-trends.

Research Information Network (2013) Finch Report: Report of the Working Group on Expanding Access to Published Research Findings. March 19. www.researchinfonet.org/publish/finch.

Ricciardi, Victor (2007) *Facilitating Research with the Social Science Research Network (SSRN): An Editor's Perspective*. SSRN Scholarly Paper ID 928110. Rochester, NY: Social Science Research Network. http://papers.ssrn.com/abstract=928110.

Ricolfi, Marco, Lynne Brindley, Claudia Dillman, Tarja Koskinen-Olsson, Toby Bainton, Anne Bergman-Tahon, Jean-François Debarnot, Myriam Diocaretz, and Olav Stokkmo (2008) *Final Report on Digital Preservation, Orphan Works, and Out-of-Print Works: I2010 Digital Libraries High Level Expert Group, Copyright Subgroup*. European Commission. www.ifap.ru/library/book305.pdf.

Rider, Fremont (1944) *The Scholar and the Future of the Research Library: a Problem and Its Solution*. Hadham Press.

Rieger, Oya Y. (2007) Select for Success. *D-Lib Magazine* 13 (7/8) (July). doi:10.1045/july2007-rieger.

Rieger, Oya Y. (2008a) Opening up Institutional Repositories: Social Construction of Innovation in Scholarly Communication. *Journal of Electronic Publishing* 11 (3).

Rieger, Oya Y. (2008b) *Preservation in the Age of Large-scale Digitization*. CLIR Publication. Washington, DC: Council on Library and Information Resources. www.bib.ub.edu/fileadmin/fdocs/pub141.pdf.

Rieger, Oya Y. (2011) Assessing the Value of Open Access Information Systems: Making a Case for Community-Based Sustainability Models. *Journal of Library Administration* 51 (5–6): 485–506.

Rieger, Oya Y. (2012) Sustainability: Scholarly Repository as an Enterprise. *Bulletin of the American Society for Information Science and Technology* 39 (1): 27–31. doi:10.1002/bult.2012.1720390110.

Riley, Jenn, and Devin Becker (2010) Seeing Standards: a Visualization of the Metadata Universe. www.dlib.indiana.edu/~jenlrile/metadatamap/seeingstandards.pdf.

Roemer, Robin Chin, and Rachel Borchardt (2012) From Bibliometrics to Altmetrics: A Changing Scholarly Landscape. *College & Research Libraries News* 73 (10) (November 1): 596–600.

Romary, Laurent, and Chris Armbruster (2010) Beyond Institutional Repositories. *International Journal of Digital Library Systems* 1 (1): 44–61. doi:10.4018/jdls.2010102703.

Ronallo, Jason (2012) HTML5 Microdata and Schema. Org. *Code4Lib Journal* (16). www.doaj.org/doaj?func=fulltext&aId=949185.

Rosa, Isaias Barreto da, Ilya Shmorgun, Sonia Sousa, Veronika Rogalevits, and David Lamas (2012) Bringing DSpace-based Digital Libraries into Mobile Devices. In *15th International Conference on Computer and Information Technology (ICCIT)*: 551–6.

Rosenthal, David S. H. (2010) LOCKSS: Lots of Copies Keep Stuff Safe. In *NIST Digital Preservation Interoperability Framework Workshop*. http://download2.lockss.org/locksswiki/files/NIST2010.pdf.

Ross, Seamus (2000) *Changing Trains at Wigan: Digital Preservation and the Future of Scholarship*. NPO Preservation Guidance Occasional Papers. National Preservation Office, British Library. http://eprints.erpanet.org/45.

Rotenberg, Ellen, and Ann Kushmerick (2011) The Author Challenge: Identification of Self in the Scholarly Literature. *Cataloging & Classification Quarterly* 49 (6): 503–20. doi:10.1080/01639374.2011.606405.

Rowlands, Ian, and David Nicholas (2005) Scholarly Communication in the Digital Environment: The 2005 Survey of Journal Author Behaviour and Attitudes. *Aslib Proceedings* 57 (6) (December 1): 481–97. doi:10.1108/00012530510634226.

Rowlands, Ian, David Nicholas, and P. Huntington (2004) Scholarly Communication in the Digital Environment: What Do Authors Want? *Learned Publishing* 17 (4): 261–73.

Rusbridge, Chris (1995) The UK Electronic Libraries Programme. *D-Lib Magazine* (December). http://dlib.org/dlib/december95/briefings/12uk.html.

Rusbridge, Chris (1998) Towards the Hybrid Library. *D-Lib Magazine* (October). www.dlib.org/dlib/july98/rusbridge/07rusbridge.html.

Rutner, Jennifer, and Roger C. Schonfeld (2012) Supporting the Changing Research Practices of Historians. ITHAKA S+R. www.sr.ithaka.org/research-publications/ supporting-changing-research-practices-historians.

Saarti, Jarmo, and Pentti Vattulainen (2013) Management of and Access to Print Collections in National and Repository Libraries in Europe: Collection for Use or for Preservation. *Library Management* 34 (4/5) (May 31): 273–80. doi:10.1108/01435121311328618.

Sadeh, T. (2007) Time for a Change: New Approaches for a New Generation of Library Users. *New Library World* 108 (7/8): 307–16.

Sadler, E. B. (2009) Project Blacklight: a Next Generation Library Catalog at a First Generation University. *Library Hi Tech* 27 (1): 57–67.

Safire, William (2009) Fat Tail. *The New York Times*, February 8, sec. Magazine. www.nytimes.com/2009/02/08/magazine/08wwln-safire-t.html.

Sale, Arthur (2006) Comparison of Content Policies for Institutional Repositories in Australia. *First Monday* 11 (4–3). http://firstmonday.org/htbin/cgiwrap/bin/ojs/ index.php/fm/article/viewArticle/1324.

Sale, Arthur (2007) The Patchwork Mandate. *D-Lib Magazine* 13 (1/2) (January). doi:10.1045/january2007-sale.

Sanderson, Robert (2013) RDF: Resource Description Failures & Linked Data Letdowns. Presented at the CNI Spring Meeting 2013, May 17. www.youtube.com/watch?v=75vEplp9uiA&feature=youtube_gdata_player.

Savenije, Bas (2010a) The Access to Information Divide: Breaking down Barriers presented at the Stellenbosch University Library 2010 Symposium. http://scholar.sun.ac.za/handle/10019.1/488.

Savenije, Bas (2010b) Gaining Momentum for Open Access. In *Open Access to the Achievements of Slovenian Scientists*, 25–36. Ljubljana: Slovenian Library Association. www.old.zbds-zveza.si/dokumenti/2010/skupno/savenije.pdf.

Savenije, Bas (2011) Libraries in the Information Society: Cooperation and Identity. In *Libraries and Society: Role, Responsibility and Future in an Age of Change*, 203–18. Chandos.

Savenije, Bas, and Annemarie Beunen (2012) Cultural Heritage and the Public Domain. *LIBER Quarterly* 22 (2): 80–97.

Schleyer, Titus, Heiko Spallek, Brian S. Butler, Sushmita Subramanian, Daniel Weiss, M. Louisa Poythress, Phijarana Rattanathikun, and Gregory Mueller (2008) Facebook for Scientists: Requirements and Services for Optimizing How

Scientific Collaborations Are Established. *Journal of Medical Internet Research* 10 (3) (August 13). doi:10.2196/jmir.1047.

Schonfeld, Roger C. (2003) *JSTOR: A History*. Princeton University Press.

Schonfeld, Roger C., and Ross Housewright (2010) *Faculty Survey 2009: Key Strategic Insights for Libraries, Publishers, and Societies*. ITHAKA. http://bibpurl.oclc.org/web/40082 www.ithaka.org/ithaka-s-r/research/faculty-surveys-2000-2009/Faculty%20Study%202009.pdf.

Schonfeld, Roger C., Ross Housewright, and Kate Wulfson (2013) *US Faculty Survey 2012*. ITHAKA S+R. http://cyber.law.harvard.edu/communia2010/sites/communia2010/images/Faculty_Study_2009.pdf.

Schrier, Robert A. (2011) Digital Librarianship @ Social Media: The Digital Library as Conversation Facilitator. *D-Lib Magazine* 17 (7/8) (July). doi:10.1045/july2011-schrier.

Schwartz, C. (2000) Digital Libraries: An Overview. *Journal of Academic Librarianship* 26 (6): 385–93.

Schwartz, Werner (1999) The DIEPER Project, Digitised European PERiodicals. *LIBER Quarterly* 9 (3): 298–304.

Seadle, Michael (2010) Archiving in the Networked World: LOCKSS and National Hosting. *Library Hi Tech* 28 (4) (November 23): 710–17. doi:10.1108/07378831011096321.

Seadle, Michael (2011) Archiving in the Networked World: By the Numbers. *Library Hi Tech* 29 (1): 189–97.

Sefton, P., and D. Dickinson (2011) Repositories Post 2010: Embracing Heterogeneity in AWE, the Academic Working Environment. *Journal of Digital Information* 12 (2). http://journals.tdl.org/jodi/article/viewArticle/1766/2165.

Shen, Xiangxing, Zhong Zheng, Shuguang Han, and Chong Shen (2008) A Review of the Major Projects Constituting the China Academic Digital Library. *Electronic Library* 26 (1): 39–54.

Shieber, Stuart (2009) The Argument for Gold OA Support. *The Occasional Pamphlet*. June 11. http://blogs.law.harvard.edu/pamphlet/2009/06/11/the-argument-for-gold-oa-support.

Shirky, Clay (2009) Newspapers and Thinking the Unthinkable. *Clay Shirky*. March 13. www.shirky.com/weblog/2009/03/newspapers-and-thinking-the-unthinkable.

Shreeves, Sarah (2009) IDEALS: Shifting to a Service Focus at the University of Illinois. In *Starting, Strengthening, and Managing Institutional Repositories: A How to Do It Manal*: 129–36. Neal-Schuman Publishers.

Shreeves, Sarah L., Thomas H. Teper, Timothy G. Donohue, Joanne Kaczmarek, and Sue Lewis (2006) *IDEALS Digital Preservation: Current Status and Future Directions*. IDEALS Preservation Working Group. UIUC Library.

http://hdl.handle.net/2142/135.

Simister, Shawn (2013) Google I/O 2013 – The Freebase APIs: Tapping into Google's Knowledge Graph. Presented at the Google I/O 2013, May 16, San Francisco CA. www.youtube.com/watch?v=r-VL7NKJqcs&feature=youtube_gdata_player.

Simons, Natasha (2012) Implementing DOIs for Research Data. *D-Lib Magazine* 18 (5/6) (May). doi:10.1045/may2012-simons. www.dlib.org/dlib/may12/simons/05simons.html.

Singhal, Amit (2012) Introducing the Knowledge Graph: Things, Not Strings. *Inside Search: The Official Google Search Blog.* May 16. http://googleblog.blogspot.com/ 2012/05/introducing-knowledge-graph-things-not.html.

Smith, Abby (1999) *Why Digitize?* CLIR Report 80. Council on Library and Information Resources. www.clir.org/pubs/reports/pub80-smith/reports/pub80-smith/pub80.pdf.

Smith, MacKenzie, Mary Barton, Margret Branschofsky, Greg McClellan, Julie Harford Walker, Mick Bass, Dave Stuve, and Robert Tansley (2003) DSpace. *D-Lib Magazine* 9 (1). doi:10.1045/january2003-smith.

Soehner, C., C. Steeves, and J. Ward (2010) E-Science and Data Support Services: A Study of ARL Member Institutions. Washington DC: Association of Research Libraries.

Somerville, M. M., and N. Brar (2009) A User-centered and Evidence-based Approach for Digital Library Projects. *Electronic Library* 27 (3): 409–25.

Spink, Amanda, and Colleen Cool (1999) Education for Digital Libraries. *D-Lib Magazine* 5 (5): 1–7.

Springer, Michelle, Beth Dulabahn, Phil Michel, Barbara Natanson, David Reser, David Woodward, and Helena Zinkham (2008) *For the Common Good: The Library of Congress Flickr Pilot Project.* Library of Congress. www.loc.gov/rr/print/flickr_report_final.pdf.

St Clair, Gloriana (2008) The Million Book Project in Relation to Google. *Journal of Library Administration* 47 (1–2): 151–63.

St Jean, Beth, S. Y. Rieh, E. Yakel, and K. Markey (2011) Unheard Voices: Institutional Repository End-users. *College & Research Libraries* 72 (1): 21–42.

Stanford University. Digital Library (2005a) *The Stanford Digital Libraries Technologies Project.* http://diglib.stanford.edu:8091.

Stanford University. Digital Library (2005b) *Information Finding Projects in the Stanford Digital Library.* http://ilpubs.stanford.edu:8091/diglib/pub/infofinding.html.

Stephens, Michael (2006) Exploring Web 2.0 and Libraries. *Library Technology Reports* 42 (4) (August): 8–14.

Stevenson, K., S. Elsegood, D. Seaman, and C. Pawlek (2009) Next-generation

Library Catalogues: Reviews of Encore, Primo, Summon and Summa. *Serials* 22 (1): 68–82.

Stewart, Darin (2012) Google's Knowledge Graph: Yeah, That's the Semantic Web (Sort of). *Gartner Blog Network.* May 17. http://blogs.gartner.com/darin-stewart/ 2012/05/17/googles-knowledge-graph-yeah-thats-the-semantic-web-sort-of.

Stirling, P., G. Illien, P. Sanz, and S. Sepetjan (2012) The State of E-legal Deposit in France: Looking Back at Five Years of Putting New Legislation into Practice and Envisioning the Future. *IFLA Journal* 38 (1): 5–24.

Stoker, David (1994) Librarians and the Internet. *Journal of Librarianship and Information Science* 26 (3): 117–20. doi:10.1177/096100069402600301.

Stone, G. (2010) Searching Life, the Universe and Everything? The Implementation of Summon at the University of Huddersfield. *Liber Quarterly* 20 (1): 25–42.

Stratton, Barbara (2011) *Seeking New Landscapes: A Rights Clearance Study in the Context of Mass Digitisation of 140 Books Published Between 1870 and 2010.* British Library. http://pressandpolicy.bl.uk/imagelibrary/downloadMedia.ashx? MediaDetailsID=1197.

Stubley, P. (1999) Clumps as Catalogues: Virtual Success or Failure? *Ariadne* (22).

Suber, Peter (2003) Bethesda Statement on Open Access Publishing. June 20. www.earlham.edu/~peters/fos/bethesda.htm.

Suber, Peter (2004) Open Access Overview (Definition, Introduction). www.earlham.edu/~peters/fos/overview.htm.

Suber, Peter (2005) How to Facilitate Google Crawling of OA Repositories. www.earlham.edu/%7Epeters/fos/googlecrawling.htm.

Suber, Peter (2009) Open Access in 2008. *Journal of Electronic Publishing* 12 (1) (February). doi:http://dx.doi.org/10.3998/3336451.0012.104.

Suchanek, Fabian, and Gerhard Weikum (2013) Knowledge Harvesting from Text and Web Sources. Max Planck Institute for Informatics. http://suchanek.name/work/publications/icde2013t.pdf.

Suleman, Hussein (2012) The Design and Architecture of Digital Libraries. In *Digital Libraries and Information Access: Research Perspectives*: 13–28. Facet Publishing.

Sumner, Tamara (2010) Customizing Science Instruction with Educational Digital Libraries. In *Proceedings of the 10th Annual Joint Conference on Digital Libraries*, 353–6. JCDL '10. New York, NY, US: ACM. doi:10.1145/1816123.1816178.

Swan, Alma (2008) The Business of Digital Repositories. In *A DRIVER's Guide to European Repositories*, 15–48. Amsterdam University Press. http://eprints.soton.ac.uk/264455.

Swan, Alma (2011) Institutional Repositories: Now and Next. In *University Libraries and Digital Learning Environments*, 119–34. Ashgate Publishing.

Swan, Alma, and Sheridan Brown (2004) Authors and Open Access Publishing.

Learned Publishing 17 (3): 219–24.

Swan, Alma, and Sheridan Brown (2005) Open Access Self-archiving: An Author Study. Monograph. Key Perspectives Ltd. http://eprints.soton.ac.uk/260999/.

Swan, D. W., J. Grimes, T. Owens, R. D. Vese Jr, and K. Miller (2013) *Public Libraries Survey: Fiscal Year 2010*. Institute of Museum and Library Services. www.imls.gov/assets/1/AssetManager/PLS2010.pdf.

Tammaro, Anna Maria (2007) A Curriculum for Digital Librarians: a Reflection on the European Debate. *New Library World* 108 (5/6): 229–46. doi:10.1108/03074800710748795.

Tang, Jie, Jing Zhang, Limin Yao, Juanzi Li, Li Zhang, and Zhong Su (2008) ArnetMiner: Extraction and Mining of Academic Social Networks. In *Proceedings of the 14th ACM SIGKDD International Conference on Knowledge Discovery and Data Mining*, 990–8.

Tanner, Simon (2009) The Economic Future for Digital Libraries: a 2020 Vision. In *Digital Library Economics: An Academic Perspective*: 291–309. Chandos.

Tanner, Simon, and Marilyn Deegan (2010) *Inspiring Research, Inspiring Scholarship*. JISC and KDCS. www.kdcs.kcl.ac.uk/fileadmin/documents/Inspiring_Research_Inspiring_Scholarship_2011_SimonTanner.pdf.

Tansley, Robert (2006) Building a Distributed, Standards-based Repository Federation: The China Museum Project. *D-Lib Magazine* 12 (7/8). doi:10.1045/july2006-tansley.

Tarrant, David, Ben O'Steen, Tim Brody, Steve Hitchcock, Neil Jefferies, and Leslie Carr (2009) Using OAI-ORE to Transform Digital Repositories into Interoperable Storage and Services Applications. *Code4Lib Journal* 6.

Tedd, Lucy A. (2002) Library Co-operation and ICT in the UK: An Overview. *Information Services and Use* 23 (4): 199–210.

Tedd, Lucy A., and J. A. Large (2005) *Digital Libraries: Principles and Practice in a Global Environment*. Walter de Gruyter.

Tennant, Roy (2004a) Digital Libraries: Metadata's Bitter Harvest. *Library Journal* 129 (12) (July 15). http://roytennant.com/column/?fetch+data/39.xml.

Tennant, Roy (2004b) *Managing the Digital Library*. Reed Press.

Ternier, Stefaan, David Massart, Michael Totschnig, Joris Klerkx, and Erik Duval (2010) The Simple Publishing Interface (SPI). *D-Lib Magazine* 16 (9/10) (September). doi:10.1045/september2010-ternier.

The Guardian (2013) Google Books Wins Case against Authors over Putting Works Online, 14 November. www.theguardian.com/books/2013/nov/14/google-books-wins-case-authors-online.

The Library Corporation (2008) TLC Introduces LS2 – a New ILS Platform: Press Release: The Library Corporation: TLC: October 28. Available from www.librarytechnology.org/ltg-displaytext.pl?BC=13600.

Thibeau, Don (2011) Introduction to OpenID and OpenID Foundation 2011 March. http://openid.net/wordpress-content/uploads/2011/03/Introduction-to-OpenID-Foundation-March-2011.pdf.

Thomas, Chuck, and Robert H. McDonald (2007) Measuring and Comparing Participation Patterns in Digital Repositories. *D-Lib Magazine* 13 (9/10). doi:10.1045/september2007-mcdonald.

Thomas, Lisa Carlucci (2012) Mobile Libraries 2012. *Library Journal* 137: 26–8.

Thompson, J., D. Bainbridge, and H. Suleman (2011) Towards Very Large Scale Digital Library Building in Greenstone Using Parallel Processing. *Digital Libraries: For Cultural Heritage, Knowledge Dissemination, and Future Creation*: 331–40.

Thornton, Elaine (2012) Is Your Academic Library Pinning? Academic Libraries and Pinterest. *Journal of Web Librarianship* 6 (3): 164–75. doi:10.1080/19322909.2012.702006.

Tonta, Y. (2008) Libraries and Museums in the Flat World: Are They Becoming Virtual Destinations? *Library Collections, Acquisitions, and Technical Services* 32 (1): 1–9.

Torzec, Nicolas (2012) The Short Life of the Open Knowledge Graph. *Zec Blog: All Things Data*. September 16. http://zecblog.com/2012/09/16/the-short-life-of-the-open-knowledge-graph.

Toyoda, M., and M. Kitsuregawa (2012) The History of Web Archiving. *Proceedings of the IEEE* 100 (Special Centennial Issue): 1441–3. doi:10.1109/JPROC.2012.2189920.

Trainor, Cindi, and Jason Price (2010) Rethinking Linking: Breathing New Life into OpenURL. *Library Technology Reports*. http://works.bepress.com/cinditrainor/2.

Trant, Jennifer (2009a) Studying Social Tagging and Folksonomy: A Review and Framework. *Journal of Digital Information* 10 (1): 1–44. http://arizona.openrepository.com/arizona/handle/10150/105375.

Trant, Jennifer (2009b) *Tagging, Folksonomy and Art Museums: Results of Steve.museum's Research*. Archives and Museum Informatics. http://arizona.openrepository.com/arizona/handle/10150/105627.

Travis, Hannibal (2010) Estimating the Economic Impact of Mass Digitization Projects on Copyright Holders: Evidence from the Google Book Search Litigation. *Journal of the Copyright Society* 57: 907–1017.

Treloar, Andrew, David Groenewegen, and Cathrine Harboe-Ree (2007) The Data Curation Continuum. *D-Lib Magazine* 13 (9/10) (September). doi:10.1045/september2007-treloar.

Tripathi, Manorama, and V. K. J. Jeevan (2013) A Selective Review of Research on E-resource Usage in Academic Libraries. *Library Review* 62 (3) (May 24): 134–56. doi:10.1108/00242531311329473.

Troll Covey, Denise (2003) The Need to Improve Remote Access to Online Library Resources: Filling the Gap Between Commercial Vendor and Academic User Practice. *Portal: Libraries and the Academy* 3 (4): 577–99.

Troll Covey, Denise (2009) Self-archiving Journal Articles: A Case Study of Faculty Practice and Missed Opportunity. *Portal: Libraries and the Academy* 9 (2): 223–51.

Troll Covey, Denise (2011) Recruiting Content for the Institutional Repository: The Barriers Exceed the Benefits. *Journal of Digital Information* 12 (3). http://works.bepress.com/denise_troll_covey/56.

Tzoc, Elías (2013) A Mobile Interface for DSpace. *D-Lib Magazine* 19 (3/4) (March). doi:10.1045/march2013-tzoc.

UNESCO Institute for Statistics (2009) Regional Totals for R&D Expenditures (GERD) and Researchers, 2002, 2007 and 2009 [data file]. www.uis.unesco.org/ScienceTechnology/Pages/red-survey-results-2012.aspx. Select 'Data Centre'.

Usherwood, Bob (2002a) Accounting for Outcomes: Demonstrating the Impact of Public Libraries. *Australasian Public Libraries and Information Services* 15 (1): 5–13.

Usherwood, Bob (2002b) Demonstrating Impact through Qualitative Research. *Performance Measurement and Metrics* 3 (3): 117–22.

Usherwood, Bob, Kerry Wilson, and Jared Bryson (2005) Relevant Repositories of Public Knowledge? Libraries, Museums and Archives in 'the Information Age'. *Journal of Librarianship and Information Science* 37 (2): 89–98.

Van de Sompel, Herbert, Ryan Chute, and Patrick Hochstenbach (2008) The aDORe Federation Architecture. *arXiv:0803.4511* (March 31). http://arxiv.org/abs/0803.4511.

Van de Sompel, Herbert, and Patrick Hochstenbach (1999a) Reference Linking in a Hybrid Library Environment: Part 1, Frameworks for Linking. *D-Lib Magazine* 5 (4). doi:10.1045/april99-van_de_sompel-pt1.

Van de Sompel, Herbert, and Patrick Hochstenbach (1999b) Reference Linking in a Hybrid Library Enivonment Part 2: SFX, a Generic Linking Solution. *D-Lib Magazine* 5 (4). doi:10.1045/april99-van_de_sompel-pt2.

Van de Sompel, Herbert, and Patrick Hochstenbach (1999c) Reference Linking in a Hybrid Library Environment: Part 3, Generalizing the SFX Solution. *D-Lib Magazine* 5 (10). doi:10.1045/october99-van_de_sompel.

Van de Sompel, Herbert, and Carl Lagoze (2000) The Santa Fe Convention of the Open Archives Initiative. *D-Lib Magazine* 6 (2).

Van de Sompel, Herbert, Carl Lagoze, Jeroen Bekaert, Xiaoming Liu, Sandy Payette, and Simeon Warner (2006) An Interoperable Fabric for Scholarly Value Chains. *D-Lib Magazine* 12 (10) (October). doi:10.1045/october2006-vandesompel.

Van de Sompel, Herbert, Carl Lagoze, Michael L. Nelson, Simeon Warner, Robert

Sanderson, and Pete Johnston (2009) Adding eScience Assets to the Data Web. In *Proceedings of Linked Data on the Web*. Madrid. http://arxiv.org/abs/0906.2135.

Van de Sompel, Herbert, Sandy Payette, John Erickson, Carl Lagoze, and Simeon Warner (2004) Rethinking Scholarly Communication. *D-Lib Magazine* 10 (9). doi:10.1045/september2004-vandesompel.

Van Eijndhoven, Kwame, and Maurits van der Graaf (2007) *Inventory Study into the Present Type and Level of OAI Compliant Digital Repository Activities in the EU*. SURF Foundation. www.driver-support.eu/documents/DRIVER%20 Inventory%20study%202007.pdf.

Van House, N. A. (2003) Digital Libraries and Collaborative Knowledge Construction. In *Digital Library Use: Social Practice in Design and Evaluation*: 271–95. MIT Press.

Van House, Nancy, Mark Butler, Virginia Ogle, and Lisa Schiff (1996). User-Centered Iterative Design for Digital Libraries: The Cypress Experience. *D-Lib Magazine* (February). www.dlib.org/dlib/february96/02vanhouse.html.

Van Houweling, Molly Shaffer (2012) Orphan Works & Mass Digitization: Obstacles & Opportunities: Atomism and Automation. *Berkeley Technology Law Journal* 27: 1471–503.

Van Orsdel, L. C., and K. Born (2009) Reality Bites: Periodicals Price Survey 2009. *Library Journal* 134 (7): 36–40.

Van Veen, Theo, and Bill Oldroyd (2004) Search and Retrieval in the European Library. *D-Lib Magazine* 10 (2) (February). doi:10.1045/february2004-vanveen.

Van Westrienen, Gerard, and Clifford A. Lynch (2005) Academic Institutional Repositories. *D-Lib Magazine* 11 (09) (September). doi:10.1045/september2005-westrienen.

Vattulainen, Pentti (2004) National Repository Initiatives in Europe. *Library Collections, Acquisition, and Technical Services* 28 (1): 39–50.

Verwayen, Harry, Jeremy Ottenvanger, Mel Collier, and Jill Cousins (2008) *Business Model Europeana 2011–2015: The Whole Is Greater Than the Sum of the Parts: Revised Working Paper August 2008*. Kennisland/Knowledgeland.

Vickery, Graham, and Sacha Wunsch-Vincent (2007) *Participative Web And User-Created Content: Web 2.0 Wikis and Social Networking*. Paris, France, France: Organization for Economic Cooperation and Development (OECD).

Waaijers, L. (2008) Copyright Angst, Lust for Prestige and Cost Control: What Institutions Can Do to Ease Open Access. *Ariadne* (57): 2.

Wacha, Megan, and Meredith Wisner (2011) Measuring Value in Open Access Repositories. *Serials Librarian* 61 (3–4): 377–88. doi:10.1080/0361526X.2011.580423.

Walsh, Mark (2011) Time Spent On Apps Outpaces Web 06/21/2011. *Online Media Daily*, June 21.

www.mediapost.com/publications/article/152706/#axzz2OHvcOd5m.

Walters, Tyler O. (2009) Data Curation Program Development in US Universities: The Georgia Institute of Technology Example. *International Journal of Digital Curation* 4 (3): 83–92.

Walters, Tyler O., Liz Bishoff, Emily Gore, Mark Jordan, and Thomas C. Wilson (2009) Distributed Digital Preservation: Technical, Sustainability, and Organizational Developments. In *Proceedings*, 10. California Digital Library. http://escholarship.org/uc/item/38g232wc.

Walters, William H. (2013a) E-books in Academic Libraries: Challenges for Acquisition and Collection Management. *Portal: Libraries and the Academy* 13 (2): 187–211.

Walters, William H. (2013b) E-books in Academic Libraries: Challenges for Sharing and Use. *Journal of Librarianship and Information Science* (January). http://lis.sagepub.com/content/early/2013/05/08/0961000612470279.abstract.

Warner, Simeon, Nathan Woody, Paul Ginsparg, and Thorsten Schwander (2009) Author Identifiers in Scholarly Repositories. In *4th International Conference on Open Repositories*. Georgia Institute of Technology. https://smartech.gatech.edu/handle/1853/28467.

Waters, Donald J. (1998) What Are Digital Libraries? *CLIR Issues* 4 (1): 5–6.

Waters, Donald J. (2007) Preserving the Knowledge Commons. In *Understanding Knowledge as a Commons: From Theory to Practice*: 145–67. MIT Press.

Watson, S. (2007) Authors' Attitudes to, and Awareness and Use of, a University Institutional Repository. *Serials: The Journal for the Serials Community* 20 (3): 225–30.

Way, D. (2010) The Impact of Web-scale Discovery on the Use of a Library Collection. *Serials Review* 36 (4): 214–20.

Weibel, Stuart L. (1995) Metadata: The Foundations of Resource Description. *D-Lib Magazine* 1 (1) (July). http://dlib.org/dlib/July95/07weibel.html.

Weibel, Stuart L. (1999) The State of the Dublin Core Metadata Initiative April 1999. *D-Lib Magazine* 5 (4). doi:10.1045/april99-weibel.

Weibel, Stuart L. (2005) Border Crossings: Reflections on a Decade of Metadata Consensus Building. *D-Lib Magazine* 11 (07/08) (July). doi:10.1045/july2005-weibel.

Weibel, Stuart L., and Carl Lagoze (1997) An Element Set to Support Resource Discovery. *International Journal on Digital Libraries* 1 (2) (September): 176–86. doi:10.1007/s007990050013.

Weingarten, Fred W. (1993) NREN and the National Infrastructure: a Personal Vision. *Internet Research* 3 (3).

White, Howard D., and Katherine W. McCain (1998) Visualizing a Discipline: An Author Co-citation Analysis of Information Science, 1972–1995. *Journal of the*

American Society for Information Science 49 (4): 327–55.

Wiggins, Andrea, and Kevin Crowston (2011) From Conservation to Crowdsourcing: A Typology of Citizen Science. In *Proceedings of the 44th Hawaii International Conference on System Sciences*, 1–10. IEEE Computer Society.

Wiggins, Andrea, and Kevin Crowston (2012) Goals and Tasks: Two Typologies of Citizen Science Projects. In *2012 45th Hawaii International Conference on System Science (HICSS)*, 3426–35. doi:10.1109/HICSS.2012.295.

Wilensky, R. (2002) Re-inventing Scholarly Information Dissemination and Use. In *III Jornadas De Bibliotecas Digitales: (JBIDI'02): El Escorial (Madrid) 18–19 De Noviembre De 2002*: 3–4.

Wilson, Bonita, and Allison L. Powell (2005) A Tenth Anniversary for D-Lib Magazine. *D-Lib Magazine* (July). doi:10.1045/july2005-wilson.

Wilson, Katie (2007) OPAC 2.0: Next Generation Online Library Catalogues Ride the Web 2.0 Wave! *Online Currents* 21 (10) (January 1): 406–13.

Wilson, Ross (2012) Volunteering for Service: Digital Co-Curation and the First World War. *International Journal of Heritage in the Digital Era* 1 (4) (December): 519–34. doi:10.1260/2047-4970.1.4.519.

Witt, Michael (2010) Implementations of ORE. *Library Technology Reports* 46 (4): 26–34.

Witten, Ian H., David Bainbridge, and David M. Nichols (2009) *How to Build a Digital Library*. Morgan Kaufmann.

Witten, I.H., R.J. McNab, S. Jones, M. Apperley, D. Bainbridge, and S. J. Cunningham (1999) Managing Complexity in a Distributed Digital Library. *Computer* 32 (2): 74–9. doi:10.1109/2.745723.

Woldering, Britta (2004) The European Library: Integrated Access to the National Libraries of Europe. *Ariadne* (38) (January). www.ariadne.ac.uk/issue38/woldering.

Wolski, Malcolm, Joanna Richardson, and Robyn Rebollo (2011) Building an Institutional Discovery Layer for Virtual Research Collections. *D-Lib Magazine* 17 (5/6) (May). doi:10.1045/may2011-wolski.

Womack, David (2003) Who Owns History? *Cabinet Magazine* (10). www.cabinetmagazine.org/issues/10/womack.php.

Yakel, E., S. Y. Rieh, B. St Jean, K. Markey, and J. Kim (2008) Institutional Repositories and the Institutional Repository: College and University Archives and Special Collections in an Era of Change. *American Archivist* 71 (2): 323–49.

Yang, S. Q., and K. Wagner (2010) Evaluating and Comparing Discovery Tools: How Close Are We Towards Next Generation Catalog? *Library Hi Tech* 28 (4): 690–709.

Yang, Seungwon, Barbara M. Wildemuth, Jeffrey Pomerantz, Sanghee Oh, and Edward Fox (2009) Core Topics in Digital Library Education. In *Handbook of*

Research on Digital Libraries: Design, Development, and Impact: 493–505. Hershey, PA: Information Science Reference.

York, Jeremy (2010) Building a Future by Preserving Our Past: The Preservation Infrastructure of HathiTrust Digital Library. In *World Library and Information Congress: 76th IFLA General Conference and Assembly*: 10–15. http://conference.ifla.org/conference/past/ifla76/157-york-en.pdf.

Zaino, Jennifer (2013) Research Libraries Take the Prize for Linked Data and SemTech Efforts – Semanticweb.com. *Semanticweb.com*. February 27. http://semanticweb.com/tag/metadata/page/2/.

Zaugg, Holt, Richard E. West, Isaku Tateishi, and Daniel L. Randall (2011) Mendeley: Creating Communities of Scholarly Inquiry through Research Collaboration. *TechTrends* 55 (1): 32–6.

Zhang, Junliang, Javed Mostafa, and Himansu Tripathy (2002) Information Retrieval by Semantic Analysis and Visualization of the Concept Space of D-Lib® Magazine. *D-Lib Magazine* 8 (10) doi:10.1045/october2002-zhang.

Zhao, D. G., and A. Ramsden (1995) Report on the ELINOR Electronic Library Pilot. *Information Services & Use* 15 (3): 199–212.

Zhou, Qian (2005) The Development of Digital Libraries in China and the Shaping of Digital Librarians. *Electronic Library* 23 (4): 433–41.

Zia, Lee L. (2000) The NSF National Science, Mathematics, Engineering, and Technology Education Digital Library (NSDL) Program. *D-Lib Magazine* 6 (10) (October). doi:10.1045/october2000-zia.

Zillman, Marcus P. (2013) Deep Web Research and Discovery Resources 2013. Virtual Private Library. www.deepwebresearch.info.

Index